Boundaries of Discourse in the International Court of Justice

Boundaries of Discourse in the International Court of Justice

Mapping Arguments in Arab Territorial Disputes

By

Michelle L. Burgis

MARTINUS NIJHOFF PUBLISHERS

LEIDEN • BOSTON
2009

On the cover: View of Israel's separation wall from Qalandia in the West Bank, July 2008, M. Burgis.

This book is printed on acid-free paper.

Library of Congress Cataloging-in-Publication Data

Burgis, Michelle L.
Boundaries of discourse in the International Court of Justice : mapping arguments in Arab territorial disputes / by Michelle L. Burgis.
p. cm.
Includes bibliographical references and index.
ISBN 978-90-04-17463-4 (hardback : alk. paper)
1. Boundary disputes. 2. Jurisdiction (International law) 3. International Court of Justice. I. Title.
KZ3684.B87 2009
341.4'2--dc22

2009002407

ISBN: 978 90 04 17463 4

PRINTED IN THE NETHERLANDS

To my parents

We rebelled against the English; we rebelled against the French...
We rebelled against those who colonized our land and tried to enslave us...
We repeated the red revolutions many times and we continued with our white revolutions over a number of years...
And for this we endured so much suffering, sustained so many losses, and sacrificed so many lives...
[But]
When we finally gained our liberty, we began to sanctify the borders they had instituted after they had divided our land...
And we forgot that these borders were but the boundaries of the 'solitary confinement' and the 'house arrest' which they had imposed upon us!

Abu Khaldun Sati' al-Husri, *al-'Uruba Awalan* [Arabism first] (1955), quoted in A. Dawisha, *Arab Nationalism in the Twentieth Century: From Triumph to Despair* (Princeton: Princeton University Press, 2003), at 286–287

Nos moyens sont certes limités. Nous le savons. Mais nous avons un moyen extrêmement important, c'est notre bon droit. C'est la foi que nous avons en cette justice même, dont vous êtes, Monsieur le Président, Messieurs les members de la Cour, le symbole et la personnification mêmes. Nous avons foi en cette justice que est égale pour tous et devant laquelle la raison du plus fort n'est pas toujours la meilleure.

[Our means are certainly limited. We know this. But we have an extremely important resource on our side. It is the faith that we have in justice itself of which you are the very symbol and personification, Mr President and members of the Court. We have faith in this justice which is equal for all and before which the arguments of the strongest do not always prevail.]

Western Sahara, Oral Statements, Mauritania, Moulaye el Hassen, 3 July 1975, vol. IV, at 309

Contents

Part II

Contentious Cases

Part III

Advisory Opinions

Preface

Journeys through Scholarly Quicksands and my Quest for Solid Ground

Writing a book is both a personal and an intellectual journey. Parts of this journey are revealed in scholarly statements, but many silences remain. Here I want to reflect on some of the agendas informing my research.

When I started out along a path shrouded in fog, few things were clear to me except my interest in all things Arab and a belief that the disciplinary boundaries of law would provide a more solid framework than the field I had abandoned, international relations (IR). I had come to find incessant disciplinary debates within IR tedious; my eyes were tired and sought other horizons. Reading critical and postcolonial international legal material extended my gaze and convinced me that I needed to step outside the IR box and move into another box, international law. International law seemed to provide a neat and easy framework: the simplicity of ICJ cases contained my focus and provided me with much-needed boundaries.

It was surprising then that my intellectual journey has taken me full-circle: after seeking solace in doctrine, I realised that all I could rely on was the knowledge that there was no solid ground. My travels through quicksand has become enduring and after some instability, I have now accepted the (im)permanency of the terrain.

I came to this research with only a general knowledge of international law and a deep-seated dislike of real property law. These were not good beginnings, but I sensed that in the collision between the law on territory and the Third World, rich material was waiting to be excavated. I was not wrong. At first, when aspects of the law confused me and led me into blind alleys, I maintained a faith in the certainty of doctrine and my own lack of experience: surely if judgments from the ICJ did not explain things clearly, this was about my own gaps of knowledge? Most commentaries on the case law seemed to maintain a faith in law's certainty, suggesting that all I needed to do was improve my own understanding. The majority of scholarship on title to territory is removed from sustained critical engagement and many authors writing about territory regard applicable laws as solid and knowable. In those cases, for example, where the Court's judgment did not cover the field, most scholarship readily completes the task; there is a clear body of rules to apply in all instances and normative indeterminacy, or norm conflict, is not countenanced.

It was in the encounter between international law and colonialism, however, that my footsteps started to falter: I needed to put on the sturdiest boots that could withstand much more than the luscious landscapes of Europe, the site where the law on territory had been forged. Three of my four case studies have taken me to some of the world's most extreme topographies: the Sahara and the Qatari peninsula. Like the rest of the world, these lands are now home to their own cartographic lines, but the law explaining these markings only told part of the story, and I needed to undertake my own expedition to make sense of these cases.

When one first enters the intricacies of a boundary dispute, there is a sense of excitement. The voluminous archival and cartographic materials obligatory in such disputes transport the reader to another time and another location. Legal teams are not only paid handsome sums to convince the Court of their side's legal merits, but they also partake in storytelling by taking us into a world of diplomatic dealings, tribal intrigues, pearl-fishing and imperial rivalries. Wading through the mounds of paper produced for a case, however, tends to cause confusion rather than clarity, not only in relation to the legal arguments but 'the' historical record as well. Even the most simple 'facts' are presented in diametrical opposition in contentious disputes, reminding us of the contingency of fact, history and ultimately, law. Mystique was compounded by illegible maps and documents. Could the Court decipher the materials any better than I could, or was this part of the strategy: to wrap the past in mystery and look to law for its clarification?

Once I became comfortable in the unknown worlds of blurry maps and smudged Osmanlıcı (Ottoman Turkish) documents, I tried to find at least some clarity in relation to the law on title to territory. Perhaps the documents were far from pristine, but the law must be better? Yet, the law was always mired in its contested relationship with the past, and, just like the documents themselves, doctrine required interpretation and translation. There was not one law, nor one history. Korhonen reminds us that '[n]orms complete with meaning and significance do not exist *a priori* as independent objects which could be picked up by whomever, whenever.'[1] Thus, once again, I found myself lost in the quicksands of legal argument: how did law hang together beyond its surface of rules and principles? Why in Third World territorial disputes were colonial practices usually condoned, and did this mean that the law itself was colonial and incapable of moving beyond its racist past?

My answers to these questions are still somewhat tentative, but I can now say at least that international law is never an exercise in resolving rules *per se*. Instead,

---

[1] O. Korhonen, 'New International Law: Silences, Defence or Deliverance?' (1996) 7 *European Journal of International Law* 1, at 1.

it always rests on deeper structures that inform its self-image, make sense of its past and imbue it with its own mix of (usually European) cultural assumptions. In the pleadings I have read, which were largely written by European lawyers, there were times when this underlying discursive framework was expanded, but only in limited ways. Perhaps because of the fear of ensuing chaos, the international system and its legal institutions are too heavily invested in particular narratives of the origins of international law to endow Third World experiences and voices with the status they seek.

Writing this book has also clarified my relationship with the Arab world. Over the course of the project, the most commonly asked question of me has been, 'what sparked your interest in the Arab world?' There are many things that roll off the tongue in response: the culture, the food, the music, and my travels there, but none of these explanations went to the core of my interest. Reading about the encounter between the European and non-European world, though, I soon came to realise that the Arab world (and parts of the wider Muslim world where I had travelled, such as Turkey, Iran and Pakistan) was my 'other'. No other part of the globe arouses such interest, such fascination and also such repulsion for me. I constantly renegotiate my relationship with the region and its culture, and in finding out more, I have come to realise just how close and yet how far I am from ever being an Arab. When I lived in Jordan, Syria and Palestine this was brought home to me, because I could never become a local and part of me did not want to: I wanted to observe and yet be part of the milieu at the same time. This is a difficult pose to strike, and it is one requiring constant re-positioning. It has meant that I am forever evaluating my own assumptions, prejudices and conceptions about the region as well as my research. I hope it is helpful in reading this book to recognise these background journeys.

Table of Cases

Nationalty Decrees Issued in Tunis and Morocco (Advisory Opinion) (1923) PCIJ, Series B, No. 4

Status of Eastern Carelia (Advisory Opinion) (1923) P.C.I.J., Series B, No. 5

The Case of the S.S. "Lotus" (France/Turkey) (1927) P.C.I.J., Series A, No. 10

Factory at Chorzów (Germany/Poland) (Merits) (1928) P.C.I.J., Series A, No. 17

Island of Palmas Case 1 RIAA 829; 4 ILR 3 [1928]

Legal Status of Eastern Greenland (Denmark/Norway) (1933) P.C.I.J. Series A/B No. 53

Reparation for Injuries Suffered in the Service of the United Nations (Advisory Opinion) (1949) ICJ Reps, p. 174

International Status of South West Africa (Advisory Opinion) (1950) ICJ Reps, p. 128

Case Concerning Rights of Nationals of the United States of America in Morocco (France/United States) (1952) ICJ Reps, p. 176

The Minquiers and Ecrehos Case (France/United Kingdom) (1953) ICJ Reps, p. 47

Admissibility of Hearings of Petitioners by the Committee on South West Africa (Advisory Opinion) (1956) ICJ Reps, p. 23

Case Concerning Sovereignty over Certain Frontier Land (Belgium/Netherlands) (1959) ICJ Reps, p. 209

Case Concerning Right of Passage over Indian Territory (Portugal/ India) (1960) ICJ Reps, p. 6

Case Concerning the Temple of Preah Vihear (Cambodia/Thailand) (1962) ICJ Reps, p. 6

South West Africa Cases (Ethiopia/South Africa; Liberia/South Africa) (Preliminary Objections) (1962) ICJ Reps, p. 319

Certain Expenses of the United Nations (Article 17, paragraph 2, of the Charter) (Advisory Opinion) (1962) ICJ Reps, p. 151

South West Africa Cases (Ethiopia/South Africa; Liberia/South Africa) (Second Phase) (1966) ICJ Reps, p. 6

Case Concerning the Indo-Pakistan Western Boundary (India v. Pakistan), Arbitral Award of 19 February 1968, (1968) ILM 633

Legal Consequences for States of the Continued Presence of South Africa in Namibia (South West Africa) notwithstanding Security Council Resolution 276 (1970) (Advisory Opinion) (1971) ICJ Reps, p. 12

Western Sahara (Advisory Opinion) (1975) ICJ Reps, p. 12

Dubai/Sharjah Border Arbitration, Arbitral Award, 19 October 1981, (1993) 91 ILR 543

Case Concerning the Continental Shelf (Tunisia/Libyan Arab Jamahiriya) (1982) ICJ Reps, p. 18

Case Concerning the Continental Shelf (Libyan Arab Jamahiriya/Malta) (1985) ICJ Reps, p. 13

Application for Revision and Interpretation of the Judgment of 24 February 1982 in the Case Concerning the Continental Shelf *(Tunisia/Libyan Arab Jamahiriya)* (1985) ICJ Reps, p. 192

Military and Paramilitary Activities in and against Nicaragua (Nicaragua/ USA) (Merits) (1986) ICJ Reps, p. 14.

Case Concerning the Frontier Dispute (Burkina Faso/Mali) (1986) ICJ Reps, p. 554

Applicability of the Obligation to Arbitrate under Section 21 of the United Nations Headquarters Agreement of June 26 1947 (Advisory Opinion) (1988) ICJ Reps, p. 12

Taba Arbitration (Egypt/Israel) (1989) 80 ILR 224

Case Concerning the Territorial Dispute (Libyan Arab Jamahiriya/Chad) (1994) ICJ Reps, p. 6

Maritime Delimitation and Territorial Questions between Qatar and Bahrain (Qatar/Bahrain) (Jurisdiction and Admissibility) (1994) ICJ Reps, p. 112

Maritime Delimitation and Territorial Questions between Qatar and Bahrain (Qatar/Bahrain) (Jurisdiction and Admissibility) (1995) ICJ Reps, p. 6

East Timor (Australia v. *Portugal) (Merits)* (1995) ICJ Reps, p. 102

Legality of the Threat or Use of Nuclear Weapons (Advisory Opinion) (1996) ICJ Reps, p. 26

Award of the Arbitral Tribunal in the First Stage of the Proceedings, Territorial Sovereignty and Scope of the Dispute (*Eritrea/Yemen*), 9 October 1998

Case Concerning Questions of Interpretation and Application of the 1971 Montreal Convention Arising from the Aerial Incident at Lockerbie (Libyan Arab Jamahiriya/United Kingdom) (Preliminary Objects) (1998) ICJ Reps, p. 9

Case Concerning Questions of Interpretation and Application of the 1971 Montreal Convention Arising from the Aerial Incident at Lockerbie (Libyan Arab Jamahiriya/United States of America) (1998) ICJ Reps, p. 115

Award of the Arbitral Tribunal in the Second Stage of the Proceedings, Maritime Delimitation (*Eritrea/Yemen*), 17 December 1999

Case Concerning Kasikiki/Sedudu Island (Botswana/Namibia) (1999) ICJ Reps, p. 1045

Case Concerning Maritime Delimitation and Territorial Questions between Qatar and Bahrain (Qatar/Bahrain) (Merits) (2001) ICJ Reps, p. 40

Land and Maritime Boundary between Cameroon and Nigeria (Cameroon/Nigeria; Equatorial Guinea Intervening) (2002) ICJ Reps, p. 303

Legal Consequences of the Construction of a Wall in the Occupied Palestinian Territory (Advisory Opinion) (2004) ICJ Reps, p. 136

Case Concerning the Frontier Dispute (Benin/Niger) (2005) ICJ Reps, p. 90

Table of Treaties

General Treaty between the East India Company and the Friendly Arabs (Oman/Bahrain), 8 January 1820, 70 CTS 463

Preliminary Treaties between the East India Company and Shargah, Ras Al-Khaimeh, Dibai, Abu Dhabi & Zyah, 8–15 January 1820, 70 CTS 471

Preliminary Treaty between the East India Company and Bahrain, 5 February 1820, 70 CTS 481

Treaty between Austria, France, Great Britain, Prussia, Russia and Turkey respecting the Straits of the Dardanelles and Bosphorus, 13 July 1841, 92 CTS 7

Treaty of Peace in Perpetuity between the Arab Chiefs of the Arabian Coast, 4 May 1853, 110 CTS 269

General Treaty for the Re-Establishment of Peace between Austria, France, Great Britain, Prussia, Sardinia and Turkey, and Russia, Paris, 30 March 1856, 114 CTS 409

Treaty Guaranteeing the Independence and Integrity of the Ottoman Empire, Paris, 15 April 1856, 114 CTS 497

Convention between Great Britain and Bahrein, 31 May 1861, 124 CTS 163

Agreements between Great Britain and Qatar and Abu Dhabi (Trucial Sheikhdoms of Oman), 12, 16 September 1868, 138 CTS 56

Treaty with Kings and Chiefs of Old Calabar, 10 September 1884, 163 CTS 182

General Act of the Conference of the Plenipotentiaries of Austria-Hungary, Belgium, Denmark, France, Germany, Great Britain, Italy, the Netherlands, Portugal, Russia, Spain, Sweden-Norway, Turkey (and the United States) respecting the Congo, 26 February 1885, 165 CTS 485

Great Britain-Trucial Sheikhdoms, Exclusive Agreements, 6/8 March 1892, 176 CTS 457

Franco-British Convention for the Delimitation of their Possessions west and east of the Niger, 14 June 1898, 186 CTS 313

Convention between France and Great Britain defining the limits of the French zone in Africa, 21 March 1899, 225 CTS 480

Agreement or Protocol between Morocco and Spain, concerning the cession of Ifni, 27 June 1900, 188 CTS 457

Accords Franco-Italiens de 1–2 novembre 1902: Echanges de letters entre M. Barrère et M. Prinetti, *Libya/Chad* Case, Libya, Memorial, 1991, International Accords and Agreements Annex, vol. 2, no. 7

Convention between France and Spain concerning Morocco, 3 October 1904, 196 CTS 353

Anglo-French Convention, 19 May 1910, Martens, *Nouveau receuil général de traités*, 3rd series, vol. 7, at 91–93

Treaty of Ouchy between the Ottoman Empire and Italy, 15 October 1912, *Libya/Chad* Case, Libya, Memorial, 1991, International Accords and Agreements Annex, vol. 2, no. 10

Convention between France and Spain respecting relations in Morocco, 27 November 1912, 217 CTS 288

Exchange of Letters between France and Great Britain respecting the Recognition and Protection of an Arab State in Syria, 9/6 May 1916, 221 CTS 323 (The Sykes-Picot Agreement)

Exchange of Notes between France and Great Britain modifying the Agreement of 9/6 May 1916, 25/30 May 1916, 222 CTS 13

Covenant of the League of Nations, 28 June 1919, 225 CTS 188

Anglo-French Convention, 8 September 1919, *Libya/Chad* Case, Chad, Memorial, 1991, Annexes, vol. II, annex 7, at 23

Bonin-Pichon Agreement, 12 September 1919, *Libya/Chad* Case, Chad, Memorial, 1991, Annexes, vol. II, annex 8/9, at 29

Treaty of Peace with Turkey (Treaty of Lausanne), 24 July 1923, no. 701, 28 LNTS 13

The Kellogg-Briand Pact, 27 August 1928, 94 LNTS 57

Treaty of Rome between France and Italy, 7 January 1935, *Libya/Chad* Case, Libya, Memorial, 1991, International Accords and Agreements Annex, vol. 2, no. 25

Franco-Libyan Treaty of Friendship and Good Neighbourliness of 10 August 1955, 162 BFSP 470

The Treaty of Good Neighbourliness and Friendship between the Republic of Chad and the United Kingdom of Libya, 2 March 1966, *Libya/Chad* Case, Libya,

Memorial, 1991, International Accords and Agreements Annex, vol. 2, no. 25

International Covenant on Civil and Political Rights (1966) 999 UNTS 171

International Covenant on Economic, Social and Cultural Rights (1966) 993 UNTS 3

Vienna Convention on the Law of Treaties, 23 May 1969, 1155 UNTS 331

The Agreement on Friendship and Co-operation, 23 December 1972, *Libya/Chad* Case, Libya, Memorial, 1991, International Accords and Agreements Annex, vol. 2, no. 34

Agreement between the Libyan Arab Republic and the Republic of Chad, Tripoli, 12 August 1974, *Libya/Chad* Case, Libya, Memorial, 1991, International Accords and Agreements Annex, vol. 2, no. 35

The Treaty of Friendship and Alliance between the Socialist People's Libyan Arab Jamahiriya and the Republic of Chad, 15 June 1980, *Libya/Chad* Case, Libya, Memorial, 1991, International Accords and Agreements Annex, vol. 2, no. 37.

Accord between Libya and Chad, 6 January 1981, *Libya/Chad* Case, Libya, Memorial, 1991, International Accords and Agreements Annex, vol. 2, no. 38

Acknowledgments

This book is a revised version of a PhD thesis completed at the Regulatory Institutions Network (RegNet), the Australian National University (ANU) and there are many people that must be thanked.

At ANU, I was lucky enough to receive invaluable assistance from a number of academics. First and foremost, I would like to thank (without adverbs!) my supervisor, Hilary Charlesworth for her commitment to my project. Her prompt responses to my endless emails, her sometimes painful (but always necessary) comments and her quiet confidence kept me going once I decided to make the move from international relations to international law. I would also like to thank members of my panel, John Braithwaite and especially, Jacinta O'Hagan. Tucked away in my old department, Cindy was a wonderful source of ideas and support. Nelly Lahoud also agreed to read my draft and offer her expertise on so many levels. Nelly answered many random Islam-related questions on our way to the swimming pool. She was also invaluable for dotting the diacritics in Arabic transliteration. Many other people have helped linguistically along the way: my sister, Alison, Jim and Professor Peter Grabosky assisted me in getting my reading of French up to speed. My occasional Arabic tutor, Muath, tolerated a terrible track record with my homework and has also been a wonderful friend.

I have been lucky enough to benefit from a number of conversations along the way. My thanks extend to Mr Abdul-Azziz Awasil, Professor Tony Anghie, Professor James Crawford, Judge Awn Al-Khasawneh, Professor Martti Koskenniemi (especially for kindly sending me all the materials for the *Libya/Chad* case), Dr Nemira Negem, Professor Piscatori and Judge Christopher Weeramantry for their time and insights. The wider ANU community, especially the Centre for International and Public Law and RegNet, was a source of countless seminars, workshops and inspiration.

In terms of IT-assistance (and occasional bike repair) I cannot thank Jin Ho at RegNet enough. I had no idea just how difficult diacritic fonts could be until I befriended Rabie during my internship at Al-Haq in Palestine and am terribly relived that he was ever generous with his time and warmth. During the final phase, I was also lucky enough to draw on the amazing proofing powers of John Kilcullen – thank you for picking up things no one else would have.

When it all became a little overwhelming, I was blessed with a wonderful network of friends both near and far. Friends who had recently finished their thesis provided encouragement and the *savoir faire* in continuing through the unknown. Thalia in particular was my beacon of support throughout the entire process. She seemed to know what I was going through even better than I did, and her friendship has been invaluable on so many levels. The examples of Shogo Suzuki and Joel Quirk encouraged me and their warmth and comic relief has been enjoyable. Both Nelly and Bina in their post-PhD wisdom kept urging me on in the spirit of faith and friendship.

Talking to other PhDers along the way was a check on my sanity at various moments and I cannot thank my doctoral colleagues enough. In particular, I would like to thank Reiko Take, Danielle Chubb, Gil Oren, Tony Foley Thuy Do, Jeremy Farral, Sarah Phillips, Edwina Thompson, Bu Wilson and Asmi Wood. As a result of a RegNet-funded writing retreat, I would like to thank its facilitator, Sally Knowles for her warmth and expertise. My friendship with Sarah Gollan was a wonderful dividend of the retreat too.

Often, the PhD is a necessary lesson in solitude. Luckily this was broken when I met Usha. Our friendship instantly blossomed beyond its TWAIL-based beginnings. Thank you ever so much, Usha, for being my dawn in the doctoral darkness.

A thesis cannot always be left in the office. For those who lived with me, I thank you: Petra Ekval, Simon Greenacre, Rebekah Grindlay and Simon Ohmsen. Friends beyond the thesis bubble never questioned my absence and always leant an ear when it was needed; thanks to Leanne Abbott, Jo Kinslor, Anna Mak, Mike and Nicole Opie, Lauren Salathiel and Lucy Taylor.

Financial assistance was vital throughout the project. I would like to acknowledge the generous support provided by the ANU through its Endowment for Excellence Scholarship, which funded my research for 3.5 years. I was also lucky enough to receive monies from RegNet and the Vice Chancellor's research fund for my conference presentation in Albany, New York in April 2007. Finally, ANU supported my enrolment in four semesters of Arabic in the Faculty of Asian Studies.

After the thesis was submitted, this final version of the book also benefited from the useful feedback of my two examiners, Professors Jean Allain and Iain Scobbie as well as a review of the manuscript by Professor Marcelo Kohen and Peter Macalister-Smith's wonderful engagement with Chapter Two.

Most importantly, I want to thank my family. First, my sister always barracked for me – thanks Al. My parents have been my constant support in all of this journey and much more. No matter how trivial or seemingly self-indulgent, they were there for me, supporting me. Perhaps more than anything else in this process, I have learnt just how limitless their love is. I cannot thank them enough.

Copyright Permissions and Acknowledgments

Some of the following chapters have been published in a modified form as journal articles including Chapter Three as '(De)limiting the Past for Future Gain: The Relationship between Sovereignty, Colonialism and Oil in the *Qatar v Bahrain* Territorial Dispute' 12 (2005–2006) *Yearbook of Islamic and Middle Eastern Law* 557; and Chapter Two as 'Faith in the State? Traditions of Territoriality and the Emergence of Modern Arab Statehood' (2009) 11 *Journal of the History of International Law*. I would like to acknowledge the permission of Oxford University Press which previously published Chapter Six as 'Discourses of Division: Law, Politics, and the ICJ Advisory Opinion on the Legal Consequences of the Construction of a Wall in the Occupied Palestinian Territory' (2008) 7 *Chinese Journal of International Law* 33. Excerpts from Chapter One also appear in 'The Promise of Solid Ground: Arab States, Territorial Disputes and the Discourse of International Law' (2008) 10(1) *The International Community Law Review* 73.

Abbreviations

AMU	Arab Maghreb Union
APCO	Anglo-Persian Oil Company
AU	African Union
BAPCO	Bahrain Petroleum Company
BFSP	British and Foreign State Papers
CE	Common Era
CTS	Consolidated Treaty Series
CUP	Committee of Union and Progress (Ottoman Empire)
GCC	Gulf Cooperation Council, or formally Cooperation Council of the Arab States of the Gulf
ICCPR	International Covenant on Civil and Political Rights
ICJ	International Court of Justice
IHL	International Humanitarian Law
ILM	International Legal Materials
IGO	Inter-Governmental Organisation
IR	International Relations, the discipline
LNTS	League of Nations Treaty Series
NAIL	New Approaches to International Law
NAM	Non-Aligned Movement
OAU	Organization of African Unity
OIC	Organisation of Islamic Conference
OPT	Occupied Palestinian Territories
PCA	Permanent Court of Arbitration
PCIJ	Permanent Court of International Justice
PCL	Petroleum Company Ltd.
POLISARIO	Frente Popular para la Liberación de Saguia el Hamra y Río de Oro
SADR	Sahrawi Arab Democratic Republic
TWAIL	Third World Approaches to International Law
UN	United Nations
UNGA	United Nations General Assembly
UNSC	United Nations Security Council
UNSCOP	United Nations Special Committee on Palestine, established 15 May 1947
VCLT	Vienna Convention on the Law of Treaties

Note on Arabic Transliteration

In transliterating Arabic words, some inconsistencies have been inevitable. For well-known places and people, I have retained their standard transliteration, such as Muhammed, instead of Moḥammad, and Qadhāfī, instead of the unmanageable 'Qadhdhāfī'. Otherwise, I have transliterated words with their diacritic marks and a simple ʿ for the 'ayn (ع) and ʾ for a ḥamza. To avoid complexity, I have not followed Arabic grammar for plurals of nouns, but have treated them like English words. Finally, I have not changed quotations to fit with this basic approach, and so the reader might find some inconsistencies as a result.

Introduction

1) *The Postcolonial Paradox*

International law is a discursive practice that both constrains and enables its central actors, states. We can understand the relationship between states and international law as an irresolvable conflict and ask the perennial question, how can sovereignty be constrained?[1] Or we can step into the discursive process and recognise that the relationship between international law and states is one of constant negotiation; international law as a language can only be understood in the context of ongoing conversations about the nature and boundaries of the discipline. When we look to the international order of contemporary nation-states, postcolonial membership suggests an expansive, inclusive international legal language. States only recently recognised as such now participate in and speak the language of international law through the guarantee of international legal personality. The boundaries of membership, however, are not clearly delimited. How should postcolonial states speak the language of international law? Further, how can postcolonial entities use the law's lexicon to ensure their selfhood and statehood in a world that denied it for so long? This is the paradox of postcoloniality: non-European states must use a discourse that has both contrained and enabled them. International law is thus premised not so much on the tension between sovereignty and rules, but on its potential for inclusion and exclusion. Who can speak the language of international law and what are its 'legal grammars' or rules of speech?[2]

Cultural diversity in a world of nation-states is not synonymous with linguistic plurality at the level of international law. Postcolonial membership offers a way of expanding the discourse of international law, but languages evolve slowly, and thus 'new' states speaking international law must either leave most of their vocabularies and grammars at the courtroom door or seek the assistance of a translator. What linguistic compromise is reached, for example in adjudication, and how has the language of international law responded to different dialects used in adjudication?

---

[1] A. Anghie, *Imperialism, Sovereignty and the Making of International Law* (Cambridge: Cambridge University Press, 2005), at 36.

[2] M. Koskenniemi, *From Apology to Utopia: The Structure of International Legal Argument* (Cambridge: Cambridge University Press, 2nd edition, 2005), at 11.

Scholars in the field of international law have confronted the question of disciplinary diversity and renewal in a number of ways.[3] In the postcolonial era, narratives about the progress and multiculturalism of international law abound, but such accounts only tell part of the story. Most scholars advance claims about the potential of international law through a particular understanding of international law that I term 'mainstream'. The word 'mainstream' lacks precision, but it is used to denote approaches to international law that tend to see law as determinate and distinct from other fields of human endeavour. The outcome of such a perspective supports a reified image of law, comprising a set of knowable doctrines and principles.[4] Unlike critical approaches to international law, sometimes termed 'New Approaches to International Law' or NAIL, which are alive to the discursive and reflexive qualities of international law, mainstream scholars characterise international law as a body of rules separate and distinct from the politics of speech. By seeing law as doctrine rather than discourse, determinacy remains uncontested. Thus, mainstream accounts see no paradox in the postcolonial condition: new states are able to harness the tools of a law that is untainted by its colonial past.

From within the critical fold, a sensibility towards Third World concerns has emerged that challenges mainstream narratives of progress after colonialism. Scholars linked to 'Third World approaches to international law', or TWAIL, seek to explore 'post'colonial continuities rather than ruptures. TWAIL research has focused on historical legacies, suggesting that Third World states and their peoples face a paradox: how can they speak the language of law and remain 'post'colonial? Resort to self-reflective, sceptical and often historical methodologies by many TWAIL scholars aligns them closely with the research agendas developed within NAIL. Thus, TWAIL scholarship is in sympathy with NAIL, but it is also distinguished by a particular commitment to Third World emancipation.

This commitment is evident in the use of the term, 'Third World'. Mickelson 'sees the Third World as occupying a historically constituted, alternative and oppositional stance within the international system. The "Third World" terminology itself may appear out-of-date, but its very contingency, involving an insistence on history and continuity, may in fact be one of its strengths.'[5] Although the term has become much more elastic since its use in the age of decolonisation,

[3] Particularly, see D. Kennedy, 'When Renewal Repeats: Thinking against the Box' (1999–2000) 32 *New York University Journal of International Law and Politics* 335.

[4] For a discussion about the reification of international law, see J. Boyle, 'Ideals and Things: International Legal Scholarship and the Prison-house of Language' (1985) 26 *Harvard International Law Journal* 327.

[5] K. Mickelson, 'Rhetoric and Rage: Third World Voices in International Legal Discourse' (1998) 16 *Wisconsin International Law Journal* 353, at 360.

Rajagopal argues that it can still serve to rally peoples, states and international lawyers. 'The nature of this "Third World" engagement with international law – of resistance, allure, exploitation and co-optation – has significantly affected the content and structure of modern international law and raises profound challenges of history, theory and method for the whole discipline of international law.'[6] TWAIL scholars regard colonialism as the unifying experience for Third World states, and the following book responds to this interest by exploring how narratives about colonialism are constructed in the courtroom.[7]

2) *Scope of the Study*

The book develops both NAIL and TWAIL agendas by focusing on the discursive practices used in International Court of Justice (ICJ) disputes. With its status as the pre-eminent international legal body, the ICJ elicits significant scholarly attention. Mainstream analyses of its doctrinal statements allow us to understand part of ICJ discourse, but they also obscure other aspects. What is the nature of debate between the bench and the bar and what patterns emerge across the cases? Through a critical understanding of law as language, these questions become easier to answer, and yet rarely does critical, and especially TWAIL, attention focus on ICJ discursive structures. Pleadings in particular are overlooked, and yet it is in this space of argumentative contest that a postcolonial law can be developed in detail.

I acknowledge that states do not speak directly in ICJ disputes. Usually foreign legal counsel hailing from a select group of First World institutions represents both First and Third World states. Why do Third World states rely on such counsel? The book is not concerned with discovering *the* position of given Third World states in some reified way. This is not possible and does not assist the broader aims of the book. Third World states are instead used as a tool for exploring the extent to which non-European experiences and legacies can be used to transform the language of international law. In its exploration of the arguments used to found title to territory, this book tries to straddle the mainstream and critical research agendas by mapping the legal grammars of

---

[6] B. Rajagopal, 'Counter-hegemonic International Law: rethinking human rights and development as Third World strategy' (2006) 27 *Third World Quarterly* 767, at 768.

[7] W. Tieya, 'The Third World and International Law' R. St. J. Macdonald & D. M. Johnston (eds.), *The Structure and Process of International Law: Essays in Legal Philosophy Doctrine and Theory* (The Hague; Boston: Martinus Nijhoff, 1983) 955–976, at 961.

discourse.[8] With rules that are indeterminate, how do postcolonial states advance their interests and which argumentative strategies and substantive claims are endorsed by the Court?

ICJ territorial disputes are the focus of the book because they allow for an extended exploration of the postcolonial paradox. Over the last few decades, the Court's docket has increased significantly and territorial disputes involving Third World states have been the most numerous. Some of international society's newest members have come to the Court in a bid to delimit the borders of their statehood through a law shaped by European domination. Thus ICJ territorial disputes are a microcosm of the broader dilemma confronting Third World states in their membership of international society. What language can be spoken in the Court to capture their experiences of colonialism? Can international law be decolonised? What narratives emerge across the cases?

3) *Central Research Questions*

The many questions raised above touch on some of the basic themes of the book. More specifically, the book rests on two central research questions. The first asks:

> What are the structures of legal argument that emerge in ICJ territorial disputes involving Arab states?

This question requires an account of the strategic and substantive uses of international law as language. It entails an analysis of pleadings and judgments to enable us to map out patterns in the process of adjudication. The second question opens up the postcolonial paradox:

> What do these structures suggest about the scope for universalising the discourse of international law?

In a world covered by independent nation-states, the jurisdictional reach of international law is now universal. Geography, however, is not necessarily synonymous with a law or a culture[9] that we can describe as both 'international' and 'universal'. Keal defines a 'universalising discourse…[as] one that either expands, or has the potential to expand, the boundaries of a community to which

[8] D. Kennedy, 'The Last Treatise: Project and Person (Reflections on Martti Koskenniemi's *From Apology to Utopia*)' (2006) 7 *German Law Journal* 982.

[9] D. Z. Cass, 'Navigating the Newstream: Recent Critical Scholarship in International Law' (1996) 65 *Nordic Journal of International Law* 341, at 349.

it refers.'[10] Territorial disputes showcasing narratives about colonialism and the conferring of membership of international society for non-European entities not only involve boundary delimitation; they also display international legal discourse being redefined and redrawn through argument. When postcolonial states choose to speak in the language of international law and offer accounts of statehood at odds with European experiences, international law will either absorb or deny such claims. Within the confines of the grammar and lexicon of international law, boundaries of the discipline can be challenged. Thus, I ask, are the boundaries to emerge suggestive of a universalising discourse? This book is concerned with international legal discourse in a postcolonial era and the cultural lens it relies on is the Arab experience. Arab states hailing from a rich and distinct cultural and legal tradition serve as a focus. By exploring one part of the geographical, cultural and discursive world, the universality of international law can be interrogated.

4) *Why Arab?*

What do I mean by 'Arab' and 'Arab world' throughout this study? Why should this term be used instead of others? States straddling the Atlantic Ocean and the Arabian Sea have variously been grouped together under the categories of the 'Middle East', the 'Near East', the 'Arab world' as well as the Muslim or Islamic World. There is little consensus on the exact boundaries of these regions; each evokes a particular set of characteristics along linguistic, cultural or religious lines. At a more conceptual level, Said speaks of the division between the Occident and the Orient, which was imagined by Europe and gave rise to Orientalist discourses. In his study of this European discourse, Said offers a basic definition and geographical location of Orientalism, which is 'mainly, although not exclusively, of a British or French cultural enterprise, a project whose dimensions take in such disparate realms as the imagination itself, the whole of India and the Levant, the Biblical texts and the Biblical lands…'[11] An awareness of the way in which these lands and their cultures were constructed by European thought and practice highlights the role that both geographical and conceptual indicators can play. European scholarship has tended to place Arab peoples in a number of culturally pre-determined regions; it is important in framing my analysis that such categories be interrogated. No category is value-free, and in choosing to study Arab states, I have singled out a particular

[10] P. Keal, *European conquest and the rights of indigenous people: The moral backwardness of international society* (Cambridge: Cambridge University Press, 2003), at 86.

[11] E. Said, *Orientalism: Western Conceptions of the Orient* (London: Penguin, 1978), at 4.

cultural and legal grouping that is sufficiently united to serve as a coherent site of study. However, it is important to be conscious of the boundary-drawing involved in such categories, and thus cultural and geographical borders of the Arab world are interrogated throughout this study.

Although the 'Middle East' (as well as its rarer variant, the 'Near East') is now used as a common point of reference by inhabitants within the region,[12] the term itself is steeped in colonialist and Orientalist overtones and is unhelpful for explanatory purposes. An American naval officer, Alfred Thayer Mahan, apparently coined the term, 'Middle East' in 1902, by referring to the area between Arabia and India.[13] The perspective reflected an era when Europe dominated the globe. The term 'Middle East' often includes non-Arab states, such as Iran and Turkey, and sometimes Pakistan and Afghanistan, largely because of their Islamic composition and geographical proximity to the centres of Islam. For the purposes of my interest in *civilisational* contributions to international law, the 'Middle East' is a term that lacks conceptual rigour and is not used in the book.

Arab states have also been subsumed under the umbrella of the Islamic world. Arab states are a part of the Islamic world, but this category is too broad for my aim of using particularism to interrogate universalism. Using the term 'Arab' allows us to separate Arab states from non-Arab states, especially as the experiences for example of Iran, Turkey, Pakistan and Afghanistan have all been distinct from those of the Levant, the Gulf and North Africa since the end of the First World War. Equally, although states typically included under the umbrella of the 'Middle East', as well as further afield in the Muslim world, have all experienced the civilising influences of Islam, it is too broad a category because it includes states as diverse as the examples of Algeria, Iran, Bosnia and Indonesia.

Both the UN and the ICJ have drawn attention to Arab civilisation in the official use of Arabic and the appointment of Arab judges. The UN's recognition of cultural diversity is rooted in the Statute of the ICJ itself. Article 38(1) catalogues the sources of international law, to include treaty law, custom and the writings of legal experts. The list also provides for application of 'the general principles of law recognized by civilized nations'.[14] Arab civilisation falls within this category, particularly in relation to the appointment of judges. Under the Statute, judges are selected not only in relation to their qualifications; they also serve as a 'representation of the main forms of civilization and of the principal

[12] In Arabic, 'Middle East' is rendered as '*al-sharq al-awsaṭ*'. For a discussion about the term 'Middle East', see N. R. Keddie, 'Is There a Middle East?' (1973) 4 *International Journal of Middle East Studies* 255.

[13] J. Allain, *International Law in the Middle East: Closer to Power than Justice* (Aldershot: Ashgate, 2004), at 3–4.

[14] Statute of International Court of Justice.

legal systems of the world'.[15] Arab civilisation should be able to contribute significantly to a culturally expansive international law of the future.

Thus I focus on 'Arab' states in my analysis, but acknowledge the limitations involved in such boundary drawing. The Arab world is a large and diverse region, but it is at least united in its use of Arabic and politically by the Arab League.[16] The Arab world can be identified as comprising North Africa: Morocco, Algeria, Tunisia, Libya, Mauritania, Sudan and Egypt; the Levant: Jordan, Palestine, Lebanon, Syria; and the Gulf: Iraq, Oman, Abu Dhabi, the United Arab Emirates, Bahrain, Qatar, Kuwait, Saudi Arabia, Yemen.[17] These states can all be understood as Arab, where Arabic is spoken, but they each contain local flavours, divergent practices of Islam, vastly uneven levels of development, as well as radically different forms of political rule ranging from the secular socialist regimes of Tunisia and Algeria, to Libya's unique form of republic, to the tribal monarchies throughout the Gulf.

Studies focusing on Arab civilisation have been torn between the tendencies of trying to depict Arab specificities while not singling out the region for cultural exceptionalism. In his study of public spheres in Jordan, Lynch is aware of balancing these two concerns. He argues that it is possible to produce research that is sensitive to the Arab position but not Orientalist in its tone about Arab uniqueness.[18] Such research cannot rise above specificity unless general theories applied elsewhere are used for the Arab world as well. Thus it is useful to develop an awareness of Arab cultural specificities, but a constant juggling act is required between appreciating regional social institutions on the one hand and local diversity at the political and legal level on the other.

Scholarship about the relationship between the Arab world and international law requires reevaluation, both from the mainstream and the 'Newstream' or NAIL.[19] Typically, mainstream attention has perpetuated Orientalist discourses

---

[15] Article 9, Statute of the International Court of Justice.

[16] The creation of the Arab League is discussed in Chapter Two at 91–93. The League's members include: Algeria, Bahrain, Comoros, Djibouti, Egypt, Iraq, Jordan, Kuwait, Lebanon, Libya, Mauritania, Morocco, Oman, Palestine, Qatar, Saudi Arabia, Somalia, Sudan, Syria, Tunisia, the United Arab Emirates and Yemen. For details, see the League's website: http://www.arableagueonline.org/las/index_en.jsp.

[17] Certain terms in Arabic correspond to these areas as well. Typically, the Arab world has been divided into its Asian and African parts by the expressions, *al-Maghreb* (for North Africa, excluding Egypt, meaning the eastern place in Arabic) and *al-Mashreq* (for West Asia, meaning the western place in Arabic). Also, a common term to connote the heart of the Arab World (that is, Lebanon, Palestine, Jordan, Syria, Egypt and the Ḥijāz, Saudi Arabia) in Arabic is *bilād al-shām*.

[18] M. Lynch, *State Interests and Public Spheres: The International Politics of Jordan's Identity* (New York: Columbia University Press, 1999), at 33–34.

[19] Generally, see Cass, *supra* n. 9.

through studies constructing the Arab world as especially averse to legalism. Terrorism is the obvious example here.[20] I use Arab experiences not to exceptionalise them but to highlight that both European and non-European experiences of authority over territory are contingent. Regions and peoples across the globe can contribute to the development of a universalising discourse of international law in their own particular way, and it is important to remember that both European and non-European experiences are particular and not necessarily transferable. Examples drawn more broadly from African ICJ territorial disputes demonstrate that the Arab world should not be treated differently *per se*. International law as a discourse created in Europe has excluded not only Arabs but also most of the world, and continues to do so in more subtle ways in the postcolonial era.

TWAIL scholarship also has overlooked the Arab experience in its project of Third World emancipation. Typically, TWAIL scholars have focused on southern Africa, subcontinental Asia or Latin America in their analyses of the 'Third World'. Straddling North Africa and West Asia, Arabs are geographically proximate to some of these locations, but are they also culturally? Are Arab states part of the Third World or not? The book suggests that we need to examine how Third World experiences – especially pertaining to colonial legacies – are explored in Arab adjudication. Do ICJ cases involving Arab states touch on concerns of the Third World more generally? What are the similarities and differences between Arab and non-Arab Third World states? These questions are particularly pertinent to Chapter Three, with its dispute between Libya and Chad,[21] and Chapter Six, where a number of Third World submissions are compared in the *Wall* Opinion.[22] I suggest that TWAIL scholarship should embrace Arab experiences in its project of interrogating the structures of international law.

5) *Case Selection*

Over its lifetime, the Court has increasingly come to hear territorial disputes arising from the Third World, including Arab states. Although the Palestinian impasse might suggest a region struggling with the relevance of international law, the Court has examined other issues, such as territorial and maritime delimitation cases.[23] Thus far, the Court has heard two contentious and two advisory

[20] I. M. Porras, 'On Terrorism: Reflections on Violence and the Outlaw' (1994) *Utah Law Review* 119.

[21] *Case Concerning the Territorial Dispute (Libyan Arab Jamahiriya/Chad)* (1994) ICJ Reps, p. 6.

[22] *Legal Consequences of the Construction of a Wall in the Occupied Palestinian Territory (Advisory Opinion)* (2004) ICJ Reps, p. 136.

[23] Aside from the case studies examined in this book, other ICJ cases involving Arab states include: *Case Concerning the Continental Shelf (Tunisia/Libyan Arab Jamahiriya)* (1982) ICJ Reps, p. 18;

territorial cases involving Arab states. This is a small sample, but it is balanced across the Court's jurisdictions, and provides sufficient scope for comparison within and across the cases. Because two of these cases hail from Africa and two from Asia, the book also highlights how Arab states operate in a broader discursive, postcolonial environment.

6) *Book Structure*

The book comprises three parts. Part I provides the conceptual and historical tools necessary to appreciate the case studies as boundary-drawing exercises not only between states but also within the language of international law itself. Chapter One introduces accounts of ICJ adjudication as well as critical studies of international legal discourse to highlight oversights in the study of territorial disputes. The tools provided by critical sensibilities to language are applied in my reading of the case studies and serve as the basis for the first central research question noted above. The second central research question is also considered in Chapter One, which explores the underlying assumptions about international law and its universality in existing literatures. To understand the particular heritage of modern Arab states, Chapter Two undertakes a broad historical review and investigates whether the Arab-Islamic tradition contains theories and practices supportive of the postcolonial territorial state. The chapter surveys the inter-relationship between public international law and Islamic international law, as well as some themes emerging from state practice across the Arab world. It also explores instances of European engagement with the Ottoman Empire to understand how the Sublime Porte and its Arab subjects were included and excluded in the emerging international system. Finally, the chapter discusses the experiences of modern Arab entities and their struggles with territorially delimited statehood to conclude that Arab history contains both opposition and support for the norm of territorial delimitation.

The analysis in Part II shifts to the case studies and looks at contentious matters before the ICJ. Part II begins with an introductory discussion about the nature of the Court's contentious jurisdiction, as well as some themes that

---

Case Concerning the Continental Shelf (Libyan Arab Jamahiriya/Malta) (1985) ICJ Reps, p. 13; *Application for Revision and Interpretation of the Judgment of 24 February 1982 in the Case Concerning the Continental Shelf (Tunisia/Libyan Arab Jamahiriya)* (1985) ICJ Reps, p. 192; *Case Concerning Questions of Interpretation and Application of the 1971 Montreal Convention Arising from the Aerial Incident at Lockerbie (Libyan Arab Jamahiriya/United Kingdom) (Preliminary Objects)* (1998) ICJ Reps, p. 9; *Case Concerning Questions of Interpretation and Application of the 1971 Montreal Convention Arising from the Aerial Incident at Lockerbie (Libyan Arab Jamahiriya/United States of America)* (1998) ICJ Reps, p. 115.

have emerged from ICJ jurisprudence on territory. Chapter Three introduces the first case, the *Territorial Dispute* between Libya and Chad.[24] The chapter's discussion showcases the different argumentative strategies available to postcolonial states through the contrasting positions of the parties. While Libya championed a non-European version of title to territory and challenged the colonial record, Chad's pleadings were reliant on the postcolonial dividends of French rule. Chapter Four's consideration of the territorial and maritime dispute between Qatar and Bahrain does not rest on such extreme positions,[25] but similar themes about the impact of consent under colonial rule, the validity of treaties and non-European modes of authority are explored. Both cases contain extensive historical discussion, and so much of Part II interrogates narratives about the legacies of colonialism in relation to territorial delimitation.

Part III turns to the Court's advisory jurisdiction and looks at two cases about territory and self-determination. After an introductory discussion, Chapter Five examines the various argumentative strategies and ideas used at the bar and the bench in the *Western Sahara* Case.[26] The case shares many themes with contentious territorial matters, but its advisory nature allowed greater participation for states and thus more scope for comparison about their respective positions. The case is renowned for its support for self-determination, but the book is more concerned with the way it can reveal discursive patterns about colonial legacies. The *Western Sahara* Case contained debates on the legal validity of non-European modes of authority, and its engagement with the Islamic tradition harks back to Chapter Two's historical themes.

The last case study in Chapter Six is most distinct, because it is not a typical title to territory matter dealing as it does with a form of neocolonialism in the UN period. The *Wall* Opinion included a large number of states from the First and Third Worlds arguing not only about territorial authority over the Occupied Palestinian Territories but also about the role expected of the ICJ and international law in the Israeli-Palestinian conflict. Due to the large number of states participating, the argumentative practices of the earlier cases are highlighted in greater relief. Although this case can be seen as being radically different form classic title to territory cases explored above, this book is most interested in the discursive similarities across the cases. The three earlier cases highlight the discursive constraints that postcolonial states face on entering the Court. By 2004, Third World states hold the indisputable majority in the UN and the chapter highlights this with its discussion of debates that took place in the UN

[24] *Case Concerning the Territorial Dispute (Libyan Arab Jamahiriya/Chad)* (1994) ICJ Reps, p. 6.

[25] *Case Concerning Maritime Delimitation and Territorial Questions between Qatar and Bahrain (Qatar/Bahrain) (Merits)* (2001) ICJ Reps, p. 40.

[26] *Western Sahara (Advisory Opinion)* (1975) ICJ Reps, p. 12.

over the advisory opinion request. However, to what extent have Third World states been able to shape the discourse of the Court itself? The chapter shows that although Third World states constituted a majority of participants whose arguments generally convinced the Court, the narrow judgment itself indicates that the position of Third World states is not wholly decolonised. Many of the more extreme argumentative gestures adopted by Third World states as well as Arab references to history were overlooked by the bench in its judgment. Thus, the final case study presents a continuum of sorts between colonial and postcolonial discourses of international law. The *Wall* Opinion is a significant step along the path of linguistic renewal, but the legal lexicon in 2004 was not entirely new.

The interrelationship between selfhood and territory is one of the most significant, underlying themes across the four cases. In a postcolonial world, there is room for some discursive variation in adjudication, but only through membership in international society. The book explores how postcolonial states can negotiate the boundaries of modern statehood through speech. With its emphasis on ICJ territorial adjudication, the book echoes Berman's question, 'Can international law, written by history's victors, muster the courage to look painfully, frankly, at the horrors of its own past?'[27] A close reading of four postcolonial territorial cases reveals the limits and the possibilities of a universalising international legal discourse. The book highlights that the options for retelling and reshaping international law are small, but significant. Language is dynamic and so, within its own conventions and biases, international law too contains the seeds of change. The first step is to understand how to speak the language of international law, and thus my aim is to map out argumentative possibilities of the discipline in a postcolonial era.

[27] N. Berman, 'In the Wake of Empire', (1999) 14 *American University International Law Review* 1515 (First Annual Grotius Lecture, American Society of International Law), at 1554.

Part I

Theoretical and Historical Background

Chapter One

Listening for Silences in and beyond the Courtroom: Methodological Tools for Understanding ICJ Territorial Disputes

1) *Introduction*

As a discursive exercise in argument, international adjudication is premised on the interrelationship between speaking and listening within the confines of a courtroom. International lawyers observe and listen to the flow of debate in assessing conflicting claims and their ultimate resolution by the international community's pre-eminent legal decision-making institution, the International Court of Justice (ICJ). An impressive body of international law scholarship attests to a wealth of devotion to the institution of the ICJ and its associated jurisprudence. A clamour of scholarly voices is never far from the corridors of the Peace Palace in various efforts to dissect and discuss the finest points of legal doctrine. Territorial disputes have been of especial interest to scholars of international adjudication, and with the rise of Third World participation in the Court, it would seem that international law is more inclusive than ever. Mainstream scholars have seized on the example of Third World territorial dispute resolution before the ICJ to illustrate broader claims about the nature of international law in this UN postcolonial era: we can now speak of a law that is universal; indeed, of a law that is truly international.[1]

A much rarer scholarly sensibility is the inclination and capacity to listen to the silences in and beyond the practice of territorial disputes. This is understandable: with the many voices of the Court's judges and regularly-appearing legal counsel, most scholars are content to focus on the more discernibly 'legal' strains resounding in the courtroom. A scholarly sub-discipline has emerged that is dedicated to studying these speech acts and judgments; perhaps the field of international law is served well enough by such efforts. Further, scholars of a more critical disposition have often perpetuated these silences by failing to develop the

[1] S. Pahuja, 'The Postcoloniality of International Law' (2005) 46 *Harvard International Law Journal* 459, at 461–462.

explanatory tools required in attuning our ears to less familiar sounds. Although both new and Third World approaches to international law (NAIL and TWAIL) have sought to develop methodologies sensitive to the silences and dark sides of international law, thus far their efforts in relation to territorial adjudication have remained under-developed. Scholarly silences are especially pronounced because of a general tendency to overlook the pleadings phase of proceedings;[2] law becomes judgment, rather than argumentation and debate.

A critical analysis of judgments, pleadings and the gaps in between is vital to an assessment of the extent to which the Court as a forum of international law allows for universalism. Thus, through an appraisal of both mainstream and critical approaches, the following chapter aims to highlight the limitations of current literatures on the nature of ICJ adjudication. The chapter will also develop the conceptual tools required for understanding the case studies.

The following analysis is structured around my central research question about the extent to which the ICJ can serve as a site for universalism in the postcolonial era. Rather than simply examining the prevailing materials on territorial adjudication and critical alternatives, this chapter refracts ideas through the prism of universalism: what are the underlying assumptions about international law as well as its universality in these literatures? One of the subsidiary research questions about how to understand the relationship between colonialism and international law in Arab territorial disputes can only be considered after a detailed examination of the theoretical and methodological foundations of international legal approaches to universalism. Accordingly, this chapter focuses on universalism and then the case studies offer specific instances of purported universalism in their exploration of colonialism and international law. It seeks to survey major trends in available international law literatures in English.

This chapter both deconstructs and reconstructs an understanding of universalism and a methodology of adjudication in five sections. In section one, I ask whether we can regard increased Third World participation in ICJ disputes as a

---

[2] Most studies of ICJ disputes fail to discuss pleadings in even the most cursory manner. Exceptions, however, are noteworthy and inform readings of the case studies in Parts II and III of the book. Of particular note is Koskenniemi's general discussion of territorial pleadings in M. Koskenniemi, *From Apology to Utopia: The Structure of International Legal Argument* (Cambridge: Cambridge University Press, 2nd ed., 2005), at 282–300, 385–387; and his detailed consideration of the *Libya/Chad* dispute as discussed in Chapter Three: M. Koskenniemi, 'L'Affaire du Différend Territorial (Jamahiriya Arabe Libyenne c. Tchad) Arrêt de la Cour Internationale de Justice du 3 février 1994' (1994) 40 *Annuaire français de droit international* 442. Knop also offers a close reading of the pleadings in the *Western Sahara* Advisory Opinion as discussed in Chapter Five: K. Knop, *Diversity and Self-Determination in International Law* (Cambridge: Cambridge University Press, 2002). Berman's insightful consideration of a PCIJ case is exceptional and indicates that much fruitful work remains even with PCIJ jurisprudence: N. Berman, 'The Nationality Decrees Case, or, Of Intimacy and Consent' (2000) 13 *Leiden Journal of International Law* 265.

triumph of universalism. Section two explores critical scholarship on the nature of legal universalism and the mainstream research agenda. Section three examines some critical characterisations of international law and language as a precursor to section four's analysis of the linguistic devices deployed in ICJ scholarship. In particular, section three develops the idea of silence, by suggesting that, rather than there being a lack of argument, it is a lack of capacity to *hear* other voices – or other dialects – that prevents universalism in the courtroom. Section four brings attention to the recurring narratives underpinning mainstream studies of ICJ disputes to understand how claims of universalism are made as well as how they can be sustained – or undermined. Section five is a return to fundamentals with its summation of my own perspective and position on international law. This chapter concludes on a cautious note by showing that international law contains only limited tools for becoming a universalising discourse. This is a start though. The key is to understand both speech as well as its silence in advancing the scope of the universalising potential of international law.

2) *Problematising Postcolonial Participation: Can We Now Speak of a 'World Court'?*

The mainstream international legal academy places faith in the progressive promise of international law. Past or ongoing weaknesses may be admitted, but vocational training also brings with it the desire to improve and strengthen the principled application of international rules. For Kennedy, no matter how 'difficult the project will be, international lawyers share an orientation to a past of sovereign states and a future of international law. The discipline looks forward, confident that we will arrive in the future with history at our side.'[3] The gaze then of the international lawyer projects itself always into a future guaranteed under a law that is more secure and inclusive in our postcolonial era. A striking example of this purported progress has been the increased participation of Third World states in ICJ disputes, and this is especially so in the sphere of territorial matters.[4] Various reasons have been offered to explain this development,

---

[3] D. Kennedy, 'When Renewal Repeats: Thinking against the Box' (1999–2000) 32 *New York University Journal of International Law and Politics* 335, at 347.

[4] For example, as noted by G. Distefano, 'The Conceptualization (Construction) of Territorial Title in the Light of International Court of Justice Case Law' (2006) 19 *Leiden Journal of International Law* 1041, at 1042; R. Y. Jennings, 'International Courts and International Politics', D. Freestone et al. (eds.), *Contemporary Issues in International Law: A Collection of Josephine Onoh Memorial Lectures* (The Hague: Kluwer, 2002) 13–28; M. Mubiala, 'La Contribution des États Africains à la Renaissance de la Cour Internationale de Justice' (1995) *African Yearbook of International Law* 173; P. M. Munya, 'The International Court of Justice and Peaceful Settlement of

and they will be explored below in an attempt to investigate whether we can now speak of a court able to listen to and speak for the world's states. The progressivist narrative of mainstream work is only capable of explaining part of this story of participation; greater consideration is still required as to why Third World states choose to come before the Court.[5]

In the English-speaking world (and especially the United States), the ICJ is often characterised as the 'World Court'.[6] How is this term commonly understood and what should a world court actually look like? First, it is important to note that the ontology of the World Court is a strange one, as it is populated almost exclusively by states.[7] Allott argues that a 'court epitomizes the *social* reality of the society in which it is an institution. A court epitomizes the *legal* reality whose legal relations it enforces.'[8] From this, it is possible to extrapolate the nature of the represented society from a given court. As applied to the ICJ, this would suggest that the Court works for a society of states, and yet, as Allott concedes, this is not really the case;[9] the Court operates in a society of many actors, but only allows a select few to speak. Despite this restriction on *locus standi*, the Court is empowered to hear any matter of international concern, and given that a fabric of independent states now spans the globe, we can see the Court as the pre-eminent tribunal for this geo-political reality.[10] Having acknowledged this

---

African Disputes: Problems, Challenges and Prospects' (1998) 7 *Journal of International Law & Practice* 159, at 189; and S. M. Schwebel, 'The Impact of the International Court of Justice', M. Shahabuddeen (ed.), *Boutros Boutros-Ghali: Amicorum discipulorumque liber: Paix, développement, démocratie*, vol. 1 (Brussels: Bruylant, 1998) 663–674, at 668.

5 Not only have scholars understudied reasons for Third World participation before the ICJ, but Romano argues that this is also the case in relation to dispute resolution *per se*: 'so far there are no comprehensive, systematic studies of the factors determining the resort by developing countries to international judicial fora.' C. P. R. Romano, 'International Justice and Developing Countries: A Quantitative Analysis' (2002) 1 *Law & Practice of International Courts and Tribunals* 367, at 370.

6 Abi-Saab points out that the expression, 'world court' is peculiar to English: G. Abi-Saab, 'The International Court as a World Court', V. Lowe & M. Fitzmaurice (eds.), *Fifty years of the International Court of Justice: Essays in Honour of Sir Robert Jennings* (Cambridge: Cambridge University Press, 1996) 3–16, at 3.

7 Article 34(1) of the Statute of the International Court of Justice states: 'Only states may be parties in cases before the Court'. There is also some provision for the involvement of international organisations: Article 34 (2–3).

8 P. Allott, 'The International Court of Justice and the idea of justice', V. Lowe & M. Fitzmaurice (eds.), *Fifty Years of the International Court of Justice: Essays in Honour of Sir Robert Jennings* (Cambridge: Cambridge University Press, 1996) 17–39, at 27.

9 Ibid.

10 Many scholars, however, question the significance of the Court, indicating that labels like 'world' court are deceptive and misrepresent the power and impact of the Court on the international stage. For example, Kennedy argues that 'the Court is one cultural and political institution among others, crafting its decision to enhance its legitimacy and pull towards compliance, the

context, we can apply Abi-Saab's definition of 'world court': 'it is expected to be universalist in its composition, outlook and vocation, truly representing and at the service of the international community in its entirety, and not dominated by the legal or social culture or special interests of any segment thereof.'[11]

Although it is relatively easy to characterise the Court in its more recent manifestation as a universal forum, both Abi-Saab and Elias point out that the jurisprudence generated by its predecessor, the PCIJ, was exclusionary in the way most cases only considered Third World states as *objects*, and not *subjects*, of international law.[12] Difficulties in denying this heritage are exacerbated by the commonly held view that despite the name change, the ICJ and the PCIJ are one and the same entity. This was felt especially keenly in the earlier period of the ICJ.[13] Bedjaoui, a former president of the ICJ, enunciates this narrative of institutional continuity: 'the present Court is but the continuation of an international justice born at the dawn of this century in the delicious coolness of this charming tree-lined city of The Hague.'[14] Other recent members of the

---

decision one drop in the ocean of world public opinion'. D. Kennedy, 'The Nuclear Weapons case', L. Boisson de Chazournes & P. Sands (eds.), *International Law, the International Court of Justice and Nuclear Weapons* (Cambridge: Cambridge University Press, 1999) 462–472, at 464. Some mainstream perspectives tend to lament the weaknesses of the Court, hoping for a stronger institution. This theme is explored below in section four of this chapter.

[11] Abi-Saab. 'The International Court as a World Court, *supra* n. 6, at 3.

[12] G. Abi-Saab, 'The Newly Independent States and the Rules of International Law: An Outline' (1962) 8 *Howard Law Journal* 95, at 98. Elias was making the point particularly *vis-à-vis* African states, but the comment applies to the majority of the non-European world: 'Africa has in one aspect or another been before the Court since the days of the League of Nations, though unfortunately more often as the object rather than the subject of international law.' T. O. Elias, *The International Court of Justice and some contemporary problems: Essays on international law* (The Hague: Martinus Nijhoff, 1983), at 299.

[13] According to McWhinney, 'The Court's deliberate intellectual orientation towards a technical, analytical, logical approach; its established clientele, from the pre-War and immediate post-War years, of politically and economically stable Western states; and the absence of any compensating political sophistication, on the part of the newly emerging, newly decolonised, Afro-Asian countries, as to the Court's potentiality for political conflicts-resolution and for remarking "old" International Law, meant that it continued to operate and to have the reputation, as a "European" tribunal well after the United Nations proper had begun to undergo fundamental changes in its personality and character as a result of the wholesale admission of new states from 1955 onwards.' E. McWhinney, *The International Court of Justice and the Western Tradition of International Law: The Paul Martin Lectures in International Relations and Law* (Dordrecht; Boston: Martinus Nijhoff, 1987), at 67.

[14] M. Bedjaoui, 'Celebration of the Fiftieth Anniversary of the International Court of Justice' (1996) 8 *African Journal of International Comparative Law* 617, at 621. For this narrative of PCIJ/ICJ continuity, see R. P. Anand, *Studies in International Law and History: An Asian Perspective* (Leiden: Martinus Nijhoff, 2004), at 159; E. McWhinney, 'The International Court of Justice and International Law-making: The Judicial Activism/Self-Restraint Antinomy' (2006) 5

Court, including Judges Jennings and Weeramantry, disagree with this characterisation of the Court.[15] Irrespective of the relative merit of these divergent perspectives, however, the image of the PCIJ serving European interests was hard to ignore for recently independent states entering international society on the eve of independence.[16]

Given these institutional characteristics of the ICJ, especially in its first few decades, European and Third World scholars have recognised the postcolonial paradox Third World states faced: to use the Court or not to use the Court.[17] The paradox for Third World states is that it could be argued that to protect themselves, they must rely on the very weapons once created by their former colonial overlords.[18] Many reasons have been advanced to account for minimal Third World ICJ engagement, but the main strands running through the literature have tended to focus on the context of the Cold War,[19] the debacle of the *South West Africa* cases,[20] under-representation of non-European judges and legal norms,

Chinese Journal of International Law 3, at 4. It is also noted by Thirlway, who argues 'it is somewhat artificial to treat... [the PCIJ] independently of the decisions of the postwar Court – an artificiality that Rosenne avoids by treating the jurisprudence of the two international courts as a seamless whole.' H. Thirlway, 'International Legal Argument in the Permanent Court of Justice: The Rise of the International Judiciary (Book Review)' (2007) 101 *American Journal of International Law* 246, at 249.

[15] R. Y. Jennings, 'The International Court of Justice after Fifty Years' (1995) 89 *American Journal of International Law* 493, at 493. Jennings' main reason for distinguishing the ICJ and the PCIJ is the fact that the ICJ functions as the primary judicial organ of the UN. See also Weeramantry on the ICJ's contextual differences: C. G. Weeramantry, 'Expanding the Potential of the World Court', N. Jasentuliyana (ed.), *Perspectives on International Law* (Boston: Kluwer, 1995) 309–346, at 341.

[16] For an informative overview of the PCIJ's jurisprudence *vis-à-vis* colonial/mandate entities, see S. Rosenne, 'Decolonisation in the International Court of Justice' (1996) 8 *African Journal of International and Comparative Law* 564.

[17] For example, Fatouros points out that in many ways international law is especially useful for Third World states as it can act as a weapon of the weak. A. A. Fatouros, 'International Law and the Third World' (1964) 50 *Virginia Law Review* 783, at 791.

[18] Generally, see M. L. Sarin, 'The Asian-African States and the Development of International Law', F. E. Snyder & S. Sathirathai (eds.), *Third World Attitudes Toward International Law: An Introduction* (Dordrecht; Boston: Martinus Nijhoff, 1987) 33–51, at 39.

[19] McWhinney especially notes this factor. Generally, see McWhinney, *The International Court of Justice and the Western Tradition, supra* n. 13; E. McWhinney, 'Western and Non-Western Legal Cultures and the International Court of Justice' (1987) 65 *Washington University Law Quarterly* 873; and E. McWhinney, '"Internationalizing" The International Court: The Quest for Ethno-cultural and Legal-systemic Representativeness', E. G. Bello & B. A. Ajibola (eds.), *Essays in Honour of Judge Taslim Olawale Elias: vol. I Contemporary International Law and Human Rights* (Dordrecht; Boston: Martinus Nijhoff, 1992) 277–289.

[20] *International Status of South West Africa (Advisory Opinion)* (1950) ICJ Reps, p. 128; *Admissibility of Hearings of Petitioners by the Committee on South West Africa (Advisory Opinion)* (1956) ICJ

as well as deep-seated Third World cultural (as opposed to political) aversion to third party dispute resolution. In relation to the last point, it is surprising how both Third and First World scholars have readily applied cultural stereotypes to the entire non-European world. Third World scholars such as Sinha and Tieya have suggested that Third World states preferred the avenues of negotiations and mediation; adjudication was not culturally appropriate.[21] Prott lends her own European assessment to the 'problem' of Third World participation by arguing that only in Western societies had there developed the requisite notion of an independent judiciary divorced from politics. Thus, non-European states expected certain 'non-legal' solutions from the Court and were unsure about how to approach it.[22] Writing much more recently and perhaps with the benefit of hindsight, Romano cautions against making such generalisations about the Third World being less culturally inclined toward litigation.[23]

Although many commentators have avoided cultural stereotypes in their accounts of Third World participation, most have at least identified the importance of diversity on the ICJ's bench in accounting for initial Third World

---

Reps, p. 23; *South West Africa Cases (Ethiopia/South Africa; Liberia/South Africa) (Preliminary Objections)* (1962) ICJ Reps, p. 319; *South West Africa Cases (Ethiopia/South Africa; Liberia/South Africa) (Second Phase)* (1966) ICJ Reps, p. 6; *Legal Consequences for States of the Continued Presence of South Africa in Namibia (South West Africa) notwithstanding Security Council Resolution 276 (1970) (Advisory Opinion)* (1971) ICJ Reps, p. 12. In 1960, Ethopia and Liberia had filed claims before the ICJ arguing that South Africa had failed to meet its requirements towards the territory of South West Africa under the League of Nations Mandate regime. In 1966 with the casting vote of the Court's Australian judge, Sir Percy Spender, standing to contest the matter was denied to Ethiopia and Liberia. With a different bench and condemnation of its 1966 judgment, in 1971 the Court ruled that South Africa's presence in the territory was illegal. Despite this ruling, Namibia (the name of the territory since 1968) only gained its independence in 1990. For discussion about the cases, see J. Crawford, *The Creation of States in International Law* (Cambridge: Cambridge University Press, 2nd ed., 2006), at 586–598.

[21] According to Sinha in relation to 'pacific settlement of disputes, the newly independent States prefer methods of negotiation, inquiry, mediation and conciliation rather than adjudication of legal rules.' S. P. Sinha, 'Perspective of the Newly Independent States on the Binding Quality of International Law', F. E. Snyder & S. Sathirathai (eds.), *Third World Attitudes Toward International Law: An Introduction* (Dordrecht; Boston: Martinus Nijhoff, 1987) 23–31, at 29. For a counter-argument, claiming that negotiations are more important than resort to the ICJ within the 'standard of civilized behaviour', see L. Nader, 'Civilization and its Negotiations', P. Caplan (ed.), *Understanding Disputes: The Politics of Argument* (Oxford. Providence, 1995) 39–63, 41.

[22] L. V. Prott, 'Role, Consensus and Opinion Analysis at the International Court of Justice' (1983) 14 *Netherlands Yearbook of International Law* 69, at 72.

[23] C. P. R. Romano, 'International Justice and Developing Countries (Continued): A Qualitative Analysis' (2002) 1 *Law & Practice of International Courts and Tribunals* 539, at 571.

reticence in using the Court.[24] Why would Third World states trust an institution unrepresentative in its officers and the laws they applied? Mainstream scholarship suggests that only once some of these characteristics changed would Third World states be willing to entrust matters before this tribunal. As Third World jurists themselves, both El-Erian and Weeramantry single out Article 9 of the Court's Statute for discussion:

> At every election, the electors shall bear in mind not only that the persons to be elected should individually possess the qualifications required, but also that in the body as a whole the representation of the main forms of civilization and of the principal legal systems of the world should be assured.

El-Erian argues that this requirement of civilisational representation is significant and is unique in the UN system, which is otherwise based on equitable geographical distribution of its personnel.[25] Weeramantry regards this provision as fundamental for the possibility of a universal Court, able to speak for and speak to the world's many civilisations.[26] Weeramantry's example of inter-civilisational jurisprudence contained in his own separate opinions is testimony to such a possibility.[27] In the words of Anghie, Weeramanty 'suggests that international law is not alien to the Third World; it is part of the heritage of Third World countries which have contributed to its development.'[28] Despite Weeramantry's efforts, however, he has recently doubted the scope for such inter-civilisational dialogue at the bench, noting that 'it has not happened thus far in any significant measure, and such input, has been miniscule.'[29]

Although genuine civilisational representation has yet to be realised, and perhaps can never be, it is clear that the issue of the ratio of European/non-European judges at the ICJ has been a continuing motif in the literature accounting for Third World reluctance especially in the early years of the Court. For Romano,

---

[24] It is striking that in reading many discussions about the representation of ICJ judges, never once did a mainstream or Third World perspective express any concern about the gendered nature of the Court; it was worrying to have only European males, but not non-European males. This oversight in understanding the concept of a representative bench is explored in H. Charlesworth & C. Chinkin, *The Boundaries of International Law: A Feminist Analysis* (Manchester: Manchester University Press, 2000), at 80–81.

[25] A. El-Erian, 'The International Court of Justice and the Concept of Universality' (1981) 19 *Columbia Journal of Transnational Law* 197, at 204.

[26] C. G. Weeramantry, *Universalising International Law* (Leiden: Martunis Nijhoff, 2004), at 3.

[27] Especially, see *Legality of the Threat or Use of Nuclear Weapons Advisory Opinion (Advisory Opinion)* (1996) ICJ Reps (diss. op. Weeramantry), at 449–555; and *Gabčíkovo-Nagymaros Case (Hungary/Slovakia)* (1997) ICJ Reps (sep. op. Weeramantry), at 96–110.

[28] A. Anghie, 'C. G. Weeramantry at the International Court of Justice' (2001) 14 *Leiden Journal of International Law* 829, at 845.

[29] Weeramantry, *Universalizing International Law, supra* n. 26, at 3.

'the issue of the distribution of seats in the ICJ has always been highly contentious, notably among the Asian group, which is representative of such a large part of the world's population but relatively underrepresented on the bench.'[30] Some useful quantitative studies highlight the continuing discrepancies in the geographical and civilisational composition of the bench.[31]

Numbers aside, however, it is difficult to establish any direct link between the ICJ's bench and its jurisprudence. Anghie reminds us that there are no specific qualities possessed by Third World judges, but they do at least bring with them certain personal experiences:

> To label a judge as a 'Third World' judge based on the positions he [sic] takes on specific issues is a relatively simple, and perhaps simplistic way of characterizing a judge. The more complex issue is the relationship between the Third World judge and international law itself, given that historically, international law has marginalized Third World peoples and legitimized their dispossession and conquest.[32]

Bedjaoui echoes this idea by arguing that the work of a judge is deeply personal; conscience, rather than political factors, influences legal determinations.[33] Other writers have dismissed any relationship between a judge's nationality and her jurisprudence, especially because most Third World jurists are themselves educated in Europe or North America and often are well-versed in the Peace Palace's markedly European culture upon arrival.[34]

Despite the fact that there are strong arguments negating a link between Third World judges and structural change within the ICJ, the South West Africa affair

---

[30] Romano, 'International Justice and Developing Countries (Continued)', *supra* n. 23, at 579.

[31] C. Harland, 'International Court of Justice Elections: A Report on the First Fifty Years' (1996) 34 *Canadian Yearbook of International Law* 303. For more recent statistics, see Romano, 'International Justice and Developing Countries', *supra* n. 5.

[32] Anghie, 'C. G. Weeramantry', *supra* n. 28, at 844–845. For an interesting study about the problems faced by Third World judges and lawyers in their municipal jurisdictions, see R. L. Abel, 'The Underdevelopment of Legal Professions: A Review Article on Third World Lawyers' (1982) *American Bar Foundation Research Journal* 871.

[33] Bedjaoui, *supra* n. 14, at 622–623. Dupuy also regards the institution of the judge as especially important in advancing the cause of the Court: 'it seems that the best way for improving the role of the ICJ as a world court rests in the hands of the judges themselves, and in the way they view the true function of the Court within the international legal system. It is more a matter of judicial policy than of technical efficiency improvements, even if it is true that some such improvements could be achieved.' P.-M. Dupuy, 'The Danger of Fragmentation or Unification of the International Legal System and the International Court of Justice', (1998–1999) 31 *New York University Journal of International Law & Politics* 791, at 802.

[34] Abi-Saab talks more broadly about the way in which many Third World jurists educated in the West are excessively positivist and incapable of questioning legal rules. Abi-Saab, 'The Newly Independent States', *supra* n. 12, at 100.

has since been explained as being very much about First World judicial bias.[35] Along with the *Nicaragua* case, these two examples are constructed as polar opposites in accounts of Third World ICJ participation.[36] This narrative of dark and light is part of ICJ literature; no study of the Court is complete without a discussion and comparison between these watersheds. Time and again, the dark days of the Court's 'betrayal' in its 1966 *South West Africa* decision are singled out in a bid to distinguish and exceptionalise this episode in the Court's practice.[37] The casting vote of a First World judge gives further weight to this extraordinary affair that prompted profound distrust across the Third World. For example, Munya rejected any notion of universalism after this episode, naming the ICJ as the 'Western Court of Justice'.[38] Rarely do accounts acknowledge the relative unimportance of the Court for Third World states *before* the *South West Africa* cases or suggest other reasons for its associations with colonial/mandatory rule at the level of international legal discourse itself.

Irrespective of this earlier context, however, narratives lauding the rise of Third World participation must show how Third World attitudes have changed radically since the unfortunate experience of *South West Africa*. The soul-searching prompted by *South West Africa* resulted in a greater awareness of the influence of Third World judges, and commentators have documented the phenomenon of Third World states lobbying for their own jurists.[39] By the time the Court was tested in *Nicaragua*,[40] the typical narrative suggests that Third World interests were vindicated: the Court could now shine for the interests of the majority world. Furthermore, in 1986 with this instance of First World reversal, the ICJ's

[35] For a nuanced and contextual consideration of the South West Africa affair and its roots in European intellectual history, see S. N. Grovogui, *Sovereigns, Quasi-Sovereigns, and Africans: Race and Self-Determination in International Law* (Minneapolis: University of Minnesota Press, 1996).

[36] *Supra* n. 20; *Military and Paramilitary Activities in and against Nicaragua (Nicaragua/ USA) (Merits)* (1986) ICJ Reps, p. 14.

[37] M. Pomerance, 'The ICJ and South West Africa (Namibia): A Retrospective Legal/Political Assessment' (1999) 12 *Leiden Journal of International Law* 425, at 430. Adede offers an example of this narrative of exception: he describes how President Judge Spender advised Judge Khan to step down for the 1966 case, thus changing the balance of the Court. Such an account may well be factually correct, but in focussing on these superficial factors, it is easier to distinguish this episode and overlook pervasive structural explanations for why it was possible at all for the Court to reach such a decision. A. O. Adede, 'Judicial Settlement in Perspective', A. S. Muller, D. Raič & J. M. Thuránszky (eds.), *The International Court of Justice: Its Future Role after Fifty Years* (The Hague; Boston: Martinus Nijhoff, 1997) 47–81, at 51–53.

[38] P. M. Munya, 'The International Court of Justice and Peaceful Settlement of African Disputes: Problems, Challenges and Prospects' (1998) 7 *Journal of International Law & Practice* 159, at 173.

[39] McWhinney, 'Western and non-Western Legal Cultures', *supra* n. 19, at 880–882; Pomerance, *supra* n. 37, at 431.

[40] Pomerance, *supra* n. 37, at 435.

Chamber also handed down its *cause célèbre* of later territorial judgements, the *Frontier Dispute*,[41] which demarcated the boundary between two African states, Burkino Faso and Mali.[42] This judgment has served as the blueprint for later Third World territorial disputes, which largely revolve around *ad hoc* agreements seeking the Court's assistance in solidifying borders. Over a decade later and with unprecedented Court activity, Judge Ajibola noted: 'This increase in the volume of cases before the Court is obviously a reflection of an increasing confidence that states now have in the Court. It suggests that states are now more amenable to submitting their differences to adjudication than they were in the past.'[43] Former events and PCIJ memories aside, then, most commentators feel confident in viewing the Court as qualitatively different from its early days, partly as a result of increased Third World participation. Perhaps, in the twenty first century, it is even possible to posit a Court universal in its reach and representation.

Third World participation in the Court is noteworthy, but it does not prove the Court's universalism or legitimacy. Rarely have scholars celebrating the Court's 'relevance' advanced convincing structural reasons for the seeming shift in Third World arbitral proclivities. For example, most mainstream accounts about the work of the Court disregard quotidian realities for Third World decision-making about adjudication.[44] Concerns about representation, language, time delays and funding nevertheless are real.[45] For example, little attention has been paid to the impact that an almost exclusively European bar must have on the choices available to states.[46] Some scholars especially from the Third World are alive to these limitations and biases, but rarely is this feature acknowledged elsewhere. Pellett is a notable exception, when he concedes that 'in the small world of public international law we may speak of the "mafia" of the International

[41] Distefano, *supra* n. 4, at 1042.

[42] *Case Concerning the Frontier Dispute (Burkina Faso/Mali)* (1986) ICJ Reps, p. 554. The case is discussed briefly in Part II's Introduction, at 97–114.

[43] B. A. Ajibola, 'Dispute Resolution by the International Court of Justice' (1998) 11 *Leiden Journal of International Law* 123, at 124.

[44] In a discussion about some of the difficulties and drawbacks of ICJ litigation, see G. Guillaume, 'The Future of International Judicial Institutions' (1995) 44 *International & Comparative Law Quarterly* 848.

[45] Sinclair notes state concern over delays as an important reason for avoiding ICJ litigation: I. Sinclair, 'The Court as an Institution: Its Role and Position in International Society', D. Bowett et al., *The International Court of Justice: Process, Practice and Procedure* (London: The British Institute of International & Comparative Law, 1997) 21–26, at 23.

[46] For some illuminating statistics about non-European lawyers at the Court, see K. T. Gaubatz & M. MacArthur, 'How International is "International" Law?' (2000–2001) 22 *Michigan Journal of International Law* 239, at 250–260.

Court of Justice'.[47] Reasons for this situation are many, but one factor is the way in which lawyers well-versed in the Court's languages of English and French will *ipso facto* feel more at home than some of their counterparts. In a rare discussion about the impact that language restrictions have on participants, Judge Oda described the difficulties he has faced in keeping pace with native English or French speakers on the bench.[48] Many Third World lawyers and judges possess the Court's official languages as mother tongues too, but this is not always the case.[49]

Of similar neglect is the factor of litigation expenses preventing Third World participation. The ICJ Statute requires states to fund the costs of a case,[50] and these may be prohibitive for many Third World states. On the initiative of the Non-Aligned Movement (NAM) at the UN,[51] the General Assembly introduced the Secretary-General's Trust Fund derived from the voluntary contributions of member-states to support needy states in covering litigation costs for contentious cases founded on a *compromis*. Jennings argues that the 'fund is clearly an important step in enabling poorer countries to take advantage of the Court for the disposal of disputes within its contentious jurisdiction, where the parties are able to make a special agreement.'[52] Such an initiative – even though limited in its accessibility and future liquidity – is commendable and could serve as another factor in boosting Third World participation before the Court. Bekker, however, laments the lack of scholarly or media attention on the fund's impact thus far.[53]

---

[47] Quoted in Romano, 'International Justice and Developing Countries (Continued)', *supra* n. 23, at 561, note 79. This point is also made by McWhinney, '"Internationalizing" the International Court', *supra* n. 19, at 288.

[48] S. Oda, 'Comment', D. Bowett et al. (eds.), *The International Court of Justice: Process, Practice and Procedure* (London: The British Institute of International & Comparative Law, 1997), at 94–101.

[49] The relevance of language is rarely noted in the literature, but an exception is Richard Falk, who discusses 'Western cultural hegemony' as symbolised by the Court's location in The Hague working only in French and/or English. R. Falk, *Reviving the World Court* (Charlottesville: University Press of Virginia, 1986), at 180.

[50] Article 64, Statute of the International Court of Justice.

[51] T. Bien-Aime, 'A Pathway to The Hague and Beyond: The United Nations Trust Fund Proposal' (1989–1990) 22 *New York University Journal of International Law & Politics* 671. For a brief overview of the scheme, see 'United Nations: Secretary-General's Trust Fund to Assist States in the Settlement of Disputes through the International Court of Justice' (1989) 28 ILM 1589.

[52] Jennings, 'The International Court of Justice after Fifty Years', *supra* n. 15, at 501.

[53] P. H. F. Bekker, 'International Legal Aid in Practice: The ICJ Trust Fund' (1993) 87 *American Journal of International Law* 659, at 660. It has been very difficult to access detailed information about the fund's beneficiaries, but I am aware that the fund was used by Burkino Faso and Mali in the *Fronter Dispute* in applying the Chamber's boundary determination, and Chad drew on funds in its dispute with Libya in the *Territorial Dispute*, discussed in Chapter Three

Factors such as the increased representation of Third World judges and the *Nicaragua* judgment have bolstered the Court's legitimacy, but it remains unclear whether this can account for why Third World states now rely on the Court more than ever before. Many mainstream scholars have praised the Court for its postcolonial progress and now invoke the narrative of universalism, but critical scholarship, introduced in the next section, questions not only the arguments advanced, but also the methods used, in constructing such a narrative.

3) *NAIL and TWAIL on the Politics of Law and the Possibility of Universalism*

Mainstream accounts of the Court's universality rest on assumptions about the nature of international law. This is equally true of those voices questioning and challenging such a depiction of the ICJ. Thus, debates about the nature of the Court are part of a broader disciplinary debate about how to study international law.[54] Methodology is an exercise in boundary-drawing and a conscious choice about which knowledges to privilege and which to silence.[55] It is the task of critical scholars to probe these 'blind spots' within the discipline to deny the naturalness and inevitability of prevailing power relations,[56] including those constructed through the discourse of international law in and beyond the courtroom. International law is structured by a dynamic of difference and NAIL and TWAIL scholars have highlighted this dynamic in a number of ways.[57] Reappraisals of binary oppositions such as masculine/feminine, colonial/postcolonial,

below. In his 2002 survey, Romano notes that since its inception, four requests for assistance have been made. Romano, 'International Justice and Developing Countries (Continued)', *supra* n. 23, at 554.

[54] For a good illustration of some of these contrasting methodologies, see the special issue dedicated to method in international law: (1999) 93 *American Journal of International Law*. In particular, see the editorial comments: S. R. Ratner & A.-M. Slaughter, 'Appraising the Methods of International Law: A Prospectus for Readers' (1999) 93 *American Journal of International Law* 291; and A.-M. Slaughter & S. R. Ratner, 'The Method is the Message' (1999) 93 *American Journal of International Law* 410.

[55] H. Charlesworth, 'Feminist Methods in International Law' (1999) 93 *American Journal of International Law* 379, at 368 & 381. This idea is also explored in relation to terrorism and international law, see I. M. Porras, 'On Terrorism: Reflections on Violence and the Outlaw' (1994) *Utah Law Review* 119.

[56] The idea of disciplinary blind spots is invoked by a number of critical scholars, who speak of mainstream methodological oversights. Some examples include: Charlesworth, *supra* n. 55, at 386; and Kennedy, 'When Renewal Repeats, *supra* n. 3.

[57] For example, as elaborated in A. Anghie, 'Colonialism and the Birth of International Institutions: Sovereignty, Economy, and the Mandate System of the League of Nations' (2002) 34 *New York University Journal of International Law and Politics* 513, at 518–519.

universal/particular and law/politics demonstrate how difficult it is to speak of universalism. By studying the dark side of dichotomies at play in international legal discourse,[58] this section problematises the narrative of universalism and progress as explored in section four's consideration of some themes in the literature about the ICJ. The section first surveys some basic characteristics of NAIL scholarship before considering TWAIL's particular perspective on Third World concerns revolving around colonialism.

Summaries inevitably simplify scholarship and this perhaps is especially so in relation to NAIL, which seeks to open up, rather than contain and confine, international legal research.[59] Thus, instead of attempting a survey of NAIL literatures, some relevant themes are explored instead so as to problematise the self-image of international law within the discipline as well as to raise questions about universalism.[60]

Critical approaches rose to prominence in the eighties especially with the work of David Kennedy and Martti Koskenniemi.[61] Kennedy described his approach, and those of his peers, as 'Newstream', and this was a term that encapsulated critical reappraisals of the discipline until its later metamorphosis in the nineties into 'NAIL'. Critical scholars are concerned with exploring the inner workings of the discipline of international law. Excavations have revealed

[58] The idea of the dark side is noted by Koskenniemi when he discussed the need to deconstruct the promise of liberalism and appreciate those it overlooks in this world of endless consumer choice: 'Not to fall under the spell of that shopping mall requires focusing on its dangers, discontinuities and mechanisms of exclusion. If "deconstruction" is able to bring out that dark side, the reality of the mall at night, it may provide a means for critical identification and practice.' M. Koskenniemi, 'Letter to the Editors of the Symposium' (1999) 93 *American Journal of International Law* 351, at 361. David Kennedy also explores this image in a number of his writings, the most extensive being: D. Kennedy, *The Dark Sides of Virtue: Reassessing International Humanitarianism* (Princeton: Princeton University Press, 2004).

[59] This is pointed out in T. Skouteris, 'Fin de NAIL: New Approaches to International Law and its Impact on Contemporary International Legal Scholarship' (1997) 10 *Leiden Journal of International Law* 415, at 418, footnote 6.

[60] For some surveys of NAIL contributions, see J. A. Beckett, 'Countering Uncertainty and Ending Up/Down Arguments: *Prolegomena* to a Response to NAIL' (2005) 16 *European Journal of International Law* 213; D. Z. Cass, 'Navigating the Newstream: Recent Critical Scholarship in International Law' (1996) 65 *Nordic Journal of International Law* 341; Kennedy, 'When Renewal Repeats', *supra* n. 3; A. L. Paulus, 'International Law after Postmodernism: Towards Renewal or Decline of International Law?' (2001) 14 *Leiden Journal of International Law* 727; N. Purvis, 'Critical Legal Studies in Public International Law' (1991) 32 *Harvard International Law Journal* 81. For a brief discussion and bibliography of NAIL scholarship, see T. Skouteris & O. Korhonen, 'Under Rhodes' Eyes: The "Old" and the "New" International Law at Looking Distance' (1998) 11 *Leiden Journal of International Law* 429.

[61] Especially see the work of Koskenniemi listed in the bibliography; and D. Kennedy, 'A New Stream of International Law Scholarship' (1988) 7 *Wisconsin International Law Journal* 1.

'biased discursive structures,' usually hidden under the veil of liberalism,[62] which is typically depicted as normatively neutral in a system straddling sovereignty and its constraint.[63] Critical scholars challenge liberalism's promise of equality by revealing the 'background conditions and norms' of international law, which generate not only disciplinary blind spots and biases, but also exclusion for actors on the ground.[64]

Critical approaches are alive to the effects generated by the perpetuation and seeming naturalness of dichotomies and none more so than the tension between law and politics. By separating law from politics, mainstream scholars can construct an image of international law untouched by considerations of power and domination. In so doing, the bulk of international legal scholarship perpetuates ongoing exclusion and silence in a gesture that is – at least covertly – fiercely political. Conversely, critical scholars elide law with politics, showing us that the two cannot be separated; international law is a 'tradition and a political project',[65] played out in a special institutional and discursive setting that provides it with particular meaning. Thus for Koskenniemi, law 'is a surface over which political opponents engage in hegemonic practices, trying to enlist its rules, principles and institutions on their side, making sure they do not support the adversary.'[66] For international lawyers, the 'point is…not to be ashamed of…underlying choices but to make them in the open, to open them up for critique and rebuttal.'[67] Kennedy suggests that we ask not '*whether* politics or *where* politics, but *what* politics.'[68]

Once law is understood as a discursive political practice, it is impossible to regard rules as objective or to resolve definitively conflicts over competing norms in a horizontal system; international law becomes indeterminate. The consequences of this position have resulted in profound mainstream mistrust. Thus, Skouteris notes that '[d]espite the growth of NAIL writing, engaged scholarly response has been spectacularly absent.'[69] Political ramifications within NAIL are also internally destabilising, as its call for context can also be deconstructed,

[62] This term is used in C. Thomas, 'Critical Race Theory and Postcolonial Development Theory: Observations on Methodology' (2000) 45 *Villanova Law Review* 1195, at 1219.

[63] See generally, Koskenniemi, *From Apology to Utopia, supra* n. 2; and M. Mutua, Keynote Address, Third World Approaches to International Law, Albany Law School, 20–21 April 2007.

[64] Kennedy, 'When Renewal Repeats', *supra* n. 3, at 409–410.

[65] M. Koskenniemi, 'The Fate of Public International Law: Between Technique and Politics' (2007) 70 *Modern Law Review* 1, at 1.

[66] M. Koskenniemi, 'International Law and Hegemony: A Reconfiguration' (2004) 17 *Cambridge Review of International Affairs* 197, at 200.

[67] Paulus, *supra* n. 60, at 753.

[68] Italics in the original, Kennedy, 'When Renewal Repeats, *supra* n. 3, at 412.

[69] Skouteris, *supra* n. 59, at 419–420.

making it impossible to know which account to favour.[70] The consolation at least is that NAIL is alive to the politics of choice in its methodological schemes. Ultimately, NAIL provides the conceptual tools for exposing structural biases and contingencies at the heart of international law. Whether it can serve as a political platform for progressive change is still to be seen, especially in relation to law as a universalising discourse.

A number of approaches based around identity have taken up the themes of NAIL in various shades of harmony and dissonance.[71] For example, both feminist and Third World concerns have their roots in earlier projects, but they have often combined these along a broader critical trajectory, so that it is possible to note a whole range of critical subfields within NAIL.

TWAIL is one critical approach which shares many similarities with earlier Third World as well as NAIL scholarship in its quest to interrogate the universality of international law. Kennedy identifies the central TWAIL concerns as being:

> How is domination and inequality reproduced?
> What has international law got to do with it?
> How can we fight this domination?[72]

Chimni echoes this by pointing out that TWAIL's focus is centred on struggles of Third World peoples; he argues, however, that a NAIL tendency toward rejecting all rules and offering no alternatives is unhelpful.[73] TWAIL began as a movement in the mid nineties, but draws heavily on the consciousness and practice of earlier Third World jurists seeking to advance the rights of the developing world in the context of decolonisation.[74] Gathii notes that these earlier scholars, or TWAIL I scholars, were largely concerned with how to reform international law so that it could fulfil its promise of equality and universality in a postcolo-

---

70 Paulus, *supra* n. 60.

71 As noted in Kennedy, 'When Renewal Repeats', *supra* n. 3, at 391–392 and especially footnote 22.

72 D. Kennedy, Keynote Address, Third World Approaches to International Law, Albany Law School, 20–21 April 2007.

73 B. S. Chimni, 'Towards a Radical Third World Approach to Contemporary International Law' (2002) 5 *International Centre for Comparative Law and Politics Review* 14, at 23–24.

74 Baxi suggests that 'Third Worldism offers histories of mentalities of self-determination and self-governance, based on the insistence of the recognition of radical cultural and civilisational plurality and diversity.' U. Baxi, 'What may the "Third World" expect from International Law?' (2006) 27 *Third World Quarterly* 713, at 714. An emphasis on development is also an important element in Third World work as argued by L. Marasinghe, 'Third World Jurisprudence of the Twenty-First Century', A. Anghie & G. Sturgess (eds.), *Legal Visions of the 21st Century: Essays in Honour of Judge Christopher Weeramantry* (The Hague: Kluwer, 1998) 49–71, at 55.

nial world.[75] Although a nationalist strand rejected international law altogether, an integrationist strand advanced a multicultural law, built on European and non-European norms.[76] A number of first and Third World scholars therefore focused on an historical account of the pre-colonial origins of international law and many argued and continue to argue that international law was once based on the interaction between European and non-European independent states. Colonialism and its denial of international legal personality cannot be ignored, but with its demise, many scholars were keen to show how international law was also culturally rich and non-discriminatory.[77] Such studies have contributed to our understandings of the history of international legal relations and their contribution is touched upon in Chapter Two.

'TWAIL II' scholarship is more cautious about embracing optimistic narratives of a postcolonial international law:[78] structural biases continue to exclude and silence much of the Third World, but in different ways from those of the colonial period. Thus, TWAIL II has channelled its energies in exploring the legacies of colonialism to show that colonialism is a constant[79] and that international law is a 'medium of conquest and domination'.[80] Particular attention has been paid to understanding how international law is not a practice based on regulating relations between sovereign states; instead, it is structured by an ongoing dynamic of cultural difference.[81] Continuity, rather than change, is highlighted, and so it becomes much more difficult to speak of an era *after* colonialism. Pahuja captures this idea when she posits that the '"post" in postcolonial designates

[75] J. T. Gathii, 'Alternative and Critical: The Contribution of Research and Scholarship on Developing Countries to International Legal Theory' (2000) 41 *Harvard International Law Journal* 263, at 265.

[76] Ibid., at 273.

[77] For example, Abi-Saab speaks of the period of decolonisation as a re-acquisition of sovereignty for the Third World: Abi-Saab, 'The Newly Independent States', *supra* n. 12, at 103–104. See also M. A. Ajomo, 'International Law, the United Nations and Decolonization', E. G. Bello & B. A. Ajibola (eds.), *Essays in Honour of Judge Taslim Olawale Elias: vol. I Contemporary International Law and Human Rights* (1992) 77–92, at 79; P. C. Jessup, 'Diversity and Uniformity in the Law of Nations' (1964) 58 *American Journal of International Law* 341; M. Shahabuddeen, 'Developing Countries and the Idea of International Law', McDonald, R. St. John (ed.), *Essays in Honour of Wang Tieya* (Dordrecht; Boston: Martinus Nijhoff, 1994) 721, at 726.

[78] For some discussions of the basic differences between TWAIL I and TWAIL II approaches, see B. S. Chimni, 'Towards a TWAIL Theory of Interpretation: Some Notes', Conference Paper, TWAIL III, Albany Law School, 20–21 April 2007.

[79] A. Anghie, *Imperialism, Sovereignty and the Making of International Law* (Cambridge: Cambridge University Press, 2005), at 315.

[80] M. Mutua, 'Critical Race Theory and International Law: The View of an Insider-Outsider' (2000) 45 *Villanova Law Review* 841, at 843.

[81] Anghie, *Imperialism, supra* n. 79, at 4–5.

a state neither clearly beyond nor after the colonial.'[82] Our consciousness as international lawyers and the experience of Third World peoples cannot escape the reality that 'first of all there was colonialism'.[83] Although TWAIL is devoted to the interests of Third World peoples (as opposed to Third World states),[84] Mickelson reminds us that colonial legacies are no less important for the First, as opposed to the Third, World, especially regarding the distribution of wealth.[85] More recent European narratives of good governance are remarkably similar to the nineteenth century's 'standard of civilisation,'[86] and so current TWAIL research is especially intrigued with the cultural implications of persisting economic inequalities for Third World peoples.[87]

Perhaps because TWAIL II emphasises economic relations in a bid to expose the public/private dichotomy of liberalism, little attention has been given to territorial adjudication. To date, no TWAIL scholars have offered a close reading of Third World pleadings before the ICJ, confining themselves instead to the Court's judgments.[88]

---

[82] Pahuja, *supra* n. 1, at 469.

[83] V. Nesiah, 'Placing International Law: White Spaces on a Map' (2003) 16 *Leiden Journal of International Law* 1, at 21.

[84] B. S. Chimni, 'Third World Approaches to International Law: A Manifesto', A. Anghie et al. (eds.), *The Third World and International Order: Law, Politics and Globalization* (Leiden: Martinus Nijhoff, 2003) 47–73, at 51; and A. Anghie & B. S. Chimni, 'Third World Approaches to International Law and Individual Responsibility in Internal Conflicts' (Leiden: Martinus Nijhoff, 2003) 2 *Chinese Journal of International Law* 77, at 78.

[85] K. Mickelson, 'Rhetoric and Rage: Third World Voices in International Legal Discourse' (1998) 16 *Wisconsin International Law Journal* 353, at 409–410.

[86] The 'Standard of Civilisation' is discussed in more detail below in Chapter Two, at 77–79.

[87] Anghie discusses the notion of 'good governance' as the new standard of civilisation in Anghie, *Imperialism, supra* n. 79, at Ch. 5. Chimni makes the same point in Chimni, 'Third World Approaches', *supra* n. 84, at 61. Other work drawing on TWAIL sensibilities has also characterised postcolonial World Bank and International Monetary Fund interventions as a new regime of capitulations for some of the non-European world. For example, see A. Anghie, 'Civilization and Commerce: The Concept of Governance in Historical Perspective' (2000) 45 *Villanova Law Review* 887; A. Anghie, 'International Financial Institutions', C. Reus-Smit (ed.), *The Politics of International Law* (Cambridge: Cambridge University Press, 2004) 217–237; D. P. Fidler, 'A. Kinder, Gentler System of Capitulations? International Law, Structural Adjustment, and the Standards of Liberal, Globalized Civilization' (2000) 35 *Texas International Law Journal* 387; D. P. Fidler, 'The Return of the Standard of Civilization' (2001) 2 *Chicago Journal of International Law* 137; J. T. Gathii, 'Neoliberalism, Colonialism and International Governance: Decentring the International Law of Governmental Legitimacy' (2000) 98 *Michigan Law Review* 1996.

[88] Some (re)considerations of ICJ territorial judgments must be noted: J. T. Gathii, 'Geographical Hegelianism in Territorial Disputes Involving Non-European Land Relations: An Analysis of the *Case Concerning Kasikili/Sedudu Island (Botswana/Namibia)*' (2002) 15 *Leiden Journal of International Law* 581; and Nesiah, *supra* n. 83.

Although we cannot speak of one Third World approach or one Third World,[89] both TWAIL I and TWAIL II scholars have used this label as a tool of resistance in working out how to understand the relationship between international law and its universality. Kennedy reminds us that critical approaches encounter a dilemma: 'frame breakers are generally either interpolated back into the disciplinary vocabulary or placed outside the field'.[90] There is thus a distinction 'between people operating within the disciplinary lexicon and people pursuing criticism and reform outside it.'[91] TWAIL scholars cannot be placed in one camp, but it is clear that there is discomfort for some TWAIL scholars about how to work with or work against international law. The structural implications, particularly of TWAIL II scholarship, provide little hope for a law that can transcend its exclusionary dynamics, and yet Anghie argues that TWAIL must continue to ask not if but *how* to 'construct an international law that is responsive to the needs and aspirations of the peoples of the Third World.'[92]

The tension between hope and despair within TWAIL scholarship complicates its approach to universalism. When reading TWAIL accounts of colonialism's continuing legacy, it is unclear if international law is being abandoned or if there is an attempt to change it. Writers disagree on this, but both Chimni and Anghie, for example, argue that international law cannot be rejected: 'International law is a field of contestation over meanings, approaches, solutions, remedies, and one that TWAIL cannot surrender.'[93] Pahuja has noted this irresolution in the work of Anghie, arguing that 'the concept of universality is under-theorised.'[94] Anghie himself has conceded this point: there is the will for universalism within many TWAIL accounts, but no robust theoretical mechanism advanced about how to move beyond the imperialising structures of international law.[95] It would seem then that especially TWAIL II scholarship has perhaps been too successful in revealing the dynamics of difference. Some of TWAIL's leading figures have shown us how to understand inequalities at the heart of international law, thus fulfilling the first two questions raised by Kennedy above. They have also made a convincing call to resistance,[96] and Kennedy argues that the way to fight

[89] Chimni, 'Towards a Radical', *supra* n. 73, at 14.

[90] Kennedy, 'When Renewal Repeats, *supra* n. 3, at 460.

[91] Ibid., at 463.

[92] Anghie, *Imperialism, supra* n. 79, at 2.

[93] Anghie & Chimni, *supra* n. 84, at 101.

[94] S. Pahuja, 'Review: Antony Anghie, Imperialism, Sovereignty and the Making of International Law' (2006) 69 *Modern Law Review* 486, at 488.

[95] Anghie, *Imperialism, supra* n. 79, at 317.

[96] For example, see B. Rajagopal, *International Law from Below: Development, Social Movements and Third World Resistance* (Cambridge: Cambridge University Press, 2003); B. Rajagopal, 'Counter-hegemonic International Law: rethinking human rights and development as Third World strategy' (2006) 27 *Third World Quarterly* 767.

back is in producing new legal maps.[97] Given the persistent tension in TWAIL scholarship over law's universalism, we need to draw new maps. By considering the specific case of Arab territorial adjudication, this book will map out the possibilities for universalism before the Court.

4) *Speaking in Tongues: International Law as Language*

The most important conceptual tool for reading this book is a critical sensibility towards the discursive qualities of international law.[98] One of the hypotheses informing my research is that the construction of law in the courtroom is a process of argumentation. Such an assumption is just as relevant outside the courtroom in academic discussion: institutional particularities and conventions influence ICJ disputes, but otherwise, they are a part of the discursive practice that is international law writ large. This section reviews NAIL approaches to language so that we can then apply them first in our reading of ICJ scholarly literature in the chapter and then to ICJ territorial disputes in mapping the scope for universalism within international law.

Critical international legal scholarship has shown us not only that language matters, but that international law itself is language; there 'is no escape from language.'[99] For Cass, '[i]f law is a set of arguments generated by language then it is the discussion or conversation about the arguments that creates the concepts themselves, not the actual behaviour of states, their consent, or their beliefs.'[100] Thus, language does not describe behaviour and rules; it actually constitutes them. In the words of linguist Joshua Fishman:

> Language is not merely a *means* of interpersonal communication and influence. It is not merely a *carrier* of content, whether latent or manifest. Language itself is content, a referent for loyalties and animosities, an indicator of social statuses and personal relationships, a marker of situations and topics as well as of the societal goals and the large-scale value-laden arenas of interaction that typify every speech community.[101]

---

[97] Kennedy, 'Keynote Address', *supra* n. 72.

[98] Constructivists from within the field of International Relations have also explored some of these concerns., For example, see F. Kratochwil, 'Thrasymmachos Revisited: On the Relevance of Norms and the Study of Law for International Relations' 37 (1984) *Journal of International Affairs* 343; and C. Reus-Smit, 'The Politics of International Law', C. Reus-Smit (ed.), *The Politics of International Law* (Cambrdige: Cambridge University Press, 2004), 14–44.

[99] Cass, *supra* n. 60, at 361.

[100] Ibid., at 359.

[101] Italics in original, J. Fishman, 'The Sociology of Language', N. Coupland & A. Jaworski (eds.), *Sociolinguistics: A Reader and a Coursebook* (New York: St Martin's Press, 1997 (1972)), quoted in Y. Suleiman, *A War of Words: Language and Conflict in the Middle East* (Cambridge: Cambridge University Press, 2004), at 14.

This understanding of language is applicable to any form of discourse, including international law, and it is echoed by Boyle's work on international law. Like Fishman, Boyle denies the possibility of language as something *a priori*, or as an incontestable representation of social 'fact'. In relation to international law debate about sources, Boyle argues that '[t]he idea of finding the essence or the real source of law distracts us from the reality that, in a very important sense, it is being created by our categories and definitions rather than being described by them.'[102]

Once we apply this sensibility about language to international law, the result is indeterminacy: there can be no external reference point and no rule that is beyond choice; all rules are rooted in politics. Koskenneimi's scholarship is particularly intrigued with the discursive indeterminacy of international law. Responding to a request for methodological comment in a special issue of the *American Journal of International Law*, Koskenniemi reveals his understanding about language and indeterminacy:[103]

> Legal styles are styles of argument, of linguistic expression. The accounts of method contained in the symposium readily accept this and seek to establish a firm relationship between that language and the world that it is assumed to reflect. In order to describe or assess the relationship between language and the world, however, there should be some way that is independent of language to which the forms of language could be compared. There is, however, no such way. The languages create worlds and do not 'reflect' them.[104]

Koskenniemi thus shows us that law cannot be separated from its linguistic and political context.

Although NAIL encourages international lawyers to grapple with this indeterminacy, it is also reassuring for those lost in this vision of Babel: international law is at least imperfectly structured by a series of conventions and dominant narratives that limit what is professionally preferable.[105] According to Kritsiotis, 'in the same way as power itself, international law prescribes its own limitations as a language and discipline – in the methods and arguments it allows, in its sources, in the interpretations and principles it accepts, and in its own modus operandi.'[106]

---

[102] J. Boyle, 'Ideals and Things: International Legal Scholarship and the Prison-house of Language' (1985) 26 *Harvard Journal of International Law* 327, at 332.

[103] Koskenniemi's work explores the theme of international law as language. For a more detailed list of his work in this regard, please consult the bibliography.

[104] Koskenniemi, 'Letter to the Editors', *supra* n. 58, at 359.

[105] This idea is also reflected in Chimni's notion of permissible interpretations of treaties, discussed in Chimni, 'Towards a TWAIL Theory', *supra* n. 78.

[106] D. Kritsiotis 'The Power of International Law as Language' (1997–1998) 34 *California Western Law Review* 397, at 403. Reisman echoes these ideas when he writes, 'International law requires, among other things, a limited common language of signs, symbols and values which can permit elites in different territorial communities to ascertain what their common interests are and to

International lawyers are political actors, but Koskenniemi recognises that '[w]e don't choose to use the concepts of international law when we enter international legal discourse. Rather we must take a pre-existing language, a pre-existing system of interpreting the world and move within it if we wish to be heard and understood.'[107] The use of the first person pronoun here is important because international law is necessarily a community-generated discourse. International lawyers are therefore members of an 'interpretive community' rewriting the rules of their own success.[108] For Korhonen, international lawyers must be mindful of the socialising function of international law:

> In order to be able to make a meaningful argument in international law one has to adapt to the meaning-structures, the already-defined problematic, and the direction of epistemic interest that together amount to the world-view of the discipline.[109]

What are the structures of international legal argumentation and what is the world-view of the discipline? The book does not answer these questions comprehensively, but the case studies are a start in this process.

From these observations, it follows that success in legal argument is not founded on the presentation of compelling doctrinal 'evidence,' but rather on the ability to recognise and perhaps refashion underlying linguistic structures of international law. 'Therefore, an organized conception of…situational limitations is indispendisable for the international lawyer.'[110] International law is no different from other languages in the way it is built on a set of rules of syntax and grammar, and this is acknowledged by its practitioners. The mistake made by many lawyers, however, is to recognise only those rules expressed at the level of doctrine; instead, doctrine needs to be understood as a malleable tool of argument in the hands of those lawyers fluent in the language of international law.[111] Thus, the 'politics of international law is what competent international lawyers

---

arrange for means for implementing them.' W. M. Reisman, 'Islamic Fundamentalism and Its Impact on International Law and Politics', M. W. Janis & C. Evans (eds.), *Religion and International Law* (Cambridge, MA: Martinus Nijhoff, 1999) 357–384, at 357.

107 Koskenniemi, *From Apology to Utopia, supra* n. 2, at 12.

108 Both Kennedy and Chimni touch on this idea of interpretive communities. For example: Kennedy, 'When Renewal Repeats', *supra* n. 3, at 346; and Chimni, 'Towards a TWAIL Theory', *supra* n. 78.

109 O. Korhonen, 'New International Law: Silences, Defence or Deliverance?' (1996) 7 *European Journal of International Law* 1, at 6.

110 Ibid.

111 This idea is also expressed by Koskenniemi, who argues that the key is not so much which argument is used, but 'what rules govern the production of arguments and the linking of arguments together in such a familiar and conventionally acceptable way and why it is that no definite resolution of standard problems can be attained.' Koskenniemi, *From Apology to Utopia, supra* n. 2, at 8.

do. And *competence is the ability to use grammar in order to generate meaning by doing things in argument.*'[112]

This book is a study of international law and not linguistics *per se*, but it is instructive to set out some definitions of language that are applied in my readings of the case studies. As discussed above, language is both an open and closed system of the communication of and generation of meaning; language is dynamic and adaptive, but it is only comprehensible within certain limits of grammatical and lexical usage. Thus, the language of international law has developed and changed in response to the speech of its interlocutors, international lawyers, but their speech has also been structured and limited by the discipline of international law. The book builds on the notion of 'grammar' employed by Koskenniemi and it interprets the term to mean those general rules of language that structure how words or phrases gain meaning. For example, in English, with its minimal inflectional endings, syntax or word order fulfils a grammatical function, helping us identify the subject and object of a verb.[113]

At a more abstract and perhaps less systematic level, international law also has its rules or grammars of usage. The book is particularly intrigued by discursive constraints around the relationship between law and politics. As will be shown in the case studies, a variety of devices are drawn on in adjudication to provide definition and certainty to the field of international law and the ICJ by the separation of law from politics. Because doctrine is indeterminate, determinacy is provided in part by the grammar of the law/politics dichotomy. Specific words forming the lexicon of international law assist this communicative process of limiting indeterminacy. Thus, words and phrases carry a particular meaning within the language of international law. The case studies also highlight the extent to which new words and new meanings generated by Third World states participating in ICJ adjudication are comprehensible in the Peace Palace. Thus 'lexicon' is used to express utterances that are meaningful within the discourse of international law. For example, what does 'consent' mean within the context of treaty formation? What incidents and events are permissible in arguing for consent or its absence? In Chapter Three where Libya's argument about its lack of experience vitiating consent is discussed, is such an idea comprehensible within

[112] Italics in original, Ibid., at 571. Kennedy 'present[s] international law as a series of professional performances rather than an edifice of ideas, doctrines, and institutions recasting the discipline's intellectual tools as a lexicon of argument about reform and disciplinary renewal, as well as professional affiliation and disaffiliation. For international lawyers, the performances of renewal, criticism, and reform are central to professional identity and *competence*...' Italics added. Kennedy, 'When Renewal Repeats, *supra* n. 3, at 337.

[113] For example, with its word order, 'the cat saw the girl' conveys meaning in English by the speaker knowing that the subject usually precedes the object. Thus, the cat is the subject of the verb, and the girl, its object.

the disciplinary discourse? Are there words in the lexicon of international law that can capture Libya's experiences under Italian colonial rule?

Because of linguistic and experiential diversity, the practice of international discourse is about more than speaking in a lawyerly mother tongue; it is also about translation. As international law is a limited language, experiences outside its parameters must be spoken anew in a tongue that is intelligible. According to Koskenniemi, '[t]he question of the justiciability of international disputes is then a question about the possibility of *translating* values and priorities that contestants in a dispute advance, into the ideolect of international law as one aspect of such modernity.'[114] Related to this notion of translation is the question of whether international law is actually capable of speaking for various peoples, ideas and experiences: can all dialects and languages be rendered in legal language? Partly as a result of the dichotomy between law and politics, speech that upholds this distinction is invoked to portray law as objective and unaffected by (political) indeterminacy. Thus, 'the translation of the disputants' languages into the ideolect of formal rules and principles, rights and claims, is expected to produce a distancing effect under which a settlement becomes possible irrespective of the quality and intensity of the passions it triggers.'[115] Yet certain experiences challenge legal language to such an extent that translation is impossible; they are silenced by their situational incomprehensibility.

Aside from the structure provided by its grammar, international law as language is also constrained by the particular institutional biases in which it is articulated. Thus, international law as invoked in ICJ territorial disputes will carry with it particular conventions that are somewhat distinct from international law more generally. A competent lawyer in ICJ disputes accordingly should not only be able to understand the grammar of international law, as well as translate her client's needs, but also speak in a particular way to suit the sensibilities of the Court. If we apply Korhonen's scholarship about situationality, we can argue that a competent and successful international lawyer engaged in ICJ dispute resolution must be cognisant not only of the general parameters of international legal discourse but of those particular to the ICJ.[116]

Shalakany has explored the effect of institutional conventions in the context of Third World arbitration. Shalakany notes that disputes over natural resources could have been decided in a number of ways because 'the institution and the doctrines [of arbitration] are indeterminate enough to assist either party inter-

[114] Italics added, M. Koskenniemi 'The Silence of Law/The Voice of Justice', Boisson de Chazournes, Laurence & Sands, Philippe (eds.), *International Law, the International Court of Justice and Nuclear Weapons* (Cambridge: Cambridge University Press, 1999), 488–510, at 507.

[115] Ibid., at 501.

[116] Korhonen, 'New International Law', *supra* n. 109, at 4–9.

changeably.'[117] Why then have Third World states consistently lost when trying to maintain ownership of their resources? Shalakany points to assumptions underpinning arbitration, such as the belief that arbitration is removed from the political sphere because of its structure between equal, consenting parties.[118] For example, Shalakany ascribes Libya's arbitral failures to its refusal to maintain the law/politics divide: 'Once Libya's actions were associated with politics and the coercive exercise of sovereign powers in an unequal relationship, Libya was simply denied access to a whole set of legal interpretations that could have been more favorable to its position.'[119]

Arbitration possesses its own distinct set of disciplinary sensibilities, but the basic idea is useful in considering why certain themes for discussion are avoided at the ICJ's bench, especially in majority judgments. Although territorial disputes are based on the language of sovereign power, the broader quest within international law for separation from politics means that rarely is a court willing to listen to accounts about the effects of power inequalities on the creation of treaties or the importance of natural resources for a party's case. The case studies in the book all present narratives about the struggle over natural resources and it will be shown that Shalakany's typology of denial applies equally to these disputes: generally, states do not acknowledge the presence of oil, gas or water lying just below the surface of courtroom proceedings.[120]

In another institutional performance of the law/politics dichotomy, Koskenniemi points out that emotion is also shunned in ICJ speech acts.[121] Emotions are hard to render into 'rational' speech and thus, many experiences will necessarily remain untranslatable and silenced. For example, in the Court's Advisory Opinion in the *Nuclear Weapons Case*, law was simply unable to encapsulate or speak about the horror of such weapons: 'For a voice of justice to be heard,

---

[117] A. A. Shalakany, 'Arbitration and the Third World: A Plea for Reassessing Bias under the Specter of Neoliberalism' (2000) 41 *Harvard International Law Journal* 419, at 424.

[118] Ibid., at 455.

[119] Ibid., at 456.

[120] Boyle makes a similar point in relation to the quest for a-political language in international law: 'The scholars of the Western countries have modelled international law along the familiar lines of liberal state theory. Their utopian vision is that politics can somehow be constrained by (a-political) rules. This vision leads them to attempt to show that language can somehow provide a neutral conduit for power. The state's consent is to something called "a rule." This rule is made up of words and the words can be interpreted in a non-political way. Thus, ideological conflict can be separated from legal argument and the nation state can logically give its obedience to the resulting "objective" structure.' Boyle, *supra* n. 102, at 347.

[121] Koskenniemi provides the example of Bosnia's US legal counsel, who was replaced in the *Case Concerning Application of the Convention on the Prevention and Punishment of the Crime of Genocide (Bosnia-Herzegovina v Yugoslavia)* (2003). See CR 93/12, available from the Court's website: http://www.icj-cij.org/. Koskenniemi, 'Letter to the Editors', *supra* n. 58, at 360.

law must sometimes remain silent.'[122] The parties and judges of the ICJ in the cases explored in the book all display different levels of emotional outburst and restraint in their attempts of limiting and expanding the linguistic parameters of international law.

5) *Interrogating Conventions within Mainstream ICJ Literatures*

Section two explored some recent mainstream reactions to the Court's increased docket, suggesting that this development can be distinguished from the Court's overly-European past; it is now possible to speak of a World Court upholding universal norms. A number of structural factors, however, challenge such an account. This section explores some contributions from the large body of literature about the institutional and jurisprudential nature of the ICJ, as well as intersecting studies on territory, and juxtaposes these with critical perspectives. Through an application of the tools discussed in sections two and three, the following section will show that despite a voluminous literature, accounts of the Court's processes of argumentation and the possibility of universalism obscure as much as they reveal. After describing the scholarly conventions of mainstream ICJ and territorial scholarship, this section then explores three inter-related narratives informing the literature: the maintenance of the law/politics dichotomy, particular readings of the relationship between the past and the present, and faith in a progressive international law.

Most writings on the practice of the Court are remarkably similar and can even be described as formulaic.[123] Countless books and articles contain near-identical accounts of the Court's procedures and summaries of its jurisprudence. Special anniversary volumes or *festschriften* are regularly produced to mark the latest milestone, and often the themes contained in such tomes differ very little from previous publications.[124] Nostalgic personal accounts of time spent within the

---

[122] Koskenniemi, 'The Silence of Law', *supra* n. 114, at 489.

[123] Collier discusses how studies on the ICJ and dispute settlement tend to follow a recognisable pattern: J. G. Collier, 'The International Court of Justice and the peaceful settlement of disputes', V. Lowe & M. Fitzmaurice (eds.), *Fifty years of the International Court of Justice: Essays in Honour of Sir Robert Jennings* (Cambridge: Cambridge University Press, 1996), 364–372.

[124] Some examples of these anniversary and *festschrift* editions consulted here include: E. G. Bello & B. A. Ajibola (eds.), *Essays in Honour of Judge Taslim Olawale Elias: vol I Contemporary International Law and Human Rights* (Dordrecht; Boston: Martinus Nijhoff, 1992); D. Bowett et al. (eds.), *The International Court of Justice: Process, Practice and Procedure* (London: The British Institute of International and Comparative Law 1997); B. Cheng & E. D. Brown (eds.), *Contemporary Problems in International Law: Essays in honour of Georg Schwarzenberger on his eightieth birthday* (London: Stevens & Sons, 1988); Goodwin-Gill, Guy S. & Talmon, Stefan (eds.), *The Reality of International Law: Essays in Honour of Ian Brownlie* (Oxford:

Peace Palace also appear, serving to remind us of the selective authorship typical of this field.[125] Although some authors have questioned the power and role of the Court, the bulk of ICJ scholarship continues to display both optimism and respect for this pre-eminent 'world' court. This is partly a result of authorship: writings about the Court tend to come from international law practitioners (often appearing at the Peace Palace), academics or even judges themselves. The 'decorum' required of lawyers and judges in the Peace Palace is often mimicked in later appraisals and this is especially so in relation to British scholars.[126] American scholars, on the other hand, permit more policy perspectives in their writings, but even with such concessions, themes addressed usually differ little from those penned across the Atlantic.

Studies devoted to the law on territory differ little from those on the ICJ. Generally, Ratner points out that the 'equation of international law with international adjudication is nowhere more pronounced as in the area of territorial sovereignty.'[127] Why then undertake yet another study of territorial disputes when so much literature already exists? The point of this research is to show

---

Clarendon Press, 1999); R. St J. Macdonald (ed.), *Essays in Honour of Wang Tieya* (Dordrecht; Boston: Martinus Nijhoff, 1994); J. Makarczyk (ed.), *Theory of International Law at the Threshold of the 21st Century: Essays in Honour of Krysztof Skubiszewski* (The Hague: Kluwer, 1996); A. S. Muller, D. Raič & J. M. Thuránszky (eds.), *The International Court of Justice: Its Future Role after Fifty Years* (The Hague; Boston: Martinus Nijhoff, 1997); V. Lowe & M. Fitzmaurice (eds.), *Fifty years of the International Court of Justice: Essays in Honour of Sir Robert Jennings* (Cambridge: Cambridge University Press, 1996); R. S. Pathak & R. P. Dhokalia (eds.), *International Law in Transition: Essays in Memory of Judge Nagendra Singh* (Dordrecht; Boston: Martinus Nijhoff, 1992); C. Peck & R. S. Lee (eds.), *Increasing the Effectiveness of the International Court of Justice: Proceedings of the ICJ/UNITAR Colloquium to Celebrate the 50th Anniversary of the Court* (Boston: Martinus Nijhoff, 1997); M. Shahabuddeen (ed.), *Boutros Boutros-Ghali: Amicorum discipulorumque liber: Paix, développement, démocratie*, vol. 1 (Brussels: Bruylant, 1998). Some notable exceptions, containing more contextualised and critical perspectives are A. Anghie & G. Sturgess (eds.), *Legal Visions of the 21st Century: Essays in Honour of Judge Christopher Weeramantry* (The Hague: Kluwer, 1998); and L. Boisson de Chazournes & P. Sands (eds.), *International Law, the International Court of Justice and Nuclear Weapons* (Cambridge: Cambridge University Press, 1999). Cf Forsythe, who argues that there have been very few reviews of the Court on the occasion of its fiftieth anniversary because of its marginal role international relations: D. P. Forsythe, 'The International Court of Justice at Fifty', A. S. Muller, D. Raič & J. M. Thuránszky (eds.), *The International Court of Justice: Its Future Role after Fifty Years* (The Hague; Boston: Martinus Nijhoff, 1997) 385–405, at 385.

125 For an example of a personal account, see H. Thirlway, 'The Drafting of ICJ Decisions: Some Personal Recollections and Observations' (2006) 5 *Chinese Journal of International Law* 15.

126 Carty argues, 'Particularly in Britain, the discipline of international law is overwhelmingly formalist.' A. Carty, 'Review Article: Visions of the Past of International Society: Law, History or Politics?' (2006) 69 *Modern Law Review* 644, at 644.

127 S. R. Ratner, 'Land Feuds and their Solutions: Finding International Law beyond the Tribunal Chamber' (2006) 100 *American Journal of International Law* 808, at 808.

how existing literatures on both the Court and territorial disputes only tell part of the story of universalism and this is especially so in relation to analyses about territory. For example, within the literature on territorial title and disputes, it is surprising how often the jurisprudence of the Court is simply presented for summary and overview, with perhaps some doctrinal additions. Few analyses of territorial adjudication have studied the process of argumentation between the Court and the parties and this is shown by a general lack of attention towards the pleadings. The same is true, not only in relation to recognition of the political context outside the courtroom, but also inside it: discursive practices are explored only at the level of doctrine and, where criticism is offered, it is almost always within the strict confines of 'law' as opposed to 'politics'. Brownlie also points to a dissonance between territorial scholarship and its subject matter: '[m]any of the standard textbooks, and particularly those in English, classify the modes of acquisition in a stereotyped way which reflects the preoccupation of writers in the period before the First World War.'[128] This is despite the fact that the ICJ does not rely on this typology; it instead usually engages in a weighing up exercise of competing claims to effective control where treaties are less than dispositive.[129]

a) *Maintaining the Law/Politics Dichotomy*

We saw in sections two and three that law cannot be separated from politics, particularly when we understand international law as a language. Despite this inseparability, both ICJ jurisprudence and scholarship about the Court have often tried to maintain this distinction in various ways. It is easy enough to point to a number of mainstream accounts acknowledging the place of politics in the courtroom,[130] but the epistemological assumptions informing such accounts are still premised on dichotomy and distinction. We can understand mainstream writings as suggesting that politics and law remain qualitatively different in both their origins and their practice. Critical approaches, however, would question such distinctions and ask why it is necessary to maintain such a division.

Literatures on ICJ jurisprudence and adjudication are replete with repetitive discussions about the law/politics divide, and this is partly a product of the

---

[128] Brownlie, quoted in Distefano, *supra* n. 4, at 1048.

[129] Ratner, *supra* n. 127, at 815. Post endorses Jennings' earlier idea, by arguing that 'adjudication on territorial title is a sixth traditional mode of acquisition of territory in international law.' H. Post, 'Adjudication as a mode of acquisition of territory? Some observations on the Iraq-Kuwait boundary demarcation in light of the jurisprudence of the International Court of Justice', V. Lowe & M. Fitzmaurice (eds.), *Fifty years of the International Court of Justice: Essays in Honour of Sir Robert Jennings* (Cambridge: Cambridge University Press, 1996) 237–263, at 237.

[130] For a survey of various examples, see A. Coleman, 'The International Court of Justice and Highly Political Matters' (2004) 4 *Melbourne Journal of International Law* 29, at 30.

practice of adjudication itself. Coleman details how there emerged a distinction between 'political' and 'legal' (or justiciable) disputes at The Hague Conferences of 1899 and 1907.[131] Mosler adds that the 'need to distinguish legal disputes from disputes of another character – whether called "political" controversies of "interests" or simply "non-justiciable" – arose in connection with attempts to make judicial settlement compulsory.'[132] Aspirations of compulsory arbitration and adjudication foundered, however, and remain as elusive as ever. Under Article 35, 'The Court shall be open to states parties to the present Statute' of the ICJ.[133] It may also hear advisory cases that relate to 'any legal question'.[134] This phrase has encouraged a practice in pleadings, judgments and commentaries about debating the 'legal' in contrast to 'political' nature of the dispute at hand.[135] Kennedy invites us to think not so much about whether disputes are definable as 'legal' or 'political'. Instead when arguments are raised in support or opposition of the Court's jurisdiction, we need to ask who is making the claim, with what purpose, for what project and to persuade whom.[136] The case studies explore this law/politics tension in discussions over jurisdiction, especially in Chapter Six on the *Wall* Advisory Opinion.[137]

Commentators have acknowledged that the Court's choice about whether to exercise its jurisdiction as well as state participation is political,[138] but often there remains the idea that at least some aspects of the Court's practice and procedure are free from the taint of power politics. Jennings asks whether it is 'possible to make a clear distinction between legal and political disputes and if

---

131 Ibid., at 32–33.

132 H. Mosler, 'Political and Justiciable Legal Disputes: Revival of an Old Controversy?', B. Cheng & E. D. Brown (eds.), *Contemporary Problems in International Law: Essays in honour of Georg Schwarzenberger on his eightieth birthday* (London: Stevens & Sons, 1988) 216–229, at 220.

133 Article 35(1).

134 United Nations Charter, Art. 96(1); Statute of the International Court of Justice, Art. 65(1).

135 This is discussed further in Part III's Introduction, at 185–186.

136 Kennedy, 'When Renewal Repeats, *supra* n. 3, at 467.

137 *Legal Consequences of the Construction of a Wall in the Occupied Palestinian Territory (Advisory Opinion)* (2004) ICJ Reps, p. 136.

138 '[T]here is really no way of escape from the fact that international courts, like domestic courts indeed, will for a good deal of the time find themselves having to decide upon legal questions in respect of which their decision, however technical in form, must have great political significance.' R. Y. Jennings, 'International Courts and International Politics', D. Freestone et al. (eds.), *Contemporary Issues in International Law: A Collection of Josephine Onoh Memorial Lectures* (The Hague: Kluwer, 2002) 13–28, at 15. In relation to state participation, Shaw argues that 'recourse itself to the Court constitutes a political as well as a legal act and as such may add to political and other pressure upon an opponent with the hope that the pressure in total may lead to a resolution of the problem in question.' M. N. Shaw, 'Peaceful Resolution of 'Political Disputes': The Desirable Parameters of ICJ Jurisdiction', J. Dahlitz (ed.), *Peaceful Resolution of Major International Disputes* (New York: United Nations, 1999) 49–75, at 55.

so, by what criteria'.[139] In trying to answer this, he harks back to the context of early arbitration, where the 'classical idea, that was enunciated by no less an authority than Westlake, that it is possible to classify claims as being either legal or political, was an academic fantasy born of the desire to establish general compulsory court jurisdiction in isolation from the problem of better machinery for political decision.'[140] Like his more recent counterpart, Higgins, Jennings is realistic about the presence of political choices and implications, depicting law as an exercise in reduction:

> the rubric of 'legal dispute' should be understood as indicating not only something about the objective character of a dispute submitted to a court, but much more the highly technical procedure whereby the Court and the parties together reduced their dispute into a form which renders it manageable in an adversarial procedure in a court of law...[141]

Higgins also overlooks the dichotomy in favour of an emphasis on procedure:

> there is little reality in any definition of a political, or legal, question; what is relevant is the distinction between a political method and a legal method of solving disputes.[142]

Sugihara cites these authors to stregthen his eventual conclusion in support of a discerning ICJ, occasionally called on to decline its jurisdiction where politics challenges 'its proper bounds as a judicial body.'[143]

Such accounts seem to differ little from Koskenniemi's idea of legal language, but in fact they point to an enduring belief that law can detach itself from the realm of particular interest, through neutral procedures.[144] Like critical approaches, mainstream ideas noted above distinguish law from politics through language and practice, but their corollary could not be more different: in limited spaces law *can* escape politics, and thus, at least the adjudicative performance

---

139 Jennings, 'International Courts and International Politics', *supra* n. 138, at 14.

140 R. Y. Jennings, 'The Proper Work and Purposes of the International Court of Justice', D. Raič & J. M. Thuránszky (eds.), *The International Court of Justice: Its Future Role after Fifty Years* (The Hague; Boston: Martinus Nijhoff, 1997) 33–45, at 43.

141 Jennings, quoted in T. Sugihara, 'The Judicial Function of the International Court of Justice with Respect to Disputes Involving Highly Political Issues', A. S. Muller, D. Raič & J. M. Thuránszky (eds.), *The International Court of Justice: Its Future Role after Fifty Years* (The Hague; Boston: Martinus Nijhoff, 1997) 117–138, at 118.

142 Higgins, quoted in Ibid.

143 Ibid., at 137.

144 On the nature of procedure, Sathirathai argues, 'the fact that procedure and substance can yield contradictory results affecting states' participation demonstrates that any attempt to move from substance to procedure reveals and mirrors the inseparability of law and politics.' S. Sathirathai, 'An Understanding of the Relationship between International Legal Discourse and Third World Countries' (1984) 25 *Harvard Journal of International Law* 395, at 402.

itself remains pure from interest. Underlying conflicts at the heart of disputes are obscured and silenced to preserve a semblance of legitimacy for the process of legal dispute resolution.

This attempt at quarantine is found also at the level of doctrine in territorial disputes and accompanying academic commentaries. The degree of diversity and complexity generated in this area of international law demonstrates that territorial disputes are often far from easily resolved. Diverging accounts found in both pleadings and commentaries strengthen the observation that practitioners must rally an impressive arsenal of arguments in their quest for success. Oppositional stances therefore are constructed around an elaborate evocation of legal doctrine, and commentaries pointing out weaknesses in litigation reinforce this theme by faithfully suggesting more robust readings of available rules and precedents. Such an understanding of legal dispute resolution is based on the belief of solid ground: that a rigorous application of the rules will generally result in the 'correct' result.[145] Rather than recognising the indeterminacy underneath, along with the accompanying spectre of political partiality, a resort to doctrine serves to bolster an image of law that is insulated and safe from its other: power.

Faith in the solace of doctrine is not only adopted by lawyers from the privileged European world. A number of Third World academics as well as the pleadings of Third World states are informed by a re-evaluation of colonial title with the help of European-generated laws on title to territory.[146] These accounts invoke such legal principles in a bid to expose the illegality of the colonial erasure of Third World legal personality. Through such a gesture, these Third World scholars and states suggest that international law can function as a legitimate form of regulation, but only where it is insulated from power politics.

b) *Reading History into International Law*

In contrast with the recurring motif of the law/politics divide, literatures on the ICJ and international law more generally are less likely to delve into the annals of history. Mainstream narratives of progress discussed further below, however, are steeped in particular readings of the historical record.[147] As in the case of law *vis-à-vis* politics, mainstream images of current international legal

---

[145] I also discuss this idea in the Preface at xiii–xv.

[146] Some Third World state perspectives are explored below in my examination of pleadings contained in its case studies. For a recent example of this, see Udombana's consideration of the Scramble for Africa, N. J. Udombana, 'The Ghost of Berlin Still Haunts Africa! The ICJ Judgment on the Land and Maritime Boundary Dispute between Cameroon and Nigeria' (2003) *African Yearbook of International Law* 13, at 51–52.

[147] For a critical appraisal of the field's oversight of history and its under-theorisation (but with some optimism about more recent efforts), see C. Miéville, *Between Equal Rights: A Marxist Theory of International Law* (London: Pluto, 2005), at 153–156.

structures rely on a radical rupture with the past, allowing us to speak of the law/history dichotomy as well. Kennedy's discursive exploration of disciplinary themes shows us, however, that this narrative of change and progress provides only one possible reading of history.[148] Further, it serves to mask the perpetuation of practices at the heart of the international law project. In his study of the nineteenth century, for example, Kennedy posits how 'the modernism, pragmatism and progressivism of today's international law is more rhetorical effect and polemical claim than historical achievement, and more part of the internal dynamic of the field's development than artefact of a distant era.'[149] In her appraisal of NAIL literatures, Cass suggests that NAIL's scholarly excavation in pursuit of reinterpreting doctrine has been its most important contribution.[150] This is especially so for TWAIL accounts of the colonial record, which have probed pervasive legal structures of inequality and exclusion.[151]

Despite a general historical sensibility infusing NAIL, TWAIL as well as some IR literatures, comparatively few writers have delved into the rich historical veins of territorial litigation. Yet Merrills reminds us that 'as the Court's case law demonstrates, in territorial and boundary cases, the historical record is usually the key to applying the law. For this reason, if for no other, evidence of this type will always be significant.'[152] This section notes the silences in ICJ scholarship, as well as renderings of the historical 'background' found in works on title to territory.[153] It also notes the conceptual tools provided, and yet rarely applied to, territorial disputes by critical perspectives. To fill this gap in approaching the process of historical argumentation at the ICJ, the following section develops a method of how to read history *into* territorial disputes. I briefly examine the nature of historical inquiry, as well as the scope for interdisciplinary dialogue between international law and IR, before applying these insights to a discussion of narratives of progress in ICJ literatures.

One of the most important themes emerging from the case studies is the desire

[148] For example, see D. Kennedy, 'International Law and the Nineteenth Century: History of an Illusion' (1996) 65 *Nordic Journal of International Law* 385.

[149] Ibid., at 389–390. For another discussion deconstructing the myth of nineteenth century rupture and difference from the present, see S. N. Grovogui, *supra* n. 35, at ch. 1.

[150] Cass, *supra* n. 60, at 375. Whereas Paulus is mistrustful of this historical turn, suggesting that critical scholars are in fact escaping into the past. Paulus, *supra* n. 60, at 739.

[151] Anghie, 'Civilization and Commerce', *supra* n. 87, at 891.

[152] J. G. Merrills, 'The International Court of Justice and the Adjudication of Territorial and Boundary Disputes' (2000) 13 *Leiden Journal of International Law* 873, at 895.

[153] For example, in the words of Justice Lachs, 'Evidence of fact is... tantamount to a resurrection of history.' M. Lachs, 'Evidence in the Procedure of the International Court of Justice: Role of the Court', E. G. Bello & B. A. Ajibola (eds.), *Essays in Honour of Judge Taslim Olawale Elias: vol. I Contemporary International Law and Human Rights* (Dordrecht; Boston: Martinus Nijhoff, 1992) 265–276, at 267.

on the part of Third World states to rewrite the historical record, suggesting that there can be no one historical truth informing the self-image of international law. Allott also argues that in relation to the discipline of international law, there are in fact two strains of history: intrinsic history, or accounts of law's internal development, and extrinsic history, based on the relationship between international law and general histories.[154] Allott acknowledges the role of choice in renderings of the past,[155] but still seems to construe history as ontologically distinct from the present: we can explore the interrelationship between the past and present in an objective manner. Thus, according to Allott, history is a 'dream of a past which is not our own, history nevertheless becomes our own, and ceases to be a dream, when we live in the reality it has formed.'[156] Once conceived, history can take on a life of its own, structuring consciousness, but not vice versa. This sense of reification in Allott's typology is also evident in his bifurcation of intrinsic and extrinsic histories, suggesting that practices within international law can be distinguished from their broader context.

Both Berman and Douzinas extend our appreciation of the 'past', by showing that like language, there can be no escape from historical and personal preference: what is required is a recognition of the complicity of choice.[157] Douzinas' general definition of history informs later explorations of historical issues in the cases:

> [H]istory is not a timeline. It is a modality of time that presses against the present. Memories live not in a historically rigid sequence but in simultaneity in which we may choose from many possibilities to create the present. As in Heidegger, the past is a modality of the present; indeed the past is a potentia or the potential of the present in its nearness to the future. But this potentia exists not as the ever-present denying and withholding, nor as the inescapable nearness of the past, future and present but as a stain of past and present in the Now.[158]

When we apply these insights to international law, there is no longer *one* account of international law. In fact, interrogating the place of history in international legal scholarship returns us to the dilemma of the law/politics dichotomy, suggesting that all international law scholarship is shaped by competing claims to 'past' and 'present', 'stasis' and 'change'. Methodologically, Berman advocates a

---

[154] P. Allott, 'International Law and the Idea of History' (1999) 1 *Journal of the History of International Law* 1, at 1.

[155] Ibid., at 16. See also for this point: Y. Onuma, 'When was the law of International Society Born? – An Inquiry into the History of International Law from an Intercivilizational Perspective' (2000) 2 *Journal of the History of International Law* 1, at 5–6.

[156] Allott, 'International Law and the Idea of History', *supra* n. 154, at 3.

[157] Historical narratives necessarily are reductions of the past, but the possibilities for such reduction are open-ended. See C. Douzinas, 'Theses on Law, History and Time' (2006) 7 *Melbourne Journal of International Law* 13, at 19.

[158] Footnotes omitted, Ibid., at 25.

genealogical reading for international lawyers, which 'sees international law – its doctrines as well as its participants – as normatively impure, culturally heterogeneous, and historically contingent.'[159] We need to ask how and why history is used and link understandings about international law's past with the political desires of both participants and judges in ICJ territorial disputes.

Although territorial disputes are steeped in history, ICJ judges are unlikely to become discerning historians;[160] their focus is on the 'law' and not 'history'. Merrills is correct when he argues that we cannot expect the ICJ to engage in all historical material raised: questions of time and resources limit ICJ historical enquiry.[161] This book is alive to such considerations, but still regards the common practice of historical obfuscation as troubling: what histories are being silenced and why? It is also important to problematise the issue of 'choice' by pointing out the seeming irony of post-colonial states presenting an arsenal of evidence formed from an often-uncritical acceptance of colonial archives. Is this complicity with colonialism or deference to ICJ conventions requiring voluminous historical 'evidence', which is less plentiful in Arab tribal societies?

International Relations (IR) historical work on international law should also be noted. Beginning in the 1990s, a large body of literature in the fields of international law and IR has explored the possibilities of inter-disciplinary collaboration.[162] Some of these contributions have developed the research projects

---

[159] N. Berman, 'In the Wake of Empire' (1999) 14 *American University International Law Review* 1515 (First Annual Grotius Lecture, American Society of International Law), at 1524.

[160] Douzinas discusses this relationship between the judge and history in trials reviewing the past as a 'transformation from history as the judge to the judge as historian'. Douzinas, *supra* n. 155, at 15.

[161] Merrills, *supra* n. 152, at 895.

[162] Some inter-disciplinary examples include: K. Abbott, 'Modern International Relations Theory: A Prospectus for International Lawyers' (1989) 14 *Yale Journal of International Law* 335; W. J. Aceves, 'Institutionalist Theory and International Legal Scholarship (1997) 12 *American University Journal of International Law and Policy* 227; A. Arend, 'Do legal rules matter? International Law and International Politics' (1998) 38 *Virginia Journal of International Law* 107; J. Barker, *International Law and International Relations* (London & New York: Continuum, 2000); R. J. Beck, 'International Law and International Relations: The Prospectus for Interdisciplinary Collaboration' (1995) 1 *Journal of International Legal Studies* 119; D. Bederman, 'Review Essay: Constructivism, Positivism, and Empiricism in International Law: Legal rules and international society' (2001) 89 *Georgetown Law Journal* 469; M. Byers, 'Custom, Power and the Power of Rules: Customary International Law from an Interdisciplinary Perspective (1995) 17 *Michigan Journal of International Law* 109; M. Byers (ed.), *The Role of Law in International Politics: Essays in International Relations and International Law* (Oxford & New York: Oxford University Press, 2000); C. A. Cutler, 'Critical Historical Materialism and International Law: Imagining International Law as praxis', S. Hobden & J. M. Hobson (eds.), *Historical Sociology of International Relations* (Cambridge: Cambridge University Press, 2002) 181–199; M. Finnemore, 'Are legal norms distinctive?' (2000) 32 *New York University Journal of International Law and Politics* 699; R. Keohane, 'International Relations and International Law:

of both fields, but a number of interdisciplinary studies follow a standard formula and fall into the trap of stereotype and simplification. Klabbers captures this tendency when he writes that 'inter-disciplinarity often... presumes a flat, one-dimensional vision of the discipline-to-relate-with, yet such a one-dimensional view will rarely if ever, be persuasive.'[163] Diversity within the IR 'canon' is simplified so that many international lawyers employing IR tools are often drawing on only a small area of IR, and this is usually the dominant schools of (neo)realism or neo-liberal institutionalism. Such schools offer little in this chapter's quest for historical awareness,[164] but beyond the 'neo-neo' paradigm of IR,[165] contributions from constructivism, and especially the English School, are useful in broadening our understanding about the evolution of international law as an institution within international society.[166] The book does not embrace the inter-disciplinary project *per se*, but it does acknowledge the contribution of IR, especially in Chapter Two in its discussion of debates over the European nature of international society.[167]

Two Optics' (1997) 38 *Harvard International Law Journal* 487; S. Scott, 'International Law as Ideology: Theorizing the Relationship between International Law and International Politics' (1994) 5 *European Journal of International Law* 313; S. V. Scott, *International Law in World Politics: An Introduction* (Boulder, CO: Rienner, 2004); J. K. Setear 'An Iterative Perspective on Treaties: A Synthesis of International Relations Theory and International Law (1996) 37 *Harvard International Law Journal* 139; A.-M. Slaughter Burley, 'International Law and International Relations Theory: A Dual Agenda' (1993) 87 *American Journal of International Law* 205; A.-M. Slaughter, A. S. Tulumello & S. Wood, 'International Law and International Relations theory: A new generation of interdisciplinary scholarship' (1998) 92 *American Journal of International Law* 367.

163 J. Klabbers, 'The Relative Autonomy of International Law or The Forgotten Politics of Interdisciplinarity' (2005) 1 *Journal of International Law & International Relations* 35, at 37. Compare Simpson's considered comparison between IR and international law in G. Simpson, 'The Situation on the International Legal Theory Front: The Power of Rules and the Rule of Power' (2000) 11 *European Journal of International Law* 439.

164 For example, Koskenniemi is unnecessarily dismissive of IR's research agenda and I think this is because of his definition of IR being largely based on American realism or liberalism. See M. Koskenniemi, *The Gentle Civilizer of Nations: The Rise and Fall of International Law 1870–1960* (Cambridge: Cambridge University Press, 2002), at 485.

165 R. Powell, 'Review Article: Anarchy in International Relations Theory: The Neorealist-Neoliberal Debate' (1994) 48 *International Organization* 313.

166 For example W. Bain, *Between Anarchy and Society: Trusteeship and the Obligations of Power* (Oxford: Oxford University Press 2003); G. Gong, *The Standard of "civilization" in International Society* (Oxford: Clarendon Press, 1984); P. Keal, *European Conquest and the Rights of Indigenous Peoples: The Moral Backwardness of International Society* (Cambridge: Cambridge University Press, 2003); E. Keene, *Beyond the Anarchical Society: Grotius, Colonialism and Order in World Politics* (Cambridge: Cambridge University Press, 2002).

167 Some useful quantitative studies of territorial disputes in the fields of IR and Political Science also provide useful statistical data. For example, see B. A. Simmons, 'Capacity, Commitment, and Compliance: International Institutions and Territorial Disputes' (2002) 46 *Journal of Conflict*

c) *Narratives of Progress and Untapped Potential*

Perspectives on how to approach the past are important when speaking of international law's progress and development, especially since the establishment of the UN. In relation to the ICJ, we saw in section two how writers noted the moribund state of the Court especially in the sixties and seventies, but that a 'renaissance' signalled a significant shift in the fortunes of the Court.[168] This is particularly so in 'in the field of territorial and boundary disputes, [where] the Court has had notable successes' in the opinion of various mainstream scholars.[169] Further, we also saw how greater Third World participation has been linked to legitimacy and universalism on the part of the Court. How, though, is this conceptual link made, and what assumptions inform such an account? How are images of the Court related to perceptions of international law more generally within the literature? The preceding discussion on history showed us how, in relegating history to the shadows, international lawyers can dissociate their field from earlier practices, which are now regarded with disdain. Thus, although mainstream accounts of the Court and international law more generally overlook historical discussion, a mixed account of progress and untapped potential suggests both a faith in a better Court and a progressivist conception of international law,[170] able to look to the future, rather than the past. Here, we return to the notion of a Court more universal and legitimate. This literature, based either on the Court's fulfilled or yet-to-be fulfilled potential, cannot grasp the elusive quality of universalism. Instead, approaches beyond mainstream ICJ literature must be developed.

Most scholarship about dispute resolution is characterised by a world-view that places law at the centre of social enquiry. Through its grammar of dichotomy, mainstream international law separates itself from politics and then offers an account of social reality that ascribes substantial weight to legal explanation. Other 'non-law' factors are downplayed and overlooked in these scholarly exercises of living in a world *through law*. Frankenberg captures this analytical tendency in his exposition of the idea of 'legocentrism'. Legocentrism means that 'law is treated as a given and a necessity, as the natural path to the ideal, rational or optimal conflict resolutions and ultimately to social order guaranteeing peace and harmony.'[171] Legocentrism particularly informs many accounts of

Resolution 829; and M. W. Zacher, 'The Territorial Integrity Norm: International Boundaries and the Use of Force' (2001) 55 *International Organization* 215.

[168] Guillaume, *supra* n. 44.

[169] Schwebel, 'The Impact of the International Court of Justice', *supra* n. 4, at 663.

[170] Korhonen notes more generally that '[i]nternational law has a tradition of enthusiasm, hope, and a longing for positive accounts.' O. Korhonen, 'Liberalism and International Law: A Centre Projecting a Periphery' (1996) 65 *Nordic Journal of International Law* 481, at 484.

[171] G. Frankenberg, 'Critical Comparisons: Re-Thinking Comparative Law' (1985) 26 *Harvard International Law Journal* 411, at 445.

adjudication, which are noteworthy for the absence of contextual, 'non-legal' considerations.

Much of the literature devoted to adjudication has applauded the recent upsurge in Third World participation and the Court's docket as a whole, because of legocentrism, combined with a deep-seated faith in adjudication. At the level of language, Colson points out that the very term 'dispute settlement' suggests that matters have been resolved.[172] Faith in the dividends of dispute resolution infuses a literature that sometimes displays a vision of peace through adjudication: once states present themselves before the Court, matters will improve.[173] For example, some authors lament comparisons, arguing that fewer Advisory Opinions from the ICJ, as compared to the PCIJ are an unmitigated retrogression: the world needs more law as voiced by the Court.[174] Others hold up either compulsory arbitration or at least greater accession to the 'optional clause'[175] as the answer.[176] Jennings cautions against such hope, however, pointing out not only that calls for compulsory arbitration have gone unheeded since 1899, but that today's Court cannot possibly achieve everything; its settlement role is necessarily limited.[177] Furthermore, in relation to the Court's increased docket, Jennings suggests that this is partly a product of a world with many more states[178] and the recognition of the Court's *limited* parameters: 'one reason for the recent welcome increase of the resort by governments to contentious jurisdiction of the Court...is precisely that there is already a better realization amongst governments that the adjudication process is an excellent way of dealing with *certain kinds*' of disputes.[179]

[172] E. Colson, 'The Contentiousness of Disputes', P. Caplan (ed.), *Understanding Disputes: The Politics of Argument* (Oxford: Providence, 1995) 65–82, at 66.

[173] This faith is expressed by Anand in his dichotomy between the evils of untrammelled sovereignty and the pacification offered by the Court: Anand, *supra* n. 14, at 176–179.

[174] M. S. M. Amr, *The Role of the International Court of Justice as the Principal Judicial Organ of the United Nations* (The Hague; New York: Kluwer, 2003), at 378. Justice Schwebel is more discerning, arguing, 'However, the question is not whether the Court is busy; it is whether the Court is effective – whether each of its judgments or advisory opinions leaves the world – or even a small corner of it – a better place.' Schwebel, *supra* n. 4, at 668.

[175] Article 36(2), Statute of the International Court of Justice. On this point, also see Forsythe, *supra* n. 124, at 401–402. The basic function of the optional clause is discussed in Part II's Introduction, at 98–99.

[176] ABILA Committee on Intergovernmental Settlement of Disputes, 'Reforming the United Nations: What About the International Court of Justice?' (2006) 5 *Chinese Journal of International Law* 39, at 42.

[177] Jennings, 'The Proper Work' *supra* n. 140, at 41.

[178] Jennings, 'The International Court of Justice after Fifty Years', *supra* n. 15, at 494.

[179] Italics in original, 'The Proper Work', *supra* n. 140, at 45. Guillaume echoes this idea by pointing out that the Court has established itself as particularly adept at hearing 'middle-range disputes'. Guillaume, *supra* n. 44, at 851.

Despite Jennings' sober words, a number of mainstream and Third World scholars hold firm to the notion of peace through law, presenting the Court's untapped potential as a product of political factors beyond the Court's reach. Shahabuddeen articulates this theme, when he points out that '[t]hrough no fault of its own, the World Court has not realized the more ambitious of the aspirations of some of its well-wishers.'[180] Other writers' belief in the Court's potential suggests a Court and an international law full of progressive promise.[181] Perhaps it has failed thus far to fulfil this promise,[182] but there is still 'enormous potential for the use of the Court'.[183] Third World participation in territorial disputes is one example of this potential, serving as a barometer of legitimacy; surely this portends a Court able to act for all states equally in the postcolonial era.

6) *Conclusion: Law as Argument and Contestation about the Quest for Universalism*

In this section, we return to the search for a place and time lived through a universal international law. From the review above, it is now possible to settle on the basic tools employed throughout the book. Most fundamentally, this research operates not only on the premise of the situationality of law,[184] but also its (re)construction through the practice of argument. The book will explore and interrogate this process of argument through the study of ICJ territorial disputes involving Arab states. How do Arab states depict international law, are there recurring themes, and how are these taken up or rejected by the Court? The book also accepts the challenge first raised by Koskenniemi in 1989 of mapping legal grammars. In his recent appraisal of the impact of Koskenniemi's seminal

---

[180] M. Shahabuddeen, 'The International Court of Justice: The Integrity of an Idea', R. S. Pathak & R. P. Dhokalia (eds.), *International Law in Transition: Essays in Memory of Judge Nagendra Singh* (Dordrecht; Boston: Martinus Nijhoff, 1992) 341–361, at 361.

[181] For example, in his consideration of the Court's suddenly increased docket, Highet depicts the ICJ as a 'hot court' after the Nicaragua episode. K. Highet, 'The Peace Palace Heats Up: The World Court in Business Again?' (1991) 85 *American Journal of International Law* 646, at 654.

[182] Anand, *supra* n. 14, at 162; Falk, *supra* n. 49, at 7; S. W. Tiefenbrun, 'The Role of the World Court in Settling International Disputes: A Recent Assessment' (1997) 20 *Loyola of Los Angeles International & Comparative Law Journal* 1, at 20 & 25.

[183] R. Higgins, *Problems and Process: International Law and How We Use It* (Oxford: Clarendon Press, 1994), at 187.

[184] Koskenniemi, *From Apology to Utopia*, *supra* n. 2, at 26; Korhonen, 'New International Law', *supra* n. 109, at 4–9; O. Korhonen, *International Law Situated: An Analysis of the Lawyer's Stance towards Culture, History and Community* (The Hague: Kluwer, 2000) at 129.

work, *From Apology to Utopia*, Kennedy argues that Koskenniemi's invitation to delineate international legal grammars has yet to be accepted.[185]

Discussion above has shown that scholars are torn about the universalist qualities and potentiality of international law. Some regard the engagement of Third World states with the ICJ as enough. Others doubt the ability of existing structures to speak for and from the margins. Still others suggest that international law's indeterminacy and malleability allows for both optics: international law nurtures imperialist and anti-imperialist tendencies.[186] At the very least, however, universalism must mean the possibility to speak in many tongues, of many experiences and of contested histories. It must also mean that such narratives can in some way be heard and appreciated, as for example, by the ICJ's bench. Scholarship lauding the ICJ's recent record, or even international law's progressive future more generally, is inadequate for explaining why Third World – and particularly in this book, Arab – states come before the Court, how they use it and what the results are. Conversely, despite providing us with an array of conceptual tools, critical scholars have so far failed to expand our knowledge of the grammars of legal argumentation employed at the Peace Palace. The book acknowledges the particular discursive contours of the Court, and seeks to explore the nature of dialogue generated about international law's past, present and future, particularly through the prism of colonialism. Thus, this study embraces the critical call to map out the legal grammars informing Arab ICJ disputes. In so doing, it challenges critical and mainstream scholars alike to expand the research agenda of international law by interrogating spaces and silences where both universalism and particularism lie. Having reviewed the conceptual tools informing this book, the next chapter provides the historical tools for reading the case studies by exploring notions of territoriality in the Arab-Islamic tradition.

---

185 D. Kennedy, 'The Last Treatise: Project and Person (Reflections on Martti Koskenniemi's From Apology to Utopia) (2006) 7 *German Law Journal* 982.

186 M. Koskenniemi, 'International Law and Imperialism', D. Freestone, S. Subedi & S. Davidson (eds.), *Contemporary Issues in International Law: A Collection of the Josephine Onoh Memorial Lectures* (The Hague: Kluwer, 2002), at 197. Rajagopal echoes this idea when he argues that international law can be both hegemonic and counter-hegemonic: Rajagopal, 'Counter-hegemonic International Law', *supra* n. 96, at 768.

Chapter Two

Between Faith and Place: Arab-Islamic Approaches to Authority over Territory in Theory and Practice

1) *Introduction*

Chapter One highlighted tensions faced when studying international adjudication in a postcolonial world and it raised the question of whether we can speak of an international law that is universal. Third World states now participate in ICJ matters more than ever before, particularly in relation to territorial disputes. Arab states have mirrored this trend over the last few decades, suggesting that, like the rest of the Third World, they are willing to accept colonialism's legacy, the nation-state.

The following chapter tries to make sense of the Arab world's engagement with international law and adjudication in three ways. First, the chapter provides a narrative overview and commentary about the emergence of Arab statehood. In particular, ideas about the link between territory and modes of authority in the Arab-Muslim tradition are explored so that we can appreciate both the similarities and differences between Arab and European trajectories of statehood. Second, the chapter is intrigued with the interplay between the Arab and European world/s for understanding the rise not only of the state, but also, international law and membership in international society. All of the case studies explore the extent to which international law and international legal personality was the privilege of European entities. Here, we can challenge notions of cultural difference, especially in looking at Ottoman-European relations and their combined contribution to the formation of international law. Third, the chapter considers the development of Islamic international law as a practice and as a field of recent scholarship within the discipline of public international law. Have Islamic legal norms and institutions evolved to reflect changes in international society and models of statehood? What is the role of Islamic law in modern international adjudication and to what extent can Islamic norms inform public international law? We can also ask, are current approaches within the scholarship of international law adequate for understanding the link between Islamic law and public international law?

The following discussion traces the concept of Arab statehood from the era of the Prophet to the present, but it does not pretend to offer a definitive account of Islamic legal history. Further, Piscatori asserts that it 'is nearly impossible to say with authority at any one moment what Islam is and what it is not.'[1] The following section explores particular choices and interpretations shaping the chapter's narrative about Islam, the West and the development of international law. I also interrogate scholarly agendas informing historical accounts in order to understand how dominant narratives about Islam, international law and Arab states shape research within and beyond the international legal academy. The chapter is therefore concerned more with the uses and abuses of history than with a quest for historical 'truth'. After exploring the nature of historical enquiry, the chapter then applies these insights to three historical periods: the origins of Islam and the rise of the Caliphate; Arabs under Ottoman and colonial rule; and finally, Arab forms of statehood and dispute resolution in the modern era since the institution of the Mandates.

2) *How Should International Lawyers Study Islamic Law and its Contribution to International Law?*

(a) *Linking International Law with Historical Contingency*

Before considering the Arab-Islamic experience of statehood and the rise of international law, it is important to gain an awareness of how Islamic legal and political history has been constructed. While interest in Islamic studies has grown enormously over the last few decades for scholars working in both international relations and international law, much of it is superficial and repetitive. Specialised studies outside international law therefore can assist in developing an Islamic theory of statehood and international law. However, it is important to note particular shortcomings and biases of such scholarship. Perhaps because of a real or imagined linguistic and cultural gulf, non-specialist scholars have readily accepted dominant narratives about Islamic law and civilisation. In this section, the nature of historical and legal scholarship on Islam is discussed.

We saw in Chapter One that historical understandings play a role in the argumentation and judgment of territorial disputes. We also saw that, although states and judges acknowledge history's relevance, rarely do they concede the subjectivity of choice or the structuring effects of the law/history dichotomy. Like the law/politics dichotomy, international legal scholarship tends to separate law from history, but with radically different effects. The separation between law and politics allows law to be portrayed as neutral and free from the contingencies

[1] J. Piscatori, *Islam in a World of Nation-States* (Cambridge: Cambridge University Press, 1986), at 9.

of interest. Typically, however, when history is enlisted in international legal scholarship, it is not so much as an 'other' but as a one-dimensional ally to arguments founded on law. Like choices informing doctrinal arguments, historical narratives are depicted as unmediated accounts of the past. Rarely are these accounts seen as worthy of comment or criticism; as Korhonen reminds us, it 'is not common to question the discipline's sense of history.'[2]

Despite dominant narratives about international law's origins, as well as familiar watersheds or 'critical dates', international law can never escape scholarly agendas in linking the past with the present. Because the discipline of international law is built on narratives about its progressive development, for example, it is necessary to render particular accounts of the past to support certain readings of the present. Kennedy illustrated this in his study of 'primitive' international law, when he showed that conventional paradigms identifying the origins of international law in 1648 with the Treaties of Westphalia require a body of thought markedly distinct from 'modern' examples.[3] Simplicity behoves us to focus on certain historical events and forget others, but we should at least be alive to the choices involved when constructing an account of international law that is based, for example, on the familiar milestones of 1648, 1789, 1815, 1856, 1885, 1914, 1918, 1939 and 1945. It is all too easy to project current realities onto the past, thereby obscuring subaltern voices and experiences.[4]

Dominant European narratives about international legal history contain both rupture and stability: the present must be contrasted with the past, but the dynamism of the past must also be stabilised into a manageable, 'frozen' form.[5] Once history is both compartmentalised and paralysed, it can then be used as an unproblematic tool of legal scholarship. According to Korhonen, a 'common stance towards history seems to assume that the jurist has some way of reaching the past as it once was, i.e. unmediated by intervening circumstances and undistorted by the accumulation of layers of temporally alternating meanings and lenses of prejudices.'[6] Korhonen rejects this approach and instead calls on lawyers to recognise their own relationship with both temporality and international law's dynamism.[7] Although international lawyers typically strive to 'minimise outside

2 O. Korhonen, *International Law Situated: An Analysis of the Lawyer's Stance towards Culture, History and Community* (The Hague: Kluwer, 2000), at 129.

3 D. Kennedy, 'Primitive Legal Scholarship' (1986) 27 *Harvard International Law Journal* 1, at 1–3.

4 Y. Onuma, 'When was the law of International Society Born? – An Inquiry into the History of International Law from an Intercivilizational Perspective' (2000) 2 *Journal of the History of International Law* 1, at 25.

5 Korhonen, *supra* n. 2, at 136.

6 Ibid., at 129–130.

7 Ibid., at 135.

contamination' and to 'appear as impartial and non-predisposed as possible', this is unattainable.[8] Ultimately, Korhonen suggests that international lawyers abandon the ideal of objective history, because the

> International jurist is not situated in any middle ground towards history. She uses and abuses history in different ways, negotiates continuity and change, and works facing a number of schisms – producing reality effects, striking conventions about history and law, and having to let them shift... The international jurist is often in a key position in managing these stabilisations and shifts and she strives to make sense of them. She has to negotiate a convoluted situational web where no uniform solution can last eternally and where she therefore has to understand the various conditions involved.[9]

With this sensitivity about the relationship between history and international law, it is now possible to explore the relationship between international law and Islamic history.

(b) *Linking Islamic Law with Public International Law*

Partly in response to the phenomenon of Islamic 'fundamentalism,' and partly out of a desire to expand the discipline's universal underpinnings, there is now a growing body of literature devoted to exploring the historical inter-relationship between international law and Islam. Despite this development, Mayer laments its quality, arguing that the 'existing literature does not always treat problematic issues in an objective and coherent fashion or adequately analyze methodological questions.'[10] Westbrook also argues that scholarship on Islamic international law has been disappointing because 'these attempts either fail to address the concerns of public international law or fail to locate authority in Islam – fail, that is, to be substantively Islamic.'[11] Some of these difficulties can be attributed to the methodology of comparison,[12] and Westbrook recognises that writing 'comparative law is always difficult because communication is largely about shared meanings, and comparative law explores the difference of meanings.'[13] Does the Islamic tradition contain, for example, terms that can be rendered in public international law terminology? How can we find common meanings across different lexicons?

---

[8] Ibid., at 151.

[9] Ibid., at 206.

[10] A. E. Mayer, 'War and Peace in the Islamic Tradition and International Law', J. Kelsay & J. T. Johnson (eds.), *Just War and Jihad: Historical and Theoretical Perspectives on War and Peace in Western and Islamic Traditions* (New York: Greenwood Press, 1991) 195–226, at 199.

[11] D. Westbrook, 'Islamic International Law and Public International Law: Separate Expressions of World Order' (1993) 33 *Virginia Journal of International Law* 819, at 821.

[12] Especially see: G. Frankenberg, 'Critical Comparisons: Re-Thinking Comparative Law' (1985) 26 *Harvard International Law Journal* 411.

[13] Westbrook, *supra* n. 11, at 821–822.

Particularly with so few international lawyers educated in Arabic and the principles of *fiqh* or Islamic jurisprudence, it is perhaps unsurprising that sophisticated comparative frameworks are rare. Problems of translation abound. Beyond this, Strawson points out that 'English texts do not merely present Islamic law, they construct it.'[14] The first step required then in appreciating the similarities and differences as well as historical interplay between European international law and Islamic law is for scholars to possess substantial knowledge beyond the confines of European theory and state practice. Without this knowledge, there will not be incentives for international lawyers to develop alternative narratives to the dominant one which locates the birth of international law exclusively within European domains. This will also assist the project of universalising the discourse of international law. Bedjaoui pointed out that not only Western scholars are to blame here; 'even Arab and Muslim jurists themselves are completely unaware of the Islamic conception of international law or confine it to the ghetto'.[15] He appeals to both Western and Muslim lawyers to reverse this oversight by engaging with the rich body of material available.[16] The recent work of Judge Weeramantry in his inter-civilisational project attests to the potential of such work,[17] but most scholarship still remains under-developed.

Even where detailed accounts are offered, however, much of this scholarship is problematic. For example, a dominant approach championed by scholars versed in Arabic and the *sharīʿa* has been to effect a reconciliation between Islam and international law at all costs.[18] These scholars readily acknowledge dissonances such as the doctrine of *jihād* and the issue over enduring peace between the Muslim and non-Muslim worlds. However, their ultimate goal of

---

[14] J. Strawson, 'Islamic Law and English Texts' (1995) 6 *Law and Critique* 21, at 21.

[15] M. Bedjaoui, 'The 1980–1988 Gulf War and Universal Law: The Severe Judgment of World Legal Scholarship upon the Belligerents', I. F. Dekker & H. H. G. Post (eds.), *The Gulf War of 1980–1988: The Iran-Iraq War in International Legal Perspective* (Dordrecht: Martinus Nijhoff, 1992) 279–299, at 295.

[16] 'And I can restrain myself no longer from *appealing to all jurists in the Muslim world to take greater personal responsibility and mobilize more efficiently in a decisive effort of creativity, instead of confining themselves to an attitude of slavish imitation* [*taqlīd*?] *which often results in strapping lifeless artificial limbs of foreign origin on living human communities.*' Italics in original, Ibid., at 296.

[17] C. G. Weeramantry, *Islamic Jurisprudence: An International Perspective* (Kula Lumpur: The Other Press, 2001).

[18] One striking example of anachronism is Al-Ghunaimi's classification of seventh century Arabian city-states as analogous to modern nation-states: 'the city of Medina was possessed of the required elements – population, territory and government – to be classified as a state under the principles of modern international law.' Given that the nation-state model had yet to emerge anywhere else, it seems forced to make such an anachronistic argument. M. T. Al-Ghunaimi, *The Muslim Conception of International Law and the Western Approach* (The Hague: Martinus Nijhoff, 1968), at 55.

aligning Islamic law and public international law entails that certain elements of Islamic law are purged in this apologist project.[19] Points of difference have to be overlooked, whereas points of similarity are over-emphasised. Westbrook summarises this approach as an

> obsession with the world of Islam and a monolithic world outside; a tendency to explain 'Islamic law' within the categories of Western international law (even using Latin); a predilection to apologize for the practice of Muslim states, combined with often harsh critiques of Western states; the desire to adopt superficially understood conceptions of Western politics; and the tendency to give elaborate and tenuous historical arguments for the priority of something 'Islamic' in existing public international law, however hegemonic and loudly un-Islamic it may currently be.[20]

International lawyers illustrative of Westbrook's criticisms note that the Islamic tradition includes the principle of *pacta sunt servanda*,[21] and developed a sophisticated body of international humanitarian law centuries before the Hague Conferences. *Jihād*, just war and humanitarianism are all in vogue.[22]

Fascination with certain aspects of Islamic law is linked to the way in which the contemporary application of *sharīʿa* has become confined to particular spheres of society's regulation. Most Arab legal systems have adopted a hybrid system of law, retaining the *sharīʿa* only for private sphere matters and favouring European, civil law models for public governance. The regulation of personal status, family relations and inheritance has continued to reflect *sharīʿa* principles. On the other

---

[19] W. S. D. Cravens, 'The Future of Islamic Arguments in International Boundary Disputes between Islamic States' (1998) 55 *Washington & Lee Law Review* 529, at 541.

[20] Westbrook, *supra* n. 11, at 858.

[21] Cravens argues that although Islam contains a doctrine akin to *pacta sunt servanda*, it lacks the breadth of the meaning contained in public international law: Cravens, *supra* n. 19, at 570. Ford also argues that Islamic and public international law definitions are not in complete parity: C. A. Ford, 'Siyar-ization and its Discontents: International Law and Islam's Constitutional Crisis' (1995) 30 *Texas International Law Journal* 499, 521. For scholars generally supportive of the existence of *pacta sunt servanda* in the Islamic tradition, see Al-Ghunaimi, *supra* n. 18, at 212; Mayer, *supra* n. 10, at 201; Weeramantry, *supra* n. 17, at 141. Boisard goes even further, suggesting that 'Islam not only reinforced the validity of the axiom, *pacta sunt servanda*, but also introduced it to international relations, making possible the systematic development of conventional law, which became a partial substitute for custom,' M. A. Boisard, 'On the Probable Influence of Islam on Western Public and International Law' (1980) 11 *International Journal of Middle East Studies* 429, at 441–442.

[22] Moinuddin argues that Western scholars have tended to over-emphasise the importance of *jihād* and Islamic supremacy in classical sources. He points out, however, that a number of Muslim scholars have tried to show how the *siyar* is about much more than this narrow focus. H. Moinuddin, *The Charter of the Islamic Conference and Legal Framework of Economic Co-operation among its Member States* (Oxford: Clarendon, 1987), at 19–20.

hand, public law, including international law, has lagged far behind.[23] Scholars wishing to acquaint themselves with Islamic notions of international law must therefore grapple with realities on the ground: very few modern examples of Islamic international law are available. Yet the Islamic legal tradition contains a wealth of learning about international issues from earlier eras, allowing contemporary research a platform from which to develop and strengthen a body of modern Islamic international legal norms and practices. Studies about the *pacta sunt servanda* norm exist, and considerations of *jihād* abound,[24] but Islamic international law needs concerted invigoration lest it remain an under-developed and somewhat skewed field of study bent on treaty law and the laws of war.

Perhaps the biggest challenge faced in studying the history of international Islamic law is the tension between theory and practice. For example, it is important to recognise the primacy of early Islam and its enduring legacy on the evolution of Islamic law. The period of the Prophet's life (d. 632) generated the two main sources of Islamic law: the *Qur'ān* and the *Sunna*. Furthermore, for Muslims, 'the great age of early Islam served as an image of what the world should be'[25] Although Islamic polities have never since emulated this golden age, certain scholarship turns to this era for guidance, thus overlooking the significance of later state practice and the evolution of certain legal theories. Hallaq does not regard this fascination with early Islam as innocent, despite its indisputable significance to Islamic thought: the 'choice of concentration on one area or another is a function of relevance'[26] For example, Hallaq points out that

[23] According to Bedjaoui, 'the Islamic law which rose out of the religious revolution of the seventh century has historically suffered from the brake being applied in the public domain and from being kept in leading strings in the private domain. This has resulted in an unbalanced evolution, in that its public (international) law limb has been virtually amputated and its private law limb allowed to develop in a somewhat ingrowing manner.' Bedjaoui, *supra* n. 15, at 296–297. Also, see S. Zubaida, *Law and Power in the Islamic World* (London: I. B. Tauris, 2003), at 2.

[24] Some examples of literatures in English surveying Muslim laws of war include: J. D. R. Cockayne, 'Islam and International Humanitarian Law: From Clash to a Conversation between Civilizations' (2002) 84 *International Review of the Red Cross* 597; J. Kelsay, 'Al-Shaybani and the Islamic Law of War' (2003) 2 *Journal of Military Ethics* 63; J. Kelsay & J. T. Johnson (eds.), *Just War and Jihad: Historical and Theoretical Perspectives on War and Peace in Western and Islamic Traditions* (New York: Greenwood Press, 1991); J. Rehman, *Islamic State Practices, International Law and the Threat from Terrorism* (Portland: Hart, 2005); and H. M. Zawati, *Is Jihād a Just War? War, Peace, and Human Rights under Islamic and Public International Law* (Lewiston, NY: Edwin Mellen Press, 2001).

[25] A. Hourani, *Arabic Thought in the Liberal Age 1798–1939* (Cambridge: Cambridge University Press, 1962, reissued 1983), at 8.

[26] W. B. Hallaq, 'The Quest for Origins or Doctrine? Islamic Legal Studies as Colonialist Discourse' (2003) 2 *UCLA Journal of Islamic and Near Eastern Law* 1, at 3.

the work of Schacht[27] tended to explore either Islam's early phases or its most recent; at least half a millennium, and especially the Ottoman era,[28] remains 'depressingly a terra incognita'.[29] In focusing on the early period in the context of 'debts and borrowings', old-school Orientalists like Schacht could portray Islamic law as 'at best, heavily indebted to the legal traditions of the cultures that gave birth to Western civilization and, at worst, little more than a replica of these traditions.'[30]

Other studies continue this quest for non-indigenous sources of Islamic civilisation by over-emphasising the impact of European ideas and institutions on the Arab world in the wake of colonialism. Thus, Hourani opined that scholarship has 'been wrong in laying too much emphasis upon ideas which were taken from Europe, and not enough upon what was retained, even if in a changed form, from an older tradition.'[31] We can see from the opinions of Hallaq and Hourani that a balance is required in appreciating Islamic culture within the context of changing internal and external conditions.

Focusing on only certain periods of Islam's history aids the production of a distorted and monolithic image of Islamic law and civilisation. As we saw *vis-à-vis* comparative scholarship generally, it is difficult to preserve dynamism and diversity when studying two or more subjects; often one will be reduced to a cliché of its former self. Boisard questioned accounts of Islam's link with public international law for their tendency to construct both the West, as well as Islam, as monoliths. Instead, we need to appreciate the significant interaction and cross-fertilisation that took place, as well as the role of intermediaries, such as Jews.[32] Beydoun echoes these sentiments when he characterises depictions of a cohesive Islamic community as neo-Orientalist simplifications of the diversity and dissonance within Islamic communities.[33] According to Barakat, Orientalist accounts of the Arab world typically have regarded religion as the central determinative force in social life, thus creating a static and reified conception of 'Arab

---

[27] His classic works being: J. Schacht, *An Introduction to Islamic Law* (Oxford: Clarendon Press, 1964); and J. Schacht, *The Origins of Mohammadan Jurisprudence* (Oxford: Clarendon Press, 1979, new ed.).

[28] This relative lack of scholarship on the Ottoman era is also noted in A. Hourani, 'How Should We Write the History of the Middle East?' (1991) 23 *International Journal of Middle East Studies* 125, at 129.

[29] Hallaq, *supra* n. 26, at 4.

[30] Ibid., at 5. Here, Hallaq is referring to typical narratives of either Near Eastern or Hellenistic creative impetus of Islamic civilisation.

[31] Hourani, 'How Should We Write', *supra* n. 28, at 128.

[32] Boisard, *supra* n. 21, at 432–434.

[33] K. A. Beydoun, 'Dar al-Islam Meets "Islam as Civilization": An Alignment of Politico-Theoretical Fundamentalisms and the Geopolitical Realism of this Worldview' (2004–2005) 4 *UCLA Journal of Islamic & Near Eastern Law* 143, at 146.

society' as well as 'Islamic law'.[34] For Piscatori, rather than over-determining the role of culture,[35] and so as to avoid essentialism, 'even a religious code such as Islam must be accepted as variable and evolving with changing circumstances.'[36] Historical accounts must probe under-studied periods as well as the pervasive role of political choice, whether in the evolution of Islamic legal norms or scholarly accounts of such laws.

How can the needs for historical specificity and conceptual continuity be reconciled when seeking to understand the link between the historical development of Islamic law in theory and practice? For instance, is it anachronistic to apply concepts such as 'state' and 'secularism' to Islamic history? First, it is important that particular scholarly agendas be acknowledged when constructing an historical account. In this chapter, my reading of mainly secondary material was framed by a desire to understand how Islamic communities have lived out the relationship between territory and authority. The conceptual framework informing my learning in the subject matter was premised on the desire to identify non-European models of political authority over territory. I also wanted to probe stereotypical accounts of Islamic societies perpetuated in the West. Typically, the Arab-Muslim world has been distinguished from the European experience on account of its tribal structure and the role of religion in society, but is such an understanding accurate?[37] I was also interested in tracing the development and evolution of ideas and practices that have allowed Arab states today largely to accept the nation-state model. Aside from surmisable realist explanations about the interests of state elites, are there earlier experiences and theories from the Arab-Islamic tradition sympathetic to and supportive of institutions such as the nation-state model, public international law and dispute resolution? Widespread contact across the Mediterranean world produced a variety of institutional and theoretical models, and it is on these examples that the chapter will focus while exploring the three points highlighted in the introduction.

Second, the chapter embraces some of the methodological devices developed by Piscatori in his 1986 study, which asked the question, 'is there something about

[34] H. Barakat, *The Arab World: Society, Culture, and State* (Berkeley: University of California Press, 1993), at 120.

[35] J. Piscatori, 'Order, Justice, and Global Islam', R. Foot et al. (eds.), *Order and Justice in International Relations* (Oxford: Oxford University Press, 2003) 262–292, at 265.

[36] Ibid., at 267.

[37] It is common for studies of Arab society to amplify the importance of tribalism. Hourani's scholarship points out that the 'structure of Islamic thought and society developed, however, not primarily in the Hijaz [the birthplace of Islam, Arabia], but in the great areas of high civilization which were incorporated into the caliphate.' Hourani, 'How Should We Write', *supra* n. 28, at 131. For Hourani's application of his premise, see A. Hourani, *A History of the Arab Peoples* (London: Faber & Faber, 1991).

Islam which makes it incongruous with the idea of nationalism and with the institution of the nation-state?'[38] Piscatori answered this question in the negative: there is room for compatibility between the territorial state and Islam through an historical approach able to surmount essentialism by marrying Islamic theory and practice. One of the four tenets of Islamic law is *ijmāʿ*, or consensus, and Piscatori applies this to his own concepts of *ijmāʿ al-qawl* (consensus of speech) and *ijmāʿ al-faʿil* (consensus of action).[39] Piscatori suggests that it is best to see Islam 'as the political beliefs and conduct of Muslims, what they say as well as what they actually do,'[40] rather than holding fast to ahistorical stereotypes. In the following three sections, Islamic law and history will be explored as both a product of speech and action, within and beyond the diversity of *dār al-islām*, the abode of Islam or peace.

3) *In the Wake of the Prophet's Message: Conquests, Caliphs and the Development of Islamic International Law*

The purpose of this section is twofold: to introduce some basic aspects of Islamic law and history in the first few centuries of Islam; and from this basis, to discuss classical Muslim notions of authority over territory. Because the book is concerned with the process of argumentation at the ICJ, it does not pursue the agenda of effecting some sort of resolution between public international law and Islamic law *per se*. Secondary scholarship is drawn on only for its attention to the international legal dimensions of Islam and the extent to which Islamic practice contributed to the development of international law, which is explored below. Of more importance is an appreciation of Islamic approaches to territory and authority as well as the centrality of the Caliphate because these ideas are drawn on by a number of parties in three of the four case studies: Libya in Chapter Three, both Bahrain and Qatar in Chapter Four and Algeria, Mauritania and Morocco in Chapter Five.

Like any other monumental historical moment, the story of Islam's birth can be told in many ways. For our purposes, appreciating how a narrative is constructed and applied to legal argument is far more important than isolating an indisputable rendering of the Prophet's life and the revelation of Islam. Why is it important to return to the Prophet's life? How can theories of rule and laws emerge out of such an – often idealised – image?

---

[38] Piscatori, *Islam in a World of Nation-States, supra* n. 1, at vii.

[39] Ibid., at 45.

[40] Ibid., at 14.

Allah's message was revealed to his last prophet, Muhammed in Arabian Mecca and Medina in the early part of the seventh century. Although the Islamic message was intended to be the definitive guide for faith into the future, it was also a product of its environment. Thus, Islam draws not only on its Arab, tribal origins, but also on the other monotheistic traditions of Judaism and Christianity. The Prophet acted as Allah's deputy on earth, combining secular and divine rule over his followers. The community that emerged under Muhammed came to be known as *al-umma*, or the community of the believers, all united in their commitment to Allah's message as revealed to his Prophet and later compiled in the *Qur'ān*.

Although Allah's ultimate authority remained uncontested, controversies emerged almost immediately as to the nature of rule on earth. Khadduri points out that societies based on religious rule have erroneously been described as theocracies. He argues that

> a distinction ... must be made between an authority which is directly derived from and exercised by God, and an authority which is derived from a divine code endowed by God but enforced by His viceregent (or by a secular ruler) which is equally binding upon the latter and the people.[41]

Thus, Khadduri suggests that it is best to understand the society established by Muhammed as a divine universal nomocracy, grounded in Allah's revelation, the *Qur'ān*. Foda disputes this account, suggesting that sovereignty on earth resided in the *umma*, and was expressed through the relationship between the *umma* and Allah's law, or *sharī'a*.[42]

Despite the primacy of the *umma* in a theoretical sense, it is the theory and practice of the Caliphate that best reveals the interrelationship between religion and politics, and helps explain tensions in Islamic perspectives on authority. Even with over ten wives, Muhammed died in 632 leaving only daughters and a controversy over who should succeed him. The word *khalīfa*, or caliph, derives from the Arabic verb *khalafa*, meaning to follow or succeed. This was expressed by the first caliph himself, Abu Bakr, who said: 'I am not a successor to God, I am successor to God's Messenger [Muhammed]'.[43] There were disputes and political differences following the death of the Prophet, but later Muslims sought to overcome these early differences by depicting the period of the first four caliphs as one of consensus and harmony. Hence it is referred

[41] M. Khadduri, *War and Peace in the Law of Islam* (Baltimore: John Hopkins Press, 1955), at 14.

[42] E. Foda, *The Projected Arab Court of Justice: A Study in Regional Jurisdiction with Specific Reference to the Muslim Law of Nations* (The Hague: Martinus Nijhoff, 1957), at 99.

[43] Contained in Mawardi's *al-aḥkām al-sulṭāniyya*, quoted in S. Mahmassani, 'The Principles of International Law in the Light of Islamic Doctrine' (1966) 117 *Recueil des Cours* 201, at 233.

to as the era of *al-khulafā' al-rāshidūn*, or the [four] rightly-guided caliphs.[44] On Mu'āwiyya's defeat of 'Alī, the Prophet's son-in-law and the figure who would become associated with Shi'ism, the first Muslim empire was established in Damascus: the Ummayad Caliphate (661–750). Following on from earlier conquests, caliphal rule came to be associated with a ruler's ability to maintain and extend the Prophet's message through conquest and empire. Because of its dominance politically and theoretically both in an historical sense and for the cases, the rest of this chapter will only explore the Sunni practice of rule.

After rapid territorial expansion, Abbasid caliphs (750–1258) in particular had to confront a world not only far from universally Muslim, but also a Muslim world comprising multiple caliphs and sects.[45] It was therefore during this period that rulers and scholars explored the relationship between territory and authority under the Caliphate in detail. Hourani captured the tension between theory and practice confronting scholars of the period, when he wrote:

> The caliphate had been one, at least in principle; it had been universal, resting on a formal equality of rights and functions as between all believers; its head had been, by his own claim and general recognition, the successor of the Prophet in his political function, and he had exercised his function in accordance with the *Shari'a*. None of this was true of the sultans who had taken over power. Their rule was territorially limited.[46]

Scholars of the classical era laid out the requirements for caliphal rule, and despite its theoretical ilk, it is clear that such work reflected an increasingly splintered and divided system of governance, both geographically and institutionally.[47] Piscatori concedes that 'much of classical and medieval theory supports the view that Islam is pre-eminently concerned with the creation of a universal community and is intolerant of those who are not Muslim.'[48] However, he also suggests that this period contains the germ for the later idea of the nation-state and that we should not confine ourselves to a formulaic interpretation of a universalistic Caliphate. For example, Ibn Taymiyya (1263–1328) argued that religious unity was not synonymous with political unity; separate Muslim entities were permitted. Ibn Khaldun's (1332–1406) sociological study of the rise

---

[44] Abu Bakr (632–634), 'Umar (634–644), 'Uthmān (644–656) and 'Alī (656–661). For a general history of the Caliphate, see I. Lapidus, *A History of Islamic Societies* (Cambridge: Cambridge University Press, 2nd edition, 2002), at 45–66.

[45] For example, Al-Ghunaimi illustrates that while the Abbasids ruled from Baghdad, the Ummayads in Cordoba, Spain also declared a caliphate under 'Abd al-Rahman III in 909 and the Fatīmīds in Cairo under 'Ukayd-allah in 929. Al-Ghunaimi, *supra* n. 18, at 67–68. This is also noted by Onuma in his study of Islam in international law, Onuma, *supra* n. 4, at 21.

[46] Hourani, *Arabic Thought, supra* n. 25, at 12.

[47] For example, al-Mawardi's (972–1058) principal work on political theory, *al-aḥkām al-sulṭaniyya* (*On the Ordinances of Government*).

[48] Piscatori, *Islam in a World of Nation-States, supra* n. 1, at 44.

and fall of societies also suggests that it was natural for Islamic empires to wax and wane;[49] what should not change, however, was faith in the application of Allah's message through the *sharīʿa*.

Muhammed's lifetime had ushered in the two main sources of *sharīʿa*, the *Qurʾān* and the *Sunna*, or traditions of the Prophet, but it was not until much later that *sharīʿa* was systematised, especially in its international form of the *siyar*.[50] Although we can characterise the *siyar* as somewhat of an afterthought, it still followed *sharīʿa* practices and principles.[51] Codified rules suitable for application to complex societies were rare in Islamic law's primary sources, the *Qurʾān* and *Sunna*. In response, *uṣūl al-fiqh* (ways of interpretation) were developed, which laid out how to identify rules through the interplay of primary as well as secondary sources, namely *ijmāʿ* (consensus of legal scholars) and *qiyas* (analogical reasoning). Given the relative lack of material found in the *Qurʾān* and *Sunna* on international issues, the *siyar* was especially dependent on these secondary sources and it also reflected the political realities of Abbasid rule. In addition, because of the gradual shift from *ijtihād* (innovative reasoning) in the early centuries to *taqlīd* (imitation), the evolution of legal norms failed to keep pace with international developments. For this reason, the classical *siyar* as developed by *mujtahids*, or practitioners of *ijtihād*, must not be portrayed as the sum total of Islamic internationalism. Instead, it is necessary to factor in state practice in combination with a flexible approach to the evolution of earlier scholarship and *sharīʿa* principles. The importance of state practice and adaptation was especially relevant under the Ottomans, and this is explored in the next section after a brief overview of the characteristics of *siyar*.

What is the *siyar* and how did it conceptualise the relationship between territory and Caliph in a world containing both believers and non-believers? Although Al-Shaybānī (748–805) developed *siyar* more than any other scholar in the early centuries of Islam,[52] it was not until Al-Sarakhsī (d. 1101) that a clear definition emerged:

> The *siyar* is the plural of *sīra*…It describes the conduct of the believers in their relations with the unbelievers of enemy territory as well as with the people whom the believers had made treaties, who may have been temporarily (*mustaʾmins*) or permanently (*Dhimmīs*) in Islamic lands; with apostates, who were the worst of the unbelievers…and with rebels…[53]

---

[49] Ibid., at 47–48.

[50] See generally, W. B. Hallaq, *The Origins and Evolution of Islamic Law* (Cambridge: Cambridge University Press, 2005), at chs. 5–7.

[51] Khadduri, *War and Peace, supra* n. 41, at 47.

[52] For a discussion of these other theorists, especially in relation to *jihād*, see M. Khadduri, *The Islamic Law of Nations: Shaybānī's Siyar* (Baltimore: John Hopkins Press, 1966), at 38–39; and Mahmassani, *supra* n. 43.

[53] Khadduri, *The Islamic Law of Nations, supra* n. 52, at 40.

It was understood that the *sharīʿa* applied to Muslims as members of the *umma*, but a different body of law was required for non-Muslim peoples and lands. Bifurcated jurisdiction was a product of the prevailing Islamic worldview, which distinguished *dār al-islām* (land of peace or Islam) from *dār al-ḥarb* (land of war). Many writers have discussed this dichotomy and the implications, not only for separation between Muslims, but also for amicable relations across confessional lines. Because the division suggests perpetual conflict, as encapsulated in the concept of *jihād*,[54] many commentators regard the *siyar* as incapable of adapting to a system of nation-states under the norm of sovereign equality. Other authors tend to downplay classical *siyar's* exclusionary effects through a series of reconciliatory gestures discussed above.

The failure to achieve worldwide conquest and the inability to wage constant wars of conversion had necessitated agreements with non-Muslim powers, for example through treaty. Sunni schools of jurisprudence did not develop a uniform position on this, but it was generally agreed that treaties of peace could be concluded for a period of up to ten years.[55] The resulting regime was called *dār al-ṣulḥ*, the land of reconciliation or treaty. The Prophet himself had entered into treaties, and so at least temporary versions were supported in the centuries to follow.[56]

This practice of temporary truces, however, did not support treaties between Muslim powers (both operating in *dār al-islām*) or the notion of permanent peace between Muslims and non-Muslims. Further difficulties arose in relation to treaty relations with non-Muslims because of the issue of territorial dominion: Which laws were applicable in lands under treaty? Were Muslims in the land of war able to enforce the *sharīʿa*? What was the status of non-Muslims within *dār al-islām*?[57] Some of these questions are explored in relation to Ottoman practice below, and they were also the subject of numerous classical treatises.

Debate continues about the nature of Islamic authority over territory as developed in the classical period. Parvin and Somner distinguished between legal and territorial rule:

---

[54] *Jihād* is derived from the Arabic verb, *jahada*, which connotes an action requiring exertion, strain, effort, trouble. *Jihād* is typically translated as 'holy war', but can refer to any sort of religious struggle, such as a personal one of the conscience. The word, *ijtihād*, or independent legal reasoning, is derived from the same root.

[55] A. A. Abū Sulaymān, *Towards an Islamic Theory of International Relations* (Herndon, VA: The International Institute of Islamic Thought, 2nd edition, 1994), at 20.

[56] The most famous treaty during the Prophet's lifetime was *ṣulḥ al-ḥudaybiyya* (the Treaty of Ḥudaybiyya), formed between Moḥammed and the Meccans in 628. For a general discussion of treaties, see Zawati, *supra* n. 24.

[57] Generally, see Khadduri's translation of Al-Shaybāni on such issues: Khadduri, *The Islamic Law of Nations, supra* n. 52.

> Dar al-Islam is not... inherently a territorial concept. Rather, it is a legal construct that has a territorial dimension: a territorial expression of the *umma*... which itself has a political component. Thus, the dar al-Islam can be considered a political-territorial expression of that community in which the Islamic religion is practiced and where it is protected by a Muslim ruler. Similarly, the dar al-sulh can be described as an area in which the practice of Islam is permitted but not under the protection of a Muslim ruler. In the dar al-harb, though Islam might be practiced, it does not enjoy the protection of the non-Muslim ruler.[58]

While the relationship between ruler and territory was vital, contemporary authors are divided as to the nature of a caliph's rule: was it territorial or personal? Crone, for example, points out that the word, *khalīfa* refers only to the caliph's office and not his polity or his control over a geographical area.[59] The authority of the caliph's office derived from his application of the *sharīʿa* to the *umma* and not from effective territorial control *per se*. However, under classical doctrine this could also mean that Islamic law followed a community regardless of political authority:

> since the concept of territorial sovereignty had not yet developed under Muslim law and since the Muslims were bound by the law regardless of the country or the territory they resided in, it follows, at least in Muslim legal theory, that the jurisdiction of the Islamic state would extend to Muslims, regardless of their place of residence.[60]

Other authors are more flexible in their fusion of theory and practice, arguing that territory was at least a factor in the development of jurisdiction and authority.[61]

The question of Islam's territorial nature involves conceptual tools and assumptions which are not static. The Caliphate cannot simply be aligned with the modern state, but it is necessary to forge a credible theoretical basis between classical scholarship and modern practice as explored in the next section. It is possible to show that some appreciation of territorially limited dominion emerged during the classical era which could inform later theory and practice. It

[58] M. Parvin & M. Sommer, 'Dar Al-Islam: The Evolution of Muslim Territoriality and its Implications for Conflict Resolution' (1980) 11 *International Journal of Middle East Studies* 1, at 4–5.

[59] P. Crone, *God's Rule: Government and Islam* (New York: Columbia University Press, 2004), at 3.

[60] M. Khadduri, 'International Law', M. Khadduri & H. J. Liebesny (eds.), *Law in the Middle East: Origin and Development of Islamic Law, vol. 1* (1955) 349–372, at 360.

[61] For example, Parvin and Somner argue that 'Muslim jurisdiction, and therefore the dar al-Islam, was coextensive with *secure*, nonoppressed Muslim inhabitation and, while the character of Islamic law had a personal rather than territorial cast... the system was nonetheless binding on groups, which perforce, have a territorial distribution, as well as on individuals.' Italics in original, Parvin & Somner, *supra* n. 58, at 3. See also, Al-Ghunaimi, *supra* n. 18, at 64.

is also important not to superimpose pre-conceptions on this contested terrain. According to Foda, it 'seems that the concept of a personal and non-territorial sovereignty of the Muslim State – held by some jurists – is mainly derived from the regime of the capitulations which appeared as a complete system and the régime in the Islamic world towards the end of the 18th century.'[62]

The institutions of the Caliphate and capitulations continue to elicit controversy in the quest for Muslim approaches to territorial authority. We saw above that classical theory based on universal personal rule of the caliph increasingly had to accommodate the realities of multiple Muslim and non-Muslim entities. Thus, on their rise to predominance eight centuries after the Prophet's death, the Ottomans were left a legal legacy far from settled. In their control over much of the Arab world, as well as in their relations with Europe, the Ottomans substantially developed the rules of *siyar*, and this forms the subject of discussion below.

4) *Caliphs, Capitulations and Colonialism in Ottoman Lands*

An appreciation of the Ottoman legacy is necessary in exploring the traditions of territoriality in the Arab-Muslim world and the extent to which these inform Arab state practice *vis-à-vis* international law. Additionally, three of the case studies hail from lands at least nominally under Ottoman authority: Libya, Palestine and the Gulf states.[63] Historical research about Ottoman rule and its relations with Europe as well as its management of its Arab populations indicates that much untapped archival material remains to be evaluated.[64] A number of works accounting for the emergence of international law in Europe tend to treat the Sublime Porte as an occasional interlocutor in an otherwise Christian world. Yet, Faroqhi has argued that we must abandon such misunderstandings because 'there was no "iron curtain" separating the Ottoman elites and their tax-paying subjects from the world outside the borders of the Empire.'[65] Ottoman-European interaction contributed substantially to the law we now know as international law. International legal scholarship has conceded some role to

[62] Foda, *supra* n. 42, at 108.

[63] By the sixteenth century, all Arabic-speaking lands were under Ottoman control with the exception of Morocco, Sudan and parts of Arabia. However, Faroqhi reminds us that 'Ottoman central control, while substantial in certain aspects of life and also in some geographical regions, in no way covered the entire surface of the Empire in an even and regular fashion.' S. Faroqhi, *The Ottoman Empire and the World Around It* (London: I. B. Tauris, 2004), at 48.

[64] See M. M. İlhan, 'The Ottoman Archives and Their Importance for Historical Studies: With Special Reference to Arab Provinces' (1991) C. LV *Belleten* 415.

[65] Faroqhi, *supra* n. 63, at 2.

the Ottomans in standard accounts of international law's 'birth', but usually in historically inaccurate projections of a Power weakened by the late nineteenth century. For example, the regime of capitulations and the Sublime Porte's 1856 'entry' into international law are regularly invoked to bolster narratives advancing an image of European origin: European predominance accounts for Turkish capitulation in both these episodes.

A closer reading of the historical record undermines such a narrative and suggests a *dialogue* between multiple cultures and polities. This section's sketch of Ottoman-European relations seeks not only to dispel some common misunderstandings, but also to link classical Islamic conceptions of territory with Ottoman dominion: for example, were capitulations consistent with the classical *siyar*, and did they contribute to its evolution? Was international society and international law exclusively European? What was the nature of Ottoman international legal personality? The following section considers Ottoman membership within international society by interrogating the practice of capitulations and the 1856 Treaty of Paris before moving on to the idea of the caliphate and Islamic authority in the late Ottoman period.

We saw above that the nature of Islamic jurisdiction is based on a community of belief, and it was for this reason that practices were devised for regulating relations with non-believers both within and beyond Muslim lands. Islam always permitted a space for peoples of the book, or *dhimmīs*.[66] In exchange for accepting Muslim dominion and the imposition of the poll tax or *jizya*, resident Jewish, Zoroastrian, Sabean and Christian communities were able to apply their own laws for communal matters.

Circumstances, however, were very different for non-residents, such as traders. Under classical doctrine, *dār al-islām* had to secure itself against threats from *dār al-ḥarb*, including from aliens, or *ḥārbīs*. For *ḥārbīs* wishing to enter *dar al-islām*, it was necessary either to convert to Islam or to secure *amān*, which was a form of protection.[67] Any Muslim within *dar al-islām* could grant *amān*, which would transform a *ḥārbī* into a *musta'min* (or bearer of *amān*; protected person) for the period of one year. With this device, traders, for example, were able to conduct their business deep into Muslim lands, avoid the *jizya* and, over time, have many legal matters settled extra-territorially. In his study of the origins of international law, Ago showed how there emerged a complex web of relations between three great powers in the Mediterranean from the ninth century, generating the seeds of modern international law, through mechanisms

[66] For consistency and lack of confusion, I use Arabic spelling even though many words were often rendered differently in Turkish.

[67] For a consideration of *amān*, see M. C. Bassiouni, 'Protection of Diplomats under Islamic Law' (1980) 74 *American Journal of International Law* 609.

such as inter-state negotiations, treaties and customary law.[68] Thayer mentioned this in his study on capitulations when he wrote that the 'Arab, Saracen and Christian nations of the Mediterranean seem to have granted extraterritoriality freely from an early time, in the paramount interest of commerce.'[69]

Particularly with the penetration of merchants from the Italian city-states throughout the Mediterranean, it was necessary to assure a conducive climate for commerce, including those agreements between Muslim and Christian rulers that later came to be known as capitulations.[70] Although the word 'capitulation' might suggest to an English speaker the idea of concession, it is actually derived from the Latin word for chapter, *capitulum*, because these agreements were subdivided into chapters, or articles.[71] The first capitulatory agreement was between Morocco and the maritime republic of Pisa in 1133, followed by Valencia in 1149, and then a number of Italian city-states seeking to augment Mediterranean trade thereafter.[72] By the time the Ottomans had engulfed the Byzantines in their capital in 1453, there was already a well-established Muslim-Christian practice of capitulations. It was only under the Sublime Porte, though, that this regime was systematised and fully developed in the centuries to follow.[73] On their capture of Constantinople, the Ottomans set the tone of their relations with non-Muslims by entering into agreements with *dhimmīs* and gradually consolidation of earlier trade links with Italian powers.[74]

Especially later Ottoman *siyar* indicates that this sizeable part of the *umma* had abandoned the classical ideal of universal Muslim rule advanced through *jihād*. By the sixteenth century, conquest still continued, but within a limited

[68] These three powers were the Frankish-Lombard Empire of Charlemagne, the Byzantine Empire and the Muslims from Spain to Syria. R. Ago, 'Pluralism and the Origins of the International Community' (1977) *Italian Yearbook of International Law* 3, at 13.

[69] L. E. Thayer, 'The Capitulations of the Ottoman Empire and the Question of their Abrogation as it Affects the United States' (1923) 17 *American Journal of International Law* 207, at 208.

[70] 'Finding their legal basis in the principle of the personality of the law, the capitulations reflected the economic need of encouraging commerce between Arab-dominated areas and the states in Italy and the Western Mediterranean.' H. J. Liebesny, 'The Development of Western Judicial Privileges', M. Khadduri & H. J. Liebesny (eds.), *Law in the Middle East: Origin and Development of Islamic Law*, vol. 1 (Richmond, VA: William Byrd Press, 1955) 309–333, at 314.

[71] Ibid., at 313.

[72] For a list of these early agreements, see ibid., at 312–315.

[73] Ibid., at 315.

[74] For example, in 1453 just after the fall of Constantinople and the birth of İstanbul, Mehmed signed an imperial decree, or *ahdname*. In this document, he granted the Genoese Council and its people in the neighbourhood of Galata a degree of political and legal autonomy and trading rights in exchange for a surrender of weapons and the muffling of church bells. D. Goffman, *The Ottoman Empire and Early Modern Europe* (Cambridge: Cambridge University Press, 2002), at 172. This is also discussed in Liebesny, *supra* n. 70, at 315.

framework softened by a growing deference to treaties of peace.[75] With the collapse of the Abbasid Caliphate in the thirteenth century Islamic history had first witnessed a number of smaller competing dynasties, out of which emerged two dominant powers: the Sunni Turks and Shiʿite Persia. In this period, 'the division of Islam...became permanent and the divisions were consolidated by the trends of political development within Islam as well as by its relationships with the Christian world. The Islamic universal state became transformed into an Islamic state system.'[76] Thus, a world once divided into *dār al-islām* and *dār al-ḥarb* gave ground to new conceptualizations of space: an enlarged *dār al-ṣulḥ* without, and the *umma* spread across numerous empires and states within.

Initially, for non-believers on Turkish soil, *ahdname* or decrees of the sulṭan were unilaterally granted to foreign powers for the protection of their nationals. In keeping with classical doctrine, these instruments were limited to ten-year periods or, later, to the lifespan of the sulṭan.[77] These capitulatory agreements could be renewed on the accession of a new sulṭan, and so European powers regularly renewed the growing body of treaties to arise from this process.[78] From the eighteenth century onwards, there also emerged some treaties of perpetual peace, indicating the rejection of a future world united under Islam.[79] Far from being instruments of European domination, these treaty regimes can instead be seen as Ottoman largesse in dealing with far weaker powers eager to expand their commercial opportunities. The Islamic theory informing them, however, was not necessarily appreciated equally by both sides; they 'signified one thing to the Ottoman mind and quite another to the alien European one.'[80]

Over time, perceptions of power started to inform the capitulations regime in new ways so that increasing European strength resulted in ever more extensive jurisdictional as well as territorial concessions from İstanbul. Where once *ahdnames* had been unilateral decrees granted by the sulṭan, they increasingly took on the shape of bilateral agreements between equal and, later, unequal powers.[81] As communications between Europe and the Porte developed, so too

---

[75] For an overview of Ottoman treaties with non-Muslims especially, see V. Panaite, 'The Re'ayas of Tributary-Protected Principalities (the 16th–18th Century)' (2003) 1 *Romano-Turcica* 83.

[76] Khadduri, *The Islamic Law of Nations, supra* n. 52, at 61.

[77] Liebesny, *supra* n. 70, at 327.

[78] For a list of such renewals, see Thayer, *supra* n. 69, at 211–212.

[79] The first perpetual treaty of peace was between the Porte and Russia in 1711. However, this practice was far from consistent, as Quataert points out that the Treaty of Belgrade between the Turks and Russia and Austria was limited to a period of 27 lunar years. D. Quataert, *The Ottoman Empire 1700–1922* (Cambridge: Cambridge University Press, 2nd edition, 2005), at 78.

[80] Goffman, *supra* n. 74, at 175.

[81] Cf. Menage on the bilateral nature of certain early Ottoman capitulations: V. L. Menage, 'The English Capitulation of 1580: A Review Article' (1980) 12 *International Journal of Middle East Studies* 373.

did the number and subject matter of these agreements, which were modeled on treaties covering the jurisdictional rights of foreigners signed by France and the Porte between 1535 and 1740.[82] According to Faroqhi, it was in the eighteenth century that 'the so-called capitulations . . . were increasingly turned into a source of privilege particularly by French and English consuls or ambassadors.'[83]

European privilege increased further during the nineteenth century. The gradual loss of Ottoman lands, as well as the spread of nationalist movements in Europe, inspired Christian powers to 'protect' co-religionists in lands under Muslim rule. Examples include Russia's many treaties with the Porte regarding its Christian Orthodox populations and France's connection with the Maronites of Mount Lebanon, which persists to this day.[84] With the advantage of historical hindsight, the gradual relinquishment of territorial control can be traced across the centuries, but such a method would overlook the perspectives of Ottoman rulers during those periods when their power was equal or greater to that of their European counterparts. In fact, it 'was not until the middle of the nineteenth century that the Sultans seem to have regarded these concessions as a disparagement on their sovereignty.'[85]

It is ironic that in an age witness to the consolidation of a territorially limited Muslim empire – or Caliphate – the Ottomans suffered such an assault on their jurisdiction. While the Porte gained formal European recognition of its sovereignty in the 1856 Treaty discussed below, jurisdiction within its territories was emasculated more and more by capitulatory agreements. A related anomaly informs the familiar narrative of international law's evolution: Europe welcomed the Porte into its exclusive club in an era of unprecedented interference and disregard for the Porte's territorial integrity. How can we account for these contradictions? What do they suggest about the evolution of the idea of statehood within and beyond Arab-Ottoman lands?

Although centuries of accelerated Ottoman-European interaction had generated greater cultural awareness and familiarity, increasing power disparities forged identities ever more in opposition with each other. In the earlier phases of European-Ottoman relations, when only a nascent European states-system existed, intermittent relations based on trade or war gave rise to an emerging body of regional custom. Over time, such practices developed, but also conjoined with a European discourse based on cultural superiority and the positivist doctrine of recognition. The construction of identity through 'othering' relies

[82] Thayer, *supra* n. 69, at 216.

[83] Faroqhi, *supra* n. 62, at 60–61.

[84] Piscatori discusses some of these agreements: Piscatori, *Islam in a World of Nation-States, supra* n. 1, at 52–53.

[85] Thayer, *supra* n. 69, at 213.

on enough knowledge to generate caricatures of one's 'other', and this in turn requires a degree of interaction. When we combine this idea with the historical context of increasingly intermeshed European-Ottoman relations and European imperialism elsewhere, the imposition of cultural norms on Turkey becomes more explicable. According to Quataert, on 'each side proximity structured a complex identity formation process of repulsion and attraction. After all, a people comes to perceive of itself as distinct and separate with particular and unique characteristics, often through using the "other" as a means of defining what it is and, equally, what it is not.'[86]

For many scholars, the high-point of Ottoman 'othering' occurred in the mid-nineteenth century with the imposition of the 'standard of civilisation' on Turkey's entry into 'international' society in 1856. For this book's focus, the 1856 episode allows us to consider the place of Arab and non-European peoples within the international legal community. For example, in Chapter Three, Libya draws on Ottoman membership of international society to rebut European control over North Africa. The Ottoman presence is also explored in Chapter Four's discussion about imperial rivalries in the Gulf. European powers could only dictate boundaries if local Arab and/or Ottoman personality was defeated through argument. Thus, is it accurate to conceive of an international society populated exclusively by European or European-invited states?[87]

The controversy over membership of international society has been especially important for raising questions about the universality of international law. Alexandrowicz, for example, rejected the narrative of international law's European origins by offering a counter-narrative of equality between European and Asian powers before the nineteenth century.[88] It was only from the late eighteenth

---

[86] Quataert, *supra* n. 79, at 6.

[87] Wight captures the typical narrative: 'The orthodox answer, then, to the question about the limits of the states-system, is that it was originally confined to Western Christendom out of which it grew; that the European colonies in North and South America became peripheral members of it when they attained independence; that the first non-European state to be admitted was the Ottoman Empire in 1856; that Persia, Siam, China and Japan (but not Ethiopia or Liberia) were admitted with different degrees of grudging patronage in the later part of the nineteenth century; that this extension of the system beyond Europe and America first received legal recognition in the Hague Conferences of 1899 and 1907; and that the transformation of the Western European system into a world system was finally performed through the League of Nations and the United Nations.' M. Wight, *Systems of States: Edited with an introduction by Hedley Bull* (Leicester: Leicester University Press, 1977), at 117.

[88] According to Alexandrowicz, 'Though the Europeans had sailed to the East Indies since the end of the fifteenth century and though they had at first intended to discover and occupy lands, and where necessary, to establish their territorial possessions by conquest, they had in practice to fall back on negotiation and treaty making in preference to resorting to war. In fact they found themselves in the middle of a network of States and inter-State relations based on traditions

century that the law of nations 'started contracting into a regional (purely European) legal system, abandoning a centuries old tradition of universality based on the natural law doctrine.'[89] Many Third World scholars, especially in the advent of decolonisation, advanced similar arguments to demonstrate that they were not simply citizens of 'new' states;[90] independence was only the latest moment in re-claimed statehood.[91] Such accounts are based on benign assumptions about pre-nineteenth century legal custom and thought.[92] Koskenniemi suggests that such perspectives place too much emphasis on the 'universalism' of earlier writers, such as Grotius and Vattel.[93] In his study of Vitoria's thought, Anghie echoes such sentiments by showing that the European natural law tradition shared with positivism a rejection of cultural equality.[94] Furthermore, in the pre-nineteenth century world, it is difficult to speak of one international

---

which were more ancient than their own and in no way inferior to notions of European civilization.' C. H. Alexandrowicz, *An Introduction to the History of the Law of Nations in the East Indies (16th, 17th, 18th Centuries)* (Oxford: Clarendon Press, 1967), at 224.

89 Ibid., at 2. For a similar perspective, see P. C. Jessup, 'Diversity and Uniformity in the Law of Nations' (1964) 58 *American Journal of International Law* 341. Grewe refuted this position in articulating the dominant international law narrative of its origins: what 'happened in the nineteenth century was certainly not the narrowing of a universal law of nations to a regional, European law of nations, as Alexandrowicz asserted. On the contrary, the European law of nations gradually grew into a global legal order, the members of which were, it is true, only the "civilised nations". This development cannot be interpreted as a "regionalisation" or "Europeanisation". Rather, the dualism of the Christian-European law of nations and the natural law-based universal law of nations dissolved into a single, universal legal system, albeit one which had been deprived of its natural law foundation by the rise of positivism. This universal legal system introduced a new differentiation through the criterion of civilisation, thus laying the foundation of a new, colonial law of nations separate from the general one.' W. H. Grewe, *The Epochs of International Law*, M. Byers (trans) (New York; Berlin: de Gruyter, 2000), at 466.

90 Alexandrowicz's 'reversion' thesis distinguishes certain Asian states from African ones. In relation to the former, he suggests that a 'State can hardly drop out of the Family of Nations because of ideological change in the structure of the Law of Nations... [Whereas] unlike the case of countries of the East Indies, there is generally no room for a claim to their [African] classification as original States. Most of the African entities are new States in the present-day meaning of the word, and reversion to sovereignty has no application.' C. H. Alexandrowicz, 'New and Original States: The Issue of Reversion to Sovereignty' (1969) 45 *International Affairs* 465, at 471; 473.

91 For a discussion of pre-colonial African state formation, see C. Okafor, 'After Martyrdom: International Law, Sub-State Groups, and the Construction of Legitimate Statehood in Africa' (2000) 41 *Harvard International Law Journal* 503.

92 See for example, G. Abi-Saab, 'International Law and The International Community: The Long Road to Universality', R. St. J. Macdonald (ed.), *Essays in Honour of Wang Tieya* (Dordrecht: Martinus Nijhoff, 1994) 31–41.

93 M. Koskenniemi, *The Gentle Civilizer of Nations: The Rise and Fall of International Law 1870–1960* (Cambridge: Cambridge University Press, 2002), at 131.

94 A. Anghie, 'Francisco de Vitoria and the Colonial Origins of International Law' (1996) 5 *Social and Legal Studies* 321.

law at all. Instead, Onuma suggests a world comprising multiple regional legal systems only interacting intermittently.[95] Such regional systems included those comprising the Sublime Porte and European states.

It is important to recognize that narratives about Ottoman 'entry' into 'international' society can help interrogate and unsettle prevailing conceptions of the 'European' origins of international law. Europe and the Sublime Porte forged an extensive network of legal relations, based on treaties relating to peace, trade and the protection of Christian populations. These treaties spanning centuries cannot simply be understood as a product of European domination.

Narratives emphasising European domination rely particularly on the centrality of the 'standard of civilisation' in the nineteenth century.[96] Although it is possible to view the 'standard of civilisation' as symbolic of an onerous and racist European (international) law, the record is more complex. We must concede some agency to the 'old man of Europe', especially at the internal level, where significant domestic pressure contributed to Ottoman reform efforts in the nineteenth and early twentieth centuries.[97] It is also problematic to speak of a clearly defined 'standard of civilisation'.[98] For Koskenniemi,

> The existence of a 'standard' was a myth in the sense that there was never anything to gain. Every concession was a matter of negotiation, every status dependent on agreement, *quid pro quo*. But the existence of a *language of a standard* still gave the appearance of fair treatment and regular administration to what was simply a conjectural policy.[99]

---

[95] Onuma, *supra* n. 4, at 8.

[96] For a general discussion about the 'standard of civilisation', see G. Gong, *The Standard of "Civilization" in International Society* (Oxford: Clarendon Press, 1984). Fidler's scholarship on capitulations and their links with the present stresses the link between European domination, capitulations and the standard: 'Capitulations were the primary tool used by the Western countries to implement the standard of civilization, and they were the catalysts for reforms in non-Western countries that would bring such countries closer to membership in the civilized world'; and 'The economic and legal harmonization stimulated by capitulations were indicators of the transformation of non-Western countries into Western clones. Capitulations were the epicenter of a radical remaking of the way the world was organized. And international law was a primary instrument in setting up capitulatory regimes and placing the standard of civilization at the center of civilizational customary international law.' D. P. Fidler, 'The Return of the Standard of Civilization' (2001) 2 *Chicago Journal of International Law* 137, at 142, 143. Grewe also discusses the relationship between civilisation and capitulations: Grewe, *supra* n. 89, at 457.

[97] For an overview of this period, particularly the Tanzimat reforms, see, K. H. Karpat, 'The Transformation of the Ottoman State, 1789–1908' (1972) 3 *International Journal of Middle East Studies* 243.

[98] For an overview of the linguistic origins of 'civilisation' in Europe, see Grewe, *supra* n. 89, at 446–451.

[99] Emphasis in original, Koskenniemi, *supra* n. 93, at 134–135.

The 'standard of civilisation' was and remains a slippery one, and it is more fruitful to consider other historical practices in exploring Ottoman membership of international society.

Accounts about the European nature of international society are never complete without mentioning the 1856 Treaty of Paris, with its reference to Ottoman 'entry' into 'international society'. Does the Treaty of Paris mark a momentous shift in the political and legal position of the Sublime Porte? Or, is it better to regard the Treaty as only part of the rich fabric of Ottoman-European relations that began many centuries before? If we see Ottoman 'entry' as a result of the Treaty, then we also accept the positivist doctrine of recognition and, therefore, the 'standard of civilisation'. Conversely, by seeing the Treaty as simply one of many agreements between the Porte and Europe, the narrative of membership becomes more nuanced: perhaps international law was always more than European. An appreciation of the Sublime Porte's place in the international system is not only useful for an understanding of the status of its Arab territories discussed later in the case studies. It is also useful in considering whether international law is premised only on European experiences of statehood.

Authors differ as to whether we should regard 1856 as the moment of membership into international society for the Ottoman Empire, according to their respective positions about international law, positivism, the 'standard of civilisation' and approaches to history. It is easy enough to locate contemporary sources suggesting European rejection of Turkish civilisation and culture both before *and after* 1856.[100] These accounts frame their enquiry around the role of (European)

[100] This is argued by Alexandrowicz, 'New and Original States', *supra* n. 90, at 466. It is worth quoting Richard Cobden in 1836 about Turkish 'barbarity': 'Turkey cannot enter into the political system of Europe; for the Turks are not Europeans. During nearly four centuries that that people have been encamped upon the finest soil of the Continent, so far from becoming one of the families of Christendom, they have not adopted one European custom. Their habits are still Oriental, as when they first crossed the Bosphorus. They scrupulously exclude their females from the society of the other sex; they wore the Asiatic dress; sit cross-legged, or loll upon couches, using neither chair nor bed; they shave their heads, retaining their beards; and they use their fingers still, in the place of those civilised substitutes, knives and forks. Equally uninfluenced, after nearly four hundred years' contact... is the Osmanli's [sic] condition by the discoveries and improvements of modern times. A printing press may be said to be unknown in Turkey; or, if one be found in Constantinople, it is in the hands of foreigners... Literature and science are so far from finding disciples amongst the Turks, that that people have been renowned as twice the destroyers of learning: in the splendid though corrupt remains of Greek literature at Constantinople; and by extinguishing the dawn of experimental philosophy, at the subversion of the Caliphate'. R. Cobden, *The Political Writings of Richard Cobden*, cited in Grewe *supra* n. 89, at 453. It is also instructive to quote an excerpt from the later PCIJ *Lotus* Case. By 1927 the Ottoman Empire was no more, and on a wave of secular reform Turkey submissively embraced European models of law and governance. Before the Court, Mahmout Essat Bey declared, 'Monsieur le Président, Messieurs de la Cour, la Turquie a voulou faire

recognition and the 'standard of civilisation': here, the Standard is regarded as the gatekeeper, rather than as simply one of many devices available to Powers pursuing their interest in the context of an emerging international system.

Within the European states system, threats to the preservation of the balance of power were managed through treaties and diplomacy, and so the 1856 Treaty should be understood against the backdrop of Russian and Ottoman rivlary over the eastern Mediterranean. Russia's attempts to gain access to the Mediterranean via the Bosphorus and Dardenelles, as well as its moves against the Porte more generally, were the basis of the 'Eastern Question'.[101] This episode from the Russo-Ottoman wars of the late eighteenth century saw other European powers forge various alliances in support of the Porte to deflect Russian encroachment and its threat to the balance of power.[102] European intercessions confirmed Ottoman sovereignty as a counterweight to Russian aspirations. In the 1841 Straits Convention, for example, the Great Powers undertook 'to respect this determination of the Sultan [regarding Ottoman control of the Straits], and to conform themselves to the principle above declared.'[103] A breach of the territorial

---

partie de la grande famille des nations; elle en a réclamé et obtenu tous les droits; mais elle a aussi accepté, de grand coeur, toutes les obligations; elle vient de metre en vigeur le Code civil suisse, le Code des obligations suisse, le Code pénal italien et le Code de commerce allemend. Sa legislation modernisée se heurte, dès les premiers jours, à des obstacles. La Turquie veut bien remplir toutes les obligations qui découlent du droit international; elle ne veut pas qu'on exige d'elle quoi ce soit au delà de ces obligations. Vous allez prendre votre décision au nom des principes du droit international, au pays de Grotius. Votre sentence sera respectée par la Turquie; elle ne veut pas séparer son sort de celui de la civilisation européenne.' Quoted in M. Shahabuddeen, 'The World Court at the Turn of the Century', A. S. Muller, D. Raič & J. M. Thuránszky (eds.), *The International Court of Justice: Its Future Role after Fifty Years* (The Hague; Boston: Martinus Nijhoff, 1997) 3–29, at 10.

101 Quataert summarises the 'Eastern Question' as 'how to solve the problem posed by the continuing territorial erosion of the Ottoman empire…[which] continued to be addressed over the course of the nineteenth century. On the one hand, many European leaders came to understand the grave risks that total Ottoman collapse posed to the general peace. And so they agreed to seek to maintain its integrity, for example, reversing the potentially devastating results of war at the negotiating table and, in 1856, admitting the Ottoman state into the "Concert of Europe". Thus, the European consensus that the empire should be maintained, tottering but intact, helped preserve the Ottoman state. On the other hand, through their wars and support of the separatist goals of rebellious subjects, European states abetted the very process of fragmentation that they feared and were seeking to avoid.' Thus the norm of territorial integrity was far from clear-cut in this period. Quataert, *supra* n. 79, at 56.

102 1768–1774 and 1787–1792.

103 Treaty between Austria, France, Great Britain, Prussia, Russia and Turkey respecting the Straits of the Dardanelles and Bosphorus, 13 July 1841, 92 CTS 7. Quoted in D. J. Bederman, 'The 1871 London Declaration, Rebus Sic Stantibus and a Primitivist View of the Law of Nations' (1988) 82 *American Journal of International Law* 1, at 6–7.

status quo would not only violate territorial interests of the Porte but European interests as a whole.[104]

A similar undertaking appeared in the Treaty of Paris, which concluded the 1853–1856 Crimean War between Russia and Turkey and their allies.[105] Scholars in particular look to Article 7 for indications of Turkish 'entry' into the fold:

> Sa Majesté la Reine du Royaume Uni de la Grande-Bretagne et d'Irelande, Sa Majesté l'Empereur d'Autriche, Sa Majesté l'Empereur des Français, Sa Majesté le Roi de Prusse, Sa Majesté l'Empereur de toutes les Russies, et Sa Majesté le Roi de Sardaigne, déclarent la Sublime Porte admise à participer aux avantages du droit public et du concert Européens. Leurs Majestés s'engagent, chacune de son côté, à respecter l'indépendence et l'integrité territoriale de l'Empire Ottoman: garantissent en commun la stricte observation de cet engagement: et considéront, en consequence, tout act de nature à y porter atteinte comme une question d'intérét general.[106]

In his close reading of the Treaty and its wider context, McKinnon Wood argues that this provision did not mark a radical break with the past; we cannot retrospectively deem Turkey to have been outside of international society and international law before 1856. 'Throughout the record there is no trace that the participants were conscious that Turkey was not already a subject of international law, or that they were proposing to confer that status upon her'.[107] He also argues that there was little change in state conduct after the Treaty.[108] Finally, in relation to Article 7, he suggests that the provision was not about international law at all, but rather it was 'an act of admission to what today might be called a regional understanding'[109] – the Concert of Europe. We can understand the Treaty as a manifestation of Great Power management more than anything else. 'Donc, il est faux de dire qu'en 1856 la Porte Ottomane ait été admise pour la première fois au droit international en viguer en Europe.'[110]

There was no radical rupture in 1856. The notion of Ottoman territorial integrity remained contested in the face of supportive and subversive European

---

[104] Ibid., at 7.

[105] After mounting tensions between Russia and the Sublime Porte as well as Britain, hostilities broke out between Russia and Turkey in late 1853. After Russia failed to back down to their demands, France and Britain declared war in March 1854 alongside the Ottoman Empire.

[106] Italics added, quoted in H. McKinnon Wood, 'The Treaty of Paris and Turkey's Status in International Law' (1943) 37 *American Journal of International Law* 262, at 262–263. Treaty Guaranteeing the Independence and Integrity of the Ottoman Empire, 15 April 1856, 114 CTS 497.

[107] Ibid., at 267.

[108] 'There seems...to be evidence that governments and political opinion in the contracting countries were quite unaware that the Treaty of Paris had effected a fundamental change in Turkey's status in international law.' Ibid., at 269.

[109] Ibid., at 274.

[110] T. Toyoda, 'L'aspect universaliste du droit international européen du 19ème siècle et le statut juridique de la Turquie avant 1856' (2006) 8 *Journal of the History of International Law* 19, at 33.

'allies'.[111] International law of the nineteenth century was more than European, but it is difficult to specify this any further given the complex role of culture and positivism in an age of burgeoning empires. Ultimately, conclusions about the nature of international law in the nineteenth century are indeterminate.

Before completing our discussion of the contested Ottoman legacy, this section comes almost full circle by returning to the idea of the Caliphate and its relevance not in classical Islamic thought and practice but in the later period of Turkish rule. For many Muslims, the Mongol's destruction of Abbasid Baghdad in 1258 had sounded the Caliphate's death knell, or, at the very least, significant confusion as to the location of any future, nominally universal, successor.[112] Upon conquering Mamluk Egypt and Syria in 1516–1517, Selim I inherited the title of *khādim al-ḥaramayn al-sharīfayn*, or the servant of the two Holy Shrines, and Ottoman control of these sites in Mecca and Medina was confirmed by Süleyman the Magnificent's seizure of Arabia in 1534.[113] Ottoman sulṭans were not models of caliphal ideals. They could not trace their lineage back to Muhammed's tribe, the Quraysh, and neither could they portray themselves as examplars of the *sharīʿa's* strict application. They could, however, lay some claim to the Caliphate as the dominant Sunni power[114] (alongside the Mughals in India) with control over the Holy Sites and the annual pilgrimage, or *ḥajj*.[115]

[111] According to Moinuddin, 'It could...be argued that centuries of peaceful contacts and commercial relations between Islamic and non-Islamic states prior to the admittance of the Ottoman Empire to the Concert of Europe in 1856 had led to the emergence of a body of 'regional' or 'Islamic' customary rules which provided for the underlying basis of such relations.' Further, in relation to custom, he argues that 'it could still be argued that regular peaceful contacts throughout the ages, whether on the basis of unilateralism or principles of equality and reciprocity, provided a fertile ground for the eventual development of a consistent legal policy applied by Islamic States in their external relations with other States. This legal policy, which was reflected in treaty relations between Islamic and non-Islamic States and which was based on principles of equality and reciprocity could be said to have become a general and widely accepted practised "customary" policy by 1856.' Moinuddin, *supra* n. 22, at 39–40.

[112] Quataert, *supra* n. 79, at 83.

[113] H. Kayali, *Arabs and Young Turks: Ottomanism, Arabism, and Islamism in the Ottoman Empire, 1908–1918* (Berkeley: University of California Press, 1997), at 17.

[114] For an excellent discussion comparing Moroccan and Turkish competing claims to the Caliphate, see A. El-Moudden, 'The Idea of the Caliphate between Moroccans and Ottomans: Political and Symbolic Stakes in the 16th and 17th Century-Maghrib' (1995) 82 *Studia Islamica* 103.

[115] Hourani quotes Zabidi (1732–1791) on this point, who argued that the sulṭan's claim 'was based not on apostolic succession from the Prophet, but on the divine right of those who had established their *effective power* and used it in the interests of Islam. The sultan defended the frontiers against Christians and Shi'is; he protected the Holy Places and organized the Pilgrimage with care; he paid respect to the Shari'a and its guardians [the *'ulema*].' Emphasis added, Hourani, *Arabic Thought, supra* n. 25, at 27.

The institution of the Caliphate at this time also provided a point of contrast with the Turks' main Muslim and Shi'ite rival, Safavid Persia.[116]

We have seen that Ottoman rulers combined Islamic principles of *siyar* with pragmatism in their relations with Europeans, and such flexibility was underwritten during periods of Ottoman strength. Although the Porte's Islamic identity was never questioned, it was not until its position came under serious international and internal strain that the Caliphate was evoked as a tool of legitimacy and control. According to Deringil, the 'continuous, indeed almost monotonous, acclamation of the sultan's caliphal title dates clearly to the period of decline at the end of the 18th century.'[117] The late eighteenth century did not only witness significant Ottoman international pressures as a result of the Russo-Ottoman Wars mentioned above. During this period, Ottoman legitimacy was also threatened from within, through the efforts of Muhammed ibn 'Abd al-Wahhāb (1703–1792) and his call for a return to 'pure' Islam. 'Both the spiritual claims of the Wahhābī reformers as the heirs of true Islam and their early nineteenth-century seizure of Mecca and Medina seemed to undermine Ottoman legitimacy.'[118] The Wahhābī threat was felt particularly near its power base in the Arabian Peninsula, providing the Ottomans with another reason to strengthen their presence in the Gulf, as discussed in Chapter Four.

The use of the Caliphate as a tool of legitimacy gained even more importance by the late nineteenth century when the loss of European territories meant that the majority of Ottoman subjects were Muslim and/or Arab. Later on, Arab nationalism threatened the Porte's link with its Arab population, but this was not because of any deficit in Islamic credentials; it was more an Arab reaction against the policies of Turkification and secularisation instigated especially under the Young Turks administration after 1908.[119] Ottoman calls in Arabic for a universal Caliphate were targeted particularly at Arabs across the Empire.[120] Certain prominent Arab intellectuals at this time were supportive of Turkish rule for the very reason that the Caliphate was seen as uniting Muslims against European encroachment. This idea was articulated by the prominent intellectual,

[116] According to Faroqhi, 'Whenever treaties were concluded from a position of strength, such as the peace of Amasya (1555/962–3), it was usually demanded that the Iranians cease the ritual cursing of the early caliphs Abū Bakir, 'Omar and 'Othmān, whom the Shi'ites considered as usurpers and the Sunnis, by contrast, as "rightly guided"'. Faroqhi, *supra* n. 63, at 36 (footnotes omitted).

[117] S. Deringil, 'Legitimacy Structures in the Ottoman State: The Reign of Abdülhamid II (1876–1909)' (1991) 23 *International Journal of Middle East Studies* 345, at 346.

[118] Quataert, *supra* n. 79, at 84.

[119] See generally, M. Haddad, 'The Rise of Arab Nationalism Reconsidered' (1994) 26 *International Journal of Middle East Studies* 201.

[120] Hourani, *Arabic Thought, supra* n. 25, at 106.

Rashīd Riḍā, in his 1919 memorandum to British Prime Minister, Lloyd George,[121] where he contrasted foreign rule unfavourably with Ottoman protection of the Muslim Holy Sites.[122] Even from its earliest days, Islam had straddled faith and power, and thus Ottoman stewardship of the *umma* and its lands was preferred over non-Muslim dominion. Perhaps the distinction between *dār al-islām* and *dār al-ḥarb* had given way to modern realities, but it still served as a powerful device in linking authority over territory, not only through effective control but also through the legitimacy of religious symbolism. After its defeat in the First World War the Ottoman Empire was succeeded by the Turkish Republic and a host of foreign territories that would come under Mandate rule. In 1922, the caliphate was stripped of all its temporal power, and in 1924 it was abolished altogether.[123] Henceforth, it would serve only as an ideological counterpoint to the rising forces of nationalism and the so-called nation-state across the Arab world.

Despite the demise of the Caliphate and the Ottoman Empire, Islamic and Arab traditions have continued to inform more recent Arab approaches to authority over territory. We saw that although Ottoman personality may have been contested, it was still sufficient *as an idea* to inspire arguments about Ottoman authority and the relevance of the Caliphate in later ICJ pleadings. We also saw that international law was more than a European discourse, but that its exact boundaries are mired in controversies that reflect particular agendas of contemporary international legal scholarship. In the final section, I trace how

[121] For an overview of Riḍā's thought, see ibid., at ch. 9.

[122] 'The great minister should know that his government's declaration which expresses respect for the Islamic holy places in the Hijaz, Jerusalem, and Iraq and continued Muslim control of them has no positive effect on the Muslims whatsoever. Such a declaration is even painful... since it implies that the holy places are under foreign sovereignty and consequently worship there depends upon the will of the foreigner. He [the prime minister] no doubt knows that contrary to British expectations, recognizing the independence of the Hijaz and proclaiming the amir of Mecca a king did not have a positive effect on the Muslims. That was the case because the Hijaz is one of the poorest and weakest Muslim countries. It is not a land of sovereignty and temporal authority, but of worship. Muslims were not concerned that their holy places would be demolished or access to them denied; their real concern was for Islamic [political] sovereignty without which Islam itself and its mosques could not be safe. The preservation of this sovereignty is a desire mixed in the blood of every Muslim who regards the survival of his religion as dependent upon the existence of an independent strong [Islamic] state subject to no foreign influence. This is why most Muslims in the world passionately cling to the Turkish state and consider it as representative of the Caliphate although it lacks al the Caliphate conditions except power and independence.' Rashīd Riḍā translated and quoted (italics and additions in translation) in M. Haddad, 'Arab Religious Nationalism in the Colonial Era: Rereading Rashīd Riḍā's Ideas on the Caliphate' (1997) 117 *Journal of the American Oriental Society* 253, at 271.

[123] Ibid., at 272, 276.

Arab states have made sense of Ottoman and Islamic legacies in constructing practices of territoriality and dispute resolution in the region.

5) *From the Mandate Period to the Present: Independence, the Failure of Regionalism and the Place of Adjudication*

In contrast to much of the Third World, the majority of Arabs only experienced European rule in the twentieth century with the establishment of the Mandates under League of Nation auspices in 1922.[124] The case studies of Western Sahara and Libya/Chad remained under direct colonial rule and the Arab Gulf was nominally under a protective rather than colonial regime. Thus although the Mandate period was seminal in the Arab consciousness, it only directly touches on one case in the book, Palestine as discussed in Chapter Six. Rather than explore the period for its direct link with the cases, this section considers its symbolic legacy for Arab states on gaining independence. We should see the League of Nations era as a transitionary one along a path towards today's Arab states and their borders. We should also recognize, however, that the legacies of the Mandate persist, having had lasting effects on the nature of territoriality across the region.

In this final section, the rise of Arab nation-states is depicted against the backdrop of earlier Islamic practice and theory and European colonialism. What legacies of territoriality and international law did Arabs draw on after their independence? Why has the state been such a contested model across the region? Aside from Arab experiences under numerous Islamic empires, particularly the Ottomans, it was the encounter with European control, either directly in the form of colonialism or indirectly with the Mandate, that was seminal in shaping the contours of Arab international legal personality. After describing modes of Mandatory rule, this section will explore Arab nationalism *vis-à-vis* territorial notions of authority before considering Arab regional responses to territorial disputes and international legal fora more broadly. Given the many, interrelated experiences of international legal governance at hand, how have Arab states negotiated their place in international society and the international legal system? Is there a continuing role for Islamic principles, and how can these be realized in a postcolonial era?

Like other moments in international law's past, the Mandate period has been singled out as a milestone, marking a significant shift for at least some peoples from colonial exploitation to international legal protection. Although self-determination was granted to European peoples of the former German and

[124] Hourani, *A History of the Arab Peoples, supra* n. 37, at 318–319.

Ottoman Empires, other territories came under French and British control. These territories were classified into 'A', 'B' and 'C' Mandates, depending on their level of social and political development. In his study which appeared only shortly after the Mandates' inception, Lauterpacht examined League of Nations provisions and concluded that the regime was radically different from colonialism. He expressed misgivings about C Mandates, but as for the more 'advanced' A and B Mandates it was incorrect to speak of annexation.[125] Sovereignty lay with the League, and consequentially Mandate territories could not be subsumed under the territory of the Mandatory.[126] Crawford's discussion of the 'received view' reinforces Lauterpacht's position. Crawford shows that the dominant narrative distinguished colonial rule from the Mandates; France and Britain did not possess sovereignty over these territories.[127] Instead, sovereignty was held 'in trust' by the League.[128]

This narrative is challenged by Anghie, who, in asking whether we should regard the institution as the negation or recreation of colonialism, favours the latter response.[129] Article 22 of the League Charter is reminiscent of nineteenth century colonialist discourses of the 'standard of civilisation' when it speaks of a 'sacred trust of civilization'.[130] Under this system, peoples were to be guided

125 H. Lauterpacht, 'The Mandate under International Law in the Covenant of the League of Nations', *International Law: Being the Collected Papers of Hersch Lauterpacht*, vol. 3 (Cambridge: Cambridge University Press, 1977), 29–84, at 37, 65.

126 Ibid., at 49.

127 J. Crawford, *The Creation of States in International Law* (Cambridge: Cambridge University Press, 2nd edition, 2006), at 573.

128 Generally, see Crawford, ibid., at ch. 13.

129 A. Anghie, *Imperialism, Sovereignty and the Making of International Law* (Cambridge: Cambridge University Press, 2005), at 146.

130 The relevant text of Article 22 reads:

> To those colonies and territories which as a consequence of the late war have ceased to be under the sovereignty of the States which formerly governed them and which are inhabited by peoples not yet able to stand by themselves under the strenuous conditions of the modern world, there should be applied the principle that the well-being and development of such peoples form a sacred trust of civilisation and that securities for the performance of this trust should be embodied in this Covenant.
>
> The best method of giving practical effect to this principle is that the tutelage of such peoples should be entrusted to advanced nations who by reason of their resources, their experience or their geographical position can best undertake this responsibility, and who are willing to accept it, and that this tutelage should be exercised by them as Mandatories on behalf of the League.
>
> The character of the mandate must differ according to the stage of the development of the people, the geographical situation of the territory, its economic conditions and other similar circumstances.
>
> Certain communities formerly belonging to the Turkish Empire have reached a stage of development where their existence as independent nations can be provisionally recognized subject to the rendering of administrative advice and assistance by a Mandatory until

along a single trajectory of eventual independence; diversity was not permitted in this schema as, instead, those 'not yet able to stand by themselves' were ushered into a system of seeming sovereign similitude. This paradox of enforced 'freedom' is captured by Anghie:

> In seeking to liberate the mandate peoples from the 'strenuous conditions of the modern world', the system instead entraps the mandate peoples within those conditions. The peculiar cycle thus creates a situation whereby international institutions present themselves as a solution to a problem of which they are an integral part.[131]

For Arabs, two mandate(d) legacies are particularly relevant when considering statehood and territoriality. First, it was during the Mandate period that the seeds were sown for the ongoing conflict over Palestine, as discussed in relation to Arab nationalism later in the chapter and in Chapter Six. Second, it was under French and British rule that lines on maps were drawn, and these borders – despite many challengers – have remained largely unchanged.[132]

Although 'the idea of the nation-state has emerged as a veritable *Grundnorm* in modern Muslim [or Arab] political and religious discourse',[133] it has not always been so. Why was territorial integrity so difficult to accept for many Arab states and why did it ultimately triumph? In trying to answer these questions, context must influence any response, because although we can now speak of general Arab acceptance of the bounded nation-state, the Arab world still contains many challengers to the *status quo* of confined territoriality.[134] Compared with Europe, for example, Arab states are not nearly as secure in their statehood. Numerous violations of territorial borders, external interference and non-state actor violence all occur on a regular basis.[135] These phenomena symbolise a shaky system that

---

> such time as they are able to stand alone. The wishes of these communities must be a principal consideration in the selection of the Mandatory.

Covenant of the League of Nations, 28 June 1919, 225 CTS 188.

131 Anghie, *supra* n. 129, at 178.

132 Some other important factors to note from the Mandate period would be its impact on the shape of Arab legal systems today, languages of instruction and school curriculum, as well as persisting commercial and personal ties.

133 S. A. Jackson, *Islamic Law and the State: The Constitutional Jurisprudence of Shihāb al-Dīn al-Qarāfī* (Leiden: Brill, 1996), at xiii.

134 M. Barnett, 'Sovereignty, nationalism, and regional order in the Arab states system' (1995) 49 *International Organization* 479, at 509.

135 There are simply too many examples to list here, but some deserving attention not discussed below in relation to territorial adjudication include: Jordan's occupation of the West Bank between 1949 and 1967; Israel's ongoing occupation of the West Bank, East Jerusalem, Gaza Strip, Golan Heights and Sheba'ā farms; Israel's former occupation of the Sinai and southern Lebanon as well as its 2006 war against Lebanon; Iraq's invasion of Kuwait in 1990; the use of Lebanon as a site of regional conflict during its civil war, 1976–1990; Morocco's ongoing

has been able to survive, thanks largely to modern tools of state repression[136] along with substantial foreign aid.

Until European rule, most Arabs were content to live under a fragmentary political system; being part of the *qawm*, or (Arab) people was a belief carried only by a small elite.[137] Part of the sense of pan-Arabism or *al-ʿarabiyya al-qawmiyya* was fuelled in opposition to Turkification within the Ottoman Empire.[138] Nascent nationalist sentiments were to intensify greatly with the imposition of European rule as well as the arbitrary demarcation of much of the Arab world into French and British controlled spheres. Ayubi argues that it 'was the colonial encroachment on the Arab East, combined with the accelerating demise of the Ottoman state, which contributed more than anything to the politicisation of Arab nationalist ideas there.'[139] Although the French and British had tried to mollify Arab interests through the local leadership of prominent Hashemites, such as King Abdullah in Jordan and King Faisal in Iraq, this was not sufficient to stem the tide of growing opposition to European interference. Once independence was gained by most of the Arab world after World War II, Arab heads of state nominally ruled their assigned states but were expected to work in the interests of the Arab people as a whole and not only their citizens.[140] According to Barnett, if 'the institution of sovereignty instructed the newly independent Arab states to recognize each other's borders and authority over its population, the institution of pan-Arabism sanctioned just the opposite.'[141] Arab states and Arab leaders thus operated in a normative universe pitting visions of state sovereignty against those of Arab nationalism.

The conflict between these competing tendencies up until 1967 highlights how weak the territorial norm was in the Arab world, especially compared with other regions of the non-European world. For example, although Africa remains embroiled in its own struggles over statehood, most of its rulers chose to reject any systematic reevaluation of the colonial legacy from as early as 1964 with the Cairo Declaration.[142] This was not the case with the Arab world, as instead there took

occupation of Western Sahara and its confrontations with Algeria as discussed in Chapter Five; the US invasion of Iraq in 2003; and the use of non-state violence to destabilise the region.

136 F. G. Gause, III, 'Sovereignty, Statecraft and Stability in the Middle East' (1992) 45 *Journal of International Affairs* 441, at 461.

137 E. Karsh & I. Karsh, *Empires in the Sand: The Struggle for Mastery in the Middle East 1789–1923* (Cambridge, MA: Harvard University Press, 1999), at 352.

138 N. N. Ayubi, *Over-stating the Arab State: Politics and Society in the Middle East* (London: I. B. Tauris, 1995), at 137.

139 Ibid., at 138.

140 M. Barnett, 'Institutions, Roles, and Disorder: The Case of the Arab State System' (1993) 37 *International Studies Quarterly* 271, at 282.

141 Ibid., at 283.

142 The Cairo Declaration is discussed more in Part II's Introduction, at 110.

place a veritable 'cold war' of ideologies in the first few decades of independence over how to order the Arab system.[143] 'Sovereignty failed to produce stabilizing outcomes in the Middle East as in Africa because pan-Arabism assigned to the Arab state a contradictory role and associated behavioral expectations.'[144]

One of the most important events to challenge the territorial *status quo* in the region was the Arab defeat in the 1948 conflict with Zionist forces, who successfully declared the state of Israel on 14 May 1948. Immediate effects of 1948 produced many Palestinian refugees and the emigration of Sephardic Jews resident in the region for millennia. Politically, the fallout took a little longer to materialise, but it was profound. A combination of shock arising from Arab defeat as well as a rejection of Europe's legacy of a divided Arab world saw a number of regimes fall in revolutions during the 1950s. The most significant shift occurred with the Egyptian Free Officer revolution of 23 July 1952, which after internal struggles saw Nāṣir emerge triumphant, not only as Egypt's leader, but as leader of the Arab people as a whole. This revolution deposed Egypt's King Farouk and challenged the region's other conservative regimes, such as those of Jordan, Iraq and the Gulf.

Like Barnett, Nahas suggests that we need to view that moment of 1952 in the development of Arab nationalism through the prism of normative institutions vying for predominance. 'The rise of the Egyptian revolutionary challenge to the dynastic Middle Eastern state-system was more a function of stress in the structure of ideas and norms governing the system than any dramatic shift in the balance of power in the area.'[145] Especially with the nationalisation of the Suez Canal in 1956, Nāṣir and his promise of Arab nationalism stole the hearts of Arabs far beyond Egypt's borders. Further, in 1958, the 'apogee of Pan-Arabism',[146] the Iraqi monarchy was overthrown by pan-Arabist officers and Egypt and Syria formed the United Arab Republic (UAR), suggesting that the dream of Arabs united under one state might be realised.[147] However, this 'success' and other attempted unions were bittersweet; rather than indicating that the region's leaders were willing to abandon parochial interests, it simply confirmed that even in its heyday, Arab nationalism was far from the normative default. In his study of the Arab state system, Owen suggests that in fact the territorial state was the main reference point from the colonial period onwards.[148] Further,

[143] M. Kerr, *The Arab Cold War: Gamal 'Abd Al-Nasir and his Rivals, 1958–1970* (London: Oxford University Press, 3rd ed, 1971).

[144] Barnett, 'Institutions, Roles, and Disorder', *supra* n. 140, at 290.

[145] M. Nahas, 'State-Systems and Revolutionary Challenge: Nasser, Khomeini, and the Middle East' (1985) 17 *International Journal of Middle East Studies* 507, at 512.

[146] Gause, *supra* n. 136, at 445.

[147] The UAR only lasted until 1961.

[148] R. Owen, *State, Power and Politics in the Making of the Modern Middle East* (London: Routledge, 2nd edition, 2000), at 18.

'the drive for unity was always more ambivalent than is usually presented. Just as important, any scheme for greater interstate co-operation was underpinned by a basic Arabism, a sense of kinship between the Arabic-speaking peoples, which remained a central fact of Middle Eastern life whatever else might be going on.'[149] It is also important to recognise that many Arab states were, and are, not simply a reflection of colonially determined borders. Harik argues that significant state formation had occurred before the colonial period, and although his suggestion of fifteen precolonial states is overdrawn, it does indicate a need to acknowledge the vital role of local allegiances and institutions that bolstered the eventual triumph of the territorial state after 1967.[150]

After 1948 Israel's presence in the heart of the Arab world was the most significant challenge to pan-Arabism, and with the devastating Arab defeat of 1967 died the dream of a united Arab polity. Not only did the Arab world and Nāṣir suffer humiliation; geo-strategic factors were of great concern now that Egypt had lost the Sinai, Syria the Golan Heights and the Palestinians the remainder of their territory to Israeli occupation. Reasons for such a loss were sought and 'Arabism quickly became the whipping boy for the defeat'.[151] Nāṣir resigned immediately, and a few months later Arab leaders met in Khartoum to evaluate options for regional rule in the future. By September and the summit's conclusion, the normative landscape had irrevocably changed: '*wataniya* [state-based nationalism] had been consecrated as the dominant ideology, regulating inter-Arab relations on the principle of state sovereignty.'[152] The region would no longer be caught between contradictions, and the 'hitherto destabilizing thrust of pan-Arabism was replaced by a general acceptance of the autonomy and legitimacy of the modern state.'[153] The promise of pan-Arabism did not simply disappear after 1967, but it is undeniable that never again could it rally such support. Arab leaders and their people continued to nurture a shared Arab identity, but increasingly this identity was grounded within the confines of separate states, bolstered by repressive tools in the hands of the region's rulers as well as economic consolidation.

Thus, although we have seen that much of the twentieth century was one of reaction against European models of statehood, it was also a period of consolidation of the state. Arabs had reacted against the colonial and Mandatory legacies

---

149 Ibid., at 71.

150 I. Harik, 'The Origins of the Arab State System', G. Salamé (ed.), *The Foundations of the Arab State* (London: Croom Held, 1987) at 22.

151 M. N. Barnett, *Dialogues in Arab Politics: Negotiations in Regional Order* (New York: Columbia University Press, 1998), at 162.

152 A. Dawisha, *Arab Nationalism in the Twentieth Century: From Triumph to Despair* (Princeton: Princeton University Press, 2003), at 286.

153 Y. Sayigh, 'The Gulf Crisis: Why the Arab Regional Order Failed' (1991) 67 *International Affairs* 476, at 490.

of bounded states by supporting pan-Arabism. Yet we also saw that the Arab world could draw on its own tradition of territoriality that would feed into future models of the nation-state in the region. By considering Islam in the post-1967 environment, as well as regional organisations, the final section evaluates the options available to Arabs in solidifying their selfhood and statehood as well as dispute resolution mechanisms for settling territorial matters.

Once pan-Arabism was tested and defeated in 1967, Islam increasingly became the main source of inspiration for alternative visions to the Arab predicament of statehood. Like Egypt's revolution in 1952, Iran's very different revolution of 1979 demonstrated the fragile appeal of secular nationalism, or *waṭaniyya*, across the wider Muslim world. Although Iran was never part of the Arab system, the impact of Khomeini's success not only terrified authoritarian Arab regimes, but it also provided an alternative transnational, non-territorial vision: unity not through an Arab state or *qawm*, but through the *umma*, free from illegitimate, corrupt and 'un-Islamic' rulers.[154] It is simplistic to depict modern Islamic movements in monolithic hues as was the case in our historical overview; modern Islam is manifested in a startling array of political and non-political forms. Many Islamically-inspired groups operate effectively within the postcolonial context of the territorial state, partly because it has become so entrenched.[155] As a result, the vision of an *umma* united under the Caliphate is often tempered with political realities; if we choose to speak of a modern *siyar*, we would glimpse many tensions between theory and practice, between universalism and bounded territoriality.

No account of the triumph of Arab statehood would be complete without considering the Arab League, which embodied its participants' predilections for territorial integrity softened only by pan-Arabist rhetoric and ineffectual responses to regional crises. Studying the Arab League provides a deeper appreciation of regional trends regarding statehood as well as mechanisms for dispute resolution. If we cast our gaze back to the League's origins during wartime meetings in 1944, the institution that emerged a year later promised a great deal. It also brought together member states culturally and linguistically closer than most other regions. Despite the appeal of pan-Arabism, particularly from the 1950s onwards, the formation of the League took place in a context where state elites could advance parochial interests largely unhindered by the appeal of transnationalism. Many models of integration were flagged during these years,[156] but

[154] D. Armstrong, *Revolution and World Order: The revolutionary state in international society* (Oxford: Clarendon Press, 1993), at 191.

[155] D. F. Eickelman & J. Piscatori, *Muslim Politics* (Princeton: Princeton University Press, 1996), at 139.

[156] Possible models included: 1) the League as a single international person representing all Arab

only 'Syria was in favour of full-fledged Arab unity, and was prepared to surrender her sovereignty, as well as to accept compulsory means for the settlement of disputes.'[157] Eventually, the seven founding members of the League adopted the Arab League Pact on 22 March 1945,[158] which must be seen as a triumph of sovereignty over transnationalism.

Because the Arab League was formed by states unwilling to concede any sovereignty, the institution has contributed little to most of the region's conflicts, especially those over territory. In 1957, Foda wrote that '[b]order disputes are of long standing between the Asian Arab States by virtue of the *unnatural partition* of this part of the world after the First World War.'[159] Although we have seen that these borders became more secure, the twentieth century has witnessed a number of Arab territorial disputes.[160] Many of these have since been settled, but very rarely has the Arab League played a decisive role in their resolution.[161] This is despite the fact that by 1950 a Draft Statute for an Arab Court of Justice had been devised by the League, as first suggested by Iraq.[162] The need for a strong and independent court, however, conflicted with Article 5 of the Pact, which severely curtailed instances when dispute settlement mechanisms could trump state sovereignty:

---

countries; a federation based on the partial cession of Arab sovereignty; or a loose confederation based on co-operation and consent. Foda, *supra* n. 42, at 6–7.

[157] H. A. Hassouna, *The League of Arab States and Regional Disputes: A Study of Middle East Conflicts* (Leiden: Oceana, 1975), at 6.

[158] The full text of the Pact can be found at the League's website: http://www.arableagueonline.org/las/index_en.jsp.

[159] Italics added, Foda, *supra* n. 42, at 30.

[160] For an excellent overview of some of these disputes and their adjudication in the colonial and postcolonial period, see J. Allain, *International Law in the Middle East: Closer to Power than Justice* (Aldershot: Ashgate, 2004), at ch. 8.

[161] Some examples include: The Buraimi dispute: J. B. Kelly, 'The Buraimi Oasis Dispute' (1956) 32 *International Affairs* (Royal Institute of International Affairs) 318; Morocco's 1963 invasion of Algeria as discussed in Chapter Five; the Saudi-Yemen border issue: A. H. Al-Enazy, '"The International Boundary Treaty" (Treaty of Jeddah) Concluded between the Kingdom of Saudi Arabia and the Yemeni Republic on June 12, 2000' 96 (2002) *American Journal of International Law* 161; and the Taba Arbitration between Egypt and Israel: *Taba* Arbitration (Egypt/Israel) (1989) 80 ILR 224. For background to this dispute, see M. ElBaradei, 'The Egyptian-Israeli Peace Treaty and Access to the Gulf of Aqaba: A New Legal Regime' (1982) 76 *American Journal of International Law* 532; and R. Lapidoth, 'The Strait of Tiran, the Gulf of Aqaba and the 1979 Treaty of Peace between Egypt and Israel' (1983) 77 *American Journal of International Law* 84. Some other pertinent disputes, such as the Eritrea/Yemen arbitration, are discussed *vis-à-vis* the case studies, at Chapter Three & Chapter Four.

[162] Foda *supra* n. 42, at 13.

> Should there arise among them a dispute that does not involve the independence of a State, its sovereignty or its territorial integrity, and should the two contending parties apply to the Council for the settlement of this dispute, the decision of the Council shall then be effective and obligatory.[163]

The creation of a Court was widely promoted even though conflict remained over its jurisdiction. 'In fact, the creation of this Arab court has been the subject of numerous discussions and even more numerous resolutions.'[164] Foda explained that the League's failure to realise the Court was a product of Arab attitudes regarding arbitration; Arab states have tended to favour reconciliation over arbitration, even though arbitration is central to the Islamic tradition.[165] After over half a century later, the Court's inception seems less likely than ever. Thus even though the Arab world could draw on planned arbitral institutions, a rich legal tradition as well as at least some support for arbitration, it seems that international adjudication bodies have come to serve as the only viable option for arbitration in the region.

Arab League states straddle a number of regional affiliations and many are members of other organizations. Multiple regional memberships need not necessarily weaken the League, but especially for Arab-African states, comparatively greater reliance and success underscore the lack of trust held by certain Arab states for the League's capabilities. More recently smaller regional groupings have emerged in the Arab world, indicating further gaps in the League's capacity to fulfill certain, more parochial, aspirations.[166]

Of greater relevance in our discussion of regional arbitration initiatives is the Organisation of Islamic Conference (OIC) and its support for the creation of an Islamic International Court of Justice.[167] Although the OIC has a much larger membership than the League, both share an institutional framework endorsing

---

163 This state-centric theme of the Pact was only reinforced in the 1950 Joint Defence and Economic Co-Operation Treaty, available from the Arab League's website: http://www.arableagueonline.org/las/index_en.jsp.

164 B. Boutros-Ghali, 'The Arab League (1945–1970)' (1969) 25 *Revue égyptienne de droit international* 67, at 82.

165 Foda, *supra* n. 42, at 49–50.

166 These include the Arab Maghreb Union (AMU) and the Gulf Cooperation Council (GCC). Neither of these bodies is particularly effective and this is especially so regarding the AMU, which has been paralysed by the Algerian-Moroccan stand off over Western Sahara. These organisations are discussed further in Chapter Five and Chapter Four respectively. For a comparative analysis of the two bodies, see M. Cammett, 'Defensive Integration and Late Developers: The Gulf Cooperation Council and the Arab Maghreb Union' (1999) 5 *Global Governance* 379.

167 For an interesting discussion of arbitration for private law matters in the Islamic world, see C. N. Brower & J. K. Sharpe, 'International Arbitration and the Islamic World: The Third Phase' (2003) 97 *American Journal of International Law* 643.

the sovereignty norm and no real mechanisms for dispute resolution.[168] The OIC was established in Rabat, Morocco, on 25 September 1969, after a 'Zionist arson attack upon *Al-Aqsa* mosque complex in occupied Jerusalem on 21 August 1969.'[169] The OIC was motivated to defend Islam, its Holy Sites and its peoples and so from its inception the OIC was closely associated with the Palestinian issue and anti-colonialism in general, as enshrined in its Charter. Although the OIC can be characterised as a modern manifestation of the *umma*, the organisation has rejected this radical vision. Thus,

> It is incorrect to identify the OIC as operating within the Islamic concept of *Ummah*... The OIC is an international inter-governmental organization composed of sovereign states therefore working within the common structure of international law where member states are the main subjects.[170]

This idea is reflected in the Draft Statute of the Islamic International Court of Justice, which seeks to marry the application of *sharīʿa* with optional jurisdiction on the part of its member states.[171] Although the Court was first suggested in the 1980s, few developments have boosted its prospects of realisation more recently. Perhaps like the Arab Court of Justice it will remain little more than a dream in the minds of Arab states when seeking the assistance of the ICJ. Territorially bounded states and international, rather than regional, forms of adjudication reflect the dominant approach in the region. Is it possible for Arab states to introduce their particular heritage and experience of authority over territory, as will be shown in the cases? Is the ICJ a forum capable of sustaining such inter-cultural debates? Are the experiences of Arab territoriality comprehensible inside the Peace Palace?

6) *Conclusion*

Given the rich and diverse history of the Arab-Islamic world, locating the source of ideas and their application has been a difficult task. This chapter has

---

168 According to Moinuddin, 'The emphasis laid by Member States of the OIC on the principle of sovereignty is an unequivocal and emphatic 'no' to supranationalism. Following precedents of the OAS, OAU and the Pact of the Arab League, the OIC Charter underlines the dominant role of the principle of sovereignty, independence and territorial integrity in inter-Islamic relations,' Moinuddin, *supra* n. 22, at 93. See also S. Akbarzadeh & K. Connor, 'The Organization of the Islamic Conference: Sharing an Illusion' (2005) 12 *Middle East Policy* 79.

169 Rehman, *supra* n. 24, at 27.

170 M. Lombardini, 'The International Islamic Court of Justice: Towards an International Islamic Legal System?' (2001) 14 *Leiden Journal of International Law* 665, at 667.

171 For an overview of the Court's Statute, see, ibid. I could only find a copy of the draft Statute in Arabic: http://www.islamonline.net/Arabic/doc/2000/10/article32.shtml.

highlighted that Arab states inherited a number of legacies that were both supportive and dismissive of the nation-state model. We also saw that it is simplistic to essentialise 'Islamic international law' and 'public international law'; neither should be reified into a body of norms applicable across time and continents. This is especially the case for the legal relations that evolved between and across Christian Europe and its Ottoman 'other'. Later projections have overshadowed a complex interplay between cultures and faiths, particularly during the slow demise of the Sublime Porte. There can be no definitive historical account of Ottoman international legal personality, but a significant body of material allows contemporary scholars to construct the story of membership in a number of ways. The story of the evolution of international law was more complex than the familiar narrative of exclusive European creation suggests.

Earlier too, despite a classical Islamic theory redolent of faith-based universalism, practice instead indicated a growing acceptance of territorially limited and delimited entities. Thus it is possible to speak of an Arab-Islamic tradition informing contemporary manifestations of the state in the region that contains a number of different normative visions for configuring authority over territory. Although the last few decades have witnessed a consolidation of the sovereignty norm by Arab state elites, earlier legacies of Islamic international law suggest that there is significant space for renegotiating the boundaries of statehood where willingness for dialogue exists. International lawyers can assist in this process by continuing to question the construction of international law's past and present configurations to develop a discipline alive to the wealth of legal traditions informing the modern state system.

Part II
Contentious Cases

Introduction to Part II

Constituting the Self through Territory: The Law and Practice of Territorial Disputes and Boundary Drawing

We saw in the previous chapter that the relationship between territory and statehood in the Arab-Islamic tradition is complex, both supporting and rejecting European models of authority. Notwithstanding this tradition, the nature of international society today is far less variegated; the nation-state is the only model of membership available to political entities at the international level. It is therefore no surprise that Arab states have largely rejected the alternative of pan-Arabism in preference for well-demarcated nationhood and statehood. This is especially so in relation to natural resources, because defined borders are an ideal way of preserving national wealth. ICJ territorial cases have enabled a variety of Third World states, both Arab and non-Arab, to entrench their interests through the certainty provided by boundary delimitation. The practice of ICJ argumentation requires these states to construct particular narratives about not only their statehood but its relationship with norms relating to international legal personality more generally. Thus, territorial adjudication rests on detailed historical accounts[1] interwoven with the specific law relating to title to territory.

To place the two cases studied in Part II into this context of historical and legal argumentation, the following discussion aims to provide the reader with an understanding about the nature of ICJ contentious cases as they relate to territory. This introductory section raises themes of relevance for both the contentious and advisory cases considered below. The following section will explore matters relating to history as well as boundary delimitation, especially the norm of *uti possidetis juris*. The introduction to Part III, on the other hand, will only explore the nature of self-determination *vis-à-vis* ICJ adjudication in Advisory Opinions. This might seem counter-intuitive at a conceptual level; the self precedes any relationship grounded in territory. Doctrine and practice, however, have tended to reflect this approach as expressed by Brownlie:

---

[1] Merrills, for example, argues that 'the historical record is usually the key to applying the law.' J. G. Merrills, 'The International Court of Justice and the Adjudication of Territorial and Boundary Disputes' (2000) 13 *Leiden Journal of International Law* 873, at 895.

> [T]here is a complementarity between *uti possidetis* and the principle of self-determination. It is *uti possidetis* which creates the ambit of the pertinent unit of self-determination, and which in that sense has a logical priority over self-determination.[2]

This tension between the self and territory is particularly pronounced across the African continent, as highlighted in Chapters Three and Five below. The choices confronting both African and Arab states at decolonisation are thus explored below in relation to borders and the role of the ICJ in this project. Because territorial adjudication relies on certain legal and historical interpretations, this section also overviews the relevant jurisprudence to highlight how limited the choices are for postcolonial states seeking selfhood. Before opening up the discussion to these broad considerations of history, doctrine and policy, however, the following section will first outline the procedural aspects of ICJ contentious adjudication.

The Statute of the International Court of Justice is based on optional jurisdiction only available to states.[3] For parties seeking to found a jurisdictional link between their particular dispute and the capacity of the Court to exercise its mainline jurisdiction, a number of options are available.[4] First, states may accept the general jurisdiction of the Court through Article 36(2) or the 'optional clause',[5] which allows states to issue a unilateral declaration, either 'made unconditionally or subject to reservations which are not incompatible with the purposes of the optional clause.'[6] Although the Court recently celebrated its sixtieth anniversary, the optional clause is still 'underused' by the bulk of the world's states as only

---

2 I. Brownlie, 'Boundary Problems and the Formation of New States', D. Freestone, S. Subedi & S. Davidson (eds.), *Contemporary Issues in International Law* (The Hague: Kluwer, 2002), at 191.

3 Article 34(1) of the Statute reads: 'Only states may be parties in cases before the Court.'

4 The other main way of conferring jurisdiction not discussed in the text is through a compromissory clause contained in both multilateral and bilateral treaties. None of the case studies or the other cases discussed at length arise from this practice.

5 This provision reads:

> The states parties to the present Statute may at any time declare that they recognize as compulsory ipso facto and without special agreement, in relation to any state accepting the same obligation, the jurisdiction of the Court in all legal disputes concerning:
> the interpretation of a treaty;
> any question of international law;
> the existence of any fact which, if established, would constitute a breach of an international obligation;
> the nature or extent of the reparation to be made for the breach of an international obligation.

6 S. Rosenne, *Rosenne's The World Court: What it is and how it works*, T. D. Gill (ed.), 6th edition (Leiden: Martinus Nijhoff, 2003), at 74. For a full list of these states, see http://www.icj-cij.org/jurisdiction/index.php?p1=5&p2=1&p3=3.

sixty five states have accepted this provision.[7] Perhaps out of any regional grouping, Arab states have the worst record of accepting the Court's jurisdiction under Article 36(2). To date, Egypt is the only Arab state, out of a possible twenty two, to have accepted the Court's jurisdiction.

This Third World, and particularly Arab, aversion to the optional clause is reflected in Part II's cases, which both stem from a framework agreement or *accord cadre*. Such agreements are an open-ended form of *compromis*, allowing either unilateral application or a pair of applications outlining the nature of the dispute. The benefit of such an approach is that it allows parties to specify and limit the matters under dispute as well as the law applicable. Where framework agreements are vague, however, the Court can step in, framing the scope of its enquiry as well as determining whether it should exercise its jurisdiction at all. The *Qatar/Bahrain* dispute in Chapter Four demonstrates that, even with framework agreements, consent is far from certain and that a state's eventual participation in proceedings should not simply be interpreted as its comprehensive acceptance of the Court's functional legitimacy. Once the practice of territorial adjudication is reviewed below, this section will conclude by returning to the themes of consent, choice and legitimacy for postcolonial parties in a world of nation-states.

It is one of the paradoxes of globalisation that delimiting the territorial confines of the state remains of singular importance – especially for postcolonial states.[8] As more recent members of the international system, Third World states are increasingly supportive of its dictates, which through the juridical support of territorial boundaries provide some protection from increasingly porous economic borders. Challenges to the nation-state are still evident, but usually at the sub-state, rather than the national level, and this is because territory as defined through law 'constitutes the tangible framework for the manifestation of power by the accepted authorities of the State in question.'[9] In a world comprising parcelised jurisdiction, territory 'plays not only a definitional role, but a constitutive one historically as well. It is the link between a people, its identity as a state, and its international role.'[10] In the wake of decolonisation, Third World states have struggled with this relationship, and adjudication has only been called on occasionally in contests over identity, territory and resources. We saw in Chapter One, however, that Third World states have increased their

[7] R. Y. Jennings, 'The International Court of Justice after Fifty Years' (1995) 89 *American Journal of International Law* 493, at 495.

[8] M. N. Shaw, 'The Heritage of States: The Principle of *Uti Possidetis Juris* Today' (1997) 67 *British Yearbook of International Law* 75, at 75.

[9] M. N. Shaw, *Title to Territory in Africa: International Legal Issues* (Oxford: Clarendon Press, 1986), at 1.

[10] Ibid., at 3.

participation in ICJ territorial matters, highlighting at the very least that other means, such as military conflict, negotiations, or regional institutions, have often failed to achieve the desires of many Third World states.

Recent Third World ICJ territorial litigation forms part of a well-established and largely European tradition of adjudication and arbitration. Although adjudication has never been the default for settling disputes over territory, it has played an important role in a number of contests over boundaries and territorial control. Especially since the nineteenth century, a number of arbitrations have taken place between European powers in relation to their colonies in the Americas, Asia and Africa.[11] Grewe points out that arbitration during this period was typically used for mid-range territorial matters in an institutional setting increasingly juridical, compared to earlier practices centring on diplomacy.[12] During the early twentieth century this trend continued with a number of arbitrations as well as the hearing of many cases – often of a colonial nature – before the Permanent Court of Justice (PCIJ).[13]

Since its inception in 1946, the ICJ has drawn on this jurisprudential heritage and has further developed the law and practice regarding title to territory. There is a clear trend arising from this litigation, which began with intra-European disputes and then gradually embraced intra-Latin American, intra-Asian and lastly intra-African cases.[14] As outlined in Chapter One, the 1986 *Frontier Dispute* marked a watershed for Third World territorial adjudication; the caseload of the Court remains heavily tilted in favour of African, Latin American and Asian states invoking colonial legacies to secure postcolonial statehood. Yet Franck argues that such a quest for certainty is 'illusory' because territorial disputes contain competing norms that cannot be resolved by adjudicatory methods.[15]

---

[11] S. Rosenne, 'Decolonisation in the International Court of Justice' (1996) 8 *African Journal of International and Comparative Law* 564, at 565.

[12] W. H. Grewe, *The Epochs of International Law*, M. Byers (trans) (New York; Berlin: de Gruyter, 2000), at 519–520.

[13] Rosenne, 'Decolonisation', *supra* n. 11, at 564–565.

[14] *Minquiers & Ecrehos (France/United Kingdom)* (1953) ICJ Rep 47; *Sovereignty over Certain Frontier Land (Belgium/Netherlands)* (1959) ICJ Rep 209; *Arbitral Award made by the King of Spain on 23 December 1906 (Honduras/Nicaragua)* (1960) ICJ Rep 192; *Temple of Preah Vihear (Cambodia/Thailand)* (1962) ICJ Rep 6; *Frontier Dispute (Burkina Faso/Mali)* (1986) ICJ Rep 554; *Land, Island and Maritime Frontier Dispute (El Salvador/Honduras; Nicaragua intervening)* (1992) ICJ Rep 351; *Territorial Dispute (Libya/Chad)* (1994) ICJ Rep 6; *Kasikili/Sedudu Island (Botswana/Namibia)* (1999) ICJ Rep 1045; *Maritime Delimitation and Territorial Questions between Qatar and Bahrain (Qatar/Bahrain)* (2001) ICJ Rep 40; *Land and Maritime Boundary between Cameroon and Nigeria (Cameroon/Nigeria; Equatorial Guinea Intervening)* (2002) ICJ Rep 303; *Case Concerning Sovereignty over Pulau Ligitan and Pulau Sipadan (Indonesia/Malaysia)* (2002) ICJ Rep 625; *Case Concerning the Frontier Dispute (Benin/Niger)* (2005) ICJ Rep 90.

[15] T. M. Franck, 'Postmodern Tribalism and the Right to Secession', C. Brölmann et al. (eds.), *Peoples and Minorities in International Law* (The Hague: Kluwer, 1993), at 4.

Perhaps in a bid to obscure such norm conflict, an elaborate practice has emerged in territorial cases, providing the international lawyer with a clear path to pursue when no argumentative deviation is desired. For example, Ratner argues that judicial settlement of territorial matters advantages those able to invoke certain rules and speak in a highly specialised style, or competence.[16] Some of these techniques are showcased later in this section, but here we can at least identify the centrality of doctrine over and above wider contextual concerns. More broadly, we can identify typical argumentative techniques as perpetuating a 'legocentric' approach to history and territory. Such an approach in the courtroom is to be expected, but it has substantive effects. Not only does a doctrinal preference overlook complexities, but it also tends to suggest that conflicts can be settled without resort to 'less significant' issues. The difficulty with such an approach, however, is the boundary drawing required in defining 'law'. Time and again, ICJ pleadings and judgments have centred on usually European treaties,[17] thus creating a hierarchy of 'relevant' legal evidence and also separating instances of 'hard' law from its 'softer' variants, like indigenous occupation of the land. In his study of ICJ territorial cases, Sumner confirms this institutional practice – or bias. He points out that the court 'manifests a hierarchical preference for treaty law, *uti possidetis*, and effective control, respectively.'[18]

Another important instance of such discursive boundary-drawing is highlighted by references to the modes of acquisition as well as the distinction between territorial delimitation and boundary demarcation. Ratner argues that the modes of acquisition, namely, conquest, cession, occupation, prescription and accretion, are often invoked in treatises on territory, but tend to be overlooked in judgments in preference for considerations of effective control and historical consolidation.[19] Although it is correct to depict an adjudicative style more flexible than a set of limited categories,[20] these modes of acquisition still provide a powerful framework in guiding and limiting analysis in even the most recent cases. Given their

[16] S. R. Ratner, 'Land Feuds and their Solutions: Finding International Law beyond the Tribunal Chamber' (2006) 100 *American Journal of International Law* 808, at 814.

[17] In his separate opinion in the *Kasikili/Sedudu Island* Case, Judge Kooijmans objects to the majority's approach in choosing to prioritise a specific treaty under examination above general rules and principles of international law. Kooijmans J. (sep. op.) *(Botswana/Namibia)* (1999) ICJ Rep 1045, at 1144–1152.

[18] B. T. Sumner, 'Territorial Disputes at the International Court of Justice' 53 (2004) *Duke Law Journal* 1779, at 1780.

[19] Ratner, *supra* n. 16, at 815. Koskennieimi also makes this point. He argues that it has been difficult to keep the modes of acquisition distinct, and so tribunals have tended to favour effective possession and consolidation. M. Koskenniemi, *From Apology to Utopia: The Structure of International Legal Argument* (Cambridge: Cambridge University Press, 2nd edition, 2005), at 283.

[20] A clear statement of the preference for effective control is found in the *Eastern Greenland* Case, which defined title as the combination of 'the intention and will to act as sovereign, and some

contested nature, especially when applied to the colonial period, such a legal framework cannot be free from scholarly censure. However, they provide both litigants and the bench with a useful and artificial means of clarifying points of contention. The Court took up the opportunity most recently in its 2002 judgment about control over the Bakassi Peninsula. In contrast to Cameroon's reliance on European treaty law, one of Nigeria's claims to title was based on historical consolidation.[21] In retaliation, the majority judgment defended itself through doctrine, declaring that 'the theory of historical consolidation is highly controversial and cannot *replace the established modes of acquisition of title under international law*'.[22]

The Court has been more flexible with issues of delimitation and demarcation, suggesting that the line between territorial and boundary disputes is not exact; the difference is one of degree rather than kind.[23] Again, it would seem that treatises are more formulaic, as shown in Merrills' categorisation of territorial disputes.[24] When contrasting textbook analyses and ICJ judgments, discrepancies soon emerge, suggesting that the Court is less emphatic about the need for such a distinction. Ultimately, however, these controversies and others are of limited importance in trying to understand the dynamics of argumentation in territorial adjudication. Jennings was right in 1963 when he argued that international law is concerned not so much with changes in the occupation of territory but rather with changes in the *right* to territorial sovereignty.[25] Thus, 'where a new State arises the law has looked chiefly at the emergence of the new subject rather than the incidental transfer of territory; it has looked to the sovereign, rather than the territorial element of territorial sovereignty.'[26] These observations shift the analysis away from facts or definitional debates and remind us that control over territory is ultimately about the relationship between international rules and the constitution of international legal personality.

---

actual exercise or display of such authority.' *Legal Status of Eastern Greenland (Denmark/Norway)* (1933) P.C.I.J. Series A/B No. 53, at 46.

[21] *(Cameroon/Nigeria; Equatorial Guinea Intervening)* (2002) ICJ Rep 303, at 349–352. For discussion on this point, see N. J. Udombana, 'The Ghost of Berlin Still Haunts Africa! The ICJ Judgment on the Land and Maritime Boundary Dispute between Cameroon and Nigeria' (2003) *African Yearbook of International Law* 13, at 33–35.

[22] Italics added, *(Cameroon/Nigeria; Equatorial Guinea Intervening)* (2002) ICJ Rep 303, at 352.

[23] *(Burkina Faso/Mali)* (1986) ICJ Rep 554, at 563.

[24] J. G. Merrills, 'International Boundary Disputes in Theory and Practice: Precedents Established', J. Dahlitz (ed.), *Peaceful Resolution of Major International Disputes* (New York: United Nations, 1999), at 99–101.

[25] R. Y. Jennings, *The Acquisition of Territory in International Law* (Manchester: Manchester University Press, 1963), at 14.

[26] Ibid., at 8.

Most postcolonial territorial disputes are rooted in colonial practice of the nineteenth century, thus requiring detailed explorations about the link between membership of international society and territorial title. Debate about the treatment and personality of non-European peoples during this period remains fierce. If we adopt an approach like that of Alexandrowicz's and certain TWAIL scholars,[27] we can see the colonial period as exceptional; as an instance of European disavowal of fundamental international legal principles. Such a stance suggests that European states breached established modes of acquisition as well as norms about treaty law and coercion. If we take the view that European practice at this time was part of international law's evolution, however, colonialism begins to appear as both politically *and* legally acceptable. This latter perspective is captured by Miéville in his discussion of unequal treaties:

> Let us be clear – these unequal treaties were not ostensibly but *really* legal, they *created* the general principles of international law: they are not fraudulent, but the truth of nineteenth-century international law. That is the law we inherited.[28]

The following overview of European colonialism thus highlights one of the central themes of this research: that doctrine must always be understood in relation to scholarly reconstructions of the past. We cannot determine a pure past or a pure law, only its interpretation and application in ongoing legal controversies.

With the gradual expansion of European control across the globe in the nineteenth century, a variety of discourses and practices emerged both to explain and regulate territorial aggrandisement. In the preceding centuries expansion had been driven by trading companies, because 'European states did not want to take on the burdens of colonial rule. There was... no explicit international law *of colonies*'[29] after the age of 'discovery' and before the rise of imperialism. Whereas the European encounter with the 'new world' was framed through the discourse of Christianity and *jus gentium*, nineteenth century explanations centred on civilisation, positivism and recognition. Nineteenth century authors as well as contemporary commentators have contrasted these regimes in a bid to distinguish America's 'discovery' from Africa's through the trajectory of

[27] I briefly discuss Alexandrowicz's argument about pre-nineteenth century non-European international legal personality in Chapter Two, at 76–78. Also see M. A. Ajomo, 'International Law, the United Nations and Decolonization', E. G. Bello & B. A. Ajibola (eds.), *Essays in Honour of Judge Taslim Olawale Elias: vol. I Contemporary International Law and Human Rights* (Dordrecht: Martinus Nijhoff, 1992) 77–92; and M. L. Sarin, 'The Asian-African States and the Development of International Law', F. E. Snyder & S. Sathirathai (eds.), *Third World Attitudes Toward International Law: An Introduction* (Dordrecht: Martinus Nijhoff, 1987) 33–51.

[28] Italics in original. C. Miéville, *Between Equal Rights: A Marxist Theory of International Law* (London: Pluto, 2006 (2005), at 246–247.

[29] Emphasis in original. Miéville, Ibid., at 232, also see 248–256.

'progress'. Conquest had been the dominant mode of acquisition meted out to the Ameridians. Papal grants in the latter part of the fifteenth century had encouraged the spread of Christianity via conquest secured through territorial dominion.[30] By the nineteenth century, however, Andrews argues that the 'immorality of acquisition of territory by conquest' encouraged either cession or occupation of *terrae nullius* instead.[31]

The problem here, however, is that cession and occupation as modes of acquisition relied on understandings of legal personality and therefore the doctrine of recognition. Many entities, especially in Africa, were simply not regarded as *worthy* of recognition; they were deemed to be *terrae nullius* or non-state entities of some sort. This notion is expressed by Schwarzenberger in stark terms: 'rights and duties under international law exist only between subjects of international law'; whether 'communities outside the pale of international law submit peacefully or otherwise is irrelevant.'[32] Even when non-European societies were recognised for the purpose of cession, this was often exclusively for European interests; cession was used as a *factual* antecedent for European *inter se* agreements delimiting respective spheres of influence.[33] Thus these treaties were the tools of European powers able to secure their interests without the need for military conquest. In the words of Herbst, it 'was boundary creation on the cheap.'[34]

Some modern authors regard treaties of cession as puzzling: how was it possible that European powers could enter into agreements with entities they saw as less than sovereign?[35] To answer this question, it is essential that strict categories of legality be abandoned. It is easy enough to portray European colonial practice today as technically illegal or alegal. What is more difficult is to understand the relationship between legal categories and their application in a given historical context. Anghie

[30] S. Korman, *The Right of Conquest: The Acquisition of Territory by Force in International Law and Practice* (Oxford: Clarendon Press, 1996), at 42–47.

[31] J. A. Andrews, 'The Concept of Statehood and the Acquisition of Territory in the Nineteenth Century' (1978) 94 *Law Quarterly Review* 408, at 410. One notable exception in Africa was the conquest of Madagascar in 1896 as noted by Korman, *supra* n. 30, at 65.

[32] G. Schwarzenberger, 'Title to Territory: Response to a Challenge' 51 (1957) *American Journal of International Law* 308, at 314. Schwarzenberger draws on the PCIJ's Eastern Greenland judgment for the idea that conquest is operative between sovereigns and thus in some ways, later practices of colonialism that denied the need for conquest can be seen as regressive, rather than progressive: *Eastern Greenland Case* (1933) P.C.I.J., Ser. A/B, No. 53, at 50.

[33] J. Castellino & S. Allen, *Title to Territory in International Law: A Temporal Analysis* (Aldershot: Ashgate, 2003), at 91.

[34] J. Herbst, 'The creation and maintenance of national boundaries in Africa' (1989) 43 *International Organization* 673, at 685.

[35] D. W. Greig, 'Sovereignty, Territory and the International Lawyer's Dilemma' (1988) 26 *Osgoode Hall Law Journal* 127, at 151–152.

suggests that we read this period as one of fluid personality,[36] where non-European powers were sometimes afforded the limited capacity to form contracts at the private law level but not at the international law level:[37]

> The non-European states thus existed in a sort of twilight world; lacking personality, they were nevertheless capable of entering into certain treaties and were to that extent members of international law.[38]

Koskenniemi's analysis of the period, on the other hand, is free from the conceptual constraints imposed by cession. 'Colonial title was always original [as through occupation of *terrae nullius*] and never derivative [as through cession]: it followed from European law's qualification of the acts of European powers, not from native cession.'[39] These views as well as others highlight how difficult is the task of settling on 'the law' during the colonial period. For Koskenniemi, the 'law of territorial acquisition oscillates between basing title on effective possession (and its derivatives) and an external recognition (acquiescence).'[40] Shifting positions are also evident throughout the cases. Thus rather than seeking certainty, it is better to recognise the uses of different doctrinal evaluations in the cases explored throughout the book.

No account of colonial expansion would be complete without a discussion of the Berlin Conference of 1885, and yet,[41] as in the case of doctrinal categories, we must see this event less as a milestone and more as a crystalisation of

---

[36] 'European states adopted different views of native personality, depending on their own interests. The problem was that native personality was fluid, as it was created through the encounter with a European state which would inevitably 'recognise' the capacity of the non-European entity according to its own needs.' A. Anghie, *Imperialism, Sovereignty and the Making of International Law* (Cambridge: Cambridge University Press, 2005), at 79.

[37] According to Grewe, 'the protagonists of colonial expansion in the nineteenth century did not deny non-civilised peoples the *dominium civile*, but rather only political *imperium*; not the capacity to hold private, civil rights, but rather legal personality as a subject of international law. They did not deny that every human being had innate rights which were held independently of the stage of culture and civilisation they had achieved.' Grewe, *supra* n. 12, at 548.

[38] Anghie, *supra* n. 36, at 76. This sense of twilight is captured by Andrews in his observation of a two-tier international law of the nineteenth century between members and non-members of international society. Shaw further divides the system into three: full members and states in the Concert of Europe, non-European states and non-European peoples not recognised as states. Andrews, *supra* n. 31, at 419 and Shaw, *Title to Territory, supra* n. 9, at 45.

[39] M. Koskenniemi, *The Gentle Civilizer of Nations: The Rise and Fall of International Law 1870–1960* (Cambridge: Cambridge University Press, 2002), at 128. This position is diametrically opposed by Shaw, who suggests that most title in Africa was derivate and resulted from treaties of cession: Shaw, *Title to Territory, supra* n. 9, at 39.

[40] Koskenniemi, *From Apology to Utopia, supra* n. 19, at 286.

[41] General Act of the Conference of the Plenipotentiaries of Austria-Hungary, Belgium, Denmark, France, Germany, Great Britain, Italy, the Netherlands, Portugal, Russia, Spain, Sweden-Norway, Turkey (and the United States) respecting the Congo, 26 February 1885, 165 CTS 485.

imperial practices that occurred throughout the long nineteenth century.[42] Like Turkey's 'entry' into international society in 1856 discussed in Chapter Two,[43] a simplistic rendering of the Berlin Conference tends to place too much emphasis on this episode, signalling it out for exception. The Conference's organisers had high hopes for regulating the acquisition of the rest of Africa, free navigation and the status of the Congo, but results were far more modest, and besides, most of coastal Africa was already spoken for.[44] For European powers,[45] Berlin simply required would-be colonisers to inform each other of their intentions.[46] A degree of territorial consolidation was also necessary, but often through the most minimal displays of effective control that were little more than symbolic. Although Berlin was intended to define relations between European states as well as the law applicable to Africa, it only served to confirm the exclusively European notion of sovereignty with little detail as to its content on the continent.[47] It sanctioned a practice which was only to increase after the Conference's close: 'allowing a European power to preclude others from contesting a piece of territory that was merely under its sphere of influence.'[48]

The main territorial entity to emerge out of Berlin-style colonialism was the protectorate, which, like treaties of cession, was often based on arbitrary inter-

[42] Miéville, *supra* n. 28, at 253. Further, Koskenniemi argues that it is unclear whether events after Berlin were qualitatively different or simply the extension of earlier policies. Koskenniemi, *The Gentle Civilizer, supra* n. 39, at 117.

[43] Chapter Two, at 75–81.

[44] Herbst, *supra* n. 34, at 683.

[45] All of the participants at the Conference were from Europe (geographically or ethnically, in the case of the United States which ultimately chose not to be a signatory) or were included within the Concert of Europe, namely the Ottoman Empire. Although the Sublime Porte had been officially recognised as a member of (European) International Society since 1856, it was initially excluded from the list of Berlin participants and had to lobby for its inclusion, and this in the face of widespread and enduring Ottoman title over large parts of the African continent, *supra* n. 41.

[46] The key provisions of the General Act of the Conference on this point were:

> Article 34 – Any power which henceforth takes possession of a tract of land on the coasts of the African Continent outside of its present possessions, or which, being hitherto without such possessions, shall acquire them, as well as the Power which assumes a Protectorate there, shall accompany the respective act with a notification thereof, addressed to the other Signatory Powers of the present Act, in order to enable them, if need be, to make good any claims of their own.
>
> Article 35 – The Signatory Powers of the present Act recognize the obligation to insure the establishment of authority in regions occupied by them on the coasts of the African Continent sufficient to protect existing rights, and, as the case may be, freedom of trade and transit under the conditions agree upon.

[47] Koskenniemi, *The Gentle Civilizer, supra* n. 39, at 121, 126.

[48] Herbst, *supra* n. 34, at 684.

pretations of sovereignty and personality.[49] According to Andrews, 'there was an enormous variety in the styles of protectorate, some of which were scarcely dissimilar from colonial status in the extent of control assumed by the protecting power.'[50] Shaw explains the proliferation of protectorates through an account of how the classical ideal of protectorates increasingly gave way to colonial exigencies. Initially, protectorates were based on bifurcated sovereignty: external sovereignty for the protecting power and internal sovereignty for the protégé.[51] This classical notion of protection continued to persist throughout the colonial period, particularly in those parts of the non-European world deemed to possess certain attributes of 'civilisation'. For instance, the Trucial states of the Gulf, as discussed in Chapter Four, always maintained their internal sovereignty; but we will see how, even in such instances, that the line between internal and external sovereignty became blurred.[52]

The institution of 'colonial protectorates', which were simply colonies by another name, was much more common in southern Africa. The ICJ recently revisited the controversy over the boundary between 'colonial protectorates' and 'proper' protectorates in the dispute between Nigeria and Cameroon mentioned above. In this case, Nigeria relied on an 1884 treaty of protection between Britain and the Chiefs of Old Calabar to argue that later British alienation of Calabar lands through a treaty with Germany was of no legal effect: *nemo dat quod non habet*.[53] Despite strong dissent from some members of the bench on this issue, the Court held that the plain words of the treaty were not really about 'protection' at all, but were simply a policy choice on the part of Britain.[54] The indigenous peoples in the area lacked international legal personality and so their lands were open to colonisation.[55] Judges Ranjeva and Koroma opposed such a finding by relying on the law/politics dichotomy. They both regarded the

[49] M. Koskenniemi, 'International Law and Imperialism', D. Freestone, S. Subedi & S. Davidson (eds.), *Contemporary Issues in International Law: A Collection of the Josephine Onoh Memorial Lectures* (The Hague: Kluwer, 2002), 197–218, at 212.

[50] Andrews, *supra* n. 31, at 420.

[51] Shaw, *Title to Territory, supra* n. 9, at 47.

[52] Generally see Chapter Four.

[53] Treaty with Kings and Chiefs of Old Calabar, 10 September 1884, 163 CTS 182. *Land and Maritime Boundary between Cameroon and Nigeria (Cameroon/Nigeria; Equatorial Guinea Intervening)* (2002) ICJ Rep 303, at 404.

[54] Ibid., at 405–406.

[55] Denial of non-European international legal personality also informed Judge Huber's reasoning the *Island of Palmas* Award, where he stated: 'As regards contracts between a State or a Company such as the Dutch East India Company and native princes or chiefs of people not recognized as members of the community of nations, they are not, in the international law sense, treaties or conventions capable of creating rights and obligations such as may, in international law, arise out of treaties.' *Island of Palmas Case* 1 RIAA 829; 4 ILR 3 [1928], at 858.

majority judgment as amounting to the 'recognition of political reality rather than...an application of the treaty and the relevant legal principles.'[56] Ranjeva characterised the Court's deference to inter-temporality through the 'following maxim: "in treaty relations with indigenous chiefs, *pacta non servanda sunt*".'[57] Judge Al-Khasawneh echoed these thoughts when he argued that the Court had erred in considering the general Berlin practice of protectorates and *Island of Palmas* notions of inter-temporality[58] rather than treaty interpretation.[59] Although these three judges from the Third World reached different conclusions about Nigeria's modern claim over the territory, they all strove to apply a law free from politics in the scramble for Africa. Such a stance is common amongst TWAIL I scholars as well, who have tended to find solace in law in contrast to 'political' acts of the colonial period.[60]

Difficulties of analysis regarding the colonial era are further compounded once the requirement of inter-temporality is factored in, and yet, as in the case of the modes of acquisition, dispute persists as to how past events should be interpreted for determining the present. The classic articulation of this rule was expressed by Judge Huber in the *Island of Palmas* Award, who considered the competing claims of the Netherlands and the United States over a deserted island:

> As regards the question which of different legal systems prevailing at successive periods is to be applied in a particular case (the so-called intertemporal law), a distinction must be made between the creation of rights and the existence of rights. The same principle which subjects the act creative of a right to the law in force at

[56] *(Cameroon/Nigeria; Equatorial Guinea Intervening)*, Koroma J. (dis. op.), at 476.

[57] *(Cameroon/Nigeria; Equatorial Guinea Intervening)*, Ranjeva J. (sep. op.), at 470.

[58] For example, he argues: 'support for the contention that treaties of protection in sub-Saharan Africa allowed generally for the transfer of sovereignty to the colonial/protecting Power cannot be safely established by reference to the Island of Palmas Award nor to the alleged practice of the Berlin Conference era, a practice from which, at best, no firm inferences can be drawn and which in fact supports retention of a normative distinction between colonies and the so-called colonial protectorates and the consequent upholding of the maxim *nemo dat quod non habet.*' *(Cameroon/Nigeria; Equatorial Guinea Intervening)*, Al-Khasawneh J. (sep. op.), at 499.

[59] 'Clearly, the crucial factor is the agreement itself, and whilst it is entirely possible that such agreements vested sovereignty in the newcomers it is equally possible that they did not, in which case sovereignty was retained by the local ruler under an agreed scheme of protection or administration. These are questions of treaty interpretation and of the subsequent practice of the parties and cannot be circumvented by the invention of a fictitious sub-category of protectorates termed "colonial protectorates" where title is assumed to pass automatically and regardless of the terms of the treaty of protection to the protecting Power, for that would be incompatible with the fundamental rule pacta sunt servanda and would lead to what has been termed "institutionalized treaty breach", a situation that no rule of intertemporal law has ever excused.' *(Cameroon/Nigeria; Equatorial Guinea Intervening)*, Al-Khasawneh J. (sep. op.), at 495.

[60] The basic attributes of TWAIL I scholarship are discussed in Chapter One, at 31–33.

> the time the right arises, demands that the existence of the right, in other words its continued manifestation, shall follow the conditions required by the evolution of law.[61]

This statement remains seminal for territorial disputes, but it has not always been applied uniformly by even the ICJ itself, as shown above in relation to Nigeria and Cameroon, as well as in Chapter Four. The rule requires a particular reading of the past and the evolution of legal norms and yet such a task is fraught with difficulty when applied to the colonial period. Should we regard colonial treaties, for example, as agreements between equal sovereigns or something else? Further, how should we approach the problem of coercion in the formation of these treaties? Both Shaw and Kaikobad adopt a pragmatic approach when they argue that we must accept colonial treaties and the rights they generated because *at the time* it was permissible to impose treaties through force.[62] Kaikobad argues that this position has largely been confirmed through the International Law Commission in its drafting of the Vienna Convention on the Law of Treaties,[63] which immunises the rights arising from boundary treaties *vis-à-vis jus cogens* and the rule of *rebus sic stantibus*.[64] Thus in an era when coercion shaping treaties was permitted, the legal ramifications can carry over into the postcolonial present.[65]

The most important device of temporality for postcolonial, and especially African, states has been the doctrine of *uti possidetis juris*.[66] The practice first emerged in nineteenth century Latin America in the wake of Spanish withdrawal and the creation of independent states. So as to preserve stability, these new states succeeded from the municipal lines of Spanish administration. More

61 *Island of Palmas Case* 1 RIAA 829; 4 ILR 3 [1928], at 845.

62 Shaw, *Title to Territory*, *supra* n. 9, at 43.

63 Vienna Convention on the Law of Treaties, 23 May 1969, 1155 UNTS 331. Especially see Articles: 52, 53, 62, 64, 71 & 72.

64 Thus, according to Kaikobad, 'a rule of law which does not inhibit the reopening of frontier questions, settled in an earlier period of time, on charges of coercion would not only constitute an invitation for fresh boundary claims, but would be inconsistent with the general underlying notions of continuity of boundaries presented in the context of State succession to boundary treaties and the proviso to the doctrine of *rebus sic stantibus*. The rule, however, in favour of the continuation of boundary treaties concluded in controversial circumstances at an earlier period of time emphasizes the view that boundary treaties and regimes have lasting effects and underlines again the importance of the doctrine of finality.' K. H. Kaikobad, 'Some Observations on the Doctrine of Continuity and Finality of Borders' (1984) 54 *British Yearbook of International Law* 119, at 136.

65 Ibid., at 134.

66 J. Castellino, 'Territory and Identity in International Law: The Struggle for Self-Determination in the Western Sahara' (1999) 28 *Millennium: Journal of International Studies* 523, at 527. For an extensive study of the norm's evolution, see Shaw, 'The Heritage of States', *supra* n. 8.

recently, this principle of stability was confirmed in Asia in the *Temple* case as well as the *Rann of Kutch Arbitration*.[67] On the eve of decolonisation, African elites soon grasped the value of supporting such a norm, and it was confirmed in the heydays of independence both in the Organisation of African Union's (OAU) Charter as well as the 1964 Cairo Declaration.[68] Despite increasing African dispute settlement reliant on the norm, as epitomised by the *Frontier Dispute* and the *Benin/Niger* case,[69] numerous writers question its validity and long-term value.[70] Functionally, the virtues of stability are constantly invoked,[71] and yet the norm

> creates states by establishing new identities within rigid boundaries, the preservation of which are not always feasible, and, as evidenced by modern break-ups, that it transforms internal boundaries to international ones with disregard for any viable interconnection between the internal border and the forging or maintenance of national unity.[72]

Further, the norm not only gives legitimacy to acts 'purely on the basis that those acts occurred during the colonial era';[73] in fact, it aids the interests of contemporary domination, through the consolidation of the 'territorial state'.[74]

---

[67] Brownlie, 'Boundary Problems', *supra* n. 2, at 189. *Case Concerning the Temple of Preah Vihear (Cambodia/Thailand)* (1962) I.C.J. Reps., p. 6; and *Case Concerning the Indo-Pakistan Western Boundary (India/Pakistan)*, Arbitral Award of 19 February 1968, (1968) ILM 633.

[68] Resolution AHG/Res.16(1), on Border Disputes Among African States, adopted by the First Ordinary Session of the Assembly of Heads of State and Government in Cairo, 21 July 1964. See M. N. Shaw, 'Peoples, Territories and Boundaries' (1997) 8 *European Journal of International Law* 478, at 494. The principle of *uti possidetis* also appears in Article III (3) of the AOU Charter and paragraph 7 of the preamble. T. Maluwa, 'International Law-Making in Post-Colonial Africa: The Role of the Organization of African Unity' (2002) *Netherlands International Law Review* 81, at 94–95. All African states supported the *uti possidetis* doctrine except Somalia and Morocco. Somalia called for Greater Somalia at the OAU's opening session in May 1963 and Morocco 'reserved its position with regard to Article 3(3) of the OAU Charter.' J. Klabbers & R. Lefeber, 'Africa: Lost between Self-Determination and *uti possidetis*', C Brölmann et al. (eds.), *Peoples and Minorities in International Law* (Dordrecht; Boston: Kluwer, 1993), 37–76, at 58.

[69] *Frontier Dispute (Burkina Faso/Mali)* (1986) ICJ Rep. 554; *Case Concerning the Frontier Dispute (Benin/Niger)* (2005) ICJ Rep. 90.

[70] Especially, see Castellino, *supra* n. 66, at 527; Castellino & Allen, *supra* n. 33.

[71] Oduntan argues that 'it would appear that African States are more inclined towards the view that "good fences make good neighbours"'. G. Oduntan, 'The Demarcation of Straddling Villages in Accordance with the International Court of Justice Jurisprudence: The Cameroon-Nigeria Experience' (2006) *Chinese Journal of International Law* 79, at 99.

[72] Castellinio & Allen, *supra* n. 33, at 21.

[73] R. McCorquodale & R. Pangalangan, 'Pushing Back the Limitations of Territorial Boundaries' (2001) 12 *European Journal of International Law* 867, at 876.

[74] Shaw uses the term, 'territorial state' to describe most African states, which were created through territorial lines rather than strong social and cultural bonds usually associated with nation-states. Shaw, *Title to Territory, supra* n. 9, at 186.

Colonialism and postcolonialism take on unnerving similarities with *uti possidetis*, because it 'legitimates the action of civil officers, typically situated in foreign officers in metropolitan capitals in the middle of the nineteenth and twentieth century, who have essentially shaped the identities and destinies of colonial peoples.'[75] Given these problems, it is not surprising that several scholars from Africa suggest that 'the time for flogging dead paradigms is long past.'[76] Mutua further asserts that 'these concepts and principles may have trapped Africa in a detrimental time capsule; they now seem to be straitjackets with timebombs ready to explode.'[77]

Irrespective of these criticisms, it appears that *uti possidetis* is now firmly grounded in the practice of African states, but is this also true of Arab states? Again, discursive boundary-drawing is required in answering such a question, and here we return to the Introduction of the book and its definition of the Arab world.[78] The Arab world geographically straddles both the Asian and African continents; the cases reflect this division with Chapters Three and Five arising in Africa and Chapters Four and Six from Asia. To an extent, Arab states have been able to pick and choose different regional affiliations and priorities, as shown by Libya in Chapter Three.[79] Although it is simplistic to speak of Arab-African and Arab-Asian states, it is nevertheless clear that Arab states on the African continent have a much closer connection with the norm of *uti possidetis juris*. It is now possible to hold that *uti possidetis juris* is a regional customary norm in both Latin America and Africa, whereas the matter is unsettled in the case of Asia.[80] Because of African support for the norm, some commentators now argue that it has taken on universal relevance, but we need to look carefully at Arab practice.[81] The dispute between Qatar and Bahrain discussed in

[75] Castellino & Allen, *supra* n. 33, at 22. This idea of control from the city in the colonial and postcolonial periods is also noted by Herbst: 'The resemblance between the rule of control of the capitals of the Europeans' rule of effective control through protectorates is, of course, not accidental. Indeed, control of the capital is today simply the minimal level of government presence that the Europeans first defined at the Berlin Congo Conference.' Herbst, *supra* n. 34, at 687.

[76] Udombana, *supra* n. 21, at 59.

[77] M. Mutua, 'Why Redraw the Map of Africa: A Moral and Legal Inquiry' (1994–1995) 16 *Michigan Journal of International Law* 1113, at 1114.

[78] Discussed at 5–8.

[79] Discussed at 132–138.

[80] According to Ratner, 'the repeated assumption by the Court that *uti possidetis* is a norm of international law is probative. Without definitely opining on the issue, one may thus assume some support for regarding *uti possidetis* as a norm of regional customary law in Latin America and Africa, if not a general norm as well, in the context of decolonization.' S. R. Ratner, 'Drawing a Better Line: Uti Possidetis and the Borders of New States' (1996) 90 *American Journal of International Law* 590, at 598–599.

[81] For example, see G. N. Barrie, 'Uti Possidetis versus Self-Determination and Modern International Law: In Africa the Chickens are Coming Home to Roost' (1988) *Tijoskrif vir die*

Chapter Four explores this issue and suggests that the norm is not applicable in the Gulf. Thus, the arguments sustained in Arab territorial disputes need to be understood in the context of an emerging, but far from settled deference, to the *uti possidetis* norm.

Before finishing our overview of contentious Third World territorial adjudication, we need to consider the role of equity and the relevance of geography in ICJ jurisprudence. The Court's docket has included not only territorial but also maritime matters, and many cases actually combine these considerations in adjudication. Through a number of cases, the ICJ has developed the role of equity in maritime delimitations. Given that continental shelf and territorial cases share many similarities, it is surprising how states have shunned all resort to equity in territorial cases. The Award rendered in the *Eritrea/Yemen* arbitration is an example of equity's application to mixed maritime and territorial matters,[82] but aside from cautious application of equity *infra legem* in the *Frontier Dispute*,[83] the ICJ remains loathe to extend its jurisprudence in such a way.[84] The ICJ is limited by the wishes of the Parties, and so it would seem that

---

Suid-Afrikaanse Reg 451, at 453. Klabbers & Lefeber, *supra* n. 68, at 54, fn 69. *Taba* Arbitration (Egypt/Israel) (1989) 80 ILR 224. Cf the treatment of *uti possidetis* in the more recent arbitration between Yemen and Eritrea: Award of the Arbitral Tribunal in the First Stage of the Proceedings, Territorial Sovereignty and Scope of the Dispute (*Eritrea/Yemen*), 9 October 1998, at paras. 96–99.

[82] *Award of the Arbitral Tribunal in the Second Stage of the Proceedings, Maritime Delimitation (Eritrea/Yemen)*, 17 December 1999. This arbitration is contrasted with the Qatar/Bahrain dispute in Chapter Four. Klabbers & Lefeber suggest that the norm has now because accepted in the 'Middle East' too and they cite the *Taba* arbitration (especially Arbitrator Lapidoth's dissent) for this conclusion.

[83] *Frontier Dispute (Burkina Faso/Mali)* (1986) ICJ Rep 554, at 567–568.

[84] It is worth quoting the ICJ in the *Frontier Dispute* at length on this point:

> [T]he Chamber can resort to that equity *infra legem* which both Parties have recognized as being applicable in this case... In this respect the guiding concept is simply that 'Equity as a legal concept is a direct emanation of the idea of justice' *(Continental Shelf (Tunisia/Libyan Arab Jamahiriya)*, ICJ Reps 1982, p. 60, para. 71). The Chamber would however stress more generally that to resort to the concept of equity in order to modify an established frontier would be quite unjustified. Especially in the African context, the obvious deficiencies of many frontiers inherited from colonization, from the ethnic, geographical or administrative standpoint, cannot support an assertion that the modification of these frontiers is necessary or justifiable on the ground of considerations of equity. These frontiers, however unsatisfactory they may be, possess the authority of the uti possidetis and are thus fully in conformity with contemporary international law. Apart form the case of a decision *ex aequo et bono* reached with the assent of the Parties, it is not a matter of finding simply an equitable solution, but an equitable solution derived from the applicable law (*Fisheries Jurisdiction*, ICJ Reps 1974, p. 33, para. 78).

Frontier Dispute (Burkina Faso/Mali) (1986) ICJ Rep 554, at 633. Cf. Koskennieimi, who suggests that adjudicative examples illustrate how tribunals are quite open to the equitable balancing of interests. Koskenniemi, *From Apology to Utopia, supra* n. 19, at 262–266.

both postcolonial states and the Court have favoured the certainty and stability assured through devices such as European treaty law, *uti possidetis* and effective occupation. Given that territorial cases often involve the apportionment of land with natural resources, there is a compelling argument to raise about the need for the sharing of resources, especially in relation to poor, postcolonial states. Despite this, it would seem that postcolonial states are willing to take a gamble and stake their claims purely on 'law', rather than broader, perhaps 'political', factors invoked *ex aequo et bono*.

In territorial disputes, extreme geographical and climactic factors can modify the general requirements for effective control, but in its jurisprudence the Court has not been willing to stray far from the familiar strictures of the European nation-state. Both in polar regions and deserts,[85] the Court has acknowledged that evidence of *effectivités* will not be as systematic and widespread as in well-populated, temperate environments. The jurisprudence still favours a particular model of state control, however, so that differences in *effectivités* can only be of degree and not kind. This will be highlighted in the *Western Sahara* case in Chapter Five,[86] where the Court downplayed cultural and geographical factors to hold that instances of Moroccan and Mauritanian control were less than sovereign. Similarly, in the *Kasikili/Sedudu Island* Case Namibian arguments about the presence of indigenous tribes were found to have no bearing on the Caprivi Strip title.[87] In dissent, Judge Weeramantry adopted a contextually sensitive approach to this matter when he held that we

---

[85] For example in relation to Greenland, the PCIJ pointed out: 'It is impossible to read the records of the decisions in cases as to territorial sovereignty without observing that in many cases the tribunal has been satisfied with very little in the way of the actual exercise of sovereign rights, provided that the other State could not make out a superior claim. *This is particularly true in the case of claims to sovereignty over areas in thinly populated or unsettled countries.*' Emphasis added, *Legal Status of Eastern Greenland* (Denmark/Norway) [1933] P.C.I.J., Ser. A./B., No. 53, at 46. For a discussion of the impact of harsh conditions on proving control over territory also see Award of the Arbitral Tribunal in the First Stage of the Proceedings, Territorial Sovereignty and Scope of the Dispute (*Eritrea/Yemen*), 9 October 1998, at paras. 446–454.

[86] *Western Sahara (Advisory Opinion)* (1975) ICJ Rep 37.

[87] According to the majority, 'there is nothing that shows...that this presence was linked to territorial claims by the Caprivi authorities. It is, moreover, not uncommon for the inhabitants of border regions in Africa to traverse such borders for purposes of agriculture and grazing without raising concern on the part of the authorities on either side of the border...[75] The Court concludes...that the peaceful and public use of Kasikili/Sedudu Island, over a period of many years, by Masubia tribesman from the Eastern Caprivi does not constitute "subsequent practice in the application of the [1890] treaty" within the meaning of Article 31, paragraph 3 (b), of the Vienna Convention on the Law of Treaties.' *Kasikili/Sedudu Island (Botswana/Namibia)* (1999) ICJ Rep 1045, at paras. 74–75. For a TWAIL analysis of the case, see J. T. Gathii, 'Geographical Hegelianism in Territorial Disputes Involving Non-European Land Relations: An Analysis of the *Case Concerning Kasikili/Sedudu Island (Botswana/Namibia)*' (2002) 15 *Leiden Journal of International Law* 581.

> must not look for indicia of occupation in terms of settled housing or ordered agriculture...for the very nature of this terrain prevented settled habitation in the manner known to Western jurisprudence and tradition. At best there would have been temporary occupation...from time to time as the rains and the climate determined.[88]

Because of these conditions

> Concepts of settled occupation, in default of which a territory is deemed unoccupied and even *res nullius*, which traditional principles of international have led us to expect, must consequently be discarded [in this matter].[89]

Such sensibilities are invoked throughout the pleadings discussed in the cases below, yet rarely has the Court modified its legal findings to reflect such a perspective.

Although the Court operates within a well-established jurisprudential and institutional framework, there are still a number of ways of determining territorial disputes between postcolonial states, especially when the parties introduce experiences contrary to the European tradition. Successful contentious adjudication rests on a seamless integration of doctrine, history and fact set within the context of ICJ practice and rules. The discussion above has highlighted how territorial cases are about much more than well-informed doctrinal positions and legocentric perspectives. More importantly, they are about a party's ability to present their arguments in ways that preserve a distinction between law and politics with sufficient reference and deference to the jurisprudential heritage of the Court. This reflects Shalakany's findings on Third World arbitration as discussed in Chapter One.[90] We can now test these propositions in relation to the African territorial dispute between Libya and Chad in the following chapter.

---

[88] *Kasikili/Sedudu Island (Botswana/Namibia)* (1999) ICJ Rep 1045, Weeramantry J. (diss. op.), at para. 31.

[89] Ibid., at para. 32.

[90] A. A. Shalakany, 'Arbitration and the Third World: A Plea for Reassessing Bias under the Specter of Neoliberalism' (2000) 41 *Harvard International Law Journal* 419. Discussed at 38–39.

Chapter Three

Sanctioning Colonial Legacies in the Sahara? The Construction of Postcolonial Selfhood in the Libya/Chad *Territorial Dispute*[1]

1) *Introduction*

On 3 February 1994 far from the mountainous and sandy expanses of the central Sahara, the ICJ brought the protracted conflict between Libya and Chad to an end by ruling that the Aouzou Strip separating the two states was part of Chad. Responses to the ruling were swift; under UN auspices, Libyan troops withdrew from the territory and aside from occasional flights of rhetoric by Libya's leader, Qadhāfi, it would seem that the Court has resolved a postcolonial conflict of the most complex kind.[2] Many other methods of dispute resolution had failed to quieten neighbourly hostilities, prompting speculation about how and why international law could succeed where military conflict, regional institutions and negotiations had failed. These background factors were overlooked by the Court in its judgment, but they will be revisited throughout the chapter to explore how the parties as well as the Court drew boundaries, not only in the sand, but more importantly, between 'law' and 'politics'. Representations of the relationship between law and politics diverged considerably, and so this Case is an ideal site in which to explore the discursive options available to postcolonial states in the courtroom. Given that this research is concerned with mapping legal grammars at play in ICJ territorial adjudication, the main task of this chapter will be to evaluate patterns of argumentation employed by the Court and the parties. What does the grammar of international law proscribe for states speaking

---

[1] *Case Concerning the Territorial Dispute (Libyan Arab Jamahiriya/Chad)* (1994) ICJ Reps, p. 6, hereinafter *Libya/Chad*.

[2] Under Resolution 915, the UN Security Council established the United Nations Aouzou Strip Observer Group (UNASOG) and under Resolution 926 in June 1994, UNASOG's mandate was terminated on the successful withdrawal of Libyan troops. J. G. Merrills, 'The International Court of Justice and the Adjudication of Territorial and Boundary Disputes' (2000) 13 *Leiden Journal of International Law* 873, at 900.

about the relationship between 'law' and 'politics' and which words or lexicon can be used in such an endeavour?

Perhaps more than any other ICJ case in this book, the *Territorial Dispute* captures the postcolonial paradox confronting Third World states in their resort to international law. Parties in ICJ disputes enter a courtroom where a number of cases about title to territory have already been heard. The law applied in such cases is largely a product of European experiences of statehood; ideas of effective control, international legal personality and the validity of treaties are all framed through the prism of European dominance and predominance during the colonial period as discussed in this Part's introduction. For Third World states forged out of the colonial context, a dilemma emerges: to what extent should the postcolonial state be constituted through colonial practice and colonial history? Can postcolonial states escape the structuring device of colonialism? Libya and Chad answered these questions in diametrically opposed ways. On the one hand, Libya sought to subvert colonial legacies through an historical survey that characterised Ottoman and indigenous occupation as having continuing *legal* relevance for its title over the Aouzou Strip. Libya demonstrated how historical arguments lie at the heart of legal constructions of both personality and territory. Chad's presentation, on the other hand, is marked 'par l'absence de toute d'arguments d'ordre historique'.[3] Instead of offering an account of pre-colonial selfhood, Chad relied solely on colonial practice in the hope of succeeding to French title through colonial treaties. The Court fulfilled these Chadian hopes by delivering a judgment confined to questions of treaty interpretation. In fact, the language of limitation is regularly invoked in the judgment, suggesting a bench at pains to defend itself against the disruptive ramifications of Libya's 'politicised' position.

What were the implications of Libya's position, and why did the Court reject these ideas so stridently through its silence? The division between successful and unsuccessful adjudicative strategies suggests that the Court did not understand the language spoken by Libya; Libya had transgressed the boundaries of suitable argument and was deemed incompetent for this reason. Libya's claims challenged prevailing understandings about international law's past by offering alternative approaches to international legal personality under colonialism. More disturbingly for proponents of postcolonial stability in Africa, it questioned the value of a blind acceptance of *uti possidetis*. Could Libya have succeeded if it had toned down its arguments, or was its failure grammatically pre-determined by a language premised on the law/politics dichotomy and postcolonialism's

[3] M. Koskenniemi, 'L'affaire du différend territorial (Jamahiriya Arabe Libyenne c. Tchad) Arrêt de la Cour Internationale de Justice du 3 février 1994' (1994) 40 *Annuaire français de droit international* 442, at 453.

rupture with the past? To answer these questions, the chapter will first outline the judgment of the Court and then contrast the competing claims of Chad and Libya to determine why the Court took the position it did. Although the Court focussed on Chad's claims, the chapter seeks to redress this discrepancy by engaging with some of Libya's discursive strategies. Ideas about non-European legal personality, Islamic authority over territory and the policy implications of *uti possidetis* were at the heart of Libya's case, and these themes are also of central importance in Chapters Four and Five. Before exploring the dynamics of discourse at The Hague, however, the chapter begins in the Sahara.

2) *Corsairs, Camels and Caliphs: Historical and Geographical Background*

The frontier between Libya and Chad not only separates these two modern states; it has also signified divisions between north and 'sub-Saharan' Africa as well as well as between Arab north and 'black' southern Africa.[4] These boundaries are fluid and contested, but it is important to recognise that conceptual lines scar the map of Africa as much as the many arbitrary borders that arose out of colonialism.[5] Arab states to the north thus face choices about identity and allegiance and nowhere is this better reflected than in Libya, which has supported a number of pan-Arab and pan-African causes.[6] Is it best to consider the Maghreb states as part of the Arab world, or part of Africa, or is it best to do

---

[4] Chad covers three climactic zones: desert, savannah and sahel. For a fascinating account of the often artificial construction of racial boundaries in the Sahara, see B. S. Hall, 'The Question of "Race" in the Pre-colonial Southern Sahara' (2005) 10 *Journal of North African Studies* 339.

[5] Lydon attributes the discourse of a divided Africa to colonialism and calls for its end. 'Still a glaring knowledge gap currently impedes our understanding of African continental history and its place in world history. The African divide, product of division and conquest, is only now being questioned in the context of a current rethinking of African history. Ultimately, new meaning-making terminologies are necessary not only to bring the Sahara back into African Studies, but also to transcend the colonial legacy of ethnographic labels which have divided the continent between "white" or 'North Africa, and "black" or so-called Sub-Saharan Africa. It is lamentable that most Africanists, like their Middle East counterparts, remain ill-prepared to understand, let alone explain, the so-called 'Arab-Africa dichotomy' in situations such as the violent repression of Darfurians in the recent history of the Sudan.' This ongoing division of Africa is evident in TWAIL scholarship as well which tends to overlook Arab experiences altogether and instead, usually studies 'Africa', which is mostly southern Africa or the sub-continent. G. Lydon, 'Writing Trans-Saharan History: Methods, Sources and Interpretations across the African Divide' (2005) 10 *Journal of North African Studies 293*, at 315.

[6] An example is the Tripoli based Community of Saharan and Sahelian States (CEN-SAD), http://www.cen-sad.org/, G. Joffé, 'Libya's Saharan Destiny' (2005) 10 *Journal of North African Studies* 605, at 613. Less tangible examples include the many proposals of Libya's leader, Qadhāfī, over

away with such categories altogether? At least in the case of Chad, the answer must be the latter. As an exemplar of Shaw's African 'territorial state',[7] Chad is very much a product of colonialism: comprising over 200 ethnic groups,[8] there is no unified nation to speak of. Further, like its neighbour to the north, Arabic is an official language, and yet it would seem that other Arab states have drawn the boundary of the Arab world to Chad's north. Chad is not a member of the Arab League and is rarely classified along Arab lines.[9] Like other Third World states, Chad has experienced many teething problems, and its fervent support for colonial boundaries in Africa must be understood within the context of regional affiliations in the African Union (AU).

As we saw in this Part's introduction, *uti possidetis* is particularly important in Africa today, but does this encompass Africa *in toto* or is it of greater relevance in states like Chad which came into existence under colonialism? Is the norm less relevant for those Arab states, such as Libya, with a history of state formation, or are the porous borders common throughout the Arab world as amenable to finality as those in central and southern Africa? These questions are useful to consider in the context of Chadian and Libyan identity construction.

Historically, the Sahara has served as an important source of division, not only for the constitution of 'Arabness' but also for the allocation of international legal personality. With its sands criss-crossed by a complex of caravan routes, the Sahara was far from unimportant for African trade and culture. Yet, its harsh conditions precluded widespread communication between Mediterranean and communities south of the Sahara. In the pre-modern era, Europe was more familiar with peoples to the north of the Sahara, and treaties were established with the 'Barbary' powers in Algiers, Tripoli, Tunis and Morocco from the

---

the years, including the revival of a Fatīmid state across the Maghreb; and the elimination of borders across Africa, as advocated in 2008 in Ghana or earlier efforts at pan-Arabism.

7 M. N. Shaw, *Title to Territory in Africa: International Legal Issues* (Oxford: Clarendon Press, 1986), at 186.

8 R. W. McKeon, Jr, 'The Aouzou Strip: Adjudication of Competing Territorial Claims in Africa by the International Court of Justice' (1991) 23 *Case Western Reserve Journal of International Law* 147, at 148.

9 According to Wright, more Chadians speak Arabic than French (the other official language). 'But Chadian Arabs have not really become part of the political concept of the "Arab World", or are even generally accepted as such in the way that even the superficially Arabised non-Arab peoples of Somalia and Djibouti have been since they joined the Arab League in the 1970s. For Chad's Arabs are, for a national minority, perhaps too closely inbred with other, non-Arab neighbours, and at the same time too remote from the mainstream of modern Arab culture, society and politics to be able to claim a recognised place in the "Nasserist" Arab nation, despite Gadafi's expressed belief in the essential unity of the "Arab" peoples of Chad and Libya.' J. Wright, *Libya, Chad and the Central Sahara* (London: Hurst, 1989), at 137.

sixteenth century.[10] The exact status of the Barbary Powers was unclear; these states were not part of the Concert of Europe in the nineteenth century, but, equally, writers distinguished them at the time from southern African entities. For example, in 1801, Admirality judge, Sir Scott, stated:

> Certain it is, that the African states [of the north]...have long acquired the character of established governments, with whom we have regular treaties, acknowledging and confirming to them the relations of legal states...although their notions of international justice differ from those which we entertain we do not on that account venture to call in question their public acts.[11]

At the very least, this degree of recognition would preclude later European arguments based on *terra nullius* that were applied to other parts of Africa.

The exact status of northern Africa was further complicated on the eve of the Berlin Conference in 1885 because of Ottoman claims to the territories. For example, the Ottomans had established the Regency of Tripoli in 1551 after defeating the Knights of Malta.[12] Control of Ottoman Libya gradually fell into the hands of a locally-based monarchy, the Qaramanlıs,[13] thus becoming a vassal principality of the Ottomans until Europe began to challenge Ottoman interests across the continent.[14] By the end of the nineteenth century the Ottomans had increased their military and administrative presence in the region, and in 1899 the Sublime Porte also issued a hinterland claim to Tripolitania in a bid to halt European claims to lands north of Lake Chad. Such declarations did not dissuade Italian and French appetites for long, though. By 1912, the Sublime Porte signed the Treaty of Ouchy passing its interests on to Italy, and it lost all territorial claims on its defeat in the First World War, as confirmed by the 1923 Treaty of Lausanne.[15]

As former Italian and French colonies respectively, Libya and Chad were well aware of the colonial rivalries they had inherited as independent states in 1951 and 1960, but confrontation over the Aouzou Strip remained latent for

[10] J. A. Andrews, 'The Concept of Statehood and the Acquisition of Territory in the Nineteenth Century' (1978) 94 *Law Quarterly Review* 408, at 413. See also Libya, Memorial, 26 August 1991, at para. 4.08

[11] *The Helena* (1801) 4 Rob. 3, 5–6; 165 E.R. 515, quoted in Andrews, ibid., at 414.

[12] L. Anderson, 'Nineteenth-Century Reform in Ottoman Libya' (1984) 16 *International Journal of Middle East Studies* 325, at 326.

[13] See generally A. A. Ahmida, *The Making of Modern Libya: State Formation, Colonization, and Reisistance, 1830–1932* (New York: State University of New York, 1994), at 20–41.

[14] For a discussion of the Barbary states' relationship with the Sublime Porte, see S. Faroqhi, *The Ottoman Empire and the World Around It* (London: I. B. Tauris, 2004), at 82–84.

[15] Treaty of Ouchy between the Ottoman Empire and Italy, 15 October 1912, *Libya/Chad* Case, Libya, Memorial, 1991, International Accords and Agreements Annex, vol. 2, no. 10; Treaty of Peace with Turkey (Treaty of Lausanne), 24 July 1923, no. 701, 28 LNTS 13.

the first few decades after independence. In a context where new African states were eager to solidify colonial borders for the sake of stability, no mention was made of competing claims to the territory; instead, both states faced surmountable problems at home. Chad in particular was wracked by intermittent civil strife,[16] which was often fuelled by Qadhāfī-lead Libya after its coup of 1969.[17] The Libya-Chad borderlands were home to a number of largely autonomous Arabic-speaking tribes, and their allegiances and assistance was sought in the various factional struggles that tore at the fabric of the Chadian state.[18] Partly in response to the instability spilling across these disputed borders, Libyan troops invaded the Aouzou Strip in 1973, and from 1983 until 1987 'Qadhafi's regime conducted a broad intervention ranging from significant financial and military support for various armed factions within Chad to large-scale involvement of Libyan armed forces.'[19] At various moments, Chad had invoked the support of the UN, France and the OAU (Organisation of African Unity) against Libyan aggression.[20] Libya was anxious to retain its standing in the African regional context, and so it finally ended its 'most significant external involvement'[21] by withdrawing its forces in 1987. Two years later, Libya and Chad entered into an agreement or *Accord-Cadre*[22] on 31 August 1989, which built on earlier UN and OAU efforts to resolve the conflict peacefully. The avenue of ICJ adjudication was countenanced as a last resort if the matter was not successfully resolved in 'approximately one year', and Libya exercised this right by a letter to the Court on 31 August 1990.[23] Thus, after a century of competing claims by powers near and far as well as rich and poor, a determination was sought to settle territorial claims in a comprehensive, legal manner.

---

[16] M.-J. Deeb, *Libya's Foreign Policy in North Africa* (Boulder: Westview Press, 1991), at 83–84; 129–133.

[17] For an overview of the 1969 revolution, see R. Owen, *State, Power and Politics in the Making of the Modern Middle East* (London: Routledge, 2nd edition, 2000), at 59–62.

[18] McKeon, *supra* n. 8, at 155.

[19] A. Huliaras, 'Qadhafi's Comeback: Libya and Sub-Saharan African in the 1990s' (2001) 100 *African Affairs* 5 at 7.

[20] It was not until 1977 that Chad raised the issue of Libya's presence in the Aouzou Strip. 'Finally, on October 30, 1987, the O.A.U. convened an *ad hoc* committee to determine the nationality of the Aouzou Strip.' After a failure to resolve the dispute, momentum grew for other options, such as taking the matter to the ICJ. McKeon, *supra* n. 8, at 156–157. For an overview of the OAU peacekeeping role in Chad role, see R. May & S. Massey, 'The OAU Intervention in Chad: Mission Impossible or Mission Evaded?' (1998) 5 *International Peacekeeping* 46.

[21] Huliaras, *supra* n. 19, at 6.

[22] Available on ICJ website, http://www.icj-cij.org/docket/files/83/6687.pdf.

[23] For a brief sketch of events surrounding Libya's application to the ICJ, see generally, Huliaras, *supra* n. 19, at 9–10.

Aside from Libya's record of aggression towards its southern and much poorer neighbour, other extra-curial factors deserve attention here. As in the case of *Qatar v Bahrain*,[24] mineral wealth lay at the crux of the dispute's modern manifestation, but the parties and the Court did not choose to focus their attention on possible uranium deposits[25] and only made passing reference to Libyan intervention in Chad's civil unrest. Another significant factor influencing Libyan foreign policy at the time was its pariah-status as a result of the Lockerbie incident and UNSC-imposed sanctions, which were only lifted in 2003.[26] On the one hand, it might have seemed strange for Libya to come before the Court in the midst of such difficulties with Western powers. Its alleged connection with international terrorism and its aggression against Chad must have weighed on the minds of the ICJ's members in reaching their judgment.[27] On the other hand, however, Libya has been one of the most active Third World states at the ICJ, and in two earlier cases of delimitation the Court had ruled in its favour.[28] Perhaps in

---

[24] See the following chapter.

[25] Both Huliaras and McKeon discuss the presence of unexploited mineral reserves in the Aouzou Strip, including phosphate and uranium: Huliaras, *supra* n. 19, at 7 & McKeon, *supra* n. 8, at 147. Dunoff et al., on the other hand, argue that there was no economic potential, suggesting either that they are unaware of these uranium deposits (which is possible given that there is such scant mention of this factor in the legal literature) or that they do not regard this as an important resource. J. L. Dunoff et al., *International Law Norms, Actors, Process: A Problem-Oriented Approach* (New York: Aspen, 2002), at 3. It is interesting to note that in its opening address to the Court, Libya referred to its participation in other ICJ contentious cases to demonstrate how judicial settlement had formed the basis of natural resource exploitation between Libya and Tunisia: 'Not only did the Court in that case settle the dispute and restore peace to the region but its decision also opened the way to mutually beneficial development of resources.' Libya/Chad, CR 1993/14, 14 June 1993, Libya, Mr El-Obeidi, p. 18. Libya's faith in adjudication over natural resources was in stark contrast to its earlier arbitral experiences, as explored by Shalakany: A. A. Shalakany, 'Arbitration and the Third World: A Plea for Reassessing Bias under the Specter of Neoliberalism' (2000) 41 *Harvard International Law Journal* 419; I discuss Shalakany's ideas briefly in Chapter One, at 38–39.

[26] After Libya refused to hand over two of its nationals implicated in the 1988 bombing of a Pan-Am airliner over the town of Lockerbie, Scotland, the US and UK orchestrated UNSC sanctions: UNSC Resolution 748, 31 March 1992; UNSC Resolution 883, 11 November 1993. Sanctions were revoked under UNSC Resolution 1505, 12 December 2003. For an overview of the sanctions regime through a focus on legitimacy, see I. Hurd, *After Anarchy: Legitimacy and Power in the United Nations Security Council* (Princeton: Princeton University Press, 2007), at ch. 6.

[27] According to Koskenniemi, 'parmi les facteurs qui peuvent avoir influé directement sur le decision de la Cour, on trouve aussi le fait que la Libye était considérée comme un État à l'écart de la société internationale; a joué également un rôle le comportement antérieur de la Libye dans la bande d'Aouzou.' Koskenniemi, *supra* n. 3, at 457.

[28] *Case Concerning the Continental Shelf (Tunisia/Libyan Arab Jamahiriya)* (1982) ICJ Reps p. 18; *Case Concerning the Continental Shelf (Libyan Arab Jamahiriya/Malta)* (1985) ICJ Reps p. 13;

the Peace Palace, Libya could retreat from political pressures and advance its interests not through military means but through the arguments of its Western legal team.

3) *The Need for Certainty and Simplicity: The ICJ on Treaty Interpretation and the Finality of Borders*

Unlike its other successes as an ICJ litigant, Libya's arguments were dismissed by the Court in preference for Chad's position when it handed down its judgment in 1994. Although the judgment carefully constructed a legal edifice based on reliable principles and rules, its outcomes and policy motivations extend far beyond the confines of possible legal precedent. The judgment unequivocally endorsed the practices of the colonial past and reinforced colonial continuities by supporting the sanctity of European-created borders. The lengthy material presented by the parties provided the Court with an excellent opportunity to examine a number of controversial and unsettled areas of law.[29] Chad in particular opined that 'l'arrêt que rendra la Cour a une importance fondementale, non seulement pour le Tchad et la Libye, mais aussi pour la région et l'ensemble de l'Afrique.'[30] The Court was able to provide Chad with the ultimate assurance in confirming its claims over Libya's. However, the Court failed to respond to many of the issues raised in the pleadings. This section will provide a brief overview of the issues relating to jurisdiction, some of the basic claims of the parties, as well as treaty interpretation, before discussing the wider ramifications of the judgment. Throughout the discussion primary attention will be placed on the majority decision, but the two separate opinions of Judges Shahabuddeen and Ajibola, the declaration of Judge Ago, as well as Judge Sette-Camara's (judge *ad hoc* for Libya) dissent will be used as a point of contrast.

Despite an unusually straightforward acceptance of the Court's jurisdiction, the parties were divided over the scope of the Court's enquiry into 'their territorial dispute'.[31] Jurisdiction flowed from the fact that both 'Parties accepted

and *Application for Revision and Interpretation of the Judgment of 24 February 1982 in the Case Concerning the Continental Shelf (Tunisia/Libyan Arab Jamahiriya)* (1985) ICJ Reps p. 192. Joffé, 'Libya's Saharan Destiny', *supra* n. 6, at 609.

29 Eight seminal concerns overlooked by the Court are listed in C. J. Argüello-Gomez, 'Some Procedural and Substantive Aspects of the *Libya/Chad* Case' (1996) 9 *Leiden Journal of International Law* 167, at 172.

30 Chad, Memorial, 26 August 1991, p. 382.

31 The Court quoting Article 2 of the *Accord-Cadre*, at para. 18.

the jurisdiction of the Court on the basis of the [1989] Accord-Cadre'.[32] The *Accord-Cadre*, however, was vague enough to allow Libya to present the dispute as a territorial one requiring delimitation,[33] whereas Chad's reliance on the dispositive effect of the 1955 Treaty resulting in its call for the Court to demarcate a boundary already determined;[34] attribution of territory was outside of the Court's brief. The Court decided to address this discrepancy through a

---

[32] *Libya/Chad*, para. 22. It should be noted that Chad had proposed a subsidiary basis for jurisdiction, claiming in its letter to the Court that its jurisdiction 'is also based upon Article 8 of the Franco-Libyan Treaty of Friendship and Good Neighbourliness of 10 August 1955, 162 BFSP 470, which provides that: "Any disputes arising from the interpretation and application of the present Treaty, and which it has not been possible to settle by direct negotiation, shall be referred to the International Court of Justice at the request of either Party, unless the High Contracting Parties agree on another mode of settlement." Letter from the Minister for Foreign Relations of the Republic of Chad to the Registrar of the International Court of Justice, 1 September 1990, available from the ICJ website: www.icj-cji.org. On the other hand 'Libya regards the Accord-Cadre as the sole basis of jurisdiction.' Libya, Memorial, 26 August 1991, at 20.

[33] Libya claimed the following:

> That there exists no boundary, east of Toummo, between Libya and Chad by virtue of any existing international agreement.
> That in the circumstances, therefore, in deciding upon the attribution of the respective territories as between Libya and Chad in accordance with the rules of international law applicable in the matter, the following factors are relevant:
> That the territory in question, at all relevant times, was not terra nullius;
> That title to the territory, at all relevant times, vested in the peoples inhabiting the territory, who were tribes or other peoples owing allegiance to the Senoussi Order who had accepted the Senoussi leadership in their fight against the encroachments of France and Italy on their lands;
> That these indigenous peoples, were, at all relevant times, religiously, culturally, economically and politically part of the Libyan peoples;
> That, on the international plane, there existed a community of title between the title of the indigenous peoples and the rights and titles of the Ottoman Empire, passed on to Italy in 1912 and inherited by Italy in 1951;
> That any claim of Chad rests on the claim inherited from France;
> That the French claim to the area in dispute rested on 'actes internationaux' that did not create a territorial boundary east of Toummo, and there is no valid alternative basis to support the French claim to the area in dispute.
> 3. That, in the light of the above facts, Libya has clear title to all the territory north of the line shown on Map 105 in Libya's Memorial . . . that is to say the area bounded by a line that starts at the intersection of the eastern boundary of Niger and 18°N latitude and continues in a strict south-east direction until it reaches 15°N latitude, and then follows this parallel eastwards to its junction with the existing boundary between Chad and Sudan.
> Libya, Memorial, 26 August 1991, at 478–479.

[34] Chad's request reads:
'La République du Tchad prie respectuesement la Cour internationale de Justice de dire et juger que sa frontière avec la Jamahiriya arabe libyenee est constituée par la ligne suivante:

detailed examination of the 1955 Treaty in keeping with the direction of the pleadings themselves:

> It is recognized by both Parties that the 1955 Treaty is the logical starting-point for consideration of the issues before the Court. Neither Party questions the validity of the 1955 Treaty, nor does Libya question Chad's right to invoke against Libya any such provisions thereof as relate to the frontiers of Chad.[35]

By starting and ending with this Treaty, the Court confined itself to the narrowest possible examination of the Case and left many issues raised by both Libya and Chad unanswered.

The key provision invoked throughout the pleadings and the judgment was Article 3 of the 1955 Treaty between Libya and France:

> The two High Contracting Parties recognize that the frontiers between the territories of Tunisia, Algeria, French West Africa and French Equatorial Africa [comprising Chad at the time] on the one hand, and the territory of Libya on the other, are those that result from the international instruments in force on the date of the constitution of the United Kingdom of Libya as listed in the attached Exchange of Letters (Ann. 1).

This annex listed the following instruments:

- the Franco-British Convention of 14 June 1898;
- the Declaration completing the same, of 21 March 1899;
- the Franco-Italian Agreements of 1 November 1902;
- the Convention between the French Republic and the Sublime Porte, of 12 May 1910 [actually 19 May 1910]
- the Franco-British Convention of 8 September 1919;
- the Franco-Italian Arrangement of 12 September 1919.[36]

---

du point d'intersection du 24ème degré de longtitude Est de Greenwich avec le parellèle 19°30 de latitude Nord, la frontière se dirige jusqu'au point de rencontre du Tropique du Cancer avec le 16ême degré de longtitude Est de Greenwich; de ce denier point elle suit une ligne se dirgeant vers le puits de Toummo jusqu'au 15ême degré Est de Greenwich.' Chad, Memorial, 26 August 1991, at 383.

[35] *Libya/Chad*, at para. 36.

[36] The Court determined that out of these treaties the 1898, 1910 and 12 September 1919 agreements did 'not directly concern the frontier between Libya and Chad…[and so found] it unnecessary to take [them] further into consideration'. *Libya/Chad*, at para. 58 & 62. For the other treaties, see Franco-British Convention for the Delimitation of their Possessions west and east of the Niger, 14 June 1898, 186 CTS 313; Convention between France and Great Britain defining the limits of the French zone in Africa, 21 March 1899, 225 CTS 480; Accords Franco-Italiens de 1–2 novembre 1902: Echanges de letters entre M. Barrère et M. Prinetti, Libya, Memorial, International Accords and Agreements Annex, vol. 2, no. 7; Anglo-French Convention, Martens, *Nouveau receuil général de traités*, 3rd series, vol. 7, at

Libya challenged the validity of many of these agreements, and it further argued that the Court should look to other pre-1955 agreements.[37] Libya also requested the Court to consider the unratified 1935 Laval-Mussolini Treaty.[38] Libya conceded that the Court could not give any binding effect to this Treaty, but it argued that the treaty was illustrative of a context in which Italy and France were in agreement that the extension of Libya's boundaries was to include the Aouzou Strip.[39] Chad conversely emphasised the unratified nature of the 1935 Treaty and contrasted this treaty with the 1955 Treaty between France and Libya that had definitively determined the boundaries through a complete list of relevant international instruments.[40]

To respond to these opposing positions, the Court undertook a textual analysis of the 1955 Treaty, relying heavily on the customary rules of treaty interpretation laid out in Article 31 of the Vienna Convention on the Law of Treaties (VCLT). Article 31(1) of the VCLT was particularly useful for the majority judgment and separate opinion of Judge Ajibola:

> A treaty shall be interpreted in good faith in accordance with the ordinary meaning to be given to the terms of the treaty in their context and in the light of their object and purpose.[41]

In reading Article 3 of the 1955 Treaty, the Court 'had no difficulty either in ascertaining the natural and ordinary meaning of the relevant terms...or in giving effect to them.'[42] The clear intention of the Article and the Treaty as a whole was not only to determine *certain* boundaries between the parties (as argued by Libya), but *all* boundaries: 'no relevant frontier was to be left undefined and no instrument listed in Annex 1 was superfluous.'[43] Judge Ajibola invoked the 'special rule of interpretation of treaties regarding boundaries...that it must, failing contrary evidence, be supposed to have been concluded in order to ensure

91–93; the Franco-British Convention, 8 September 1919, Chad, Memorial, Annexes, vol. II, annex 7, at 23; Bonin-Pichon Agreement, 12 September 1919, Chad, Memorial, Annexes, vol. II, annex 8/9, at 29.

[37] Libya, Counter-Memorial, para. 3.16; *Libya/Chad*, CR 1993/15, 15 June 1993, Libya, Mr Sohier, at 63.

[38] Libya, Memorial, 26 August 1991, at paras. 5.326–5.342. Treaty of Rome between France and Italy, 7 January 1935, Libya, Memorial, International Accords and Agreements Annex, vol. 2, no. 25.

[39] Libya, Reply, 14 September 1992, at 183–184.

[40] For Chad's rebuttal of Libya's thesis on the 1935 Treaty, see Chad, Memorial, 26 August 1991, ch. 7, especially, at 372–373.

[41] Vienna Convention on the Law of Treaties, 23 May 1969, 1155 UNTS 331.

[42] *Libya/Chad*, at para. 43.

[43] Ibid.

peace, stability and finality.'[44] The Court considered the relationship between Article 3 and the annexed treaties in the 1955 Treaty to be cumulative, and that the annex should be 'taken by the parties as exhaustive as regards delimitation of their frontiers';[45] not only was it unnecessary to question the validity of these earlier, colonial treaties, but second, no other treaty, such as the 1935 Treaty, was apposite in this instance.

Libya and Chad had both discussed whether Article 3 of the 1955 Treaty could be regarded as constitutive or declaratory in its reliance on the annexed colonial treaties of delimitation. A declaratory position would require determination as to the legal effect of the earlier treaties, whereas a constitutive stance would hold that as a consequence of Libyan and French volition, earlier treaties would serve simply as the reference point and not as pre-existing binding law for delimiting their territories. The key then was not so much whether the 1955 Treaty was seen as constitutive or declaratory, but whether one regarded the earlier treaties as being legally valid *in their own right*. For Libya, the Article was 'purely declaratory of the pre-existing boundaries'[46] that had *not* been shaped by the annexed treaties. In contrast, Judge Ago argued in his declaration that he regarded the 1955 Treaty as constitutive because 'at the time of [Libyan] independence... the southern frontier... had not yet been the subject of treaty delimitation between the parties then directly concerned.'[47] The Court decided not to enter into this debate about the constitutive or declaratory nature of the 1955 Treaty, and thus the status of the annexed, colonial treaties was left unanswered.

Both the majority judgment and Judge Ajibola found additional support for their initial interpretation by reference to good faith and a narrow understanding of the Treaty's context. Judge Ajibola discussed good faith in some detail in relation to Libya's characterisation of Article 3 as failing to delimit its southern frontier conclusively.[48] As Judge Ajibola viewed the object and purpose of the Treaty as being to determine all boundaries, France (or Chad) and Libya were thus under an 'obligation not to defeat such objects and purposes of a treaty';[49] '[t]hey may not pick and choose which obligations they would comply with and which they would refuse to perform, ignore or disregard.'[50] Neither the

---

[44] *Libya/Chad* (sep. op. Ajibola), at para. 53. See also *Libya/Chad*, at para. 51.

[45] *Libya/Chad*, at para. 48.

[46] Libya, Reply, 14 September 1992, at 57.

[47] *Libya/Chad* (dec. Ago), at 43.

[48] For example: 'As its text clearly states, Article 3 provided that Libya and France recognized ("reconnaissient") something about certain boundaries; they did not determine or fix anything.' Libya, Counter-Memorial, 27 March 1992, at 48.

[49] *Libya/Chad* (sep. op. Ajibola), at para. 82.

[50] Ibid., at para. 83.

majority nor Judge Ajibola resorted to an examination of the *travaux*[51] because the Treaty was readily cognisable without such assistance.[52] Although the Court thus rejected Libyan and Chadian discussion about the negotiations between the contracting parties, it regarded the 'context' of Article 9 of the 1955 Treaty[53] concluded between France and Libya as reinforcing its findings about the reach of the 1955 Treaty.[54]

It is interesting at this point to interrogate the Court's stance in relation to the context of treaty making, for although the Court was eager to incorporate *certain* contextual considerations into its judgment, its silence in relation to French coercion and Libyan inexperience surrounding the 1955 Treaty is noteworthy. Customary law on duress as reflected in Article 52 of the VCLT seems to be clear: 'A treaty is void if its conclusion has been procured by the threat or use of force in violation of the principles embodied in the Charter of the United Nations'. In his genealogical study of the development of the norm relating to coercion and duress, however, Craven argues that complexities and contradictions continue to plague this provision. In an attempt to divorce law from politics, lawyers tend to 'rely upon a presumption of validity as a way of insulating themselves against the possibility that consent might be all too often found defective.'[55] Thus, according to Craven, it is rare to consider duress when assessing a treaty's validity, because it 'comes to operate in such a context...as an independent variable that may (or may not) render an agreement invalid, rather than something that goes to an evaluation as to whether or not there has been an agreement in the first place.'[56]

---

51 As per Article 32 of the Vienna Convention.

52 *Libya/Chad*, at para. 55; *Libya/Chad* (sep. op. Ajibola), at para. 88.

53 This provision reads:

> The Government of France and the Government of Libya undertake to grant freedom of movement to nomads from tribes that traditionally trade on either side of the frontier between Algeria, French West Africa and French Equatorial Africa, on the one hand, and Libya, on the other, so as to maintain the traditional caravan links between the regions of Tibesti, Ennedi, Borkou, Mourzouk, Oubari, Ghat, Edri and Ghadamés, on the other.

Quoted in *Libya/Chad*, at para. 53.

54 'This provision [quoted directly above] refers specifically to (inter alia) the frontier between French Equatorial Africa and Libya; and it is clear from its terms that, according to the parties to the Treaty, that frontier separates the French-ruled regions of Tibesti, Ennedi and Borkou...which are sometimes referred to as "the BET", on the one hand, and the Libyan regions of Koufra, Mourzouk, etc. on the other.' *Libya/Chad*, at para. 53.

55 M. Craven, 'What Happened to Unequal Treaties? The Continuities of Informal Empire' (2005) 74 *Nordic Journal of International Law* 335, at 377.

56 Ibid. See also, J. Crawford, 'The General Assembly, the International Court and Self-Determination', V. Lowe & M. Fitzmaurice (eds.), *Fifty Years of the International Court of Justice: Essays in Honour of Sir Robert Jennings* (Cambridge: Cambridge University Press, 1996) 585–605, at 602.

Such an approach appeared to motivate the Court, and yet Argüello-Gomez expressed surprise, not so much over the Court's silence, but Libya's. It must be remembered that in 1955 France was embroiled in the Algerian civil war and had continued to maintain its troops in Libyan Fezzan, much to Libya's chagrin. Libya conceded in its Memorial that 'the sine qua non of any treaty with France was the withdrawal of French forces',[57] and yet it never expressed the conviction that this French duress vitiated the 1955 Treaty; indeed Chad provided more information on this in its oral pleadings.[58] At best, Libya was providing some context to the Treaty's inception.[59] We can only hypothesise as to Libya's motives for abstaining from a more detailed discussion of the 1955 context, but given the difficulties it faced over the Lockerbie incident during the proceedings, as well as its record of aggression towards Chad, it is possible to suggest that it was wary of bringing attention to its own use of force.[60]

Despite the reluctance of Libya and the Court to confront the implications of the presence of foreign troops in the shadows of treaty agreements, Libya was more comfortable in discussing inequalities of legal skill and representation *vis-à-vis* France and Libya in 1955. As was the case for much of Libya's pleadings, the Court did not engage with this particular idea of Libya's, but it is useful to appreciate the Libyan position, as it tried to represent the challenges faced by newly independent states in an increasingly postcolonial world. Libya regarded Chad's assertion that Libya was well-advised and thus on an equal footing with France in 1955, as 'a preposterous suggestion.'[61] Libya instead highlighted that at the time it was 'one of the poorest nations in the world'[62] and that the 'Libyan [negotiating] team were hopelessly outclassed by their French counterparts',[63] whose 'tactic was to trick' them.[64] To conjure up the image of two parties able to discuss their grievances on an even-handed basis in the context of the threat of force rang hollow. The challenge of informal inequalities in treaty-making persists and has not necessarily eased in an era free from acknowledged forms of colonial rule. The Court chose not to explore this conundrum, reflecting international

57 Libya, Memorial, at p. 365. Also see Libya, Counter-Memorial, at 83.

58 For example: 'L'objection de M. Ben Halim [for Libya] à ce moment là, ne porte pas sur la délimitation des frontières, mais sur sa concomitance avec l'évacuation des troupes françaises du Fezzan.' *Libya/Chad*, CR 1993/32, 14 July 1993, Chad, Professor Cot, at 42.

59 According to Koskenniemi, 'Bien que la Libya n'ait pas déduit de ces elements la conclusion que la validité de Traité de 1955 pouvait être mise en cause, elle a néanmoins soutenu que, pour l'interprétation de cet instrument, il y avait lieu de tenir compte de cet ensemble de facteurs.' Koskenniemi, *supra* n. 3, at 449.

60 See also Argüello-Gomez, *supra*, n. 29, at 179.

61 Libya, Counter-Memorial, at 55.

62 Ibid.

63 Ibid., at 56.

64 *Libya/Chad*, CR 1993/14, 14 June 1993, Libya, Professor Bowett, at 25.

legal doctrine, which has tended to ignore instances of duress save in extreme and glaring cases. It is not surprising that the Court was unwilling to accept Libya's rather radical argument, but even when presented with the opportunity to offer some guidance about the law on unequal treaties, it remained mute.[65]

The majority judgment as well as the opinion of Judge Ajibola sought to consider 'the subsequent attitudes of the Parties to the question of frontiers',[66] as per Article 31 (3) of the Vienna Convention.[67] The Court examined a number of treaties and concluded that 'there is support for the proposition that after 1955, the existence of a determined frontier was accepted and acted upon by the Parties.'[68] Indeed, a number of provisions contained within treaties signed in 1966,[69] 1972,[70] 1974,[71] 1980[72] and 1981[73] indicate 'that both Parties are perfectly aware of the location and establishment of their common boundary.'[74] On the flipside, although there were many opportunities after Chad's independence in 1960, 'Libya did not challenge the territorial dimensions of Chad as set out by France.'[75] Thus, Judge Ajibola invoked the principle of estoppel to hold that as 'an acquiescent State, Libya is precluded from denying or challenging the validity of the boundary established by the 1955 Treaty.'[76] It is undeniable that Libya's position was weakened by its failure to act within a reasonable time after the

---

65 J. Castellino & S. Allen, *Title to Territory in International Law: A Temporal Analysis* (Aldershot: Ashgate, 2003), at 116.

66 *Libya/Chad*, at para. 66.

67 This provision reads as follows:

> There shall be taken into account, together with the context:
> any subsequent agreement between the parties regarding the interpretation of the treaty or the application of its provisions; any subsequent practice in the application of the treaty which establishes the agreement of the parties regarding its interpretation; any relevant rules of international law applicable in the relations between the parties.

Cited in *Libya/Chad* (sep. op. Ajibola), at para. 89.

68 *Libya/Chad*, at para. 66.

69 The Treaty of Good Neighbourliness and Friendship between the Republic of Chad and the United Kingdom of Libya, 2 March 1966, Libya, Memorial, International Accords and Agreements Annex, vol. 2, no. 33.

70 The Agreement on Friendship and Co-operation, 23 December 1972, Libya, Memorial, International Accords and Agreements Annex, vol. 2, no. 34.

71 Agreement between the Libyan Arab Republic and the Republic of Chad, Tripoli, 12 August 1974, Libya, Memorial, International Accords and Agreements Annex, vol. 2, no. 35.

72 The Treaty of Friendship and Alliance between the Socialist People's Libyan Arab Jamahiriya and the Republic of Chad, 15 June 1980, Libya, Memorial, International Accords and Agreements Annex, vol. 2, no. 37.

73 Accord between Libya and Chad, 6 January 1981, Libya, Memorial, International Accords and Agreements Annex, vol. 2, no. 38.

74 *Libya/Chad* (sep. op. Ajibola), at para. 93.

75 *Libya/Chad*, at para. 68.

76 *Libya/Chad* (sep. op. Ajibola), at para. 98.

1955 Treaty, but once again, the Court's oversight in relation to *Chad's* inaction is no less puzzling. As was briefly discussed above, the Aouzou Strip was occupied intermittently by Libyan troops from the 1970s, and yet, afforded with the ideal opportunity to set the record straight amidst treaty negotiations, Chad did not even attempt to question Libya's presence within its borders:

> Il faut alors que nos honorables contradicteurs nous expliquent comment est-ce possible – puisque d'après eux le traité de 1955 délimitait la frontière sud entre la Libye et le Tchad – qu'en décembre 1972, lors de la visite et des discussions des Tchadiens à Tripoli: 1) les Tchadiens n'aient pas protesté contre la présence libyenne dans la bande d'Aouzou; 2) qu'ils aient signé un traité d'amité, de coopération et d'assistance mutuelle avec un État qui occupait leur territoire?[77]

Argüello-Gomez also acknowledges this discrepancy and 'found it astounding that the Court…should have ignored the implications of the attitudes' as reflected in Chad's apparent acquiescence in Libya's presence in the Aouzou Strip.[78]

Thus, in a judgment 'caractérisé par une tonalité positiviste' and 'une approche purement textuelle',[79] the Court examined the specifications of the various annexed treaties in Article 3 of the 1955 treaty to determine the boundary. In its *dispositif*, the Court held

> By 16 votes to 1,
> (1)…that the boundary between…[Libya and Chad] is defined by the Treaty of Friendship and Good Neighbourliness concluded on August 10 1955 between the French Republic and the United Kingdom of Libya;
> (2)…that the course of the boundary is as…indicated…on sketch-map No. 4 [please find attached].[80]

In contrast to the majority's detached engagement with the past, Judge Ajibola acknowledged some of the Case's broader themes, even if he chose to cast his vote with the majority. It is worthwhile quoting his poetic opinion at length:

---

[77] *Libya/Chad*, CR 1993/18, 18 June 1993, Libya, Mr Cahier, at 32.

[78] This was also echoed in Libya's oral submission: 'Non seulement il y a eu silence de sa part mais il y a eu un comportement qui est en totale contradiction avec ce qu'il soutient aujourd'hui: aucun État ne signe quatre traités d'amité avec un État qui est censé occuper une partie de votre territoire et je ne mentionne même pas les remerciements d'hommes politiques tchadiens à la Libya.' *Libya/Chad*, CR 1993/28, 7 July 1993, Libya, Professor Cahier, at 62. Argüello-Gomez also discusses the puzzling attitude taken to the Court in relation to the subsequent conduct of France (on Chad's request) in failing to register the 1955 Treaty until after 'the initiation of proceedings' on Chad's request. As in the dispute between Qatar and Bahrain, discussed in Chapter Four, the Court decided not to draw any inferences from this conduct. Argüello-Gomez strongly states that this behaviour reflects negatively on the fundamental requirement of good faith in treaty formation. Argüello-Gomez, *supra*, n. 29, at 181–183.

[79] Koskenniemi, *supra* n. 3, at 443.

[80] *Libya/Chad*, at para. 77.

> For about a century, perhaps since 1885 when it was partitioned, Africa has been ruefully nursing the wounds inflicted on it by its colonial past. Remnants of this unenviable colonial heritage intermittently erupt into discordant social, political and even economic upheavals which, some may say, are better forgotten than remembered. But this 'heritage' is difficult, if not impossible to forget; aspects of it continue, like apparitions, to rear their heads, and haunt the entire continent in various jarring and sterile manifestations: how do you forget unhealed wounds? One aspect of this unfortunate legacy is to be seen in the incessant boundary disputes between African States.[81]

Perhaps overwhelmed in the face of such challenges, the Court decided it was best to take solace in the comforts provided by a dose of strict (if somewhat selective) treaty interpretation coupled with its endorsement of the stability of borders. In deeming it 'unnecessary to consider the history of the "Borderlands"',[82] the Court effectively turned away from some of the Case's most intriguing elements. The evolving arguments of both Libya and Chad, however, offered their own appreciation of the relationship between the past and the present in international law for postcolonial states. Some of these arguments are considered below.

4) *Listening to the Court's Silences: The Pleadings of Libya and Chad*

As is the case in any contentious case before the ICJ, the primary concern of each Party is to mount as strong a claim as possible by rallying all of the 'legal' materials at its disposal. Thus the arguments themselves, especially in the hands of foreign lawyers, cannot be regarded as embodying the sentiments of states directly, and it is questionable whether such an endeavour would even be possible. The historical experience and the contemporary positions of the parties simply provide a framework from which to garner the most robust of propositions. Thus, while two states may find their positions diametrically opposed in the Case itself, in many areas of state practice away from the Peace Palace they may often work in concert. To a large extent the participants operate in a tightly circumscribed scenario of storytelling where many of the rules are pre-ordained, and this is especially the case for postcolonial states, which only contributed occasionally to the development of international rules as *subjects* before their independence. Both Libya and Chad wished to walk away from this matter victorious in their opposing territorial claims. Their pleadings like those explored in the rest of the cases, however, were already framed by their historical experiences of statehood during the colonial period. Parties will always choose certain points to emphasise or obscure. But when states, such as Chad, were constituted with little thought

[81] *Libya/Chad* (sep. op. Ajibola), at para. 7.
[82] *Libya/Chad*, at para. 75.

for indigenous patterns of authority and rule, it is understandable that such a state should accept the realities of colonially-determined borders instead of instability and uncertainty. According to Libya, '[a]ll Chad had to do was to piece together the already fully prepared, well-articulated French case',[83] relying on 'an extreme pro-colonial view of international law.'[84] Libya, on the other hand, was in a much better position to draw on its rich heritage of documented control over the territories.

Thus, out of the practice of European colonialism, Libya and Chad had significantly different experiences of statehood, and consequently advanced contrasting arguments before the ICJ. In this section, some of the discursive strategies used by the parties are explored to try and understand why the Court was so dismissive of Libya's claims. What was it about Libya's case that was so unconvincing for the Court and why were Chadian arguments preferred?

a) *Discourses on Non-Western Sovereign Control in the Central Sahara*

Libya had acknowledged that the 1955 Treaty was of central importance for the Court in determining title over the Aouzou Strip. If the 1955 Treaty were definitive in marking the Chad/Libya southern border, then there would be no need to examine an account of earlier *effectivités*. Libya was willing to concede some effect to the 1955 Treaty, but only in demarcating certain parts of its borders, excluding its southern sector.[85] Libya argued that the Treaty was unclear about the status of the Aouzou Strip, and because of this deficit, other arguments had to be explored by the Court. For example, Libya pointed out that

> Determining the territorial extent of these claims, it is evident that *effectivités* – the situation on the ground and the related conduct of the various participants: the indigenous peoples, the Senoussi Order, the Ottoman Empire, France, Italy, and Great Britain – considered in their broadest aspect will have an important role to play.[86]

Here, Libya was asking the Court to reflect on the historical dimensions of the Case and move beyond the confines of the 1955 Treaty.

One of the central pillars of Libya's case rested on the idea of indigenous-Ottoman rule over the disputed territories. Libya argued that this precolonial title would defeat any subsequent French or Italian claims where indigenous-Ottoman effectiveness could be proven. Thus not only would the treaties annexed in the 1955 Treaty be invalid, but Libya also characterised its sovereign title over

[83] *Libya/Chad*, CR 1993/14, 14 June 1993, Libya, Mr Maghur, at 57.
[84] *Libya/Chad*, CR 1993/19, 21 June 1993, Libya, Professor Crawford, at 29.
[85] Libya, Counter-Memorial, at para. 3.105.
[86] Libya, Counter-Memorial, at para. 5.10.

the Aouzou Strip as founded on a direct line from this indigenous-Ottoman or Senūsī-Ottoman title and subsequent Italian succession after the collapse of the Ottoman Empire.[87] As Ricciardi argues in his magisterial study published on the eve of proceedings, this Case raises some perplexing questions about existing understandings of sovereignty's interrelationship with the contours of the postcolonial state. For although the

> [p]resent system has produced stability in African boundaries... [i]t has failed... to satisfy genuine beliefs of title, such as Libya's, that rest on notions of sovereignty that Western law traditionally has not appreciated or accommodated. Consequently, the manner in which the Court resolves this conflict will have potentially far-reaching implications for Africa and for boundary law in general.[88]

Even though the Court found it 'unnecessary'[89] to respond to Libya's arguments, the very act of Libyan articulation opens up the possibility of an international law informed by much more than Western experiences of state formation.

Libya sought to ground its title within the tradition of Islamic political thought and state practice. Perhaps concerned that the Court was unfamiliar with the lexicon it was using to describe principles about authority over territory within Islam,[90] Libya began its presentation by reminding the Court that the 'Islamic world was not primarily concerned with concepts such as boundaries or territorial sovereignty.'[91] We saw in Chapter Two that Islamic authority theoretically is grounded in allegiance between a ruler and the *umma*, rather than territorial control *per se*. In Sunni practice after the death of the Prophet, the Caliphate became the central institution of rule in the Islamic community, representing God on earth. Although Ottoman sulṭans failed to fulfil some of the required attributes of the Caliphate, the Sublime Porte gained significant legitimacy through the *idea* of the Caliphate. Even in lands not under its direct rule, the office of the Caliph still generated respect for Ottoman rule, and this was especially so during the colonial period when Islam was threatened by Christian powers. Thus, when Chad tried to portray Libya's predecessor, the Senūsī Order, as purely religious, such an argument somewhat missed the point of Libya's

[87] 'L'Italie succéda à l'Empire ottoman dans le droit souveraineté sur la totalité du territoire libyen, tel que la Porte le contrôlait précédemment, y compris donc la zone qui forme l'objet du présent différend.' *Libya/Chad*, CR 1993/16, 16 June 1993, Libya, Professor Condorelli, at 50. For an overview about Ottoman/Senūsī relations, see Ahmida, *supra* n. 13, at ch. 2.

[88] M. M. Ricciardi, 'Title to the Aouzou Strip: A Legal and Historical Analysis' (1992) 17 *Yale Journal of International Law* 301, 308.

[89] *Libya/Chad*, at para. 75.

[90] It should be noted that one of the Court's members during the case, Judge Weeramantry, is an authority on the subject of Islam and international law. See his book: C. G. Weeramantry, *Islamic Jurisprudence: An International Perspective* (Kuala Lumpur: The Other Press, 2001).

[91] Libya, Memorial, at 31.

thesis, which relied on the interplay between Senūsī and Ottoman rule and the *territorial* effects of religious authority.[92]

As has also been argued in cases such as *Western Sahara, Dubai/Sharjah, Qatar v Bahrain* and particularly, *Eritrea/Yemen*,[93] authority in Islamic societies (and in most African societies as a whole)[94] was often the product of personal allegiances based on religious affiliations. According to Lambton, who was quoted by Libya:

> The basis of the Islamic state was ideological, not political, territorial or ethnical and the primary purpose of government was to defend and protect the faith, not the state... Political boundaries were unknown to Islam except those that separated the dar al-islam, the area inhabited by Muslims from the dar al-harb,[95] the abode of war inhabited by unbelievers.'[96]

The *Western Sahara* Case was acknowledged by both Libya and Chad in this regard and will be discussed in the following section's discussion of occupation and *terra nullius*.

Although territories comprising the Libya-Chad borderlands and beyond were far from the centres of Islamic power, they were still subject to the many – often Islamic – influences that shaped nascent states in North Africa from the sixteenth century onwards. Territories on the periphery of the Ottoman Empire were only ever under its indirect rule, but its influence was significant for this Case through the examples of the nearby 'Regencies' of Algiers, Tunis, Tripoli as well as Egypt.[97] Also, prior to European colonialism, Libya asserted that 'there existed in both the Sahara and the Sudan regions of North Africa politically organized societies, closely linked by transaharian trade and cultural contacts.'[98] Libya invoked this history not only to highlight its rich and esteemed lineage

---

[92] '[L]a confrèrie [i.e. the Senoussi Brotherhood or *ikhwān*] est, sans aucun doute, sortie du rôle purement religieux que lui avait imparti son fondateur. Il n'en résulte cepedent pas qu'elle ait exercé un pouvoir souverain sur le territoire et les populations des régions [of the borderlands]'. Chad, Counter-Memorial, 27 March 1992, at 28.

[93] *Western Sahara (Advisory Opinion)* (1975) I.C.J. Reps., p. 12; *Dubai/Sharjah Border Arbitration*, Arbitral Award, 19 October 1981, (1993) 91 ILR 543; Award of the Arbitral Tribunal in the First Stage of the Proceedings, *Territorial Sovereignty and Scope of the Dispute (Eritrea/Yemen)*, 9 October 1998.

[94] '[P]olitical power in precolonial Africa was exercised not over land but over people.' J. Herbst, 'The creation and maintenance of national boundaries in Africa' (1989) 43 *International Organization* 673, at 679.

[95] These concepts are discussed further in Chapter Two at 68–69.

[96] A. K. S. Lambton, *State and Government in Medieval Islam: An Introduction to the Study of Islamic Political Theory: The Jurists* (1981), cited in Libya, Memorial, Documentary Annexes, vol. 1, Exhibit 12.

[97] The Barbary Powers are discussed in Chapter Two, at 118–119.

[98] Libya, Memorial, at 70.

in contrast to Chad's, but also to illustrate how indirect Ottoman authority and its international legal personality was an essential ingredient in this process of sovereign consolidation.[99] In relation to the Barbary powers mentioned above, Libya admitted that

> All four States enjoyed a wide degree of independence from the Porte; but they accepted the religious supremacy of the Sultan-Caliph in Constantinople as well as Ottoman sovereignty. In fact these states had entered into treaties and consular relations with other Powers and had even made war and peace with the sovereign 'Christian' Powers as far back as the 16th Century, clearly evidencing their status as subjects of international law.[100]

Here, Libya was referring to the concept of dual, or shared, sovereignty that lay at the heart of its case in relation to the Aouzou Strip.

Libya conceded that the Ottoman presence to the south of Tripoli at the turn of the twentieth century was not enough in and of itself to found title in international law; the Senūsī Order's stewardship of desert tribes provided the vital local link for Libyan claims deep into the Sahara. Conscious of this desert context, Libya pointed out that it was necessary to establish a lower threshold of effective Senūsī control over 'such barren areas'[101] as per well-developed case law on the subject.[102] Although the Senūsī Order is best characterised as a revivalist religious movement established in the 1830s to bring education and purity of faith to Muslims in north and central Africa, its development was intimately connected with the concurrent expansion of European colonialism in Africa.[103] Thus, despite the Order's disdain for all things non-Muslim, its direct and indirect

[99] '... in the early 1800s, questions of nationality and boundaries had little meaning in the Muslim regions of North Africa. What mattered was the common sharing of Islamic beliefs and loyalty to the Caliph.' *Libya/Chad*, CR 1993/19, 21 June 1993, Libya, Mr Maghur, at 18.

[100] Libya, Memorial, at 73.

[101] Libya went on to add that '[t]he nature of the Sahara Desert must be understood in the context of colonial times; only its oases were places to inhabit; it was a region to pass through'. Libya, Memorial, at 8.

[102] See especially, *Island of Palmas Case* 1 RIAA 829; 4 ILR 3 [1928] *The Minquiers and Ecrehos Case (France/United Kingdom)* (1953) ICJ Reps, p. 47; *Status of Eastern Carelia (Advisory Opinion)* 1923, P.C.IJ., Series B, No. 5; *Western Sahara (Advisory Opinion)* (1975) ICJ Rep 12. Later in its Memorial, Libya discusses perceived European double standards on this very point: 'It was a bit naïve and certainly self-serving of the French to maintain that, because evidence of Ottoman sovereignty was sparse by European standards at the time, it did not exist – and to ignore the fact that it had long pre-existed France's attempt at colonisation. At the time, only sparse control was necessary or possible in such a desert environment; but under Islamic concepts of sovereignty and boundaries it was nonetheless a very real assertion of sovereignty.' Libya, Memorial, at 32.

[103] Al Faruqi argues that the Senousi Order can be understood as an offshoot of the Arabian Wahhābi movement, as discussed briefly in Chapter Two, at 84. I. R. Al Faruqi, 'The Ideal Social Order in the Arab World' (1969) 11 *Journal of Church & State* 239, at 243.

confrontation with Christian powers provided a coherent *raison d'être*: resistance against the impending threat to Islam's presence in the Sahara's expanses.[104] It was the opinion of the Ottomans by the late nineteenth century that the 'people of this land are mostly the followers of his Holiness the Sheikh Senusi, there being a large Senusi lodge [or *zāwiyya*] venerated by many.'[105] These Senūsī

> lodges built at tribal centres, or at watering places and junctions on the trade and pilgrim routes, served as monasteries, schools, hostels, sources of advice and mediation and, in due course, as administrative centres.[106]

Thus, in the face of a French 'crusade against the Orient in general and Islam in particular under the pretext of spreading civilisation', the Senūsī sought to 'spread true civilisation and true knowledge' by instructing the 'savages' of the Central Sahara.[107] Africa was the object of more than one civilising mission, and it was not surprising that Europeans were wary of this threat to their expansion: primary sources cited by Libya engender a deep distrust and demonisation of the Order.[108] Libya's reference to this historical period can thus be appreciated as an attempt to challenge not only dominant legal doctrines but the historical assumptions informing the law as well.

Through a combination of such Senūsī control on the ground and the institution of the Ottoman Caliphate, Libya argued that territories extending even beyond Lake Chad to the South were precluded from European occupation because of the presence of dual sovereignty.[109] Essentially, Libya characterised sovereignty as comprising a local and an international dimension:

> [I]t was the Senoussi and the Senoussi peoples who held title to these regions and bore allegiance to the Caliph. The territorial rights of the Senoussi peoples were,

[104] G. Joffe, 'The Role of the Sanusi in the Central Sahara', Libya, Reply, 14 September 1992, vol. 2, at 8.

[105] The Report of Muhammad Basala, Ottoman Emissary to sub-Sahran Africa, Ottoman Archives, 11 April 1894, Libya, Memorial, Documentary Annex, vol. 6.

[106] J. Wright, *Libya, Chad and the Central Sahara* (London: Hurst, 1989), at 84, quoted in Libya, Memorial, at 44.

[107] Letter from the Senoussi Leader, Sayyid Ahmed Sherif Senoussi, published in *Il Giornale d'Italia*, 6 August 1911, Libya, Memorial, Documentary Annex, vol. 6, exhibit 47. The Senūsī 'civilising mission' was strongly supported by the Porte as well: 'The Senusi Shaikhs have rendered undeniable services for mitigating the savagery of the local peoples and for improving their morals.' Letter signed by the Grand Vizier, 11 April 1884, Libya, Reply, Documentary Annexes, vol. 3, Exhibit 8.2.

[108] Libya, Memorial, at 53–55. See also Libya's discussion of European representations of the Ottomans in North Africa in *ibid.*, at 103–104.

[109] For a good defence of the concept, see *Libya/Chad*, CR 1993/19, 21 June 1993, Libya, Professor Crawford, at 50–53; and Libya, Reply, at 223–224.

in turn, represented on the international level by the Caliph to whom they paid allegiance.[110]

Libya tried to prove this title by presenting numerous instances where the Ottoman Empire had publicly rejected French and Italian claims while increasing its own presence in the areas either directly or through its proxy, the Senūsī Order.[111] Thus, around the period when spheres of influence were being declared by European states, Libya was at pains to show that such statements could have no legal effect *erga omnes*; they were 'purely bilateral' undertakings by European powers.[112] For example: 'the Ottoman presence in the borderlands...was a substantial presence and it was continuous between 1908 and the end of 1912, and it was in direct implementation of a claim of sovereignty. It was also carried on at the invitation of and in conjunction with the Senūsī tribes and...Order.'[113] Although the Italians ultimately overran the Ottomans, Libya argued that their title passed to Italy as a consequence of the 1912 Treaty of Ouchy[114] and the 1923 Treaty of Lausanne.[115] Senūsī rights remained, with Italy acting as the

---

110 *Libya/Chad*, CR 1993/20, 22 June, Libya, Mr Dolzer, at 29. In his dissent, Judge Sette-Camara as *ad hoc* judge for Libya, was in complete agreement with the Libyan line: 'historic title over the region belonged first to the indigenous peoples, tribes, confederations of tribes, sometimes organized under the Senoussiya, and eventually passed to the Ottoman Empire before the colonial Powers set foot in the area.' *Libya/Chad* (diss. op. Sette-Camara), at 94.

111 It must be pointed out here that the nature of Ottoman-Senūsī cooperation is contested. In its pleadings, for example, Libya relied on the thesis of Evans-Pritchard, who coined the expression, 'Turco-Sanusi Condominium'. This idea remains dominant within the literature and is supported by some studies that point, for example, to Ottoman tax exemptions for the Senoussi. However, in his reappraisal of the evidence available, Le Gall questions such a simple account of mutual agreement and highlights ongoing tensions between the Senūsī Order and the Ottomans. Libya chose to overlook these discrepancies in the historical record, and it is no surprise; co-sovereignty would be harder to argue when its co-holders were in dissension. See G. Joffé, 'Qadhafi's Islam in Local Historical Perspective', D. Vandewalle (ed.), *Qadhafi's Libya, 1969–1994* (New York: St Martin's Press, 1995), 139–154, at 143; M. Le Gall, 'The Ottoman Government and the Sanusiyya: A. Reappraisal' (1989) 21 *International Journal of Middle East Studies* 91; and Ahmida, *supra* n. 13, at 89.

112 *Libya/Chad*, CR 1993/19, 21 June 1993, Libya, Professor Crawford, at 42.

113 *Libya/Chad*, CR 1993/20, 22 June 1993, Libya, Mr Dolzer, at 22.

114 '[G]râce à ce traité de cession territoriale, l'Italie acquit le droit d'exercer sa souveraineté sur l'ensemble du territoire libyen que l'Empire ottoman lui cédait' *Libya/Chad*, CR 1993/16, 16 June 1993, Libya, Professor Condorelli, p. 45. Treaty of Ouchy between the Ottoman Empire and Italy, 15 October 1912, Libya, Memorial, International Accords and Agreements Annex, vol. 2, no. 10.

115 Chad vehemently disputed this interpretation of the treaties, arguing instead that the treaties were simply concerned with the Porte's renunciation of its territorial interests, rather than about the transfer of such rights to Italy. *Libya/Chad*, CR 1993/23, 29 June 1993, Chad, Professor Cassese, at 47.

area's international overlord.[116] Thus, Libya somewhat anachronistically sought to demonstrate a direct link between its colonial and postcolonial manifestations: 'The Senoussi were Libyan: they were the very core of the new State.'[117]

Although Chad's pleadings were primarily concerned with the operation of the 1955 Treaty,[118] it still devoted considerable energy to rebutting both the factual and legal claims of Libya's Senūsī sovereignty thesis. Factually, Chad disputed the existence of a solid Senūsī-Ottoman alliance,[119] and it regarded their respective displays of effective control as inadequate for the international law of the time.[120] It also characterised Libya's hypothesis of divided sovereignty between the Ottoman Empire and the Senūsī Order as 'inventé...pour servir le but irrédentiste actuellement poursuivi par la Libye'.[121] Their summarised argument ran as follows in the oral pleadings:

---

[116] For a good summary of these arguments, see Libya/Chad, CR 1993/20, 22 June 1993, Libya, Mr Dolzer, at 26–27. Examples of treaties forged between the Senūsī Order and Italy recognising ongoing Senūsī rights include: Libya, Memorial, Documentary Annex, vol. 2, Exhibit 16 & 19.

[117] *Libya/Chad*, CR 1993/20, 22 June 1993, Professor Bowett, at 48.

[118] 'Pour le Tchad, le traité du 10 août 1955 est la clé du différend.' *Libya/Chad*, CR 1993/21, 25 June 1993, Chad, Mr Dadi, at 13.

[119] According to the French in 1934: the Ottomans 'were...in reality prisoners of the Senussi on whom they were entirely dependent, both for their supplies, their mail and their communications.' Letter from the French Minister for the Colonies to the French Foreign Affairs', 30 January 1934, Chad, Counter-Memorial, Documentary Annex, vol. 3, Exhibit 74, at 212; and see Letter from Mr Rais, Head of the Consulate-General at Tripoli to Minister of Foreign Affairs, 5 September 1899, Chad, Reply, Documentary Annexes, vol. 2, Exhibit 9, at 16. This questioning of the alliance in Chad's pleadings has much merit, since by the time Libya presented its Senūsī sovereignty thesis in oral form it had abandoned any sense of historical contingency and characterised Senūsī and Ottoman relations in crude terms, e.g. see *Libya/Chad*, CR 1993/19, 21 June 1993, Libya, Mr Maghur, at 23. There may have been a degree of collaboration between the Senūsī and the Porte, but it was also historically evident that the Senūsī Order regarded the Ottomans themselves as corrupt Muslims who had fallen from the true path of Islam; colonialism forced the two forces to compromise at times, but it is simplistic to speak in terms of a two-headed entity *per se*. See Ricciardi, *supra* n. 88, at 342.

[120] For Chad's rebuttal of the Senūsī thesis, see Chad, Counter-Memorial, 27 March 1992, at 199–238.

[121] Chad, Counter-Memorial, 27 March 1992, p. 174. Its remarks on divided sovereignty include: 'Mais même en faisant abstraction d'un éventuel accord entre les deux parties, le Mémoire libyen est mal fondé à un autre égard. Si l'on veut parler de "souveraineté partagée" entre deux sujets de droit international, il faut indiquer dę quelle manière cette souveraineté était partagé: les deux parties avaient-elles le droit d'exercer les mêmes attributs souverains? Dans l'affirmative, pouvaient-elles les exercer d'une manière concurrente, ou devaient-elles les exercer de façon alternative? Si, en revanche, il y avait une distinction de compétences, quels pouvoirs souverains pouvaient être exercés par une des parties, et quels autres pouvaient être exercés par l'autre?', Ibid., at 173.

> First that the Ottoman Empire never had title to the B.E.T., neither on the basis of effective control nor on any other basis. Second, that the Senoussi Order was never more than an intermittent source of religious influence, and to some extent political influence, ranging across northern and central Africa. This influence...was weak in the B.E.T. Third, that the failure of the Ottomans and the Senoussi Order to establish an independent source of title is not retrieved by seeking to combine the two into one form of claimed joint sovereignty. Fourth, that the indigenous peoples, whose nature has been misrepresented by the Libyans, were the bearers of rights over the territory but were insufficiently organized to possess territorial sovereignty under international law.[122]

Finally, Chad also rejected Libya's penchant for anachronism: it was 'misleading' to argue that modern Libya was a direct successor of the Senūsī even its first ruler was of Senūsī lineage.[123]

It is not necessary here to weigh up the competing historical assessments offered by Chad's rebuttal to Libya's case,[124] but it is significant that Chad's underlying assumptions about title to territory were radically different from those of its counterpart. Chad's position suggested that the grammar of international law could not support arguments about shared sovereignty or indigenous people endowed with legal personality during the epoch of European colonialism. Such a stance can be understood as illustrative of a more traditional, or realist, discourse about the implications of colonialism's past, for as Chad reminds us: 'on ne gomme pas l'histoire; le colonialisme ne peut pas être mis entre paranthèses, les peoples de les États d'Afrique ont pris acte de l'héritage.'[125] Thus, faced with the postcolonial paradox, Chad chose to use arguments typical of the coloniser to rebut Libyan links with the land. Through its arguments based on European notions of effective control and the characterisation of Senūsī-Ottoman rule as being purely religious, Chad employed grammars of argument familiar to the Court. International law is discursively flexible, but only to a degree, and when arguments are grounded in the 'hard' law of treaties, such as the 1955 Treaty, it is not surprising that the Court was convinced by the Chadian perspective.

---

[122] *Libya/Chad*, CR 1993/23, 29 June 1993, Chad, Professor Shaw, at 63.

[123] *Libya/Chad*, CR 1993/24, 30 June 1993, Chad, Professor Shaw, at 18. See also *Libya/Chad*, CR 1993/21, 25 June, Chad, Professor Pelllet, at 21.

[124] To summarise: Libya argued that Senūsī-Ottoman was effective until this title was then taken up by Italy. Libya was the later recipient of this title, and France was never successful in the requisite degree of effective control, especially in the face of persistent Senūsī revolt and Ottoman statements to the contrary. Chad, conversely demonstrated that France successfully established its control over the region. In his study of the history, Ricciardi holds that the French second occupation of the B.E.T. in 1929–1930 secured title over the territory. Ricciardi, *supra* n. 88, at 467.

[125] *Libya/Chad*, CR 1993/21, 25 June 1993, Chad, Professor Pellet, at 21.

b) *International Legal Personality for Indigenous Africans during Colonialism? Libya and Chad Compared*

In Part II's introduction, we saw how colonialism occurred within the discursive context of positivism, recognition, and the 'standard of civilisation'. Despite positivism's fixation on certainty and stability, its underlying assumptions about sovereign capacity and an international legal system based on recognition precluded entities that did not fulfil pre-ordained standards of European civilisation.[126] Thus, rules governing title to territory at the international level only applied to the subjects of international law as perceived at the time. Given that Libya asserted in this Case that the Senūsī Order attained legal personality either directly or through the support of Ottoman oversight, both Libya and Chad spent significant time debating not only whether the Senūsī Order was factually able to fulfil standards of effective control, but whether international law *at the time* had recognised it as a subject rather than an object of its jurisdiction. Instead of trying to assess the relative cogency of the two arguments, this section sketches some of the different images of international law presented in the pleadings.

In the absence of a treaty of cession, the crucial factor for determining whether the acquisition of territory was lawful rests on the status of the particular territory itself. The question that divided Libya and Chad was, 'Who was a subject of international law at the time?' Throughout the development of its submissions, Libya relied on the Court's decision in the *Western Sahara* Case to claim that the existence of analogous tribal structures in its borderlands prevented French occupation; occupation was only possible in *terra nullius*, and as in the Court's earlier decision, Libya argued that at no time had the disputed territories been *terrae nullius.*[127] Although there is significant scholarly agreement on the nexus between occupation and *terra nullius*,[128] there is far less consensus on the *definition* of *terra nullius.*[129] This was especially so during the height of European colonialism, when sovereignty was interwoven with the requirements of civilisation; (European) state practice often denied the personality of peoples in Africa[130] except to imbue them with the capacity to cede their territory through highly questionable European-imposed agreements.

---

[126] For a general discussion of this phenomenon, see A. Anghie, 'Finding the Peripheries: Sovereignty and Colonialism in Nineteenth Century International Law' (1999) 40 *Harvard International Law Journal* 1.

[127] Libya, Memorial, at para. 4.50–4.51.

[128] G. Simpson, 'Mabo, International Law, *Terra Nullius* and the Stories of Settlement: An Unresolved Jurisprudence' 19 (1993–1994) *Melbourne University Law Review* 195, at 203–204.

[129] Ricciardi, *supra* n. 88, at 394.

[130] Shaw, *Title to Territory, supra* n. 7, at 32–33.

Libya championed the rights of indigenous peoples before the Court, holding that international law could now retrospectively deem various non-European peoples the subjects of international law.[131] Chad contested Libya's hypothesis by arguing that past norms relating to conquest, as well as *terra nullius*, could not be rewritten:

> Intertemporal law does not allow us to pretend that later, more palatable laws applied in the years before these more acceptable notions had evolved. Libya insists that this must mean that 'colonial aggression' remained lawful. But as Libya well knows, this simply begs the question of what *was* regarded as 'aggression' at the time. And, palatable or not, colonial conquest and occupation was *not* regarded as 'aggression' in 1913, nor in 1919.[132]

Chad argued that state practice from the time was clear: European occupation of lands inhabited by non-European peoples was permitted in a context of unsettled law over the definition of *terra nullius*. Further, with the demise of the Ottoman presence – irrespective of its effectiveness – the borderlands were open to the claims of any European state willing to substantiate a declaration of its desires with effective control. Once again, Chad chose to rely on the discourse of colonialism to defeat Libya's expansive approach to legal personality at the end of the nineteenth century.

c) *'Closet Colonialism' before the Court?*[133] *Chad's Successful Defence of* Uti Possidetis Juris

We saw in the introduction for Part II that the norm of *uti possidetis* has received strong support from most African states since independence, and Chad and Libya are no exception; both states signed the Cairo Declaration of 1964.[134] The resort to this norm in legal argumentation is intriguing because its discursive practices tend to obscure highly political arguments behind the veil

---

[131] *Libya/Chad*, 93/24, 30 June 1993, Chad, Professor Higgins, at 33.

[132] *Libya/Chad*, 93/24, 30 June 1993, Chad, Professor Higgins, at 32. The importance of 1913 was that it followed Ottoman withdrawal from the territory. On the other hand, for 1919 Libya sought to argue that as a result of Article 10 of the Covenant of the League of Nations the international community had outlawed conquest as a mode of acquisition. Such an argument is controversial, however, as other opinions (including those of Chad) point to the wording of the provision which was only concerned with preserving the territorial inviolability of League members; it was possible that non-state entities fell outside of its protection. Article 10 reads: 'The Members of the League undertake to respect and preserve as against external aggression the territorial integrity and existing political independence of all Members of the League.', cited in *Libya/Chad*, CR 1993/19, 21 June 1993, Libya, Professor Crawford, at 54.

[133] *Libya/Chad*, CR 1993/19, 21 June 1993, Libya, Professor Crawford, at 44.

[134] Only Somalia and Morocco rejected the Declaration's call for the sanctity of territorial borders. McKeon, *supra* n. 8, at 155.

of doctrine; its use aids in the perpetuation of a restricted, international legal lexicon. By accepting colonial borders, both the ICJ and postcolonial states can avoid complex considerations of history and geography by focusing exclusively on the contours of colonial administration. Yet, reliance on *uti possidetis* is also a policy choice, and time and again its use is justified through familiar arguments based on 'stability' and 'certainty' in the face of feared anarchy and chaos.[135] These prefences can be understood as part of a grammar generative of speech acts producing a conservative worldview, and an international law free from unpleasant memories of the past. In his separate opinion, Judge Shahabuddeen acknowledged the importance of the finality of borders but cautioned against pre-empting boundaries; the policy of *uti possidetis juris* can only be followed when a clear boundary exists.[136] Here, Judge Shahabuddeen is perhaps suggesting that more caution is required in the application of *uti possidetis*. The norm (or policy) can only do so much. Also, the norm is a policy choice often hidden behind the rhetoric of law. Libya's rejection of *uti possidetis* was just as 'legal' as Chad's, but in failing to reflect the dominant discourse employed in postcolonial territorial disputes some of its arguments failed to convince a bench content with established practice.

Chad was an exemplar of *uti possidetis* not only in regard to the 1955 Treaty, but also the various annexed treaties. Through a three-pronged argument, Chad sought to demonstrate that the borders flowing from the 1955 Treaty were permanent, but that even supposing the Treaty's invalidity, the earlier treaties would be sufficient in their own right to establish French and then Chadian sovereignty over the Aouzou Strip. In the words of Libya, 'Chad now seeks to derive full benefit from the voracious appetite of the Colonial Power.'[137] Chad characterised its support for the stability of boundaries in very different terms: Libya was 'seeking to promote anarchy,'[138] and its claims constituted a threat to its very existence: 'il s'agit de son intégrité territoriale, de son unité et de son dévelopement economique.'[139] Further, Libya's attempt at boundary revision had implications beyond the immediate Case; Chad saw itself as a defender of African stability,[140] and such sentiments resonated with the Court. It is unsurprising that Chad invoked the policy of *uti possidetis juris*; it was an invaluable resource

---

[135] *Libya/Chad*, at para. 73. Chad Counter-Memorial, at para. 1.01.

[136] *Libya/Chad* (sep. op. Shahabuddeen), at 45.

[137] Libya, Reply, at 8.

[138] Libya, Reply, at 7.

[139] *Libya/Chad*, CR 1993/21, 25 June 1993, Chad, Mr Dadi, at 14.

[140] 'l'affaire d'Aouzou est un enjeu au-delà du Tchad, puisque la Libye conteste radicalement le principe du respect des frontiers héritées de la colonisation que les États africains considèrent, à la quasi-unanimité, comme une règle sacro-sainte et un rempart contre des revendications en chaîne.' *Libya/Chad*, CR 1993/21, 25 June 1993, Chad, Mr Dadi, at 18.

against the Libyan requests for a complete overview of competing indigenous and European interests in the area. Libya's claim that no boundary was in existence meant that the application of the *uti possidetis* principle was irrelevant for its argument;[141] the doctrine can only apply to boundaries reasonably settled at the time of decolonisation.[142] It is likely that if Libya had access to a treaty favourable to its interests it too would have invoked *uti possidetis juris*.

When we view Libya's wider approach to the litigation, however, it is clear that at least in this instance, its pleadings indicate a deep-set scepticism about the extent to which Africa's borders should remain a product of their colonial past in the face of non-European claims to title. The norm's entrenched position especially in Africa may well confirm the continent's borders and stave off possible conflicts, but *uti possidetis'* complicit relationship with European conceptions of authority highlights the effects of colonialism in a 'postcolonial' era. In the face of such tensions, Castellino and Allen point to a 'continuing reluctance of the existing international regime to provide an effective means of redress against the international boundaries forged by the powers in disregard of pre-colonial territorial and ethnographic parameters.'[143]

5) *An Historical Afterthought: The Implications of the Colonial Legacy in a 'Postcolonial' World*

The *Libya/Chad* Case was never about pure historical enquiry since proceedings were played out within the confines of available international legal rules and strategies. However, all participants in the matter – the bench as well as the parties – could not ignore the historical record and more importantly, the political implications of historical interpretation. This chapter' findings endorse those of Simpson, who posits that

---

[141] 'Libya's position is very clear: Article 3 of the 1955 Treaty confirmed the parties' acceptance of the *status quo* on the critical date based on the application of the principle of *uti possidetis juris* in accordance with the Article's criteria: "acts internationaux en vigeur" on the critical date. It was not intended to modify the status quo.' 'Article 3...achieved only a partial settlement of Libya's boundary problems.' Libya, Reply, at 48 & 54.

[142] The 'principle cannot be taken to mean that either an unsettled or a contested boundary can be converted into an agreed line simply by way of succession, nor may it preclude subsequent alteration with the consent of the parties concerned. However, it does mean that an agreed boundary established or confirmed in a treaty cannot be challenged simply on the grounds of a succession, and it does in reality and in practice reinforce the principle of territorial stability.' M. N. Shaw, 'The Heritage of States: The Principle of Uti Possidetis Juris Today' (1997) 67 *British Yearbook of International Law* 75, at 91–92. See also *Case Concerning the Frontier Dispute (Burkino Faso/Mali)* (1986) ICJ Reps, p. 554, at 568.

[143] Castellino & Allen, *supra* n. 65, at 117.

> one can see all the cases on acquisition as an attempt to reconcile the imperatives of law, history and politics. Each of these reconciliations has required the utilization of a number of interpretive techniques in law, and a variety of often conflicting constructions of historical truth.[144]

We cannot expect the Court to have adjudicated over the historical evidence of the parties *per se*; its mandate was to pronounce on the law, not the facts. However, territorial disputes in particular require the Court to engage in an intimate journey with the past to make sense of the legal present. Despite the possibility for a serious examination of many unsettled areas of law, the Court's judgment instead obscured these historical complexities. 'Une chose paraît claire en tout cas: la Cour répugne à attribuer un poids décisif à des faits historiques éloignés.'[145] Thus, in failing to question the colonial record while relying on colonial agreements and their consequent boundaries, the Court can be seen as a champion of colonialism's continuing hold over international law. Judge Shahabuddeen articulated the majority's view of the past as well as its relationship to the dispute:

> The case at bar recalls a world now left behind. In telling flashes, it illuminates an age when international law tended to develop as a legal construct supportive of the global projection of the power of a single region; when in important respects it was both fashioned and administered by leading members of a select community; when that community, by itself called the international community, bore little resemblance to the world as it then stood, and even less to the world as it stands today.[146]

Libya's case can be seen as an attempt to reveal how the past portrayed by Judge Shahabuddeen can and should be acknowledged in the present; the Court's construction of a radical separation between past and present reinforced their inseparable bond more than ever.

6) *Conclusion*

This Case could have been decided in a more expansive manner. The arguments of Chad and Libya could also have been different from those contained in the oral and written pleadings. Although the possibility of creative licence existed, Libya, Chad and the Court had to operate within the confines of international law's particular grammar and lexicon. In the case of the parties, they were also compelled to combine their presentation of legal doctrines with a particular

---

[144] Simpson, *supra* n. 128, at 210.
[145] Koskenniemi, *supra* n. 3, at 457.
[146] *Libya/Chad* (sep. op. Shahabuddeen), ICJ Reps, at 44.

interpretation of the colonial experience in the Aouzou Strip. For its part, Libya not only questioned the power relations behind colonial treaty formation but also challenged traditional conceptions of statehood by trying to endow the Senūsī Order with international legal personality at a time when the 'standard of civilisation' ruled supreme. Libya attempted to convince the Court that the grammar of international law could support more expansive notions of indigenous sovereignty argued on the basis of an Islamically-inspired lexicon. Chad, on the other hand, chose to thwart Libya's line through the help of a far more traditional set of utterances framed by a grammar supportive of strictly positivist treaty interpretation and the disavowal of historical context. Perhaps as a result of its haphazard and arbitrary experience of state formation, it was more difficult for Chad to construct arguments based on precolonial forms of authority over territory. Even if Chad's legal team had entertained such an approach though, it was unnecessary. Traditional international legal principles furnished Chad with more than adequate ammunition to stifle Libya's alternative position, and the Court's subsequent silence in relation to many of the substantive issues raised testifies to the strength of Chad's litigation strategy.

Through the devices of non-European legal personality, historical reinterpretation and a challenge to *uti possidetis*, Libya invited the Court to evaluate the relationship between the colonial past and the postcolonial present. The legal grammars employed on the Libyan side were more expansive in their nature as they sought to show that law should acknowledge historical and political considerations more overtly. The Case raised issues of great importance for international law as a tool of European and non-European nation-states. Koskenniemi suggests that the question asked by Libya, yet overlooked by the Court was

> Le droit international doit-il servir à effacer les consequences négatives de colonialisme sur l'ensemble des structures sociales et politiques de l'Afrique? Ou bien doit-il être considéré comme un instrument destiné à renforcer la stabilité des structures existantes, de façon à prévenir, ou à tout le moins à retarder, «des luttes fratricides».[147]

The Court chose to disavow international law's colonial complicity. Through faith in the mechanisms of strict legalism haunted by the threat of an 'anarchic' and borderless Africa, the Court indicated that the scope of legal discourse was a very narrow one. Perhaps the ramifications of Libya's position were too hard to contain, and so instead the Court barricaded itself behind the law/politics dichotomy through excessive reliance on treaty interpretation that was deaf to the colonial context. Chad's adjudicative strategy, which typified the postcolonial

[147] Koskenniemi, *supra* n. 3, at 456. Here, Koskenniemi is quoting the Chamber in the *Frontier Dispute (Burkina Faso/Mali)* ICJ Rep, p. 565, at para. 20.

paradox for Third World states intent on securing their selfhood, served its interests well. In the Case described in the following chapter, the Court was confronted with two parties closer in historical experience than Libya and Chad. Thus it will be instructive to compare Libya's and Chad's strategies with those of Bahrain and Qatar.

Chapter Four

(De)Limiting the Past for Future Gain: The Relationship between Statehood, Colonialism and Oil in the Qatar v Bahrain *Territorial Dispute*

1) *Introduction*

As in the case of the African continent, the Arab Gulf[1] is home to a number of long-standing border disputes that have only rarely been settled through adjudicative methods.[2] In contrast with much of Africa, however, the Gulf was able to sustain a significant degree of independence during the colonial period, but many of its states continue to confront difficulties in defining their borders in a region particularly unfamiliar with territorial demarcation. The discovery and exploitation of oil encouraged both foreign and local powers to construct regimes of territoriality, but how were such borders determined, and what role have legal arguments played in this endeavour? Three cases are available to answer this question: the two arbitrations between Dubai and Sharjah and Eritrea and Yemen and the ICJ dispute between Bahrain and Qatar.[3] The last case forms the subject of this chapter, but the other two cases serve as useful reference points, in exploring both local approaches to sovereign control and the link between

[1] Until relatively recently, it was conventional in the West to refer to the body of water surrounded by the Eastern side of the Arabian peninsula, and southern Iraq and Iran as the 'Persian Gulf'. However, it is common for Arabs to refer to it as the Arabian Gulf, and as things stand no resolution has been reached. Thus, I will use neither adjective when referring to the area in general. When explicitly considering Arab states in the Gulf, I will refer to it as the Arab Gulf. This is hardly a 'final solution' in Amin's opinion, but a compromise for the time being: S. H. Amin, *International and Legal Problems of the Gulf* (London: Middle East and North African Studies Press, 1981), at 32.

[2] For a discussion of territorial disputes in the Gulf region, see R. Schofield, 'Borders and Territoriality in the Gulf and the Arabian Peninsula during the Twentieth Century', R. Schofield (ed.), *Territorial Foundations of the Gulf States* (London: UCL Press, 1994), at 1–77.

[3] *Dubai/Sharjah Border Arbitration*, Arbitral Award, 19 October 1981, (1993) 91 ILR 543; *Case Concerning Maritime Delimitation and Territorial Questions between Qatar and Bahrain (Qatar/Bahrain) (Merits)* (2001) ICJ Reps, p. 40, hereinafter *Qatar/Bahrain (Merits); Territorial Sovereignty and Scope of the Dispute Award* (Phase I), 9 October 1998.

European domination and treaty law. The *Qatar/Bahrain* dispute was similar to these other cases, and yet in its judgment the Court overlooked this jurisprudence altogether. As in the case of Libya and Chad, the Court was content to adopt a narrow approach to the problems presented, but we should still ask why the Court neglected these more expansive arbitral awards and what this highlights about the discursive avenues available to states seeking redress before the ICJ.

Despite the Court's truncated response, the proceedings between Qatar and Bahrain was one of the most complex matters on the Court's docket. Indeed, this Case was procedurally one of the most protracted in the Court's history,[4] the length of the material presented was unprecedented and it was only the second case to consider both territorial and maritime claims at the merits stage.[5] After the Court rejected Bahraini opposition to the Court's jurisdiction in two preliminary judgments,[6] the scope of the Case was defined broadly to encompass all matters of contention between Qatar and Bahrain. The main territorial elements in dispute related to the states' *à titre de souverain* over the Hawar Islands[7] and Janan Island as well as the region of Zubarah on the western side of the Qatari peninsula. Following the legal principle that the land dominates the sea,[8] the Court used its territorial determination to oblige the parties' request for it to draw their maritime boundary according to general principles of international law.

Given the scope of the Case, it is not possible to examine the pleadings and the judgments with due regard to all of their discursive elements. This chapter confines itself to aspects of the Case's territorial controversies,[9] in keeping with

---

4 G. Plant, 'Maritime Delimitation and Territorial Questions between Qatar and Bahrain' 96 (2002) *American Journal of International Law* 198, at 198.

5 Ibid., at 204.

6 *Maritime Delimitation and Territorial Questions between Qatar and Bahrain (Qatar/Bahrain) (Jurisdiction and Admissibility)* (1994) ICJ Rep 112; and *Maritime Delimitation and Territorial Questions between Qatar and Bahrain (Qatar/Bahrain) (Jurisdiction and Admissibility)* (1995) ICJ Rep 6.

7 The Hawar Islands are a series of islands off the Western coast of Qatar. The largest island is simply called Hawar and can be understood as representing the group as a whole. This point was one of some dispute in the case, but for the purposes of this chapter, Hawar and Hawar Islands are synonymous in meaning except where indicated.

8 This is the maxim that especially grew out of the *North Sea Continental Shelf Cases (Federal Republic of Germany/Denmark; Federal Republic of Germany/Netherlands)* (1969) ICJ Reps, p. 3.

9 Both the Court and the Parties themselves acknowledged the primary role that the territorial claims played in the dispute, and so it is much more important to appreciate this aspect of the Case over and above maritime claims. Scholarly attention has also focused on the maritime aspects of the Case, see, B. Kwiatkowska, 'The Qatar v. Bahrain Maritime Delimitation and Territorial Questions Case' (2002) 33 *Ocean Development and International Law* 227; and Y. Tanaka, 'Reflections on Maritime Delimitation in the Qatar/Bahrain Case' 52 (2003) *International and Comparative Law Quarterly* 53.

the focus of the book on territorial disputes and the presentation of legal grammars employed, for three reasons. First, territorial matters involving issues of local authority are the best avenue through which to explore the underlying interest of the book in Arab ideas about sovereignty and colonialism. Comparisons between Arab particularism and the 'universalism' embodied by the Court will also help us in answering my second central question about international law's universality. Second, of the three main territorial issues, the chapter will limit its focus to two: the Hawar Islands and Zubarah. Janan does not raise distinct issues and was the least discussed in both the pleadings and the judgment. Third, the pleadings themselves went through many mutations, and so the chapter concentrates on the oral pleadings as expressions of the parties' final positions.[10]

A particularly difficult and novel element of the Case was the matter of 82 disputed Qatari documents. Bahrain first 'challenged the authenticity of 81 documents'[11] on 25 September 1996 after memorials had been submitted and shortly before counter-memorials were required. After many detailed reports by Bahrain, as well as an interim report by Qatar, it was agreed that Qatar would withdraw the documents and no longer rely on them in its reply or oral pleadings.[12] Despite this, Bahrain not only argued that Qatar's arguments did not reflect this change adequately, but that the affair fundamentally tainted the entire legal process. This example of evolving arguments highlights why the chapter has focused on the most recent material, namely the oral pleadings.

Finally and most importantly, rather than survey all of the claims and findings over Hawar and Zubarah, this chapter emphasises those (sometimes central) arguments concerned with either the special attributes of Arab sovereignty or the colonial legacy. Both Qatar and Bahrain fell under British 'protection' throughout much of the twentieth century, and since they are only relatively recent 'independent' entities, it is important to understand their own accounts of this process. Competing narratives over colonial histories and Arab practices will not in themselves generate a conclusive record of the past, especially since this Case was contentious. Further, given that strategic interests fuelled much of the argument, led by a largely Western legal team, it is not possible to distil any reified Arab perspective on international law.

---

[10] Each Party presented weighty memorials, counter memorials and replies as well as voluminous documents at the written pleadings stage amounting to over ten thousand pages. Hearings before the Court accounted for five weeks of testimony, which often differed in emphasis from the earlier written memorials and were sometimes wholly new.

[11] *Qatar/Bahrain (Merits)* (2001), at para. 15.

[12] For a detailed overview of the forgeries affair written by Bahrain's Agent to the *Qatar/Bahrain* case, see J. S. Al-Arayed, *A Line in the Sea: The Qatar v. Bahrain Border Dispute in the World Court* (Berkeley, CA: North Atlantic Books, 2003), at 355–393.

Nevertheless, what this Case does provide is a site where two Arab states were able to exchange ideas about their intertwined colonial histories through the prism of international law. Perhaps because of similar colonial lineages and far less pronounced disparities in wealth, the parties played more nuanced roles than the example of Libya and Chad in Chapter Three. Bahrain and Qatar manipulated the colonial record in subtle ways, sometimes favouring and sometimes rejecting the typical 'colonial' perspective. How these arguments were received and thus legitimised by the Court will be relevant in assessing the extent to which international adjudication was able to grapple with and be shaped by non-European approaches to authority. What scope was there for dialogue about non-European modes of authority over territory? Further, how was the relationship between universalism and particularism within international legal discourse resolved?

Although the Case raised many extra-legal and historical issues directly affecting the dispute, both the majority judgment as well as most academic responses overlooked these broader considerations. As the minority judgment argued, the complicated and long-contested dispute warranted a careful examination of the interrelationship between history and law to satisfy both Qatar and Bahrain. The Court, however, fell short of offering a comprehensive decision. Why did the Court fail to confront this 'sordid'[13] colonial[14] past, as revealed especially by Qatar, and did it give adequate attention to the specific regional aspects of authority? More broadly, we can also ask whether the option of international dispute settlement can adequately embrace experiences and perspectives at odds with international law's largely European origins. The main themes to emerge from this chapter are the context of coercion informing 'colonial' agreements, the legal implications of indigenous sovereignty and the uses of historical argument. These themes are similar to those explored in Chapter Three, but methods of argument and presentation produced quite different results for the parties.

The chapter begins with an account of the general history of the dispute and the proceedings as well as the ruling itself. After an overview of the respective positions of the Court and the parties, three separate sections discuss the colonial legacy, the status of Hawar and then the status of Zubarah. The chapter concludes by assessing the implications of the Case for international law in the Gulf as well as the ICJ itself.

---

[13] *Qatar/Bahrain (Merits)*, CR 2000/7, 31 May 2000, Qatar, Sir Ian Sinclair, at para. 3.

[14] For convenience, I employ the terms 'colonial' and 'colonialism' in a very loose way because technically the relations between Britain and the Gulf sheikhdoms were neither equal nor colonial. In using the word colonial, though, I am deliberately wishing to emphasise that relations were based on a dynamic of British domination.

2) *Background to the Dispute*

Although the historical backdrop to this dispute spans almost two and a half centuries, it is possible to identify some central themes, including the persistence of tribal allegiances under Ottoman and British control, the creation of special treaty relations and the discovery of oil. Bahrain, and particularly Qatar, endeavoured to depict this historical record by inundating the Court with collections of documentary evidence. This material was useful in detailing each party's claims, but its value was not wholly positive. First, documents were often haphazardly organised, illegible and repeated throughout the course of the three merits stages. Second, documents are never proof *per se* of an argument, and this is attested by the same documents being relied upon to advance conflicting claims. Third, the rationale for the inclusion of so many documents was often avoided in preference for the tendency to include anything and everything of even the most tangential relevance to the Case.[15] Fourth, although this dispute concerned contested territorial and maritime claims by two Arab states, there was very little material available from the states themselves. This was explained in the oral pleadings as resulting from the parties' hailing from an 'Arab oral culture'.[16] The unfortunate result of this, however, was an excessive deference towards the imperial records of both Britain and the Sublime Porte that arguably – and inevitably – have shaped the pleadings in a particular way. As in the dispute between Libya, and especially Chad, the parties did not acknowledge the problematic aspect of using colonial materials in the assertion of postcolonial personality.

The geographical characteristics of Bahrain and Qatar have served as a curse and a blessing over the last few centuries of regional and international relations. Bahrain's strategic location along the trade routes between Europe and 'the Far East' meant that it was favoured by many foreign powers, including the Portuguese, the Persians, the Ottomans and the British.[17] Fresh water reserves[18] enhanced its desirability in the eyes of neighbouring tribes from the Qatari peninsula and the coastal mainland of modern day Saudi Arabia. To this day, Bahrain traces its roots to the Āl Khalīfa tribe, which moved from Kuwait in

---

[15] Or in the words of Bahrain, 'Some generalization is called for at the present stage of a case [oral pleadings] that has seen the introduction of so much documentary material. Qatar, in particular, has produced four times more pages of annexes than has Bahrain (even though Qatar has only used about 50 per cent of the documents submitted).' *Qatar/Bahrain (Merits)*, CR 2000/11, 8 June 2000, Bahrain, Sir Elihu Lauterpacht, at para. 16.

[16] *Qatar/Bahrain (Merits)*, CR 2000/5, 29 May 2000, Qatar, Ms Pilkington, at para. 9.

[17] G. Joffé, 'Concepts of Sovereignty in the Gulf Region', R. Schofield (ed.), *Territorial Foundations of the Gulf States* (London: UCL Press, 1994), 78–93, at 84.

[18] This characteristic of natural underground springs account for Bahrain's Arabic name (بحرين), which means two seas.

1762 to settle on the Western coast of Qatar in 1762. Later, in 1783, a group of inhabitants from the Qatari peninsula along with the Āl Khalīfas drove out the Persians from Bahrain. This group of islands became the Āl Khalīfa 'capital' in 1796, when rule was shifted from Zubarah to Bahrain, but with a continued presence in Zubarah. Despite this Āl Khalīfa presence, Bahrain was constantly assailed by foreign and tribal powers.

Britain had first secured a foothold in the region in 1783 with the establishment of the Bushire Regency in Persia as a new commercial outpost of the East India Company.[19] In the interests of mutual British and Bahraini trade relations, a General Treaty was forged between the East India Company and Oman and Bahrain in 1820.[20] Another general treaty with other Gulf powers soon followed.[21] War was not altogether eradicated by this effort and so another treaty was established in 1853 between Britain and what came to be known as the Trucial coast.[22] The independent ruler of Bahrain himself signed 'a perpetual treaty of peace and friendship' with Britain in 1861,[23] where Bahraini assurances against piracy were balanced by British security. This relationship was enhanced by the 1892 Exclusive Protection Agreement between the Chief of Bahrain and the British Political Resident of the Gulf in Bushire.[24] The treaty stipulated that neither the Chief nor his heirs were to enter into agreement or communication 'with any Power other than the British Government'. Also, agents from other powers were denied entry into Bahrain without British permission.[25]

Largely as a result of Qatar's inhospitable terrain and small population, it was not regarded with as much interest as its Bahraini neighbour from the perspective of the British. Treaty relations were first established in 1868, and as in the case of other Trucial agreements, maritime peace was to be observed.[26] Under this agreement Qatar continued to pay tribute to Bahrain, which in turn passed these monies onto the Wahhābī forces of the mainland. Partly in response to this Wahhābī threat from the Muslim heartland, the Ottoman Empire, as the

---

[19] Joffé, *supra* n. 17, at 88.

[20] General Treaty between the East India Company and the Friendly Arabs (Oman/Bahrain), 8 January 1820, 70 CTS 463. Also see Preliminary Treaty between the East India Company and Bahrain, 5 February 1820, 70 CTS 481.

[21] Preliminary Treaties between the East India Company and Shargah, Ras Al-Khaimeh, Dubai, Abu Dhabi & Zyah, 8–15 January 1820, 70 CTS 471.

[22] Treaty of Peace in Perpetuity between the Arab Chiefs of the Arabian Coast, 4 May 1853, 110 CTS 269.

[23] *Qatar/Bahrain* (2001), at para. 39. Convention between Great Britain and Bahrain, 31 May 1861, 124 CTS 163.

[24] Great Britain-Trucial Sheikhdoms, Exclusive Agreements, 6/8 March 1892, 176 CTS 457.

[25] *Qatar/Bahrain* (2001), at para. 44.

[26] Agreements between Great Britain and Qatar and Abu Dhabi (Trucial Sheikhdoms of Oman), 12, 16 September 1868, 138 CTS 56.

self-proclaimed protector of Islam's Holy Sites,[27] had reasserted itself in the region from 1871, as was discussed generally in Chapter Two.[28] A Turkish garrison was established at Doha on the Eastern side of Qatar, but it seems from many accounts that the ruling Āl Thānī family simply flew the Ottoman flag at convenient moments and were only supportive of the Turks so as to repel other foreign powers.[29]

While the Ottoman Empire retained its largely land-based presence, Britain deepened its relations with the coastal sheikhs by establishing protection regimes.[30] With the decline of Ottoman influence in the region, Qatar entered into a treaty of protection in 1916, only three years after the Anglo-Ottoman Treaty of 1913 had guaranteed Qatari independence and with a consequent ban on Bahraini interference in its affairs.[31] The motivations behind protection agreements and their exact legal status will be considered below, but they at least set the backdrop to Britain's involvement in the parties' disputes over Zubarah and Hawar, which occurred frequently throughout the twentieth century. In the context of the growing demand for oil,[32] the need for clearly defined borders became acute, especially for the British 'protectors' as well as British and American oil companies – this in a region where tribes paid little heed to territorial boundaries and the notion of the nation-state had yet to take root.[33]

Independence from Britain in 1971 did not bring about any fundamental change for Bahrain and Qatar regarding their territorial disputes. In the past, Britain had been the sole arbiter in these affairs, but after 1971 regional Arab powers filled this vacuum. Due to turbulence created in the region over the simmering Qatari-Bahraini dispute, Saudi Arabia offered its good offices from 1976 onwards, and such efforts have continued with varying intensity through

---

[27] Of Islam's three most holy sites, two are in present-day Saudi Arabia: Mecca and Medina.

[28] 'By 1795 the Wahhabis had taken control of Central Arabia and reached the Hasa coast, and were preparing for further expansion…In 1802 the holy city of Mecca fell to the Wahhabis, and from at least 1803 until 1811 both Bahrain and Qatar were subject to the influence of…the Wahhabi Amir. The extent of this power was an embarrassment to the Ottoman Sultan, who claimed to be the titular overlord of the Hijaz and the leading Muslim sovereign with the right to control the Holy Places.' Qatar, Memorial, *Qatar/Bahrain (Merits)*, 30 September 1996, at para. 3.11. Also see 82.

[29] F. F. Anscombe, *The Ottoman Gulf: The Creation of Kuwait, Saudi Arabia, and Qatar* (New York: Columbia University Press, 1997), at 32.

[30] Qatar, Memorial, *(Qatar/Bahrain) (Merits)*, 30 September 1996, at para. 3.11, at 20.

[31] Schofield, *supra* n. 2, at 32.

[32] Oil was first discovered in commercial quantities on Bahrain in 1932. Al-Arayed, *supra* n. 12, at 161.

[33] For an overview of approaches to territory and borders in the Gulf generally, see Schofield, *supra* n. 2, at 1–77.

to the present.[34] In the course of Saudi-facilitated letter exchanges and meetings, the idea of resolving the dispute before the ICJ grew in vigour, and after drawing up a mooted framework for the hearing in 1988, Qatar accepted this 'Bahraini formula' in 1990.

3) *The Jurisdictional Stage of the Case*[35]

Although Bahrain had designed the terms for which the parties would bring their claim to the Court, it strongly resisted Qatar's unilateral application to the Court in 1991, thus creating a complex 'interlocutory' phase of the Case,[36] which considered possible bases of the Court's jurisdiction.[37] Qatar grounded its jurisdictional claim on an exchange of letters between Bahrain, Saudi Arabia and itself in 1987, which included the following points:

> All issues of dispute between the two countries, relating to sovereignty over the islands, maritime boundaries and territorial waters, are to be considered as complementary, indivisible issues, to be solved comprehensively together.

And

> In case that the negotiations provided for in the fourth principle fail to reach agreement on the solution of one or more of the aforesaid disputed matters, the Governments of the two countries shall undertake, in consultation with the Government of Saudi Arabia, to determine the best means of resolving that matter or matters, on the basis of the provisions of international law. The ruling of the authority agreed upon for this purpose shall be final and binding.

Aside from some disagreement over Zubarah, it was decided throughout the course of discussions that the dispute would be based on the Bahraini Formula. Later in 1990 at a Gulf Cooperation Council (GCC) meeting the Foreign Ministers from Bahrain and Qatar signed Minutes, whose translation was of central importance in the resulting jurisdictional hearings:

---

[34] *Qatar/Bahrain*, ICJ Reps (2001), at para. 66.

[35] For some general overviews of this stage of the case, see A. M. Campbell, 'International Law – Maritime Delimitation and Territorial Dispute – Qatar v. Bahrain, 1994 I.C.J. 112 (July 1)' (1996) 19 *Suffolk Transnational Law Review* 573; and C Reichel, 'Maritime Delimitation and Territorial Questions between Qatar and Bahrain' (1998) 26 *Denver Journal of International Law and Policy* 725.

[36] J. Klabbers, 'Qatar v. Bahrain: the concept of "treaty" in international law' (1995) 33 *Archiv des Völkerrechts* 361, at 375.

[37] For a good overview of the jurisdictional stage of the dispute, see M. D. Evans, 'Case Concerning Maritime Delimitation and Territorial Questions between Qatar and Bahrain (*Qatar v. Bahrain*), Jurisdiction and Admissibility' (1995) 44 *International and Comparative Law Quarterly* 691.

(1) to reaffirm what was agreed previously between the two Parties;
(2) to continue the good offices of the Custodian of the Two Holy Mosques, King Fahd Ben Abdul Aziz, between the two countries till the month of Shawwal, 1411 H, corresponding to May of the next year 1991. After the end of this period, the Parties may submit the matter to the International Court of Justice in accordance with the Bahraini formula, which has been accepted by Qatar, and the proceedings arising therefrom. Saudi Arabia's good offices will continue during the submission of the matter to arbitration;
(3) should a brotherly solution acceptable to the two Parties be reached, the case will be withdrawn from arbitration.[38]

The translation of *al-ṭarafān* (الطرفان), variously rendered as 'the Parties' or 'both Parties', was particularly contested as its meaning directly affected whether it was possible for Qatar to show that unilateral seisen had been contemplated in earlier agreements.[39] The Court chose not to confuse itself with this debate in any substantive way and confined itself instead to the terms of the agreements.

In its July 1994 judgment, the Court held by fifteen votes to one (Judge Oda dissenting on all four operative paragraphs)[40] first, that

> the exchanges of letters between the King of Saudi Arabia and the Amir of Qatar dated 19 and 21 December 1987, and between the King of Saudi and the Amir of Bahrain dated 19 and 26 December 1987, and the document headed 'Minutes' and signed at Doha on 25 December 1990 by the Ministers of Foreign Affairs of Bahrain, Qatar and Saudi Arabia, are international agreements creating rights and obligations for the Parties.[41]

---

[38] This translation was submitted by Qatar. Bahrain's translation is slightly different:

1. To reaffirm what was previously agreed between the two Parties.
2. The good offices of the Custodian of the Two Holy Mosques, King Fahd b. Abdul Aziz will continue between the two countries until the month of Shawwal 1411 A.H., corresponding to May 1991. The two Parties may, at the end of this period, submit the matter to the International Court of Justice in accordance with the Bahraini formula, which the State of Qatar has accepted, and with the procedures consequent on it. The good offices of the Kingdom of Saudi Arabia will continue during the period when the matter is under arbitration.
3. If a brotherly solution acceptable to the two Parties is reached, the case will be withdrawn from arbitration.

[39] For a discussion of these translation difficulties, see J. McHugo, 'The Judgment of the International Court of Justice in the Jurisdiction and Admissibility Phase of Qatar v. Bahrain: An Example of the Continuing Need for "Fact-Scepticism"' (1997) 28 *Netherlands Yearbook of International Law* 171.

[40] See his separate judgment, International Court of Justice, *Maritime Delimitation and Territorial Questions between Qatar and Bahrain (Qatar/Bahrain) (Jurisdiction and Admissibility)* (1994), (diss. op. Oda), p. 133.

[41] *Maritime Delimitation and Territorial Questions between Qatar and Bahrain (Qatar/Bahrain) (Jurisdiction and Admissibility)* (1994) ICJ Rep 112, at para. 41(1).

Second, that

> by the terms of those agreements the Parties have undertaken to submit to the Court the whole of the dispute between them, as circumscribed by the text proposed by Bahrain to Qatar on 26 October 1988, and accepted by Qatar in December 1990, referred to in the 1990 Doha Minutes as the 'Bahraini formula'.[42]

Third, that the parties could submit 'the whole of the dispute' to the Court within fixed (and very short) time limits, with the possibility of subsequent matters arising for its determination.[43] Essentially, 'the Court decided that there was a special agreement, and this special agreement was sufficient for the Court to be seised, at least preliminarily.'[44]

Although Bahrain was afforded the opportunity to frame the matter after the July 1994 Judgment, it persisted in rejecting the Court's jurisdiction and so in its second judgment the Court settled on Qatar's application for defining the dispute. Thus by ten votes to five, the Court firstly found that

> it has jurisdiction to adjudicate upon the dispute submitted to it between the State of Qatar and Bahrain

and second

> that the application of the State of Qatar as formulated on 30 November 1994 is admissible.[45]

The merits phase would be based on the following matters:

1. The Hawar Islands, including the island of Janan;
2. Fasht al Dibal and Qit'at Jaradah;
3. The archipelagic baselines;
4. Zubarah;
5. The areas for fishing for pearls and for fishing for swimming fish and any other matters connected with maritime boundaries.[46]

Despite Bahraini unease at this outcome, it decided to participate in the merits phase of proceedings so as not to prejudice its interests over the contested sites. Earlier agreements between Qatar and Bahrain had called for preservation of the

---

[42] *Qatar/Bahrain* (1994) ICJ Rep 112, at para. 41(2).

[43] *Qatar/Bahrain* (1994) ICJ Rep, at para. 41(3–5).

[44] Klabbers, *supra* n. 36, at 362. Here, Klabbers is relying on Judge Oda's dissenting opinion, *supra* n. 40.

[45] *Maritime Delimitation and Territorial Questions between Qatar and Bahrain (Qatar/Bahrain) (Jurisdiction and Admissibility)* (1995) ICJ Rep 6, at para. 50(1–2).

[46] *Qatar/Bahrain* (1995) ICJ Rep 6, at para. 47.

status quo.[47] In spite of such undertakings, there were a number of alleged breaches of the *status quo* in relation to the Hawar Islands throughout the nineties.[48]

Before reviewing the Court's decision on the merits, it is necessary to comment on the ramifications of its 1994 and 1995 judgments relating to jurisdiction. The Court's determination that two informal agreements constituted the grounds for consent disturbed a number of commentators, who have suggested that it marked the end of clearly defined parameters of consent.[49] 'The creation of commitments [even if only informal], according to the Court, by necessity implies the creation of legal rights and obligations'.[50] Chinkin points out that this ruling could induce great uncertainty on the part of many states no longer willing to enter into informal agreements, such as the minutes at the centre of the present dispute.[51] For legal doctrine more broadly, she asks 'whether the ruling...has undermined certainty in differentiating binding and non-binding agreements'.[52] On the other hand, Rosenne views the jurisdictional outcome in more positive terms:

> The framework agreement as it has developed – spasmodically – does not have the characteristics of the classic special agreement, by which the dispute is defined and the jurisdiction of the Court is established by a single event, the notification of the special agreement to the Court. The framework agreement, a form of agreement covering disagreement, has developed in response to the requirements of diplomacy which has recognized that a dispute should not be permitted to smoulder indefinitely, but which at the same time, for reasons particular to the states concerned, cannot be defined jointly and notified jointly to the Court.[53]

It is probably too early to tell whether states have altered their behaviour as a result of this ruling, but it sends a clear signal to Arab states in the Gulf to be

---

[47] For example, the Agreement of December 1987 included the following provision:

> Until a final settlement for the disputed matter is reached...:
>
> Each party shall undertake from to-date to refrain from any action that would strengthen its legal position, weaken the legal position of the other party, or change the *status quo* with regard to the disputed matters. Any such action shall be regarded null and void and shall have no legal effect...

Qatar, Memorial, *(Qatar/Bahrain) (Questions of Jurisdiction and Admissibility)*, 10 February 1992, at para. 3.27.

[48] For a collection of *notes verbales* detailing these breaches, see Qatar, Counter-Memorial, vol. 5; and Qatar, Reply, vol. 5.

[49] Generally see also Klabbers *supra* n. 36; and McHugo, *supra* n. 39.

[50] Klabbers, *supra* n. 36, at 370.

[51] C. Chinkin, 'A Mirage in the Sand? Distinguishing Binding and Non-Binding Relations Between States' (1997) 10 *Leiden Journal of International Law* 223, at 224.

[52] Ibid., at 225.

[53] S. Rosenne, 'The Qatar/Bahrain Case: What is a Treaty? A Framework Agreement and the Seising of the Court' (1995) 8 *Leiden Journal of International Law* 161, at 181.

mindful of what agreements they enter into. Although Bahrain participated in the merits phase, some of its actions outside of the Peace Palace suggest that its faith in the Court was shaky. It also remains to be seen whether the Court's less than detailed treatment of the substantive territorial claims has assuaged scepticism in the Gulf or the wider Arab world.

4) *The Court's Determination on the Merits*

After a series of lengthy pleadings, complicated by the controversy over Qatar's allegedly forged documents, the Court handed down its decision on 16 March 2001. Qatar had withdrawn the 82 disputed documents and had not relied on them in its later pleadings, and both Qatar and Bahrain submitted new versions of Qatar's Memorial and Counter-Memorial where they crossed out all discussion based on the disputed evidence.[54] The details of the judgment will be analysed in the next section, so here it is only necessary to acquaint ourselves with the central arguments of the parties and the Court's determination. Bahrain claimed sovereignty over all the areas in dispute, whereas Qatar requested the Court to declare the absence of such sovereignty rather than positively find for Qatar in the matter. Thus, Qatar's application was a negation of Bahrain's, quoted below:

> Bahrain is sovereign over Zubarah.
> Bahrain is sovereign over the Hawar Islands, including Janan and Hadd Janan.
> In view of Bahrain's sovereignty over all the insular and other features, including Fasht ad Dibal and Qit'at Jaradah, comprising the Bahraini archipelago, the maritime boundary between Bahrain and Qatar is as described in Part Two of Bahrain's Memorial.[55]

After giving fairly equal consideration to the territorial and maritime questions in a relatively brief judgment, the Court:

> (1) Unanimously... Finds that the State of Qatar has sovereignty over Zubarah;
> (2) (a) By twelve votes to five... Finds that the State of Bahrain has sovereignty over the Hawar Islands;
> (b) Unanimously... Recalls that vessels of the State of Qatar enjoy in the territorial sea of Bahrain separating the Hawar Islands from the other Bahraini

[54] It has been very difficult to determine which versions of Qatar's memorials are best to read. In the course of researching this chapter I decided to rely on Bahrain's highlighted version which still allowed me to read Qatar's crossed out claims. On general impression, the most commonly deleted material centred on regional consensus over the extent of Qatar's authority over Zubarah and the Hawar Islands.

[55] *Qatar/Bahrain (Merits)*, CR 2000/25, 29 June 2000, Bahrain, Mr Al-Arayed, at paras. 19–20.

islands the right of innocent passage accorded by customary international law;

(3) By thirteen votes to four... Finds that the State of Qatar has sovereignty over Janan Island, including Hadd Janan;

(4) By twelve votes to five... Finds that the State of Bahrain has sovereignty over the island of Qit'at Jaradah;

(5) Unanimously... Finds that the low-tide elevation of Fasht ad Dibal falls under the sovereignty of the State of Qatar;

(6) By thirteen votes to four... Decides that the single maritime boundary that divides the various maritime zones of the State of Qatar and the State of Bahrain shall be drawn as indicated in paragraph 250 of the present Judgment.[56]

Aside from the majority judgment, a joint dissenting opinion was rendered by Judges Bedjaoui, Ranjeva and Koroma as well as a separate dissenting opinion by Judge *ad hoc* Torres Bernádez (appointed by Qatar). Judges Oda, Parra-Aranguren, Kooijmans, Al-Khasawneh and Judge *ad hoc* Fortier (appointed by Bahrain) offered separate Opinions. Judges Vereshchetin, Higgins and Herczegh also issued declarations.

In relation to territorial matters, Evans argues that 'the Court took what might be thought of as the line of least resistance.'[57] The Court avoided engagement with many of the substantive arguments raised by Bahrain and Qatar in relation to title to territory, the status of various *effectivités* and the nature of consent for 'protected' states. This failure 'to give a complete ruling', in the dissenting opinion of Judges Bedjaoui, Ranjeva and Koroma signaled 'that the Court has... taken the risk not only of rendering an incorrect judgment but also of failing to give a complete ruling.'[58] The ramifications of such an outcome may well be felt beyond the courtroom in the Arab and non-Arab worlds. When the Court handed down its decision, President Guillaume stated, 'This judgment is binding, final and without appeal. It brings to an end a long-standing dispute between these two sister-States, thereby inaugurating a new stage in their relations.'[59] Whether this statement is correct can only be answered with time. However, it is possible to assess whether the criticisms rendered in the dissenting opinion were warranted. Did the Court confront all of the central issues as they related to territory, and if not, what are the possible reasons to explain its reluctance to do so? These questions will serve as a window into our discussion in the following section.

---

[56] *Qatar/Bahrain* (2001), at para. 252.

[57] M. D. Evans, 'Case Concerning Maritime Delimitation and Territorial Questions between Qatar and Bahrain (Qatar v Bahrain)' (2002) 51 *International and Comparative Law Quarterly* 709, at 712.

[58] *Qatar/Bahrain* (2001) Bedjaoui, Ranjeva & Koroma J. J. (diss. op.), at para. 14.

[59] Quoted in Kwiatkowska, *supra*, n. 9, at 232.

5) *Competing Narratives on Statehood and Colonialism in the Gulf*

This section engages directly with the reasoning contained in the parties' submissions as well as the various decisions of the Court itself. It will focus firstly on depictions of the colonial experience to problematise the historical record. It will then take up the claims advanced over the Hawar Islands and Zubarah respectively, focusing on issues relating to tribal affiliations, the status of protection agreements, communal property rights, the nature of *uti possidetis juris* in the Gulf and the relevance of Islamic norms for international law in such disputes. All of these ideas appeared in the pleadings, but often in radically different ways. A comparison will enable us to draw conclusions about the extent to which international law can be shaped and broadened by the experiences and arguments of Arab states. Harking back to my central research question about the scope for international law as a universalising discourse, we can ask here: Is international law open to particular experiences of non-European control over territory? Further, how did Qatar and Bahrain draw the boundaries of international law in their account of colonial practices?

a) *Historical Narratives on the Legacy of Colonialism*

An understanding of the complex Case between Qatar and Bahrain cannot avoid 'a long tramp through the sands of history'.[60] The centrality of the historical record was recognised not only by Qatar and Bahrain but also by the Court in its 'brief account of the complex history'.[61] Despite such recognition, historical facts were usually treated out of context and accepted at face value. This was especially so in relation to the nature of former foreign control in the Gulf. Chapter Three's discussion about the colonial histories of Chad and Libya demonstrated how there is never one historical record or one interpretation. How did the parties use historical arguments, and how did the Court respond to these accounts? Does the grammar of international law allow for historical complexity or not? This section will sketch out some contrasting historical images to show how history and international law are interdependent, but not through any pre-determined relationship. Instead, the dialectic between the two is shaped by extra-historical and extra-legal perspectives rarely averred to in the judgment or the pleadings. Yet in drawing boundaries between law and its 'others', the centrality of history, politics and culture becomes more apparent than ever.

All historical narratives recognised the influence of the British presence in the Gulf. British motivations, however, were usually described as being simply

[60] *Qatar/Bahrain (Merits)*, CR 2000/5, 29 May 2000, Qatar, Mr Salmon, at para. 9.

[61] *Qatar/Bahrain* (2001), at para. 36.

based on a 'commercial interest in protecting maritime trade routes to India.'[62] A purported increase in piracy in what came to be known as the 'Pirate Coast' 'led to the first major change in the British role in… [this] area' of 'great strategic importance'.[63] No interrogation of this British justification between the illegality of piracy and intervention was carried out by Bahrain or Qatar. Instead, the historical narratives of both Bahrain and Qatar are often uncritical in their reliance on British imperial sources, such as the reports of James Lorimer.[64]

Conversely, in *The Myth of Arab Piracy in the Gulf*, the Arab historian, Al-Qāsimī clearly states his scholarly agenda: the notion that piracy warranted Britain's intimate and 'protective' involvement in the Gulf is contestable. Al-Qāsimī refutes the claims of certain colonial and contemporary historians, such as Lorimer and Kelly, both of whom were relied upon in the memorials of Qatar and Bahrain. Al-Qāsimī's argument is forceful but was overlooked by the two states in their submissions:

> The indigenous people of the Gulf were normal people with normal human ambitions. Although poor, they were skilful. They were people practicing normal human activities, in particular trade, in which they had been involved for millennia. The only abnormal factor was the introduction of a foreign power whose aim was to dominate and exploit. The intruders were the forces of British imperialism, who knew very well and often testified that the indigenous people of the Gulf were only interested in the peaceful pursuits of pearl diving and trade.[65]

Through an unquestioning acceptance of British imperial material, Bahrain and Qatar failed to appreciate the colonial desires shaping events as well as their later depiction in the Gulf.

Al-Qāsimī's insights are confirmed in some of the Ottoman sources included in the voluminous documentary annexes of Qatar's Reply. Such inconsistent use of evidence was not only sloppy, but indicates the tendency of the parties to include as much material as possible even where it was discordant. The Ottomans were

---

[62] Bahrain, Memorial, *(Qatar/ Bahrain) (Merits)*, 30 September 1996, para. 136. Anghie discusses how norms developed in international law that gave support to the European desire for commercial expansion through trading companies. Initial justifications based on the right of free trade later gave way to fully-fledged colonial administrations. This was not the case so much in the Gulf as it was a relative latecomer to this trend, but Anghie's point does reveal the interrelationship that existed between international law, European trade and later modes of colonial rule. T. Anghie, *Imperialism, Sovereignty and the Making of International Law* (Cambridge, UK; New York, US: Cambridge University Press, 2005), at 67–69.

[63] Qatar, Memorial, *(Qatar /Bahrain) (Merits)*, 30 September 1996, at para. 3.3.

[64] For example: J. G. Lorimer, *Gazetteer of the Persian Gulf, Oman, and Central Arabia* (Calcutta: Superintendent Government Printing, 1908–1915), 2 vols. For a discussion of Lorimer's racist tendencies, see S. N. Grovogui, *Sovereigns, Quasi-Sovereigns, and Africans: Race and Self-Determination in International Law* (Minneapolis: University of Minnesota Press, 1996), at 70–73.

[65] S. M. Al-Qāsimī, *The Myth of Arab Piracy in the Gulf* (London: Routledge, 1986), at xiv.

only too aware of British ambitions in the Gulf and it was partly in reaction to such a threat that they had reasserted their control over certain Gulf territories in the latter half of the nineteenth century. The Sublime Porte's Ministry of the Interior surmised the situation in 1910 in the following terms: 'The objective of Britain is to incite the local muslims to take up arms against each other, to impose a status quo on the region and occupy the coastline, claiming that her economic commercial interests are suffering.'[66]

Such British motivations are not only unsurprising; they are to be expected. Some of the implications of colonial policy, however, were overlooked by the parties and the Court when formulating general accounts of British-Gulf relations. Britain was not simply concerned with 'protecting' its trade and Trucial partners from other powers, such as the Wahhābīs, Persians and Ottomans. This is clear when we consider the way in which treaty terms between Britain and the Arab sheikhs took on increasingly restrictive qualities, preventing any interaction between local sheikhs and non-British powers.[67]

Britain had maintained that the independence of entities such as Qatar and Bahrain was never compromised. Qatar and Bahrain advanced diametrically opposed positions on this very point and the Court struggled to formulate a clear position on the matter. It is difficult to define the international legal personality of such entities.[68] For example, the pleadings and the judgment differ as to when Qatar became an independent entity, and even then this was under the shadow of either Ottoman[69] or British control. In relation to Qatar, it was

[66] Qatar, Reply, *(Qatar/Bahrain) (Merits)*, Annexes, vol. 2, at 297. Another example of such sentiments from 1900 reads: 'it is important to establish an administration which will show the Ottomans to be in complete control; it will prevent the English making their claims elsewhere, interfering on the pretext of a few minor incidents between the sheikhs'. 'Report on Bahrain' from Council Chamber, 22 April 1900, Bahrain, Memorial, vol. 2, Annex 64(a), at 274.

[67] This is detailed in another Ottoman report: 'Despite Britain's recognition of the Bahrain Islands' independence, she considers herself privileged as regards the agreements she has made and continually repeats that she will not let any other government interfere in Bahrain's internal policy.' Report of the Foreign Minister, 27 January 1909, Bahrain, Memorial, vol. 3, Annex 75(a), at 401.

[68] See J. Crawford, *The Creation of States in International Law* (Cambridge: Cambridge University Press, 2nd, edition, 2006), at 291–292.

[69] For example, in 1898, Qatar's ruler pledged his services to the Ottomans: 'I am not a rebel and have no intention of acting against the Sultan's will. Until now I have been in the service of the Ottoman state, both with my person and my possessions, without having an ulterior motive.' Telegram from Bushire by Jassim Āl Thānī, Kaimakam of Qatar, 23 January 1898 to the Office of the Grand Vizier, Qatar, Reply, vol. 2, at 165. Although this is only a statement and does not represent the legal status of Qatar *per se*, it suggests that Qatar's independence was less than complete at the turn of the twentieth century.

common to elide Qatari identity with its imperial master,[70] but the necessary corollary of state succession after Ottoman rule was not developed. The line between Ottoman and Qatari personality is thus very hard to discern.

Despite this confusion, what remained indisputable was the impact of underlying British interests and the significant imbalance of power between such a hegemon compared to the sparsely populated sheikhdoms of the Gulf. This power dynamic influenced the possibility for freely given Arab consent. Like Libya's discussion of its relations with France in the *Libya/Chad* Case, Qatar questioned the applicability of the notion of sovereign equality in a context of quasi-colonial domination. The law/politics dichotomy upholds the notion of legal relations free from coercion and influence, but Qatar's argumentative strategy sought to break this schema down. For Qatar, Britain was never a neutral arbiter, administrator or policy advisor in the Gulf, and documentation from the annexes attests to this. For example, internal memos mooting the ownership of contested territories between Qatar and Bahrain do not rely on a rigorous categorisation of title and *effectivités*. Instead, the future control of various islands or regions was dependent on British strategic concerns,[71] and this was particularly pronounced with the advent of oil when Britain was keen to thwart American penetration in the region.[72] The exploitation of oil made it necessary to establish clear and precise boundaries between the Sheikhdoms. However, the desirability of borders was a recent phenomenon, as previously

---

[70] For example, in its pleadings, Qatar argued, 'The fact remains that Sheikh Jassim Āl Thānī ruled the entire province of Qatar, and that he governed the territory both in his own right and as surrogate for the Ottoman Empire.' *Qatar/Bahrain (Merits)*, 2000/17, 20 June 2000, Bahrain, Mr Bundy, at para. 24.

[71] An excellent example of this is some correspondence between two British officials in 1905: 'Captain Prideaux's [the author of the letter] studies have brought him to the conclusion that our record places us in a position to modify the attitude hitherto adopted in regard to this part of the Arab Coast, and that in making the change there are three alternative policies to choose from…:

> That the suzerainty of the Ruler of Bahrein should be reasserted over the whole of the Katr peninsula, except the Al Bidaa [Doha, modern-day capital of Qatar] Chiefship, the limits of which should be reduced to the narrowest possible limits.
>
> That for reasons stated we should declare the complete independence of the Maritime Arab tribes and maintain a post and Native Agent on the Katr Coast so long as the Turks remain at Al Bidaa.
>
> That we should agree to recognise the sovereignty of the Turks over the whole of the Katr peninsula on certain conditions…

Captain Prideaux favours the last.'

This extract reveals that Britain was willing to create or annihilate the legal titles of states at will. Letter from Capt. Prideaux to Maj. Cox, 16 July 1905, Bahrain, Memorial, vol. 3, Annex 71, at 355.

[72] *Qatar/Bahrain (Merits)*, CR 2000/7, 31 May 2000, Qatar, Mr. Shankardass, at para. 10.

both the Ottomans and the British asserted that to 'try and sort out boundaries at this point [at end of the nineteenth century] would not be appropriate, but would raise new problems.'[73]

Concerns about future oil concessions were vital in explaining British policy towards its protectorates in the Gulf, including Bahrain and Qatar. If these decisions had had no legal effect, there would have been little need to consider them here. However, the Court's judgment relied on British decisions without acknowledging the underlying motivations at play. In so doing, the judgment rendered the decisions of a quasi-colonial power valid under international law today. Instead of adopting a critical approach to the historical record, which could have facilitated recognition of the competing interests at play, the Court, and sometimes the parties themselves, overlooked the consequences of quasi-colonialism.

b) *Determining Sovereignty over the Hawar Islands*

i) *The 1939 Decision*

The international legal effects of British control were demonstrated most clearly in the Court's ruling on the Hawar Islands, which were 'the greatest bone of contention between the two Parties'.[74] Although the Court focused on the 1939 British award of Hawar to Bahrain, both parties based their competing claims on a number of grounds in addition to the award. Thus treatment of and reliance on the 1939 award will be reviewed first and then compared with some of the parties' other claims to demonstrate how the Court's reasoning prioritised colonial practices above evidence of local authority.

In a context framed around the urgent need for demarcated boundaries to facilitate oil exploitation, Britain issued an award in 1939, whereby it determined that Bahrain held title over the Hawar Islands. This finding was beneficial to Bahrain, and so Bahrain relied heavily on certain elements and legal principles relating to the award in its pleadings. Tensions between Qatar and Bahrain over the islands had escalated from 1937 when Bahrain occupied them and asserted its title. These events coincided with Britain's admission that 'the ownership of the

[73] Ottoman Report on the Zubarah affair, 3 May 1897, Bahrain, Memorial, vol. 2, Annex 63(a), at 269. The British echo these sentiments: 'The question of sovereign and feudal rights over places and tribes on the mainland of Arabia, opposite the Island of Bahrain, is a complicated one, and probably the Government would not deem it practicable or expedient to enter into its merits.' Letter from Lt. Col. Ross, British Political Resident, to Secretary to Govt. of India, 4 September 1873, Bahrain, Memorial, vol. 2, Annex 20, at 174.

[74] *Qatar/Bahrain (Merits)*, CR 2000/17, 20 June 2000, Qatar, Mr Salmon, at para. 1.

Hawar Group is of great importance because it is directly in...the oil "line".'[75] In anticipation of competing claims to this resource-rich area, the British had issued a 'provisional decision' in 1936 which acknowledged that 'it might...suit us politically to have as large an area of possible included under Bahrain' for oil concession purposes.[76] The details of this 'preliminary' decision by the British were never relayed to Qatar, and, furthermore, Qatar was never given the chance to rebut claims made by Bahrain, which had become the presumptive beneficiary of Britain's decision.

Notwithstanding this clandestine event, Qatar sought a settlement of the situation and entrusted that the British would confirm its sovereignty over the Hawar Islands. Thus, between 1938 and 1939, both Bahrain and Qatar submitted a series of letters to British agents outlining their respective *effectivités* and purported title over the islands. Although Qatar had participated in the process, it tried to show the Court how its involvement at the time was flawed because it had not consented to Britain alienating the territory. Qatar also went into detail about British partiality in rendering its decision in the 1939 award. Here, Qatar was trying to uphold its former status as a protected, but still *independent* state, and so in some ways the law/politics dichotomy was useful. By pointing to the treaty provisions between Britian and the Trucial states, legally the Gulf sheikhdoms were independent. On the other hand, Qatar was trying to show how in the example of the 1939 'arbitral award' that law was inherently linked with politics; the Court had to consider background agendas and not simply take the decision at face value.[77]

Despite such arguments, both the majority judgment and Bahrain characterised Qatar's consent at the time as unproblematic: the judgment failed to acknowledge the wider context of British oil interests or its undertakings towards Bahrain. Throughout its pleadings, however, Qatar was at pains to show how this episode of British 'arbitration' was tainted by self-interest and should not result in permanent consequences for two independent states in the postcolonial era. This attempt to thwart Britain's legacy was not simply a product of ICJ litigation, either: Qatar showed the Court instead how it had challenged the British decision on a number of occasions.[78] Bahrain tried to undermine Qatar's

---

[75] Letter from Captain T. Hickinbotham, British Political Agent (officiating), to the British Political Resident, 9 May 1936, Bahrain, Counter-Memorial, vol. 2, Annex 73, at 236. This was also the opinion of Loch: '[Hawar] may have considerable value now that oil has been found in Bahrain and is hoped for in Qatar', Letter from Lt. Col. Loch, British Political Agent, to Lt. Col. Fowle, British Political Resident, 6 May 1936, Bahrain, Memorial, vol. 5, Annex 247, at 1074.

[76] Quoted in *Qatar/Bahrain (Merits)* (2001) (diss. op. Bernádez), at para. 311.

[77] *Qatar/Bahrain* (2001), at para. 105.

[78] This is noted by the Court: *Qatar/Bahrain* (2001), at para. 106.

later protests by explaining them away as an instance of disappointment from an unfavourable decision. After hearing these arguments as well as summarising them in its judgment,[79] the Court chose not to engage with Qatar's challenge to consent and British authority. Although it did concede that the 1939 decision was not an arbitral award *per se*, the Court was still comfortable in affirming its 'legal effect':[80] the 1939 decision was a valid and fair reflection of Bahrain's ancient title and *effectivités*.[81]

Bahrain[82] sought to bolster 'the powerful legal position it enjoyed by virtue of the 1939 decision'[83] by relying on the principles of *uti possidetis* and *res judicata*. Bahrain had portrayed the 1939 award as an 'arbitral', or 'legal', one, and in the absence of Bahraini consent for its reconsideration by the ICJ, the principle of *res judicata* precluded reconsideration of the matter; its legal effect was irreproachable.[84] Such a gesture illustrates the use of the law/politics dichotomy well: Bahrain sought to shield British 'political' decision-making from scrutiny though resort to legal niceties. Further, in advancing this argument, Bahrain seems to have opted for international legal personality given that the concept of arbitration rests on neutral adjudication between *independent* entities. This was confirmed when Bahrain argued that any consideration of the matter would seem to bestow on the Court 'an appellate jurisdiction over the award'[85] for the first time in the ICJ's history. Thus, at least in relation to the nature of the 1939 Award, Bahrain claimed that before formal independence both Bahrain and Qatar had been independent, but 'protected', states under British care.

In contrast to notions of independence, Bahrain also invoked the idea of *uti possidetis juris*.[86] Throughout the Case, Bahrain was trying to offer as many arguments as possible even though they were incompatible: *res judicata* assumes legal independence whereas *uti possidetis* is necessarily the result of colonial administrative boundaries. In invoking the latter norm, Bahrain characterised the status of both Qatar and itself as being one of 'former British protectorates… [until] their independence in 1971.'[87] From an examination of the treaty provisions, Bahrain

---

[79] *Qatar/Bahrain* (2001), at paras. 98–109.

[80] *Qatar/Bahrain* (2001), at para. 139.

[81] *Qatar/Bahrain* (2001), at paras. 142–147.

[82] For Bahrain's presentation of the 1939 decision, see generally *Qatar/Bahrain (Merits)*, CR 2000/12, 9 June 2000, Mr Paulsson, at paras. 138–205.

[83] *Qatar/Bahrain (Merits)*, CR 2000/12, 9 June 2000, Bahrain, Mr Paulsson, at para. 201.

[84] *Qatar/Bahrain (Merits)*, CR 2000/12, 9 June 2000, Bahrain, Mr Reisman, at paras. 1–14.

[85] Ibid., at para. 14.

[86] This inherent contradiction in Bahrain's 'à la carte menu' of possible grounds for claiming the Hawar Islands is discussed by Judge *ad hoc* Bernádez in his Dissenting Opinion, *Qatar/Bahrain (Merits)* (2001), at paras. 292, 298.

[87] *Qatar/Bahrain (Merits)*, CR 2000/13, 13 June 2000, Bahrain, Mr Kemicha, para. 20. Cf. *Qatar/Bahrain (Merits)*, CR 2000/17, 20 June 2000, Qatar, Mr Salmon, at para. 7.

asserted that neither sheikhdom was able 'fully to exercise their sovereignty in domestic and foreign affairs.'[88] Perhaps aware of its inconsistent reliance on colonial dividends – was Bahrain independent or not before 1971? – Bahrain tried to smooth over its deference to British control by recognising the injustices of colonialism.[89] A critical approach to the past expressed in emotive language was fleeting, however, because Bahrain's reliance on the legality of the 1939 Award required its general acceptance of British domination. Thus, Bahrain claimed that '*the 1939 decision is indisputably an integral part of the colonial legacy...facts are facts!*'[90] There was no room for any critical interrogation of colonial practices or the legal results of such 'facts'. As in the case of Chad in Chapter Three, Bahrain confronted the postcolonial paradox by profiting from a particular, European, reading of the past.

Apart from the contestable characterisation of its colonial status, Bahrain launched a campaign in favour of the application of the *uti possidetis* norm throughout the postcolonial world. It first pointed to the Court's 1986 decision in the *Frontier Dispute*, which had characterised *uti possidetis* as a 'general principle...logically connected with the phenomenon of the obtaining of independence, wherever it occurs.'[91] From this basis, Bahrain went on to argue that *uti possidetis* is a 'universal rule' of 'customary law'[92] and 'should be the alpha and omega'[93] in the present matter.[94] Because of its 'general scope', geographical or cultural considerations are irrelevant: 'The Arab world is no exception.'[95]

---

[88] *Qatar/Bahrain (Merits)*, CR 2000/21, 27 June 2000, Bahrain, Mr Kemicha, at para. 33.

[89] 'Tens of thousands of miles of grotesque international borders in the developing world were drawn up by powerful intrusive foreigners whose entire attention was on their own political and commercial interests, with very little regard to indigenous populations. Yet these borders survive, not because they appeal to our sense of fair play, but because continued respect for such borders has avoided war.' *Qatar/Bahrain (Merits)*, CR 2000/12, 9 June 2000, Bahrain, Mr Paulsson, at para. 144.

[90] Emphasis in original, *Qatar/Bahrain (Merits)*, CR 2000/21, 27 June 2000, Bahrain, Mr Kemicha, at para. 75.

[91] *Burkina Faso/Mali* (ICJ Reps) (1986) 565, para. 20, cited in *Qatar/Bahrain (Merits)*, CR 2000/13, 13 June 2000, Bahrain, Mr Kemicha, at para. 4.

[92] *Qatar/Bahrain (Merits)*, CR 2000/13, 13 June 2000, Bahrain, Mr Kemicha, at para. 16.

[93] *Qatar/Bahrain (Merits)*, CR 2000/21, 27 June 2000, Bahrain, Mr Paulsson, at para. 8.

[94] In his separate opinion, Judge Kooijmans accepts that in those particular instances where it is applicable *uti possidetis* is a relevant consideration, but it should not outweigh other factors: 'Generally speaking, to yield too readily to its applicability would be inimical to other legally protected rights, e.g., the right of self-determination (although there is no danger of this in the present case) as well as to the very function of international courts which is not to declare, in the interests of preventing conflicts, pre-existing de facto territorial situations legal without regard to title and other relevant criterion, but to uphold justice by correcting illegalities where they occur', *Qatar/Bahrain* (Merits) (2001), at para. 8.

[95] *Qatar/Bahrain (Merits)*, CR 2000/13, 13 June 2000, Bahrain, Mr Kemicha, at para. 81.

As an Arab state itself, not only did Qatar question the general application of *uti possidetis* in the region,[96] but specifically, it challenged Bahrain's use of the norm through its portrayal of the 1939 award. Although Qatar conceded that both sheikhdoms lacked full independence before 1971, it denied that former treaty relations constituted 'a colonial-type protectorate'.[97] We saw in Part II's introduction that it was common during the scramble for Africa to mislabel colonies as 'colonial protectorates'.[98] These regimes of 'protection' rarely recognised indigenous sovereignty and were qualitatively distinct from 'real' protectorates that preserved at least internal independence. 'Colonial protectorates' were common in Africa, but not in the Gulf, and Bahrain's position of asserting colonial protection in the region was rejected by Qatar. The Court confirmed Qatar's position and held that the *uti possidetis* norm was inapplicable in the present dispute;[99] the norm was only relevant in instances of former colonial administrative decisions or explicit consent by non-colonial entities. More generally, Plant points out that the norm is only applicable in postcolonial, and not post-protectorate, situations.[100] Although doctrinal boundaries were clearly definied in this instance, Qatar's presentation demonstrated that the line between protection and colonialism in the Gulf was a blurry one.

Arguments based on the absence of consent of a protected state still possessing nominal independence was at the heart of Qatar's refutation of Bahrain's claim to the Hawar Islands. As entities that had never assented to Britain's demarcating of boundaries, or alienating territory more generally,[101] Bahrain and Qatar had to prove their consent before any decision could be binding. This was the *sine qua non* irrespective of the decision's qualities. Through analogy, Qatar relied on the 1981 Arbitral Award between Dubai and Sharjah for its examination of consent. That case had also considered a British decision delimiting the parties' borders in the Gulf. The Permanent Court of Arbitration came 'to the conclusion that the consent of the Rulers concerned was necessary before any such delimitation could have been undertaken.'[102]

---

[96] This lack of conviction about the norm's relevance to the Arab world is echoed by Judge Al-Khasawneh: 'it is still very doubtful whether even now it [*uti possidetis*] has any applicability in the Middle East', *Qatar/Bahrain (Merits)* (2001), at para. 10. Also see Part II Introduction, at 111.

[97] Emphasis omitted, *Qatar/Bahrain (Merits)*, CR 2000/17, 20 June 2000, Qatar, Mr Salmon, at para. 5.

[98] Discussed at 107–108.

[99] *Qatar/Bahrain (Merits)* (2001), at para. 148.

[100] Plant, *supra* n. 4, at footnote 79, 206.

[101] This was also the case in the *Dubai/Sharjah* Arbitration, see Judge Al-Khasawneh, *Qatar/Bahrain (Merits)* (2001), at para. 9.

[102] *Dubai/Sharjah Arbitration*, 19 October 1981, (1993) 91 ILR 543, at 567.

Qatar challenged the existence of its consent in the context of what it termed Britain's 'complex manoeuvring' over 'petroleum policy interests'.[103] First, Qatar stated that there was no agreement signed between itself and Britain authorising such authority on the part of its 'protector'. In their dissenting opinion, Judges Bedjaoui, Ranjeva and Koroma argued that any instances of Qatari deference to British actions should have been construed in the light of marked power asymmetries, rather than Qatari authorization for such wide powers.[104] Further, for Judge Al-Khasawneh, although Qatar was definitely not a colony, the 'British Government in fact exercised overwhelming control over the two Sheikhdoms' in both domestic and foreign affairs.[105] The Court overlooked such arguments to determine that consent had been established on 27 May 1938 in an exchange of letters between Qatar and Britain.[106]

We saw that the Court agreed with Qatar that the 1939 decision could not be construed as 'arbitral' between non-colonial entities, but it nevertheless held that it had 'legal effect'[107] and was binding on the parties.[108] For many members of the Court in separate opinions, as well as Qatar, however, any type of award was incapable of effect due to Qatari consent being 'vitiated by the existence of fraud'.[109] The Court failed to regard Qatar's in-depth consideration of the pressures faced from Britain *vis-à-vis* oil concessions.[110] Once again, the Court relied on the legal qualities of the award to avoid a more complex and contentious consideration of the past.

Qatar's request for Britain's assistance in settling the affair over the Hawar Islands had coincided with a very different request made by BAPCO[111] and PCL[112] –

---

[103] *Qatar/Bahrain (Merits)*, CR 2000/7, 31 May 2000, Qatar, Sir Ian Sinclair, at para. 16.

[104] 'In political terms, the nature of the relationship between the protecting Power and the protected State did not permit the use of any language other than the deferential terms in which the local rulers expressed themselves; thus to interpret that language as evidence of consent to the renunciation of territorial jurisdiction is in reality to give the opposite sense to the natural meaning of the words and conduct in 1939.' *Qatar/Bahrain (Merits)* (2001), Bedjaoui, Ranjeva and Koroma J. J. (diss. op.), at para. 38.

[105] *Qatar/Bahrain (Merits)* (2001) (sep. op. Al-Khasawneh), at para. 9.

[106] *Qatar/Bahrain (Merits)* (2001), at para. 137.

[107] *Qatar/Bahrain (Merits)* (2001), at para. 117.

[108] *Qatar/Bahrain (Merits)* (2001), at para. 146.

[109] *Qatar/Bahrain (Merits)* (2001), Bedjaoui, Ranjeva & Koroma J. J. (diss. op.), at para. 19.

[110] '[T]he Court has largely disregarded the political context which, in view of what had already been occurring, gave the Ruler of Qatar hardly any choice but to request the Protecting Power to comply with its treaty-based commitments "in light of equity and justice".' *Qatar/Bahrain (Merits)* (2001), (Kooijmans sep. op.), at para. 57.

[111] Bahrain Petroleum Company, an American company.

[112] Petroleum Concessions Ltd., a largely British-owned subsidiary of the APOC (Anglo-Persian Oil Company).

both oil companies seeking greater access to the Gulf's natural resources.[113] Much of Bahrain had already been allotted and companies were eager to secure unassigned areas, including the Hawar Islands. As the provisional decision of 1936 suggests, Britain was mindful of the stakes involved in its decision and was unable to remove itself from the pressures exerted by both Bahrain and the oil companies, who wanted the matter to be resolved with 'extreme haste'.[114] In its pleadings, Qatar had presented a significant amount of material to support its account of this 'flagrant miscarriage of justice committed by the British'[115] and it thought that the Court would agree:

> The Court will no doubt conclude that the British authorities in the Gulf had by this time become so caught up in a spider's web of their own making that they simply could not render an objective and impartial decision on the issue of title to Hawar. In effect this meant that the provisional decision of 1936 had become a final decision even before the so-called 'enquiry' into the question of title had begun.[116]

Compelling evidence aside, the Court, in what the dissenting Judges describe as a 'surreal'[117] gesture, chose to disregard all other arguments offered by the parties (such as proximity, maps,[118] *à titre de souverain* and *effectivités*) to hold that the 1939 award was based on consent and constituted a binding 'administrative' decision on the parties.

Despite the confusing nature of the legal and historical arguments presented above, it is clear that the Court's approach to the 1939 Award was simplistic and lacked critical engagement with prevailing conditions in the Gulf. Furthermore, the Judgment's unquestioning acceptance of the Award in the face of disputed consent displayed an inability to confront the reality of at least *quasi*-colonial domination, as well as a predilection for preserving the law/politics dichotomy. Conceding the centrality of 'political' motivations in arbitral decisions would render the Court's deference to such practices suspect and open to question. Instead, the Court ignored the political subtext through a textual and legalised reading of the 1939 arbitration which was similar to its handling of the 1955 Treaty in the dispute between Libya and Chad. Judges Kooijmans and Al-Khasawneh, both of whom voted in favour of Bahraini sovereignty over Hawar, still questioned the

[113] In the words of Sir Ian Sinclair, oil was at the root of the whole affair: 'The problem – the real problem – was the coincidence in time of the pursuit of the oil concession negotiations from 1936 onwards with the beginning of the "enquiry" into the appurtenance of Hawar.' *Qatar/Bahrain (Merits)*, CR 2000/19, 22 June 2000, Qatar, at para. 25.

[114] *Qatar/Bahrain (Merits)*, CR 2000/7, 31 May, Qatar, Sir Ian Sinclair, at para. 15.

[115] *Qatar/Bahrain (Merits)*, CR 2000/8, 5 June 2000, Qatar, Sir Ian Sinclair, at para. 15.

[116] Ibid., at para. 9.

[117] *Qatar/Bahrain (Merits)* (2001), Bedjaoui, Ranjeva & Koroma J. J. (diss. op.), at para. 42.

[118] Qatar in particular discussed map evidence at length, e.g. see *Qatar/Bahrain (Merits)*, CR 2000/7, 31 May 2000, Mr Bundy, at paras. 1–78.

Court's 'excessively restrictive'[119] approach. The Bahrain Formula had provided the Court with the mandate to explore *all* legally relevant matters relating to control over Hawar, and yet the majority judgment confined itself to a narrow enquiry. In the opinion of Judge Al-Khasawneh, 'the only way to dispose of the question of sovereignty over the Hawars is to embark on an enquiry into the Sheikhdoms' diplomatic history';[120] but this did not happen. Instead, 'the Judgment seems to give more weight to the position taken by that Protecting Power than to considerations of substantive law, in particular those on the acquisition of territory.'[121] In so doing, the Judgment indicated that international law remains wedded to a past premised on less than equal political, and thus *legal*, capacity between European and non-European peoples.

ii) *Regional Factors at Play in the Parties' Claims over the Hawar Islands: Communal Property Regimes and Tribal Allegiances*

Unlike the truncated decision of the ICJ, both Qatar and Bahrain offered exhaustive – even if not always convincing – accounts of their sovereign links with the Hawar Islands. Bahrain discounted Qatar's reliance on the norm of contiguity with reference to the *Island of Palmas* Case.[122] Some of the separate opinions found Bahrain's depiction of original title and continuing control convincing in itself.[123] Other judgments tended to favour Qatar's arguments based on a combination of the notion of proximity (with reference to the 1998 *Eritrea/Yemen* Award)[124] and confirmatory map evidence on the one hand with a corresponding lack of a better title by Bahrain on the other. Such general arguments presented few difficulties for traditional principles of title to territory in international law and need not be reviewed here.

---

119 *Qatar/Bahrain (Merits)* (2001), (sep. op. Al-Khasawneh), at para. 4; see also (sep. op. Kooijmans), at para. 4.

120 *Qatar/Bahrain (Merits)* (2001), (sep. op. Al-Khasawneh), at para. 12.

121 *Qatar/Bahrain (Merits)* (2001), (sep. op. Kooijmans), at para. 1.

122 (1928) 1 RIAA 829 (Arbitrator Huber) 4 ILR 3. 'In the Palmas case, Qatar leans heavily on Judge Huber's mention of islands in the territorial sea. Bahrain, on the other hand, points to those passages which stress the need for occupation or the performance of acts of authority as well as the need to maintain continuity of title.' *Qatar/Bahrain (Merits)*, CR 2000/22, 28 June 2000, Sir Elihu Lauterpacht, at para. 62.

123 Such as Judges Kooijmans and Al-Khasawneh.

124 Territorial Sovereignty and Scope of the Dispute Award (Phase I), 9 October 1998. It should be noted that Bahrain also relied on this case, but on different grounds: 'In Eritrea/Yemen Bahrain points to the criteria of exercise of jurisdiction on a continuous and peaceful basis, while Qatar points to the lesser degree of activity permitted in the case of islands that lay uninhabited and ungoverned.' *Qatar/Bahrain (Merits)*, CR 2000/22, 28 June 2000, Sir Elihu Lauterpacht, at para. 62.

Discussion about the relationship between tribal allegiances and statehood, as well as the impact of communal property rights on the ability to establish exclusive control, however, was different. These ideas required much greater exploration of the particular conditions of Arab/Muslim authority in the Gulf. Despite their common heritage, Bahrain and Qatar exploited the legal significance of cultural factors in radically different ways, thus highlighting the extent to which local traditions can be invoked for different argumentative purposes. In the following section, this dialogue about the role of legal particularism within the context of international legal universalism will be assessed through the prism of arguments about the nature of authority over the Hawar Islands.

Some *effectivités* relied upon by Bahrain were historical accounts of fishing activities, as well as judicial intervention in disputes between individuals residing on Hawar. Bahrain discussed these events within the broader context of tribal connections between Bahrain, the Hawar Islands and Zubarah. As outlined above, the Āl Khalīfa tribe that hailed from Zubarah (and ultimately Kuwait) ruled Bahrain. It was alleged that a branch of the Dowasir tribe based in the Arabian mainland had petitioned the Qāḍī of Zubarah for permission to settle on Hawar and this request was granted c.1800.[125] From this time onwards, the Dowasir resided in Hawar at least intermittently for the purpose of fishing and Bahrain argued that they were Bahraini subjects. Thus, '[a]lthough the Bahraini Dowasir were proud and independent-minded, they lived under the authority of the Rulers of Bahrain.'[126]

Before considering whether the tribe was under Āl Khalīfa authority, it is essential to consider the legal status of fishing for semi-nomadic, Muslim groups both in the Gulf and the Red Sea. Qatar argued that fishing activities could only be construed as the actions of private individuals exploiting a common resource. Bahrain, on the other hand, tried to downplay the regional institutions of communal property rights to advance that its direct connection with the Dowasir along with sustained and constant occupation of the area confirmed its sovereignty over the Islands in contention.

Qatar's case about communal fishing rights rested on a combination of general historical research as well as strikingly similar analogies from the 1998 *Eritrea/Yemen* Award. Amin's treatise on law in the Gulf is particularly pertinent here, and was invoked by Qatar throughout its written and oral pleadings:[127]

---

[125] Al-Arayed, *supra* n. 12, at 226. This historical fact is countered by Qatar, e.g. CR 2000/8, 5 June 2000, Mr Shankardass, at para. 6.

[126] *Qatar/Bahrain (Merits)*, CR 2000/13, 13 June 2000, Mr Volterra, at para. 33.

[127] Whereas Bahrain overlooked these arguments altogether, instead claiming that it was the predominant and recognised pearling power in its vicinity, including the Hawar Islands.

> The fishing activities in the Gulf have been traditionally governed by the Shariah/Islamic Law...[it] does not have a comprehensive theory in respect of fishery... all raw material, whether in land or in the sea or space...belong, exclusively, to God and *are not, in any way, subject to exclusive rights of persons*, individually or collectively.[128]

The international legal effect of such a similar regime was discussed in the *Eritrea/Yemen* Award, where it was argued that historical, cultural and geographical particularities did have legal implications. Rather than apply modern, European norms of private property or sovereign control, it was necessary to view the natural resources of the Red Sea lying between the claimant states as a *res communis*.[129] From this, Qatar argued that 'in the absence of any State control of licensing or enforcement activities, the fishing practices of individuals [would] not amount to *effectivités* as they were not acts *à titre de souverain*.'[130]

Not only did Qatar rely on local customs in relation to fishing, but it also distinguished Islamic jurisdiction from Western legal norms to argue that the Bahraini resolution of disputes between 'Hawari' individuals was not an act of sovereignty over the Islands. In its pleadings, Bahrain had furnished the Court with decisions rendered by qāḍīs in Bahrain relating to property disputes about fish traps on the islands. The question for the two parties then was how to characterise the legal effect of such decisions *vis-à-vis* Bahrain's claim to effective control over Hawar. Qatar argued that, as in the case of communal fishing rights, it was essential to distinguish qāḍī-based jurisdiction from typical, European international legal norms. '[I]t was common for Qādis in one Moslem country to settle disputes of Moslem subjects of another country or in regard to property located in another country.'[131] As long as none of the litigants involved 'objects to pleading before him', a qāḍī may be deemed competent and he can then rule on matters of property outside of the territory of the decision.[132] Thus, it was Qatar's submission that it is inappropriate to apply Western concepts to the authority exercised by a qāḍī, whose jurisdiction was only exercised *in personam*

---

128 Emphasis in the original, Amin, *supra* n. 1, at 193, cited in Qatar, Reply, *(Qatar/Bahrain) (Merits)*, 30 May 1999, at para. 4.181.

129 Territorial Sovereignty and Scope of the Dispute Award (Phase I) (*Eritrea/Yemen)* 9 October 1998, at para. 126, at 38.

130 *Qatar/Bahrain (Merits)*, CR 2000/17, 20 June 2000, Qatar, Mr. Shankardass, para. 27, This statement echoes the Arbitral Award between Eritrea and Yemen: '[such fishing activities] do not constitute evidence of *effectivités* for the simple reason that none of these functions are acts *à titre de souverain*.' *Eritrea/Yemen* Award, at para. 315.

131 *Qatar/Bahrain (Merits)*, Qatar, Reply, 30 May 1999, at para. 4.186.

132 'Legal Opinion', Judge Wassel Alaa El Din Ahmed Ibrahim, 27 April 1999, Qatar, Reply, *Qatar/Bahrain (Merits)*, 30 May 1999, Annex III.98, at 603–605.

over Muslim individuals.[133] Qatar was appealing to the Court's universalist credentials by offering a particular approach to legal authority outside of the European tradition.

While Qatar's arguments relied on the effect of non-European norms in the Gulf, they established a binary opposition between European practices of sovereignty and local practices seemingly devoid of such significance. Bahrain, on the other hand, presented a long list of (often less than dispositive) *effectivités* that were reliant on the relationship of sovereign and subject – Bahrain and the Dowasir tribe in Hawar. The respective positions of the two parties over Hawar were summarised in the eyes of Bahrain as being a contest between physical geography (Qatar's proximity argument) versus human history (Bahrain's sovereign links with the Dowasir).[134] The parties' treatment of the Dowasir tribe's status and the implications of its fishing practices could be conceived as being a contest over the characterisation of Islamic law and its relationship with overarching international legal principles about sovereignty and territory.

To begin with, almost none of the facts detailed by either Party remained unchallenged. On Bahrain's side, Qatar recognised that the Dowasir did visit the islands, but only sporadically and seasonally.[135] Irrespective of their length of stay, Qatar argued that the tribe was independent from Bahrain. Qatar also pointed out that although the Court's *Western Sahara* Advisory Opinion[136] had acknowledged tribal allegiances, a claim of sovereignty still requires these allegiances to be 'real', supported by 'acts manifesting acceptance of political authority.'[137] Thus in this instance, Qatar was relying on the Court's inflexible approach to sovereign ties in the Sahara to defeat similar arguments of statehood by Bahrain. Particularist arguments were useful for defeating the legal validity of Bahrain's position.

It is not possible to assess the legal validity of the Bahraini and Qatari perspectives on tribal authority and communal property because the Court did not consider these arguments. What can be pointed out from the discussion above, however, is that both Bahrain and Qatar relied on a particular combination of indigenous and European international legal standards to boost their respective

[133] Qatar then concludes: 'Accordingly, a Qadi sitting somewhere in Bahrain and deciding private or inheritance related disputes between Dowasir Sunni fishermen who seasonally visited the Hawar Islands, though normally resident in Bahrain, is in no sense an example of 'exercise of authority' by the Ruler of Bahrain in the Hawar Islands and such practice therefore offers no support whatsoever to Bahrain's claim of sovereignty over these islands.' *Qatar/Bahrain (Merits)*, CR 2000/8, 5 June 2000, Qatar, Mr Shankardass, at paras. 33 & 36.

[134] *Qatar/Bahrain (Merits)*, CR 2000/13, 13 June 2000, Bahrain, Mr Volterra, at paras. 3–4.

[135] *Qatar/Bahrain (Merits)*, CR 2000/8, 5 June 2000, Qatar, Mr Shankardass, at para. 15.

[136] *Western Sahara (Advisory Opinion)* (1975) ICJ Reps, p. 12.

[137] Qatar, Reply, *Qatar/Bahrain (Merits)*, 30 May 1999, at para. 4.160.

claims. It is also significant that the parties chose to present these accounts in the first place, and such a move suggests that despite its European beginnings, the Court can be a forum for the discussion about non-European legal traditions. Debate about control of Zubarah presented similar difficulties and will be considered below before this chapter's conclusion.

c) *The Case of Zubarah*

Unlike its treatment of the Hawar Islands, the Court entered into a more general, even if somewhat brief, consideration of Bahrain's and Qatar's competing claims to sovereignty over this sparsely populated region in the west of the Qatari pensinsula, Zubarah. Of interest for this book is the way in which sovereignty over Zubarah raised matters of tribalism and private property rights, as in the case of Hawar. The Court chose to focus its attention less on these factors in favour of the effect of certain treaties, purported Bahraini acquiescence to British prohibitions on its rights over the region, as well as instances of more recent Qatari *effectivités.* First, despite undeniable Āl Khalīfa links with Zubarah from its settlement in 1762, the 1868 treaty between Britain and the Sheikh of Bahrain altered any possible pretensions of Āl Khalīfa hegemony in the peninsula.[138] The 1868 treaty reflected earlier agreements regarding maritime peace in the Gulf between Britain and local sheikhdoms. After repeated 'acts and other irregularities at sea' by the Bahraini ruler's brothers, Britain imposed a number of restrictions on Āl Khalīfa endeavours beyond Bahraini shores.[139] According to the Court, 'the terms of the 1868 Agreement show that any attempt by Bahrain to pursue its claims to Zubarah through military actions would not be tolerated by the British' and that thereafter 'the rulers of Bahrain were never in a position to engage in direct authority in Zubarah.'[140]

Because of these restrictions on Bahrain, Qatar, along with its Ottoman overlord, was able to extend its control over the whole of the peninsula, as evidenced by various maps and treaties from the early twentieth century. The Court paid particular attention to the unratified Anglo-Ottoman Treaty of 1913,[141] which demonstrated the clear position of its signatories, 'Britain and the Ottoman

---

[138] Agreements between Great Britain and Qatar and Abu Dhabi (Trucial Sheikhdoms of Oman), 12, 16 September 1868, 138 CTS 56.

[139] *Qatar/Bahrain (Merits)* (2001), at para. 83.

[140] *Qatar/Bahrain (Merits)* (2001), at para. 84.

[141] The Court's reasoning was as follows:

> In view of the role played by Great Britain and the Ottoman Empire in the region in that period, it is significant to note Article 11 of the Anglo-Ottoman Convention signed on 29 July 1913 (see paragraph 45 above). This article described the course of the line agreed to separate the Sanjak of Nejd 'from the peninsula of Al-Qatar', and then went on to state:

Empire, [which] did not recognize Bahrain's sovereignty over the peninsula, including Zubarah.'[142] Although the Court did not acknowledge any source for its ability to rely on an unratified treaty, it is probable that its reasoning was founded on Qatar's use of the *Eritrea/Yemen* Award. In that case, the Arbitral Tribunal also dealt with an unratified agreement, which it deemed to be of 'diplomatic evidence…[and] of undoubted interest because it reflects what was recorded by both parties as that which they had agreed to.'[143] It should be evident at this point that the *Eritrea/Yemen* Award shared many similarities with the present Case, and it was relied upon especially by Qatar.[144] Despite these parallels both in relation to the territorial and maritime issues, the Award was not cited at all in the Court's judgment. This omission is particularly surprising given that the Award was considered in many of the dissenting and separate opinions and gave support to Qatar's claim to Hawar.[145]

Due to the Court's reliance on the above grounds, it did not consider the arguments advanced by Qatar and Bahrain about tribal loyalties in Zubarah. It is useful to examine such arguments here, however, as they can serve as a point of comparison with the preceding discussion on Hawar. Both Bahrain and Qatar depicted the Gulf before the advent of oil exploration as being a region where borders and their supporting norms of sovereignty were culturally and legally irrelevant. For example, in the words of Bahrain: 'Until well into the 20th Century, the ecology of the Arabian peninsula inhibited the emergence of States or rulers whose territory could be defined by reference to specific borders…Sovereignty over territory did not arise from a meaningless assertion of lordship of the desert.'[146] Qatar also spoke of nomadic practices, but for opposite reasons: 'The concept of a boundary, which dictates a precise separation of areas where separate sedentary populations are settled…is alien to the southern coast of the

> The Imperial Ottoman Government having renounced all its claims to the peninsula of al-Qatar, it is agreed between the two Governments that the said peninsula will, as in the past, be governed by the Sheikh Jasim-bin-Sani and his successors. The Government of His Britannic Majesty declares that it will not permit the Sheikh of Bahrain to interfere in the internal affairs of Qatar, to violate the autonomy of that country or to annex it.

Qatar/Bahrain (Merits) (2001), at para. 87.

142 *Qatar/Bahrain (Merits)* (2001), at para. 90.

143 *Eritrea/Yemen* Award, at para. 172, cited in *Qatar/Bahrain (Merits)*, CR 2000/8, 5 June 2000, Qatar, Mr Bundy, at para. 42.

144 It is also interesting to contrast Libya's arguments in Chapter Three with the Eritrea/Yemen Award. Libya invoked the unratified Laval-Mussolini Treaty of 1935 to support its claims, but unlike the Permanent Court of Arbitration, the ICJ dismissed this argument through its total reliance on the later, ratified 1955 Treaty, at 125.

145 Plant, *supra*, n. 4, at 205.

146 Bahrain, Memorial, *Qatar/Bahrain (Merits)*, 30 September 1996, at para. 64.

Gulf...The boundaries of State entities are not affected by the movement of tribes, who show a haughty disregard for them in their wanderings.'[147]

As in the case of Hawar, Bahrain wanted to show that its allegiances with the Naim tribe in Zubarah demonstrated an ongoing connection of personal authority that established sovereignty in the region. It was not possible or necessary to demarcate the exact boundaries of control; continuous settlement by the Naim with its intermittent pledges of allegiance was enough. Qatar's reference to the reality of tribal movements sought to counter Bahraini arguments by showing that, despite possible Naim allegiances and movements, these did not alter the basic sovereign title of Qatar over the peninsula,[148] which had been recognised by other states.[149] Also, Qatar sought to characterise Bahraini arguments as being overly dependent on events in the distant past, arguing that 'if certain ghosts do linger in the [Zubarah] desert, they remain ghosts, surviving only in the minds of those who believe in ghosts.'[150] Qatar's gesture here was to use the typical disregard for indigenous title within international law to boost its case of sovereignty over the peninsula. Such an adjudicative manoeuvre was a wise one, and we can also see it as another instance of the postcolonial paradox at play in the courtroom: where preferable to their argument, Third World states will readily speak in the language of their former colonisers, or 'protectors'.

In the more immediate past, while Qatar entrenched its rule over the entire peninsula throughout the mid-twentieth century, Bahrain's Āl Khalīfa rulers continued to petition their British 'protectors'[151] in pursuit of their 'honour' *vis-à-vis* Zubarah.[152] Since the 1868 treaty Britain had sought to separate Āl Khalīfa and

---

[147] *Qatar/Bahrain (Merits)*, CR 2000/5, 29 May 2000, Qatar, Mr Salmon, para. 23. It should be noted that in contrast to this general line of argument, Bahrain included testimony from Naim tribespeople confirming Bahraini control within circumscribed borders in 1937: 'we [the Naim] are within your (the Ruler of Bahrain) boundaries and we will not let them take your territory.' Letter from Chief of Naim tribe to Ruler of Bahrain, 25 April 1937, Bahrain, Memorial, vol. 3, Annex 121, at 645.

[148] '[T]ribes moved freely within a sheikh's territory without this entailing the tribe's submission to that sheikh or, inversely, transfer of the sheikh's territory to that tribe. All else being equal, it could hardly be argued that the Naim's frequenting of the Zubarah area constituted a loss of the Ruler of Qatar's sovereignty over this area.' *Qatar/Bahrain (Merits)*, CR 2000/9, 5 June 2000, Qatar, Mr David, at para. 47.

[149] Ibid., at paras. 28–38.

[150] *Qatar/Bahrain (Merits)*, CR 2000/9, 5 June 2000, Qatar, Mr David, at para. 55.

[151] For example: Letter from Ruler of Bahrain to Maj. Hickinbotham, British Political Agent, 3 February 1945, Bahrain, Memorial, vol. 4, Annex 177, at 780.

[152] The pursuit of honour and a corresponding fear about 'loss of face' was central to Bahrain's ongoing claim to Zubarah. In the words of the British Political Resident in 1946: 'If I understood him rightly he stated that he did not claim sovereignty over Zubarah but only wanted his grass and water. When I remarked that there was no profit for him in Zubarah he replied

Āl Thānī/Ottoman claims over Zubarah by stating repeatedly that Bahrain could not challenge Qatar in this matter.[153] Despite these clear barriers towards any recognition of its sovereignty, Bahrain continued to seek a solution that would encompass its claims at least in relation to private property rights. For example, in 1961, Bahrain's Ruler suggested to Britain that Qatar could retain sovereign title in exchange for Āl Khalīfa rights over immovable property, freedom of movement for its followers and jurisdiction over cases involving its followers in Zubarah.[154] The British could appreciate the basis of these claims, but could not find a solution that encompassed such competing rights.[155] Britain's inability to distinguish private law rights from rights of sovereignty in the context of a sovereign's personal rule was recognised by Bahrain in its Memorial.[156] Bahrain suggested that Britain's handling of the whole affair not only displayed confusion over the relevant facts relating to the claims of Qatar and Bahrain, more disturbingly, it arose from a belief that 'such rights had no place in the [sic] modern western notions of absolute territorial sovereignty that Britain had been trying to impose on the Middle East.'[157]

The Court's silence regarding these nuances of Arab territorial control confirmed Britain's approach to patterns of indigenous authority throughout the Trucial Coast. It is possible that the points raised by Bahrain would have had little effect even if the Court had considered them directly. However, this oversight represents a more general limitation faced by international lawyers when they seek to accommodate and balance multiple interests in territorial regions less than wholly reliant on strictly demarcated borders. In his separate opinion, Judge Kooijmans acknowledged this limitation, but could not offer any real solution:

> It is difficult to characterize the dispute concerning sovereignty over Zubarah as a dispute over territory or over the location of territorial boundaries. Even in the beginning of the twenty-first century it still carries the nature of contested hegemonic spheres or disputed entitlements to ties of allegiance rather than that of conflict-

that it was not a matter of profit as he knew that there was nothing of value in Zubarah but one of prestige.' Cited in *Qatar/Bahrain (Merits)*, CR 2000/9, 5 June 2000, Qatar, Mr Shankardass, para. 11. Also see Ibid. paras. 21. 25; Foreign Office minutes by M. Man, British Political Resident, 'Zubarah', 1 June 1960, Bahrain, Memorial, vol. 4, Annex 214, at para. 7.

153 'I emphasised that Her Majesty's Government had never recognised any claim by Bahrain to territorial sovereignty over Zubarah.' Transcript of letter from B. Burrows, British Political Resident to Foreign Office, 2 May 1954, Bahrain, Memorial, vol. 4, Annex 208(b), at 879.

154 Letter from Ruler of Bahrain to Sir George Middleton, British Political Resident, 8 February 1961, Bahrain, Memorial, vol. 4, Annex 218, at 912.

155 Foreign Office Minutes by M. Man, British Political Resident, entitled 'Zubarah', 1 June 1960, Bahrain, Memorial, vol. 4, Annex 214, at 900.

156 Bahrain, Memorial, *Qatar/Bahrain (Merits)*, 30 September 1996, at para. 314.

157 Ibid., at para. 326.

> ing claims to exclusive spatial authority over a certain piece of land. That peculiar character of this part of the dispute is even today illustrated by the fact that Bahrain neither in the written nor in the oral pleadings defined the extent of the area over which it claimed sovereignty, but simply referred to the Zubarah region.[158]

Despite these misgivings, the Court was able to delimit Zubarah's border through a Judgment devoid of doubt; international law had brought the parties certainty and finality.

6) *Conclusion*

Although this chapter has confined itself to an overview of the legal relations between Bahrain and Qatar, it must be remembered that the latter part of the dispute occurred within the context of two important regional events. The GCC's[159] formation in 1981 ushered in a new era in Gulf relations.[160] The protracted Bahraini/Qatari disagreement served as the GCC's 'test case' in 'resolving internal conflicts'.[161] Further, in the midst of discussion over the Bahrain Formula for ICJ adjudication, Iraq invaded one of the GCC's six member states, Kuwait. In neither example did the GCC's participation in these events contribute in any significant way to their resolution. Regarding Qatar and Bahrain, there was muted support from within the GCC for the adjudicative process. As for the two GCC members participating in the dispute directly, the outcome was less than ideal. Qatar's ruler described the Court's 2001 judgment on the merits as 'painful', but conceded that it would contribute 'to the stability of the region'.[162] Bahrain had already anticipated this potential pain and had taken steps before the ruling. Throughout the proceedings it proposed extra-curial options, such as negotiations, and did not arrest its commercial development of the Hawar Islands in the nineties even though it had entered into agreements pledging preservation of the *status quo* pending final settlement. As for the other four

---

158 *Qatar/Bahrain (Merits)* (2001) (Kooijmans sep. op.), at para. 33.

159 The Organisation's website contains some useful, general information: http://www.gcc-sg.org/. The six members of the GCC are Bahrain, Kuwait, Oman, Qatar, Saudi Arabia and the United Arab Emirates.

160 It was hoped in particular that the Council could play a role in resolving disputes between its member-states: 'The Council stressed that the formation of the Cooperation Council has provided the constitutional framework for settling disputes between member states when their Majesties and Highnesses approved the formation of the Authority for the settlement of disputes.' Gulf Cooperation Council, Minutes, 8 March 1982, Qatar, Counter-Memorial, *Qatar/Bahrain (Merits)*, Annexes, vol. 4, at 205.

161 F. Heard-Bey, 'Conflict Resolution and Regional Co-operation: The Role of the Gulf Co-operation Council 1970–2002' (2006) 42 *Middle Eastern Studies* 199, at 210.

162 Ibid., at 212–213.

GCC members, the ICJ ruling was welcomed. Heard-Bey muses that the reasons for this support for third party adjudication stemmed from GCC members being too connected with both of the parties to resolve the dispute definitively. 'Other constraints such as ties based on the traditional affinities of the ruling families and on centuries-old tribal relationships'[163] explain this preference for a seemingly more neutral approach.

For Qatar and Bahrain, the matter before the ICJ was not the first occasion where a third party had sought to determine territorial and maritime issues of the utmost importance. Further, although it may seem tendentious to equate the earlier motives of Britain in the Gulf with those of the ICJ, the outcomes were similar: an occasion where 'consent' was established in the face of significant protest and lingering doubt. Also, the Court's judgment closely followed the earlier position of Britain in relation both to Hawar and Zubarah. At least in contrast to the flawed and unsatisfying decisions of Britain over its protectorates, some of which were considered above, it was hoped that the ICJ would be able to settle the affair 'once and for all'.[164] To further this goal, both Bahrain and Qatar issued extensive (even if not always accurate) historical accounts of their connections with the territories in question. Indeed, the proceedings should be appreciated as much for their historical narratives as for their legal exposition.

Some of the arguments reconstructed from the annals of history, as well as their corresponding acceptance or rejection by the Court, have illustrated broader themes about how to approach the link between international law and a less than palatable colonial past. In assessing the Court's failure to render a socially acceptable judgment, Judges Bedjaoui, Ranjeva and Koroma asked, 'Why...should anyone be surprised that the taste in the mouths of the crowd, both in Bahrain and in Qatar, is a sour one?'[165] Particularly in relation to the Court's denial of underlying British motives and ongoing concerns about natural resources, it is to be expected that this judgment will be viewed partly as an endorsement of European domination over non-Europeans in the Gulf. Moreover, the majority's 'curtailed'[166] treatment of the parties' various legal grounds and historical arguments indicates unwillingness or even an inability on the part of the ICJ to embrace the legal heritage of non-European litigants. Although there was some scope for discussion about Arab approaches to authority over territory as was also the case for Libya's arguments in Chapter Three, the silence of the Court suggests that current grammars of international law are inadequate for the task of expressing such ideas. This judgment necessarily (de)limited territorial and

[163] Ibid., at 213.

[164] *Qatar/Bahrain (Merits)* (2001), Bedjaoui, Ranjeva & Koroma J. J. (diss. op.), at para. 2.

[165] Ibid., at para. 7.

[166] *Qatar/Bahrain (Merits)* (2001), (Kooijmans sep. op), at para. 4.

maritime boundaries between two small, oil-rich Arab states. On the other hand, the process of legal argumentation between Qatar and Bahrain, as well as the heated dissent from the Bench, shows that the scope of international law need not always be so limited.

Although notions of Arab/Muslim authority were unfamiliar to the Court, the case of *Western Sahara* had provided an alternative framework for conceptualising international legal personality in cultural and geographical locations far from the cooler climes of the Hague. Arguments about non-European forms of authority over territory received much greater consideration by the ICJ in its *Western Sahara* Opinion and this case forms the subject of Chapter Five after Part III's introductory discussion below.

Part III
Advisory Opinions

Introduction to Part III

Determining the Self through the ICJ's Advisory Jurisdiction: Procedures and Principles

We saw in Part II that the ICJ has heard a number of territorial disputes for Third World states through its contentious jurisdiction. The Court has also deliberated on a number of advisory cases, which have often dealt with the relationship between self-determination and territory.[1] Because of the more flexible and open-ended nature of the Court's advisory jurisdiction and its non-binding outcomes, such self-determination cases should not simply be equated with territorial delimitation. Like their contentious counterparts, however, advisory cases about self-determination are an exercise in delimiting the self (and the state) through law. Further, how the self is grounded territorially is of central importance in determining whether a people can gain international legal personality. In the case of former colonial entities, a tension arises as to whether the contours of the territory or the identity of the people form the framework for emerging legal entities. In the following introductory section, an overview of the nature of the Court's advisory jurisdiction precedes a summary of the interrelationship between self-determination, decolonisation and territory.

Advisory Opinions enable the world community to seek expert legal opinions beyond the Court's limits on *locus standi* for states in contentious cases.[2] According to Article 96 of the UN Charter:

> 1. The General Assembly or the Security Council may request the International Court of Justice to give an advisory opinion on any legal question.

---

[1] These include: *International Status of South West Africa (Advisory Opinion)* (1950) ICJ Reps, p. 128; *Admissibility of Hearings of Petitioners by the Committee on South West Africa (Advisory Opinion)* (1956) ICJ Reps, p. 23; Legal *Consequences for States of the Continued Presence of South Africa in Namibia (South West Africa) notwithstanding Security Council Resolution 276 (1970) (Advisory Opinion)* (1971) ICJ Reps, p. 12; *Western Sahara (Advisory Opinion)* (1975) ICJ Reps, p. 12; *Legal Consequences of the Construction of a Wall in the Occupied Palestinian Territory (Advisory Opinion)* (2004) ICJ Reps, p. 136.

[2] S. Rosenne, *Rosenne's The World Court: What it is and how it works*, T. D. Gill (ed.), (Leiden: Martinus Nijhoff, 2003, 6th ed.), at 86.

2. Other organs of the United Nations and specialized agencies, which may at any time be so authorized by the General Assembly, may also request advisory opinions of the Court on the legal questions arising within the scope of their activities.

This language is also used in Article 65 of the Court's Statute. Although parties disputing the Court's jurisdiction in particular cases have focused on the discretionary nature of these provisions, the ICJ has never refused a request for these reasons. Only in the earlier PCIJ matter of *Eastern Carelia* did the Court choose not to hear a matter on the grounds that it would subvert state consent.[3] Some advisory requests, including the *Western Sahara* Case, have included inter-state disputes, but the Court has tended to overlook such an issue as an obstacle in exercising its jurisdiction. According to Koskenniemi, 'giving advisory opinions is a form…of peaceful settlement of disputes, whether between the UN and its member States or between States *inter se*.'[4] The Court's consciousness of its 'duty-to-cooperate' in the UN system has meant that advisory opinions have become an important way for UN organs, particularly the General Assembly, to seek the Court's assistance and expertise in resolving matters of concern.[5]

The nature of the Court's advisory jurisdiction has elicited criticism for a number of reasons. Of interest is the way commentators have tried to define and limit the role of the Court *vis-à-vis* 'political' controversies. We saw in Chapter One that scholarship on the ICJ is characterised by ongoing negotiations over the influence and place of politics in ICJ matters. A desire to demarcate the boundaries between legal and political concerns is particularly pronounced in advisory cases for two reasons. First, under the Charter and its Statute, the Court 'may give an advisory opinion on any legal question'. This provision's inclusion of the adjective 'legal' has prompted lengthy, but often repetitive, definitions of legal *in contrast to political* disputes in both cases and commentaries. On entering the Peace Palace, it has become obligatory to justify adjudication in contradistinction to political partiality. Despite such conventions, we have seen that the Court readily embraces advisory requests, indicating that debates over

[3] *Legal Status of Eastern Greenland (Denmark/Norway)* (1933) P.C.I.J. Series A/B No. 53.

[4] M. Koskenniemi, 'Advisory Opinions of the International Court Justice as an Instrument of Preventive Diplomacy', N. Nauimi & R. Meese (eds.), *International Legal Issues Arising under the United Nations Decade of International Law* (The Hague: Kluwer, 1995), 599–619, at 604.

[5] M. Pomerance, 'The Advisory Role of the International Court of Justice and its "Judicial" Character: Past and Future Prisms', A. S. Muller et al. (eds.), *The International Court of Justice* (The Hague: Kluwer, 1997), 271–323, at 290. Further, in relation to the UNGA nature of advisory requests, Pomerance reminds us that the UNSC only sought the Court's opinion once, in 1970 over Namibia. Ibid., at 291. The UN function of the ICJ is also discussed briefly in Chapter One, especially see footnote 15, at 20.

the law/politics dichotomy serve as mere lip-service to the preservation of the ICJ's legitimacy within the international system.

Some commentators regard the Court's acceptance of advisory requests as problematic.[6] Pomerance, for example, bemoans how the Court is 'frequently turned to not for the purpose of *genuine* law-clarification and problem-solving but for *propaganda* advantages and judicial legitimation of positions already firmly taken by *political* organs.'[7] On the flip-side, there is a strong theme in scholarship on the ICJ lamenting the untapped potential of the Court's advisory function as discussed in Chapter One.[8] The caseload of the ICJ is lighter than that of the PCIJ, and this is especially so in relation to advisory opinions.

The Court has developed jurisprudence on self-determination in its contentious, and particularly its advisory, capacity. Given that only states can bring contentious matters to the Court, Advisory Opinions are the better option for considering issues about nascent state entities and questions of international legal personality. Such considerations became vital for the UNGA in the fifties, sixties and seventies when increasing Third World membership meant that decolonisation was central to its work.

Although the law and practice on self-determination has grown enormously as a result of decolonisation, a framework of earlier norms and principles helped shape the postcolonial character of self-determination.[9] The idea can be traced back to the French Revolution and was championed – at least for European

---

[6] For an overview of the literature dealing with advisory opinions and what changes to make, see Koskenniemi, *supra* n. 4; and R. Higgins, 'A comment on the current health of Advisory Opinions', V. Lowe & M. Fitzmaurice (eds.), *Fifty years of the International Court of Justice: Essays in Honour of Sir Robert Jennings* (Cambridge: Cambridge University Press, 1996), 567–581.

[7] Emphasis added, Pomerance, *supra* n. 5, at 294. For a strident defence of 'legalism' in the face of 'politics' *vis-à-vis* the *South West Africa* cases, see M. Pomerance, 'The ICJ and South West Africa (Namibia): A Retrospective Legal/Political Assessment' (1999) 12 *Leiden Journal of International Law* 425.

[8] See Chapter One, at 51. Also see Koskenniemi, *supra* n. 4, at 602.

[9] This section does not pretend to do justice to the extensive literature on self-determination, but it does note some useful sources: D. Z. Cass, 'Re-Thinking Self-Determination: A Critical Analysis of Current International Law Theories' (1992) 18 *Syracuse Journal of International Law* 21; J. Crawford, 'The Right of Self-Determination in International Law: Its Development and Future', P. Alston (ed.), *Peoples' Rights* (Oxford: Oxford University Press, 2001), 7–67; F. L. Kirgis, Jr., 'The Degrees of Self-Determination in the United Nations Era' (1994) 88 *American Journal of International Law* 304; M. Koskenniemi, 'National Self-Determination Today: Problems of Legal Theory and Practice' 43 (1994) *International and Comparative Law Quarterly* 241; K. Knop, *Diversity and Self-Determination in International Law* (Cambridge: Cambridge University Press, 2002); G. J. Simpson, 'The Diffusion of Sovereignty: Self-Determination in the Postcolonial Age' 32 (1996) *Stanford Journal of International Law* 255.

peoples – by the League of Nations after the First World War.[10] Later in Article 1(2) of the UN Charter self-determination was enshrined, but only as a *principle* and not a right.[11] 'It is only later on in both human rights and decolonization settings that official UN terminology confirms that peoples enjoy a *right* of self-determination.'[12] The UNGA issued a series of declarations linking self-determination and decolonisation. One of the most important of these was Resolution 1514 (XV), which can be read as an endorsement of self-determination within former colonial territories.[13] The provision declared that '[a]ll peoples have the right to self-determination',[14] but it then went on to state that '[a]ny attempt aimed at the partial or total disruption of the national unity and the territorial integrity of a country is incompatible with the purposes and principles of the Charter of the United Nations.'[15] Later in Resolution 1541 (XV), the UNGA set out the procedure for non-self governing territories as covered under Chapter XI of the Charter. This Resolution was relied upon in the *Western Sahara* Case because it specified the avenues available for non-self governing territories in fulfilling the right to self-determination. Under Principle VI, options included:

(a) Emergence as a sovereign independent State;
(b) Free association with an independent State; or
(c) Integration with an independent State.

Principle VII went on to require the 'free and voluntary choice by the peoples of the territory' in settling on one of these outcomes.[16]

---

[10] For a general overview of the history of the development of self-determination, see A Cassese, *Self-Determination of Peoples: A Legal Reappraisal* (Cambridge: Cambridge University Press, 1995), at ch. 2.

[11] Article 1(2) reads, 'The purposes of the United Nations are... 2. To develop friendly relations among nations based on respect for the principle of self-determination of peoples, and to take other appropriate measures to strengthen universal peace.'

[12] Italics in original, R. Falk, 'Self-Determination under International Law: The Coherence of Doctrine versus the Incoherence of Experience', W. Danspeckgruber (ed.), *The Self-Determination of Peoples: Community, Nation and State in an Interdependent World* (Boulder, CO: Lynne Rienner, 2002), 31–66, at 41.

[13] The right was confirmed a decade later in UNGA Resolution 2625 (XXV), 'Declaration on Principles of International Law Concerning Friendly Relations and Co-operation among States in Accordance with the Charter of the United Nations', 24 October 1970.

[14] Paragraph 2.

[15] Paragraph 6, UNGA Resolution 1514 (XV), 'Declaration on the granting of independence to colonial countries and peoples', 14 Dec 1960. For a general discussion of the Declaration, see S. K. N. Blay, 'Self-Determination *versus* Territorial Integrity in Decolonization' 25 (1985) *Indian Journal of International Law* 386.

[16] UNGA Resolution 1541 (XV), 'Principle which should guide Members in determining whether or not an obligation exists to transmit the information called for under Article 73e of the Charter', 15 December 1960.

For a system based on membership of states, the phenomena of self-determination and decolonisation have presented a challenge to international law. Berman captures this idea in his study of the norm's evolution, describing it as 'exceptional', because it requires 'a *limited suspension* of the usual legal norms.'[17] We have seen above that international legal personality attaches to states, but what about peoples? Berman suggests that the law sometimes becomes more flexible when it recognises the legal status of a people before they have achieved statehood. This is 'the paradox of self-determination – the assertion of a right to become a right-holder'.[18] Procedurally, such a right is difficult to fulfil within the confines of ICJ adjudication. The Court's contentious jurisdiction only allows *other* states to pursue the rights of would-be states.[19] Advisory opinions are also restrictive, because we will see that, at least in the first case study, the people seeking their self-determination, the Ṣaḥrāwīs, were prevented from presenting their case before the Court.

Perhaps the biggest obstacle in realising self-determination, however, has been definitional, rather than procedural. What constitutes a *valid* self-determination unit, or people? Further, what is the relationship between definitions of selfhood and territory? Part II's Introduction touched on these ideas through the prism of the *uti possidetis juris* norm or policy.[20] There we saw that colonialism's legacy has been enduring because of the way in which former administrative boundaries have often been transformed into international borders. Thus, when trying to balance *uti possidetis* and self-determination, the most fundamental question to ask is: what should come first, the territory or the people? In his well-known statement in the *Western Sahara* Case, Judge Dillard declared, 'It is for the people to determine the destiny of the territory and not the territory the destiny of the people.'[21] Despite this sentiment, many examples from the Court's docket as well as UNGA declarations suggest that the 'static principle' of *uti possidetis* has trumped its 'dynamic' counterpart of self-determination.[22] Further, although the Court has implicitly favoured *uti possidetis*, it has failed to acknowledge the inevitable conflict between these two norms. Yet Cassese reminds us that these

[17] Emphasis in original, N Berman, 'Sovereignty in Abeyance: Self-Determination and International Law' (1988–1989) 7 *Wisconsin International Law Journal* 51, at 58.

[18] Ibid., at 78.

[19] For example: *South West Africa Cases (Ethiopia/South Africa; Liberia/South Africa) (Preliminary Objections)* (1962) ICJ Reps, p. 319; *South West Africa Cases (Ethiopia/South Africa; Liberia/South Africa) (Second Phase)* (1966) ICJ Reps, p. 6; *East Timor (Australia v. Portugal) (Merits)* (1995) ICJ Reps, p. 102.

[20] See Part II's Introduction, at 109–113.

[21] *Western Sahara (Advisory Opinion)* (1975) (sep. op. Dillard) ICJ Reps, at 122.

[22] T. M. Franck, 'Postmodern Tribalism and the Right to Secession', C. Brölmann et al. (eds.), *Peoples and Minorities in International Law* (The Hague: Kluwer, 1993), 3–27, at 4.

two approaches are irreconcilable: 'they can coexist only if self-determination makes way for the political need to respect existing boundaries.'[23] The quest for stability through colonial legacies has resulted in an approach to self-determination limited and limiting to those wishing to achieve postcolonial personality. Two examples of the struggle for self-determination discussed below attest to this hypothesis.

[23] A. Cassese, 'The International Court of Justice and the right of peoples to self-determination', V. Lowe & M. Fitzmaurice (eds.), *Fifty Years of the International Court of Justice: Essays in Honour of Sir Robert Jennings* (Cambridge: Cambridge University Press, 1996) 351–363, at 362.

Chapter Five

Determining the Limits of Law in the Western Sahara Case[1]

1) *Introduction*

The ICJ's *Western Sahara* Advisory Opinion handed down in 1975[2] has retained a prominent place within international legal scholarship because of its confirmation of the right to self-determination at least within colonial boundaries.[3] It is ironic then that the territory along with its people, the Ṣaḥrāwīs, still lack statehood and international legal personality.[4] In spite of jurisprudential notoriety, Moroccan occupation of the territory has rendered the Ṣaḥrāwīs unable to exercise the right to choose their own form of government as guaranteed by

---

[1] The name 'Western Sahara' is derived from the great central African desert stretching from the Red Sea to the Atlantic Ocean and covering much of the northern and central parts of Africa. Sahara is derived from the Arabic word for desert, Ṣaḥrā' (صحراء) and Ṣaḥrāwī is the relative adjective used to describe a person from the place. Arabic is broadly divided into colloquial and Modern Standard (fuṣḥa) forms and some of the words in this chapter reflect this diversity. Spelling discrepancies are compounded by the fact that there are many differences between French and English transliteration. Wherever possible, the meaning of Arabic words or their English transliteration is given in the fuṣḥa/English form except in French quotations.

[2] *Western Sahara (Advisory Opinion)* (1975) ICJ Reps, p. 12; hereinafter, ICJ Reps (1975).

[3] Knop points out though that the judgment is much more than a useful account of self-determination: 'the court engaged not only the specific challenges made to the account of self-determination as free choice, but also the more general problems of interpretation of a historically Eurocentric international law and the appropriate international legal remedy for colonialism.' K. Knop, *Diversity and Self-Determination in International Law* (Cambridge: Cambridge University Press, 2002), at 116.

[4] Technically, the territory is still under the gaze of international legal regulation, but at least in relation to self-determination, the territory's legal status remains unfulfilled. As a result of Moroccan occupation, the Ṣaḥrāwīs fall under the international law of occupation as well as human rights law. The ICJ considered how these two bodies of law applied to an occupied territory in the case discussed in the next chapter on the *Wall* Advisory Opinion. For an excellent historical study of the Western Saharan struggle incorporating political and legal perspectives, see T. Hodges, *Western Sahara: The Roots of a Desert War* (Westport: L. Hill, 1983).

the ICJ over three decades ago.[5] For Castellino, the 'relevance of this case to general international law of self-determination is enormous since it is one that falls between the two categories of "salt-water" colonialism, and the issue of possibly neo-colonialism.'[6]

Although it is typical to look beyond the ICJ in understanding this denial of Ṣaḥrāwī statehood, this chapter turns to a textual analysis of the proceedings to interrogate international law's constitutive role in the impasse. Many of the reasons for the Opinion's limited effect cannot be blamed on 'political' problems outside the Peace Palace; they lie embedded *within* the framework of the proceedings and the Court itself. Especially once the reader's gaze strays from the familiar confines of self-determination rhetoric, it becomes clear that the pleadings and the Opinion represent a debate over what role international law should play in the wake of colonialism. On such considerations no *dispositif* was rendered; these contested ideas, however, lie at the heart of the various positions taken both at the bar and the bench. Confusion about international law's purpose in supporting the claims of non-European peoples and cultures pulled the Court between particularism and universalism: should the Court have embraced instances of local Moroccan and Mauritanian rule, or should the ICJ have defeated such claims by upholding the right to Ṣaḥrāwī self-determination? Although the Court ultimately remained faithful to the principle of self-determination, we should not see the Opinion simply as an endorsement of Ṣaḥrāwī rights. Rather, it was an ambivalent compromise that employed Western approaches of territoriality to silence the claims of regional powers.[7]

In the various pleadings and judicial opinions[8] competing narratives and strategies vied for credibility within the crucible of legal contestation about (post)

---

[5] The case of Palestine could also be classified as a non-self governing territory and shares many similarities with the present Case. The legal status of the current state of Palestine and unfulfilled right to self-determination as discussed in Chapter Six.

[6] J. Castellino, *International Law and Self-Determination: The Interplay of the Politics of Territorial Possession with Formulations of Post-Colonial 'National' Identity* (The Hague: Martinus Nijhoff, 2000), at 211. Elias is less circumspect describing both Morocco and Mauritania as modern day colonisers. T. O. Elias, *The International Court of Justice and some contemporary problems: Essays on international law* (The Hague: Martinus Nijhoff, 1983), at 330.

[7] Okere argues that the language used by the Court was more diplomatic than legal because of the way it supported the various States simultaneously. B. O. Okere, 'The Western Sahara Case' (1979) 28 *International & Comparative Law Quarterly* 296, at 310.

[8] Although there is a large literature devoted to the Western Sahara Opinion, few of these studies have examined the pleadings. Notable exceptions include: M. Koskenniemi, *From Apology to Utopia: The Structure of International Legal Argument* (Cambridge: Cambridge University Press, 2nd edition, 2005), at 297–300; Knop, *supra* n. 3, M. M. Ricciardi, 'Title to the Aouzou Strip: A Legal and Historical Analysis' (1992) 17 *Yale Journal of International Law* 301 and especially M. N. Shaw, 'The Western Sahara Case' (1978) *British Yearbook of International Law* 119.

colonial possibilities for the territory of Western Sahara. All arguments were structured by both general institutional biases of the Court as well as the nature of the matter at hand, especially through the questions raised by the UNGA in its request for the Opinion. Each doctrinal account was much more than an exposition of legal rules, though; strategies employed and the substance invoked were both illustrative of the range of argumentative possibilities within the Courtroom. The success of certain claims helps us to map out the legal grammars or competencies of argument in the Case, highlighting those representations of law that are most *suited* and *suitable* to their Peace Palace context. Such a focus allows us to explore my concern of mapping the grammars of argument in ICJ territorial disputes. Further, we can also begin to approach the deeper focus of the book on universalism, because the Case provides a rich array of material about the harmonies and dissonances between European and non-European approaches to authority over territory.

The chapter discusses a number of themes that have already emerged in Part II, especially the themes of historical retelling, international legal personality under colonialism and different cultural traditions towards territorial order. Perhaps because of its advisory nature, the Case is richer than those explored in Chapters Three and Four. The larger number of parties allows greater comparison not only along substantive lines, but strategic lines, namely, those strategies of discursive delivery employed by the parties. After setting the scene and summarising the Opinion itself, the chapter is divided into two halves. First, through the structuring device of the law/politics dichotomy, argumentative strategies employed by the parties and the Court are reviewed. Ever mindful of the political backdrop of the Case, all speakers constructed differing accounts of law's relationship with politics to support their respective opinions about the role expected of international law in the matter. Second, the chapter considers some matters of substance pertinent to the issue of universalism: patterns of non-Western statehood and the construction of selfhood through international law. In a case renowned for embracing the rights of colonised people, it is easy to overlook *how* the Court developed such a position. Faced with the competing claims by a number of parties and policies, the Court confirmed the Ṣaḥrāwī self through a broader denial of non-European statehood. What patterns of discourse influenced the Court in its decision and how did the Court resolve the tension between law and politics as well as particularism and universalism in its Opinion?

2) *Confusion over the Fate of Western Sahara and the Request for an Advisory Opinion*

a) *Historical Background*

The territory now known as Western Sahara is bordered by Morocco to its North, Algeria to its North East, Mauritania to its East and South and the Atlantic Ocean (along with the Canary Islands) to the West.[9] As a result of the Spanish presence, the northern segment, comprising roughly one third of the territory, is known as Saqiyyat al-Ḥamrā' (or red canal, in Arabic) and the bottom two-thirds as Río de Oro (or river of gold, in Spanish). Much of the land is incredibly dry, receiving very low rainfall throughout the year, except for its thin coastal strip, thus encouraging nomadic as opposed to pastoral habitation.[10] Western Sahara is blessed with rich fishing resources and phosphate was also discovered in abundance by Spain in 1947.[11]

Western Sahara has nourished and been nourished by numerous empires in its history, including the Islamic dynasties of the Alawites (1666-present), the Almohads (1145–1269), the Almoravids (1056–1147), the Idrisids (788–974), the Merinids (1244–1465) and the Saadians (1554–1659). It is incorrect to conceive of the entity of Western Sahara subsisting in its current form before the colonial era; this also applies to the Ṣaḥrāwī people themselves. Nevertheless, it is possible at least to point out that the territory was an integral part in the extensive trade networks spanning the Sahara in the region and broadly fell within the zone of Islamic civilisation of North-West Africa. Largely because of its desert topography, social organisation was tribally based, with numerous independent groups forging intersecting alliances across the territory and beyond. Religiously the Ṣaḥrāwīs are Sunni Muslims and their speech of the Ḥassaniyya[12] dialect of Arabic reflects this, but ethnically it is simplistic to define them as Arabs,

---

[9] Generally, see I Brownlie, *African Boundaries: A Legal and Diplomatic Encyclopaedia* (London: C. Hurst, 1979).

[10] ICJ Reps (1975), at 88.

[11] A. Cassese, *Self-Determination of Peoples: A Legal Reappraisal* (Cambridge: Cambridge University Press, 1995), at 214–215. Spain only started full-scale extraction of phosphate in 1973 and by 1975 in 'the last full year of operations', production reached 2.8 million tons annually. J. Damis, *Conflict in Northwest Africa: The Western Sahara Dispute* (Stanford: Hoover Institute Press, 1983), at 12–13. Foreign control of Western Sahara's phosphate reserves continues to this day.

[12] Damis attributes this dialect to the gradual infiltration of Maqil Bedouin Arabs, originally hailing from the Arabian Peninsula in the fourteenth century. This tribe was joined by other North African migrations so that by the end of the seventeenth century, after intermarriage with Berber tribes and conversions to Islam, local Berber tribes claimed Arab descent and spoke Ḥassaniyya Arabic. Ibid., at 5–6.

comprising as they do a rich mix of indigenous peoples as well.[13] It is common, however, to include Western Sahara within the confines of the Arab World by reason of its language and its religion. Thus, the Ṣaḥrāwīs can be regarded as African, Muslim, largely Arabo-Berber nomadic tribes with close cultural links to the neighbouring States of Morocco, Algeria and Mauritania – all of which are members of the Arab League.

While the region was well-known within the historical and cultural traditions of the Muslim world with the spread of Islam in the wake of the Prophet's death in 632 CE, Europe remained largely ignorant of the territory and its people until the Spanish Age of 'Discovery' and later, the scramble for Africa in the late nineteenth century. Spain and Portugal were the main European powers to penetrate the region, and Riedel classifies Spanish contact with Western Sahara into three historical periods: between 1385 and 1884 when relations were sporadic and focussed on Spain's fishing and trade interests in the Canary Islands;[14] Spain's declaration of a protectorate over Río de Oro, along with its consolidation in the wake of the Berlin Conference of 1884; and finally, complete Spanish occupation of the inhospitable terrain from 1934.[15] During the latter half of the nineteenth century and early twentieth century, the Spanish and French along with their British and German counterparts sought to consolidate their territorial claims in the region. Since its invasion of Algeria in 1830, and given its interests in West Africa and Morocco, France was the dominant African partner during this period.[16] Because of Spain's earlier connections with the territory of Western Sahara, however, the two European powers entered into a series of

[13] Mauritania briefly discussed the shift to Arabic in the Shinqīṭī entity: Mauritania, Oral Pleadings, International Court of Justice: Pleadings, Oral Arguments, Documents: Western Sahara, vol. IV, at 361–362.

[14] In its written memorials, Spain offered a detailed account of the various agreements created to preserve Spain's fishing interests off the coast, as well as to protect its sailors in the wake of shipwrecks. See especially, Spain, Written Submission, International Court of Justice: Pleadings, Oral Arguments, Documents, Western Sahara, vol. I, at 73–425.

[15] E. H. Riedel, 'Confrontation in the Western Sahara in the Light of the Advisory Opinion of the International Court of Justice of 16 October 1975: A Critical Appraisal' (1976) 19 *German Yearbook of International Law* 405 at 408–410. Even in relation to the post-1934 period, it is difficult to characterise Spain's presence in the area as amounting to comprehensive occupation. Shaw cites Gretton on this point, who argues that the Spanish only established complete administrative and military control in the 1960s. Shaw, *supra* n. 8, at 121. This situation was similar to that discussed in Chapter Three, where we saw that Italian occupation of Libya was paltry for decades after the formal creation of the colony.

[16] In fact, Spain's limited and essentially insignificant presence in Africa compared with its European neighbour, France, is not dissimilar to Italy's own position in North Africa and particularly Libya. Like Spain, Italy was anxious to stake a claim over a part of the continent for national glory, and Libya is perhaps the prime example of such ambitions. The nature of Italy's presence in North Africa during the same period is touched on in Chapter Three, at 137–138.

relatively amicable treaties, in particular those of 1900, 1904 and 1912, which sought to delineate their respective interests in North West Africa.[17]

Although France and Spain were both eager to ignore and override the indigenous systems of rule extant in the territory, indigenous tribes, as well as neighbouring powers, maintained connections with Western Sahara. Morocco in particular propounded a policy of 'Greater Morocco' after its independence in 1956,[18] and its most well-known spokesperson was Allal al-Fassi.[19] This ideological perspective not only justified the inclusion of Western Sahara into Morocco, but also laid claim to large parts of Algeria and the whole of Mauritania. In fact, 1963 had witnessed a border conflict between Morocco and Algeria.[20] Furthermore until 1969, Morocco refused to acknowledge Mauritania's right to exist as a separate State even in the face of significant regional opposition to such posturing.[21]

Despite the development of the self-determination norm developed in the first few decades of the UN as explored in the introduction to Part III, the norm's application to Western Sahara was complicated by Spanish intransigence[22] and competing regional claims and interpretations of its application. Spain had delayed its withdrawal from the territory for some time, thus allowing Morocco and Mauritania to develop stronger claims to the territory on its 'independence'. According to Shaw, the 'early Spanish dilatoriness was not in the context of colonial behaviour exceptional, but the claims maintained by neighbouring States were.'[23] This situation contributed significantly to the UNGA's policy difficulties;

---

[17] Agreement or Protocol between Morocco and Spain, concerning the cession of Ifni, 27 June 1900, 188 CTS 457; Convention between France and Spain concerning Morocco, 3 October 1904, 196 CTS 353; Convention between France and Spain respecting relations in Morocco, 27 November 1912, 217 CTS 288.

[18] For an overview of Morocco's regional ambitions, see Hodges, *supra* n. 4, ch. 8, 'Greater Morocco', 85–98.

[19] Damis, *supra* n. 11, at 15. Judge De Castro is the only member of the Court to discuss al-Fassi and the ideology of 'Greater Morocco'. It must be noted that this concept along with its most prominent defender did not figure in the pleadings themselves. ICJ Reps (1975) (sep. op. De Castro), at 127–128.

[20] See P. B. Wild, 'The Organization of African Unity and the Algerian-Moroccan Border Conflict: A Study of New Machinery for Peacekeeping and the Peaceful Settlement of Disputes Among African States' (1966) 20 *International Organization* 18.

[21] Z. O. A. Salem, 'Mauritania: A Saharan Frontier-state' (2005) 10 *Journal of North African Studies* 491, at 498.

[22] Mauritania argues that Spain did not comply for a number of years with UNGA requests about Western Sahara's move towards self-determination. Written Statement, International Court of Justice: Pleadings, Oral Arguments, Documents: Western Sahara, vol. III, at 7. See also Slaoui, Morocco, Oral Pleadings, International Court of Justice: Pleadings, Oral Arguments, Documents: Western Sahara, vol. IV, at 120.

[23] Shaw, *supra* n. 8, at 122.

although the Assembly had placed the situation of Sahara's decolonisation on its agenda back in 1963, its stance was far from clear on the eve of the Advisory Opinion in 1974. Such ambivalence was indicated by its choice of seeking the ICJ's assistance in the first place; it was unusual to involve the Court in decolonisation issues, and in this instance the UNGA was partly swayed by the lobbying of Morocco and its supporters. Morocco, Spain, Algeria and Mauritania all had to operate within the context of the UN's decolonisation policy, but beyond this they all pursued their own agendas. Their positions regarding a mooted referendum and the UN's role all shifted substantially over the course of the sixties up until 1975.[24] Dynamics of diplomacy within the UN, the Arab League and the OAU all influenced the formulation of policies sometimes supporting or sometimes stalling the chance for a UN-led referendum for the territory.

The impetus for the Advisory Opinion request came in the wake of intense Moroccan and Mauritanian lobbying after Spain's announcement in 1974 supporting a referendum which would have seen the Ṣaḥrāwīs determining their future in the wake of Spanish withdrawal. Keen to avoid the political fallout from a military invasion and yet mindful of time constraints in securing his hold over the territory, Morocco's King Ḥassan supported the Court's involvement as a stalling tactic. Thus, he 'would have the Western Saharan dispute submitted to the International Court of Justice at The Hague and thereby persuade the UN to postpone the referendum while the territory's legal status was under the court's laborious and time-consuming scrutiny.'[25] Initially Morocco attempted to bring a case against Spain under the Court's contentious jurisdiction, but Spain rejected such a move.[26] The UNGA was then called on by Morocco and some other Arab states to invoke the Court's advisory jurisdiction.[27] Moroccan motivations for such a strategy were easy to determine from statements made at the time and military action that continued both during and after the judgment.[28] For example, Hodges cites King Ḥassan as declaring: 'If peaceful means do not produce results, only armed struggle will remain for the Moroccan people… [and in relation to the ICJ Opinion]…whatever the result Morocco will recover its rights over its despoiled provinces no later than the end of [1975].'[29]

[24] T. M. Franck, 'The Stealing of the Sahara' 70 (1976) *American Journal of International Law* 694, at 701–707.

[25] Hodges, *supra* n. 4, 183.

[26] ICJ Reps (1975), at para. 29.

[27] Franck, *supra* n. 24, at 706; Hodges, *supra* n. 4, at 185.

[28] See Mundy for some discussion of Morocco's military exercises on the border of Western Sahara during the hearings of the Advisory Opinion: J. Mundy, 'Neutrality or Complicity? The United States and the 1975 Moroccan Takeover of the Spanish Sahara' (2006) 11 *Journal of North African Studies* 275, at 284.

[29] Quoted in Hodges, *supra* n. 4, at 207.

This deferment of the Assembly's decolonisation duties in favour of the Court was unusual: typically the Assembly assessed the situation on the ground without the assistance of the ICJ and without reference to historical considerations.[30] It was even more unusual to block planned referenda.[31] Because of widespread misgivings over such an approach, it was difficult to garner sufficient support for resolution 3292 (XXIX) seeking the Court's assistance. Many Arab States were supportive of Moroccan and Mauritanian claims over the territory, but other non-Arab African States in particular resisted any watering down of the Ṣaḥrāwī right to self-determination. For example, a Kenyan delegate to the UN stated, 'The people of Spanish Sahara should be the court'.[32] With Moroccan troops never far from the borders of Western Sahara before and during the Case, it would have been difficult to suspend belief and uphold a clear separation between law and politics.[33] Could the Court be insulated from the broader context through legal argument alone? Through its request for an Advisory Opinion of an unusually historical nature, perhaps this is what the Assembly was trying to do: maintaining faith in law as separate and distinct from politics. This tactic was also vital for the main participants in the case itself, as will be shown below.

One of the ICJ's exemplary self-determination cases was initiated in the face of widespread Third World unease about the need for adjudication, and the focus of its consideration, the Ṣaḥrāwī people, were silenced through the process.[34] We mentioned above that such silencing of non-Europeans as objects of adjudication was common to the case law of nineteenth century and PCIJ jurisprudence.[35] However, with the process of decolonisation all but finished, the Opinion reminds us of *continuities*, rather than ruptures, with former instances of colonial adjudication and silencing. A number of states would seek to speak for the Ṣaḥrāwīs, but the nature of the Court's jurisdiction permitted

[30] G. Joffé, 'The International Court of Justice. And the Western Sahara Dispute' R. Lawless & L. Monahan (eds.), *War and Refugees: The Western Sahara Conflict* (London; New York: Pinter, 1987) 16–30, at 16.

[31] Franck, *supra* n. 24, at 700–701.

[32] Ibid., at 706.

[33] During oral pleadings, Spain expressed its misgivings to this effect, but missed the irony that it had carried out such policies for almost a century in the same territory: 'Je dois donc, à ce stade, exprimer l'apprehénsion avec laquelle nous avons entendu la tenue générale de certaines interventions devant la Cour, qui n'ont pas caché leur conviction qu'un éventual avis de la Cour aurait une influence décisive dans la résolution de ce qui, sous le masque d'un litige juridique avec l'Espagne, constitute en réalité le but de s'intaller souverainement sur ce territoire africain, quelle que soit la volonté de sa population autochtone.' Sedo, Spain, Oral Pleadings, International Court of Justice: Pleadings, Oral Arguments, Documents: Western Sahara, vol. IV, at 62.

[34] Joffé, *supra* n. 30, at 16.

[35] For example, see Part II's Introduction, at 100.

no standing or rights to the people themselves.[36] Such a turn of events was a blow to the aspirations of the recently formed Polisario Front,[37] which expressed its disbelief over a judgment that would 'convey the destiny of peoples before the Court of The Hague in our total absence.'[38] In the words of a prominent Ṣaḥrāwī, 'the Sahrawis will not accept the whole world speaking for them as if they were cattle.'[39]

b) *A Summary of the Pleadings and the Opinion*

Partly because of Mauritanian and Moroccan claims to the Spanish territory in the pre-colonial period, the advice sought by the UNGA from the Court centred on the legal status of Western Sahara on the eve of Spanish colonisation and the nature of any pre-existing legal ties with neighbouring powers. Thus as per Articles 31 and 68 of the ICJ Statute and Articles 3, 87 and 89 of the Court's Rules, the UNGA asked the following questions of the Court:

1) Was Western Sahara (Río de Oro and Sakiet El Hamra) at the time of colonization by Spain a territory belonging to no one (*terra nullius*)?
2) If the answer to the first question is in the negative, what were the legal ties between this territory and the Kingdom of Morocco and the Mauritanian entity?[40]

The same resolution 3292 (XXV) acknowledged the UNGA's work in relation to decolonisation, but did not explicitly ask the Court to consider decolonisation or self-determination.[41] Perhaps it was assumed that this would be understood by the Court and other participants and in fact it was: all positions contained some exploration of this relationship. According to the Court, 'The object of the request is... to obtain from the Court an opinion which the General Assembly

[36] W. M. Reisman, 'Protecting Indigenous Rights in International Adjudication' (1995) 89 *American Journal of International Law* 350, at 354.

[37] POLISARIO, or Frente Popular de Liberación de Saguía el Hamra y Río de Oro (Popular Front for the Liberation of Saguia el-Hamra and Río de Oro) was officially established on 10 May 1973 in pursuit of independence from Spain. Once Spain left the territory, it was replaced by Morocco and Mauritania until 1979 and now only Morocco as the occupier. Polisario continues to struggle against the occupation. For general information on the origins of nationalism and Polisario, see Hodges, *supra* n. 4, at chs. 14 & 15.

[38] Ibid., at 186.

[39] Ibid.

[40] It should be noted that Mauritania was called the Mauritanian Entity, Bilād Shinqīṭī (meaning 'country of the Shinqīṭī' in Arabic) or the Shinguitti entity.

[41] The text of the resolution is reproduced in the Opinion: ICJ Reps (1975), at 13–14.

deems of assistance to it for the proper exercise of its functions concerning the decolonization of the territory.'[42]

Some procedural aspects of the Case relating to participating states should be noted. Under resolution 3292, Spain as the 'administering power' and Mauritania and Morocco as 'interested parties' were called on to submit to the Court information and documents that would be needed to clarify the two questions. These States all presented lengthy written and oral submission to the Court. Algeria also made an important contribution through its eloquent advocate, Mohammad Bedjaoui, and Zaïre made a brief but highly unconventional appearance during the oral pleadings. The Court was furnished with a dossier compiled under the auspices of the Secretary-General as per Article 65(2) of the Court's Statute,[43] but this document was insufficient for providing the necessary background, and the Court was forced to rely heavily on the materials submitted by the participating States. Finally, a number of mostly Latin American States submitted brief letters to the Court as per Article 66(2) of the Statute, generally urging the Court to be cognisant of the overriding importance of self-determination in the Case.[44]

The contentious nature of the Case was deepened during preliminary hearings about the appointment of *ad hoc* judges. The bench already included the Spanish judge Frederico de Castro y Bravo, and so the question arose regarding the rights of Mauritania and Morocco to appoint their own judges.[45] In seeking such a right,[46] Morocco invoked Article 68 of the Statute, which states, 'In the exercise of its advisory functions the Court shall further be guided by the provisions of the present Statute which apply in contentious cases to the extent to which it recognises them to be applicable.' As Morocco had attempted to bring contentious pleadings before the Court in 1974, it argued that there was 'une question juridique actuellement pendante'and that it could rely on Article 31(2) of the Statute.[47] Mauritania could not rely on the technicalities of the

---

[42] ICJ Reps (1975), at 27. In his separate opinion, Judge Dillard was relieved that the Court had chosen to place potentially non-legal questions within the context of contemporary decolonisation practice. ICJ Reps (1975) (sep. op. Dillard), at 117.

[43] International Court of Justice, Pleadings, Oral Arguments, Documents: Western Sahara, vol. 1, at 24–60.

[44] These States included: France, Panama, Nicaragua, Chile, Guatemala, the Dominican Republic, Ecuador, Costa Rica, Colombia. Ibid., at 63–72.

[45] This issue is briefly discussed in H. Charlesworth, 'Judge *ad hoc* of the International Court of Justice', T. McCormack & C. Saunders (eds.), *Sir Ninian Stephen: A Tribute* (Carleton, Vic: Melbourne University Press, 2007) 176–189, at 185.

[46] Generally, see Dupuy, Morocco, Oral Pleadings, International Court of Justice: Pleadings, Oral Arguments, Documents: Western Sahara, vol. IV, at 9–30.

[47] Dupuy, Morocco, Oral Pleadings, International Court of Justice: Pleadings, Oral Arguments, Documents: Western Sahara, vol. IV, at 17.

Statute, and instead made reference to the UNGA's recognition of its status as an interested State in various resolutions.[48]

It is interesting to contrast these two perspectives supportive of the Case's contentious nature with the views held by Spain and Algeria. Perhaps because its own judge was a member of the Court, Spain tried to dissociate the proceedings from any contentious connotations and reminded the Court of its advisory attributes.[49] Algeria also sought to steer Mauritania and Morocco from the battle lines by stressing the common ties uniting the Maghreb above particular interests. Bedjaoui declared:

> dans cette affaire qui concerne une population arabe et musulmane, je suis sûr que le Maroc, la Mauritanie et l'Algérie trouveront dans leur fraternelles relations, dans leur solidarité et dans leur génie propre, le moyen de transcender la difficulté actuelle et de dégager une solution commune, l'essentiel étant et demeurant pour tous et pour chacun la décolonisation et la libération du Sahara.[50]

Ultimately, the contentious nature of the pleadings was acknowledged only up to a point: the Court granted Morocco's request for a judge *ad hoc* by ten votes to five to balance Spain's judge, whereas Mauritania's claim was narrowly defeated with an eight to seven vote split.[51]

In contrast to these issues of procedure and jurisdiction, it is harder to identify common themes in argument regarding the two questions asked by the UNGA. Because of the pleadings' length, as well as some divergences between the oral and written stages of submission, arguments on the merits were not always clear. However, at least in relation to the first question about *terra nullius*, most participants and all judges stated that Western Sahara was not a territory *sans maître* (without a ruler, *terra nullius*). It is unfortunate that the Court did not go further in its Opinion and offer its interpretation as to who the territory's ruler might have been on the eve of Spanish 'protection'.[52] Its support for the

---

48 Salmon, Mauritania, Oral Pleadings, International Court of Justice: Pleadings, Oral Arguments, Documents: Western Sahara, vol. IV, at 32–57.

49 Generally, see Sedo & Lacleta, Spain, Oral Pleadings, International Court of Justice: Pleadings, Oral Arguments, Documents: Western Sahara, vol. IV, at 61 ff.

50 Bedjaoui, Algeria, Oral Pleadings, International Court of Justice: Pleadings, Oral Arguments, Documents: Western Sahara, vol. IV, at 60. Spain took up this rhetoric of Arab solidarity itself immediately after Bedjaoui's statement, declaring 'Permettez-moi aussi de manifester notre satisfaction devant la présence de représentants de gouvernements de pays auxquels l'Espagne est reliée par des liens d'affection, ces mêmes liens qui nous rattachent traditionnellement à tous les pays arabes.' Sedo, Spain, Oral Pleadings, International Court of Justice: Pleadings, Oral Arguments, Documents: Western Sahara, vol. IV, at 61.

51 ICJ Reps (1975), at 8.

52 M. A. Smith, 'Sovereignty over Unoccupied Territories – The Western Saharan Decision' (1977) 9 *Case Western Journal of International Law* 135, at 140; Knop, *supra* n. 3, at 126–127.

self-determination of the territory's people nearly a century later indicated its recognition for contemporary selfhood, but did the peoples of Western Sahara possess an identifiable legal personality before Spanish colonisation? The Court retroactively imposed the territorial boundaries of the Spanish territory onto the region before its colonisation, but what was the exact status of its people?[53] These questions were left unanswered by the Court, but are further examined below in the Chapter's final section.

In trying to answer the first question, Spain's position on the status of the territory was slippery and somewhat contradictory. Although it held itself up as a benevolent colonial power intent on self-determination of the Western Saharan people and dismissive of its neighbours' irredentist claims, it also displayed a degree of contempt for the capacities of the local population, and thus its exact position on the doctrine of *terra nullius* was unclear.[54] In its historical overview of the pre-colonial period, for example, there was very little recognition of an identifiable Western Saharan people constituting a separate entity. Like the Court, Spain seemed to impose boundaries onto its territory, thereby artificially cutting off Saharan tribes from regional connections. As in Chapter Four's discussion of the *Bahrain/Qatar* Case in the Gulf, the Opinion highlights the difficulties of applying concepts of bounded territoriality to cultures and places based on nomadic migrations.

Morocco's answer to the first question was in contrast to Spain's arguments and the colonial power's purported actions. In its pleadings, Morocco did not need to explore the doctrine of *terra nullius* as it applied specifically to the Western Saharan territory, because its entire case rested instead on its ability to prove Moroccan sovereignty; *terra nullius* was a *non sequitur*. A degree of compromise between the Moroccan and Mauritanian arguments is evident:[55] Morocco accommodated Mauritanian claims over the south of the territory in what must have been a bid for the two powers to effect a neat division of Western Sahara

[53] Knop also argues that although 'the court treated the population of Western Sahara as the legal "self", it is significant that it did not validate any such sociological finding. While the court did not accept Morocco's appeal to the salience of an ethnic, cultural and religious self that united Western Sahara with Morocco, neither did it endorse Spain's view that the Sahrawi... formed a coherent and distinct self at the time of colonization... As far as the court was concerned, the self effectively took its identity from the referendum and not vice versa.' Footnotes omitted, Knop, *supra* n. 3, at 118.

[54] Generally see Written Submission of Spain, International Court of Justice: Pleadings, Oral Arguments, Documents: Western Sahara, vol. I.

[55] Morocco recognised this complementarity of arguments explicitly: 'Les mémoires mauritanien et marocain ont été rédigés indépendamment l'un d'autre... Mais... le point de vue marocain et le point de vue mauritanien... sont en réalité complémentaires.' Morocco, Slaoui, Morocco, Oral Pleadings, International Court of Justice: Pleadings, Oral Arguments, Documents: Western Sahara, vol. IV, at 118.

upon Spanish withdrawal. Events after the pleadings reflected this closely. Thus for Morocco, 'il n'en reste pas moins qu'aux yeux du Gouvernement marocain il n'existe pas de *no man's land* entre la souveraineté marocaine et l'ensemble mauritanien.'[56]

Partly because Mauritania's historical record was so much weaker, it explored the doctrinal implications of *terra nullius* in some detail and the various opinions of the Court were most sympathetic to this line of argument. Algeria offered an even more rigorous and critical account of the doctrine, but the implications for international law were perhaps too radical, and the Court rejected them out of hand; in fact, the Opinion did not refer at all to the perspective offered by Algeria's counsel, Bedjaoui.[57] Mauritania conceded that the doctrine of *terra nullius* was difficult to characterise because of the many interpretations given to it in theory and practice.[58] Although Mauritania noted that some European perspectives classified many non-European entities as *terra nullius*, it rejected this by showing that state practice had largely supported treaties of cession with local rulers instead of occupation. Mauritania limited the application of *terra nullius* strictly to lands which were uninhabited or without any political coordination. Western Sahara was contrasted with this because it was 'tres structurées avec une organisation politique complexe même si elles étaient non étatiques.'[59] Thus, Mauritania tried to argue that the concept of *terra nullius* in the nineteenth century was only applicable to unorganised societies. What was less clear, however, was whether the complex structures of Saharan society had been endowed with international legal personality as discussed in the introduction to Part II. This conundrum is explored at length in the chapter's final section.

Through the application of inter-temporal law, the Court found by thirteen votes to three that Western Sahara was not *terra nullius* because European state practice during the late nineteenth century had preferred cession over occupation.[60] The Court acknowledged the fierce debate that this concept continues to elicit, but ultimately was convinced that the 'standard of civilisation' was not the applicable law *per se* at the time. 'Whatever differences of opinion there may

---

56 Morocco, Written Statement, International Court of Justice: Pleadings, Oral Arguments, Documents: Western Sahara, vol. III, at 204.

57 Judge Ammoun, however, cited Bedjaoui with approval: ICJ Reps (1975) (sep. op. Ammoun), at 85–86.

58 Generally, Mauritania, Written Statement, International Court of Justice: Pleadings, Oral Arguments, Documents: Western Sahara, vol. III, at 28–51.

59 Ibid., at 53.

60 Contrast this position with that of Koskennieimi's as discussed in Part II's Introduction, where he argued that it is best to consider European territorial control in the period as a result of occupation rather than cession. This suggests that many non-European peoples were not recognised as having any international legal personality at the time, at 105.

have been among jurists, the State practice of the relevant period indicates that territories inhabited by tribes or peoples having a social and political organization were not regarded as *terra nullius*.'[61] Crawford argues that this stance was consistent with the Court's jurisprudence: earlier cases had recognised the legal personality of entities beyond Europe.[62] Although the Court may have been following its own jurisprudence, compelling evidence was brought before the Court indicating that territories such as Western Sahara were not regarded as legal entities at the time of Spanish colonisation, and the Court's gloss over such an uncomfortable period of international law's history is troubling.[63] Some of the dissenting positions were uncomfortable with the overly historical and academic nature of the first question on *terra nullius*. Judges Dillard and Gros regarded the question as 'loaded' (read 'political')[64] and Petrén as 'pointless and consequently inappropriate'.[65] Despite this, most of the bench seized the opportunity presented to them to define the doctrine of *terra nullius* in palatable terms for the international community.

[61] ICJ Reps (1975), at 39.

[62] For example, the *US Nationals in Morocco Case* and the *Rights of Passage Case*, J. Crawford, 'The General Assembly, the International Court and self-determination', V. Lowe & M. Fitzmaurice (eds.), *Fifty Years of the International Court of Justice: Essays in Honour of Sir Robert Jennings* (Cambridge: Cambridge University Press, 1996), at 597, footnote 52. Roussellier counters this with the PCIJ's *Eastern Greenland* Case. According to Roussellier, 'The PCIJ's definition implies that *terrae nullius* are lands not claimed by any states, which again is an approach consistent with the Court's understanding of sovereignty over a disputed land as being derived from international treaties expressing consistent recognition by other states of a state's claim over a given land.' Thus, perhaps it was consistent here for the Court to recognise the international legal personality of Morocco, as it has entered into treaties with European powers at the time. However, the status of Saharan tribes was more questionable. J. E. Roussellier, 'Elusive Sovereignty – People, Land and the Frontiers of the Desert: The Case of the Western Sahara and the International Court of Justice' (2007) 12 *Journal of North African Studies* 55, at 71.

[63] See especially Bedjaoui's detailed exposition of the idea that *terra nullius* has developed in three phases: its Roman period where all lands non-Roman were *nullius*; the era of 'discovery' in the fifteenth and sixteenth centuries when all non-Christian entities were deemed as *nullius* and finally, the age in question, which regarded all the lands inhabited by non-'civilised' peoples as *nullius*. Bedjaoui, Algeria, Oral Pleadings, International Court of Justice: Pleadings, Oral Arguments, Documents: Western Sahara, vol. IV, at 455–456. See Shaw's rebuttal of Bedjaoui's arguments: Shaw, *supra* n. 8, at 129–130. Okere points out that the jurisprudence of the nineteenth century was heavily supportive of a finding of Western Sahara as *terra nullius*. Furthermore, this intellectual influence has continued in the writings of such prominent figures as Hall, Oppenheim, Schwarzenberger and Jennings. Okere, *supra* n. 7, at 305.

[64] ICJ Reps (1975) (dec. Gros), at 74; ICJ Reps (1975) (sep. op. Dillard), at 124. Some judges also regarded the second question about legal ties as 'loaded': ICJ Reps (1975) (dec. Ignacio-Pinto), at 78.

[65] ICJ Reps (1975) (sep. op. Petén), at 114.

The second question about legal ties was even more difficult to determine and it stimulated a whole range of competing perspectives about the extent to which international law can recognise non-European forms of rule over territory. Both Mauritania and Morocco asked the Court to step beyond the borders of traditional international law in trying to imagine the climatic, social, political and religious situation extant in North West Africa on the eve of purported Spanish colonisation. The Court appeared disposed to these perspectives by recognising the presence of legal ties between Morocco (fourteen votes to two) and Mauritania (fifteen votes to one) with the territory. However, as in the words of Judge Gros, the majority's ultimate decision was 'enigmatic';[66] these legal ties were less than sovereign and had no direct bearing on the prevailing legal situation. Roussellier suggests that the basis for the Court's difficulties stemmed from its failure to articulate 'what should be considered [as] acts defining the effective exercise of sovereignty.'[67] The Court was aware that its primary function was to assist in the UNGA decolonisation process, and the legal ties it had recognised did not affect this.[68] Thus the Case can best be characterised as a latent conflict between territorial integrity and self-determination. Yet again, however, the Court refused to enter the dispute directly and never ruled on how to resolve this norm conflict:[69] instead, the Court tried to accommodate many perspectives and thus failed to offer a clear position on these issues. There was no determinate position provided by doctrine, but this was just as well for the goal of the Court in affirming self-determination at all costs – even a confirmation of European approaches to authority over territory.

3) *Playing with the Rules: Strategies of Argument before the Court*

At the heart of all positions presented in the *Western Sahara* Case was an exploration of the relationship between law and politics as set out in Chapter One. Some *substantive* examples of this dichotomy are explored below in relation to colonialism and non-European modes of authority over territory. These substantive positions about the place of colonialism within international law, however, can only ever succeed by speaking the language of their context with competence: *how* arguments are presented is as important as their *substance*. Because the substance of law is itself indeterminate and requires constant redefinition

66 ICJ Reps (1975) (dec. Gros), at 75.

67 Roussellier, *supra* n. 62, at 61. Further, for a very useful tabulation of the respective arguments of the Parties and the bench regarding *effectivités*, see Ibid., at 62.

68 Shaw, *supra* n. 8, at 149.

69 Koskenniemi, *From Apology to Utopia, supra* n. 8, at 300.

vis-à-vis politics, a crucial device in advancing substantive claims is the ability to construct a legitimate and authentic account about the relationship between law and its perceived antitheses, such as morality, history, emotion, fact and especially, politics. Although these dichotomies are often inconsistent or are transposed throughout any one narrative, they at least highlight the *strategies* employed by the various participants. This in turn indicates competing characterisations of law, raising questions such as: can law speak the same language as the social sciences, and what is the role of emotion? This section will evaluate some of the strategies – or legal grammars – employed at the bench and the bar in staking an authentic characterisation of the relationship between law and politics. Such strategies include, but are not limited to, recognition of the institutional rules of the Court; attempts to make law distinct from other forms of social enquiry, especially history; problems of interpretation and language; and the use of European comparisons as a way of making sense of Arab-Islamic culture.

Debate devoted to preliminary questions about *ad hoc* judges, the Court's jurisdiction and the procedural differences between contentious and advisory proceedings all displayed different perspectives on the relationship between law and politics in the courtroom. International law as embodied in the practice of the Court rests on a paradox: it is separate from politics, but requires the consent of international society's pre-eminent political entities, states. The structure of the provisions of the ICJ Statute initiating proceedings is based on a *Lotus*-esque vision of international law,[70] which is then substantially watered down once States *choose* to submit to its jurisdiction.[71] Typically, significant energy and time is spent disputing and/or justifying the Court's jurisdiction *vis-à-vis* consent. Often these parts of the pleadings and judgments are heavily formulaic and discussions about the Court's jurisdiction vary very little across the cases. This was acknowledged by Morocco in the Peace Palace: 'il est certaines questions spécifiques que l'on doit aborder et que la Cour, normalement, se pose à l'occasion de l'interprétation qu'elle doit faire de la demande qui lui est addressée.'[72] Morocco applied this assessment of the etiquette of exposition in support of the Court's jurisdiction.[73]

---

[70] *The Case of the S.S. "Lotus" (France/Turkey)* (1927) P.C.I.J., Series A, No. 10.

[71] See Part II's Introduction, at 100–101.

[72] Dupuy, Morocco, Oral Pleadings, International Court of Justice: Pleadings, Oral Arguments, Documents: Western Sahara, vol. IV, at 140.

[73] These rules are identified as: 'On se trouve là un domaine juridique très circonscrit car, semble-t-il, deux principes se dégagent de l'examen de votre jurisprudence: les questions, d'une part, doivent avoir été rédigées dans des termes précis et, d'autre part, l'interprétation qui doit évidemment être menée par la Cour ne doit pas aboutir à la formulation de nouvelles questions.' Ibid.

In the Opinion a number of judges tried to confine the Case within the perceived limits of its advisory jurisdiction so that the issue of consent could be put to the side, but in fact many remarks indicate that the Court's jurisdiction was difficult to define. Spain identified the contentious nature of the pleadings perhaps in a bid to boost its arguments against jurisdiction. Spain characterised the contentious quality of Morocco's case 'non seulement par les thèses qui ont été soutenues, mais aussi [more importantly for this section's focus] par l'emploi de certaines expressions de la procédure contentieuse, car on a parlé du «mémoire marocain», pièce écrite qui, selon l'article 44 du Règlement, est présentée par les demandeurs dans la procédure en matière contentieuse; on a parlé de «l'agent» de ce gouvernement'.[74] Morocco's response drew attention to similar postures on the part of Spain, and argued that the Statute does not establish such a neat separation of the Court's jurisdiction.[75] Judge Petrén disagreed on this point by stating that the presentation of evidence was significantly different in the two types of proceedings.[76] Judge De Castro agreed by pointing out that the states in the present Case should have acted as *amici curiae* in an advisory capacity, and because they did not stricter rules of evidence should have been applied.[77] Thus the Court uncomfortably straddled its advisory and contentious capacities:

> we had three States submitting to the Court abundant historical and cartographical documentation the significance of which was the subject of much dispute. The same events, the same treaties, the same legislative and administrative acts, and the same religious, cultural and linguistic phenomena were represented in a variety of ways, which were often contradictory. On many a point the Court was invited to choose between differing contentions.[78]

Judge De Castro regarded this as repugnant to the Court's advisory role: the bench was not sufficiently empowered to verify the evidence presented and the

---

[74] Arias-Salgado, Spain, Oral Pleadings, International Court of Justice: Pleadings, Oral Arguments, Documents: Western Sahara, vol. V, at 46.

[75] '...le conseil du Gouvernement espagnol tire cette conclusion des termes *mémoire, agent*, que nous avons utilisés parfois dans nos écrits ou dans nos déclarations orales...l'article 44 du Règlement...lequel énumère les actes de la procédure contentieuse, sans pour autant leur conférer un sens exclusif, opposer les articles 68 du Statut, 87 du Règlement, qui posent le principe général d'une assimilation des procédures contentieuse et consultative...On pourrait tout aussi bien invoquer le lapsus, assez naturel devant une jurisdiction, d'autant plus qu'il serait tout aussi possible d'en citer des exemples dans la bouche des conseils espagnols, qui ont également parlé notamment de *memoire*.' Dupuy, Morocco, Oral Pleadings, International Court of Justice: Pleadings, Oral Arguments, Documents: Western Sahara, vol. V, at 187.

[76] ICJ Reps (1975) (sep. op. Petrén), at 112.

[77] ICJ Reps (1975) (sep. op. De Castro), at 142.

[78] ICJ Reps (1975) (sep. op. Petrén), at 112.

impact of its ruling was *erga omnes* rather than applicable only to the participating States.[79]

A number of members of the Court as well as Spain not only queried the advisory parameters of the Case but also asserted that the questions formulated by the UNGA were outside the Court's mandate; the questions were too academic or 'un-legal'.[80] These perspectives indicate a division between law and non-law through the medium of the Court: the Court was not fashioned to hear 'purely academic'[81] or historical arguments and was not competent to do so.[82] From the various statements about the historical evidence, it is also clear that the Court did not feel competent or confident to handle much of the material. Conclusions, however, should not be formulated solely on the historical nature of the material. Perhaps the Court was also deeply ambivalent about its ability to assess and even redress the wrongs of the past.

Unease about international law's boundaries is an enduring theme throughout the Case and efforts to allay this sensation by constantly restating dichotomies only entrenched the impossibility of quarantining the Opinion from its political context. Aside from the dichotomies of law/politics and legal enqiry/academic enquiry mentioned above, the extent to which morality should inform law was a prominent consideration among the non-European participants as well as the Lebanese judge, Fouad Ammoun. Because so much of the submissions centred on the colonial record, there was a desire on the part of these speakers to refashion the law by acknowledging and moving beyond the past. For example, in his discussion of secret treaties carving out spheres of influence for European appetites, Judge Ammoun asserted that 'international morality has always condemned them; and it is the precepts of morality that have justly received the consecration of positive law in this case as in so many others.'[83] For Herman, Judge Ammoun delivered his opinion 'somewhat emotionally' and it is

---

[79] De Castro noted that under Article 50 of its Statute, the Court may seek external material: 'The Court may, at any time, entrust any individual, body, bureau, commission, or other organization that it may select, with the task of carrying out an enquiry or giving an expert opinion.' He also recognised its general powers under Article 48, which states: 'The Court shall make orders for the conduct of the case, shall decide the form and time in which each party must conclude its arguments, and make all arrangements connected with the taking of evidence.' ICJ Reps (1975) (sep. op. De Castro), at 138. Castellino & Allen also agree that the evidence presented by the various parties was compelling, J. Castellino & S. Allen, *Title to Territory in International Law: A Temporal Analysis* (Aldershot: Ashgate, 2003), at 152.

[80] For example, Spain, Written Submission, International Court of Justice: Pleadings, Oral Arguments, Documents: Western Sahara, vol. I, at 222.

[81] ICJ Reps (1975) (dec. Gros), at 74.

[82] ICJ Reps (1975) (sep. op. De Castro), at 141–142.

[83] ICJ Reps (1975) (sep. op. Ammoun), at 90.

clear that this is something to be avoided.[84] Spain conversely prided itself on its dispassionate and 'neutral' presentation of 'pure law' because such a claim would appear to add to the Spanish position's authenticity: 'perspective politique... n'a sa place devant une cour de justice.[85] In contrast, Moroccan representatives were comfortable with 'd'une certaine émotion',[86] and Mauritania even conceded that '[l]a délégation mauritanienne a été amenée par la force des choses à s'addresser à l'Espagne avec une certain passion.'[87]

Despite occasional concessions to emotion, however, most of the parties (with the notable exception of Zaïre and occasionally Algeria)[88] were keen to limit their passions; it was important to preserve at least a veneer of objectivity. Morocco's representative, Benjelloun, was acutely aware of this requirement:

> je l'ai fait avec le désir sincère de rétablir la vérité, avec le seule volonté de rappeler les faits avec clarté et de démonstrer l'échelonnement des événements avec une *totale objectivité*. En aucun cas, je n'ai voulu accuser ou émettre des reproches, mon but étant avant tout d'exposer *sans passion* les mobiles de notre action et les motifs de nos prétensions et de nos réclamations.[89]

Members of the Court were also anxious to preserve law's objectivity. For example, Judge Gros championed the positivist position, declaring 'It is the duty of a court to establish facts[90]... [t]he Court cannot attribute a legal nature to facts which do not intrinsically possess it; a court does not create law, it establishes it.'[91]

---

[84] L. L. Herman, 'An Analysis of the World Court Judgment in the Western Sahara Case' (1976–1977) 41 *Saskatchkewan Law Review* 133, at 138.

[85] González Campos, Spain, Oral Pleadings, International Court of Justice: Pleadings, Oral Arguments, Documents: Western Sahara, vol. V, at 95.

[86] Benjelloun, Morocco, Oral Pleadings, International Court of Justice: Pleadings, Oral Arguments, Documents: Western Sahara, vol. IV, at 189.

[87] El Hassen, Mauritania, Oral Pleadings, International Court of Justice: Pleadings, Oral Arguments, Documents: Western Sahara, vol. V, at 300.

[88] Zaïre's brief appearance before the Court in its oral proceedings was both shocking and refreshing: ICJ convention of delivery and subject were thrown to the winds in a radical attempt to upset the framework of the nation-state and private ownership in Africa with an 'authentic' language based on nature. Although the Court did not respond to these arguments, they are worth extracting here: 'le souci constant de garder contact avec la terre est la seule clé qui permette de comprendre la philosophie proper à l'Afrique au subjet de la tenure foncière. Partout en Afrique authentique la terre n'a jamais fait l'objet d'appropriation individuelle. La propriété foncière était toujours et est toujours collective et jamais la terre ne pouvait faire l'objet d'aliénation car, vendre la terre équivaudrait à vendre son âme, ses forces propres, ses forces cosmiques.' Bayona-Ba-Meya, Zaïre, Oral Pleadings, International Court of Justice: Pleadings, Oral Arguments, Documents: Western Sahara, vol. IV, at 444.

[89] Emphasis added. Benjelloun, Morocco, Oral Pleadings, International Court of Justice: Pleadings, Oral Arguments, Documents: Western Sahara, vol. IV, at 243.

[90] ICJ Reps (1975) (dec. Gros), at 76.

[91] Ibid., at 77.

Judge Gros, however, failed to explain *how* one could establish such a neutral law, especially in the context of dissension over even the most basic information. Judge De Castro was more alive to these difficulties and pointed out that interpretation of the materials was vital in reaching a decision.[92]

Different constructions of the law/politics divide are particularly pronounced in an examination of language as a tool of argumentation. Language here refers not only to the type of language employed, such as 'French' or 'emotive', but also an understanding about the process of how expressions and words within any language are never *a priori* or pre-discursive; instead, we saw in Chapter One that international law *as language* is constituted by the process of argument within the Peace Palace.[93] The Court was confronted with definitional difficulties almost immediately because the concept of 'legal ties,'[94] contained in the UNGA's second question, was regarded as a 'non-legal' expression requiring legal 'translation'; it was outside international law's lexicon. The ICJ was also uncomfortable with the concept of 'entity'[95] in describing Mauritania, because such an expression was not common in legal discourse and its qualities were largely unknown compared with more familiar concepts such as 'state' or 'nation'. These two small examples of interpretative – or rather, constitutive – speech acts serve to highlight the ways in which language is limited and controlled in the continuous process of constructing the law/politics dichotomy. International law's lexicon is a limited one and it has often been forged out of the European experience of statehood.

---

[92] ICJ Reps (1975), (sep. op. De Castro), at 141.

[93] See Nesiah on this point in relation to the constitution of territory in the Western Sahara case and the Frontier Dispute. V. Nesiah, 'Placing International Law: White Spaces on a Map' (2003) 16 *Leiden Journal of International Law* 1, at 8. Also see Chapter One, at 34–40.

[94] De Castro recognises that it is necessary to define this term within the context of the case and interprets it to mean ties of a sovereign quality. ICJ Reps (1975) (sep. op. De Castro), at 135. Blaydes contrasts the absence of definition for the expression 'legal ties' with the clearly known one of *terra nullius*. However, as Mauritania, Morocco, Algeria and Zaïre have demonstrated, *terra nullius*, like other legal terms, is open to widespread controversy as well. L. E. Blaydes, Jr., 'International Court of Justice does not find "legal ties" of such a nature to affect self-determination in the decolonization process of Western Sahara' (1976) 11 *Texas International Law Journal* 354, at 362–363.

[95] ICJ Reps (1975), at 63. Bedjaoui also conceded that 'Le terme «ensemble mauritanian» n'est certainement pas usuel dans le terminologie du droit international. Sans doute les débats à l'Assemblée générale des Nations Unies doivent-ils permettre d'éclairer la portée et d'indiquer quelle réalité sociologique et quelle structure politique ce terme recouvre.' Bedjaoui, Algeria, Oral Pleadings, International Court of Justice: Pleadings, Oral Arguments, Documents: Western Sahara, vol. IV, at 485. Shaw further holds that although Mauritania's use of 'entity' represented an attempt to move from 'the sociological to the legal field and thus establish the existence of a political community…[he regarded] the facts…[as showing] that no such entity did exist in this sense.' Shaw, *supra* n. 8, at 138.

Under Article 39 of the Statute, parties are permitted to work in French or English or another language at their request. All parties chose to speak in French, including the former French colonial, Arabic-speaking countries of Algeria, Morocco and Mauritania as well as Zaïre. Of course, there was no recognition of the colonial legacy by the parties in their choice of language and perhaps this is a moot point, because the Court's rules are reflective of the international power dynamics extant at the time of the Court's formation.

Divergences in linguistic frameworks, however, became clearer when various Arab parties attempted to describe the particularities of non-European rule on the eve of colonialism. Many of the agents were native French speakers without Arabic themselves, but Algeria, Morocco and Mauritania also struggled to translate and render intelligible *concepts* not necessarily analogous to the European experience. This linguistic barrier was evident in occasional differences in Arabic translation[96] or Arabic terms, such as '*umma*' and 'sulṭan', which remained untranslated in the text of the written and oral pleadings. More substantively, European terminology such as 'state' and 'border' with its particular connotations was necessarily used despite narrative dissonance with local conditions. In fact, this resort to European terminology entailed a cooption of Arab experience into the more familiar confines of Western statehood. Especially when trying to explain the concept of overlapping authority in nomadic societies under Islam, the parties evoked European models from feudalism for comparison. Further, Mauritania acknowledged the difficulties of conceptualising the 'Shinqīṭī Entity' (the rough pre-colonial equivalent to modern day Mauritania), and so it assisted the Court through comparison between the territory's many autonomous tribes and the league of city-states in Classical Greece.[97] There was a sense that the particularist discourse of international law could only respond to, and comprehend, non-European experiences through European analogy, suggesting a discourse weak in its universalising tendencies.

Of greater significance was the heavy reliance placed on materials from the social sciences, such as ethnography, sociology and cartography. The inclusion of such material in turn required interpretations about the extent to which law as a discipline could accommodate the arguments and assumptions of other conceptual frameworks. Does the grammar of law enable speakers to draw on tools of argument beyond the confines of doctrine? Disagreement over the relative value and compatibility of such 'non-legal' evidence reinforces the argument of this section, highlighting the need for constant redefinition of allegiances in the law/politics contest.

---

[96] For example, see ICJ Reps (1975) (sep. op. Ammoun), at 88.

[97] Salmon, Mauritania, Oral Pleadings, International Court of Justice: Pleadings, Oral Arguments, Documents: Western Sahara, vol. IV, at 431.

The example of cartographic evidence exemplifies the central role of perspective and interpretation in the submission of material. For Spain, more than another other party, the maintenance of law as objective, and thus in contrast with politics, was vital. It chastised other States (especially Mauritania) for their misguided use of subjective or 'non-legal' sociological and ethnographic data.[98] Mauritania in turn challenged such a distinction between law and non-law by arguing that le 'droit est fait pour servir le social. Le droit n'est qu'une superstructure qui s'adapte au social. Vouloir renverser les termes, c'est vivre dans le formalisme et l'illusion.'[99] Despite such ideas, Spain continued to embrace formalism by arguing that maps were more objective than the social scientific material employed by Morocco and especially Mauritania. Spain conceded that cartographic material 'n'est pas le droit', but it nevertheless regarded maps as the *sine qua non* in any territorial matter and it never doubted their objective nature. In fact, Spain argued that the maps' objectivity was irreproachable because, rather than coming from the hands of Spanish geographers, they instead were creations of other Europeans.[100] Spain failed to recognise that the nationalities it cited in support of its argument hailed from most of the main colonial powers at the Conference of Berlin; for Spain, there was no possibility of colonial designs tainting the drawing of maps in Africa.[101] Nesiah reminds us, however,

[98] 'la méthode qui inspire les arguments de la Mauritanie tout au long de ses exposés pourrait être caractérisée comme l'emprise absolue de la sociologe sur le droit.' Lacleta, Spain, Oral Pleadings, International Court of Justice: Pleadings, Oral Arguments, Documents: Western Sahara, vol. V, at 114.

[99] Salmon, Mauritania, Oral Pleadings, International Court of Justice: Pleadings, Oral Arguments, Documents: Western Sahara, vol. V, at 293. Salmon also argues that in relation to 'quel niveau doit s'exercer le droit des peoples à disposer d'eux-mêmes reste une problème pour lequel le droit est pratiquement impotent: de fait, c'est une question d'une histoire, c'est une question de politique, c'est une question de force...Ces réflexions montrent, dès l'abord, la complexité du problème, son opacité, l'importance des données, de fait: culturelles, économiques et politiques, la primauté du politique. Le juriste doit faire preuve de discrétion et d'humilité.' Salmon, Mauritania, Oral Pleadings, International Court of Justice: Pleadings, Oral Arguments, Documents: Western Sahara, vol. IV, at 312. Morocco also accuses Spain of formalism: Dupuy, Morocco, Oral Pleadings, International Court of Justice: Pleadings, Oral Arguments, Documents: Western Sahara, vol. V, at 186.

[100] 'les cartes présentées par l'Espagne ne sont pas l'œuvre de géographes espagnols, mais elles ont été établies par des géographes réputés de nationalité anglaise, française, allemande ou autre. De ce fait, nous sommes en face d'un point important et plusiers fois relevé dans les décisions arbitrales ou judiciaries, à savoir l'objectivité des données géographiques et les cartes elles-mêmes nous indiquent les références d'après lesquelles elles ont été établies.' Arias-Salgado, Spain, Oral Pleadings, International Court of Justice: Pleadings, Oral Arguments, Documents: Western Sahara, vol. V, at 52.

[101] Judge De Castro also has faith in such maps, but seeks to reinforce his argument by relying on other colonial evidence from the period, such as contemporary written testimony. ICJ Reps (1975) (sep. op. De Castro), at 152–153.

that the development of geography as a scholarly discipline in Europe directly coincided with the colonisation of Western Sahara.[102] Moroccan scepticism about such colonially-crafted cartography reflects this fact: 'Toute la cartographie antérieure présentée par le Gouvernement espagnol repose sur des renseignements fantaisistes, voire legendaries.'[103]

Maps were used in an attempt to illustrate the nature of territorial control in Western Sahara, but history was an even more useful tool of argument. The flexible uses of history are evident by the way in which each narrative position contained often radically different emphases, nuances and evidence. In the eyes of Spain, history, like maps or law itself, could carry an objective truth through 'une analyse scientifique' in contrast with disciplines like sociology and ethnography.[104] History was vital for the Spanish case, and Spain devoted more energy than any other party in reviewing its own record in the territory of Western Sahara. Detailed examination was offered about the period preceding colonisation when Spanish mariners, pursuing the rich fishing resources off the coast, would enter into agreements with local powers. The colonial period was also surveyed, and the impression that this account produces is one of benevolent interaction between relative equals.[105]

Although Spain was largely incapable of appreciating the inevitably biased flavour of historical enquiry,[106] for those states that had lived under European historical 'realities' the desire to decolonise and rewrite the historical record was palpable.[107] According to Morocco, it was not enough to rely on European models whether in the past or present because

[102] Nesiah, *supra* n. 93, at 10.

[103] Isoart, Morocco, Oral Pleadings, International Court of Justice: Pleadings, Oral Arguments, Documents: Western Sahara, vol. IV, at 257–258.

[104] Arias-Salgado, Spain, Oral Pleadings, International Court of Justice: Pleadings, Oral Arguments, Documents: Western Sahara, vol. V, at 43.

[105] This narrative runs throughout Spains's written pleadings: Written Pleadings, International Court of Justice: Pleadings, Oral Arguments, Documents: Western Sahara, vol. I.

[106] In an historical study about the region, Lydon details how French colonial administrators in West Africa discounted valuable Arabic sources, choosing to confiscate some of them. G. Lydon, 'Writing Trans-Saharan History: Methods, Sources and Interpretations Across the African Divide' (2005) 10 *Journal of North African Studies* 293, at 299.

[107] Koskenniemi advances this idea of the decolonisation of the past in his exploration of post-communist East European States looking 'backwards into a mythical past.' M. Koskenniemi, 'National Self-Determination Today: Problems of Legal Theory and Practice' (1994) 43 *International and Comparative Law Quarterly* 241, at 258. Spain also attributes the idea of 'décoloniser l'histoire' to the historian, A. Laraoui: González-Campos, Spain, Oral Pleadings, International Court of Justice: Pleadings, Oral Arguments, Documents: Western Sahara, vol. V, at 95.

> La portée des titres marocains sur le Sahara occidental doit s'apprécier en tenant compte de l'environnement social et économique maghrébin. S'il est vrai que l'imitation des modèles européen et nord-américain ne permet pas nécessairement au XXᵉ siècle de résoudre les problèmes du tiers monde, à plus forte raison une approche juridique coupée des réalités locales risqué de fausser l'interprétation des faits survenus au siècle précédent.[108]

In their written and oral submissions, Algeria and especially Mauritania and Morocco gave their own interpretation not only of European international law during colonialism but, more importantly, the nature of European control and domination in North West Africa. Colonialism in all its brutality was revealed before the Court, and international law was either contrasted with European avarice (in continuation of the law/politics divide) or shown to be complicit in the scramble for the Sahara.

European historical evidence was critiqued in the pleadings for its failure to appreciate the complex societies of Arab North Africa, and Mauritania and Morocco especially used the forum of the Court to present a richer and more informed account. Greater historical understanding of the region assisted the presentation of their shared central claim: that at the time of Spanish colonisation, Western Sahara was controlled by the Moroccan Sharīfian Empire to the North and the Shinqīṭī entity to the South.[109] In contrast with Spain's thesis, both Mauritania and Morocco claimed that Western Sahara had no separate identity:[110] nomadic tribal life meant that overlapping allegiances were formed across the territory and beyond.

Spanish, Mauritanian and Moroccan characterisations of the historical record were necessarily simplified, but the reliance on anachronism is startling. Morocco and Mauritania depicted themselves one hundred years earlier as nearly *identical* to their present form. Morocco even described the people inhabiting Western Sahara in the nineteenth century as Moroccan.[111] Spain countered such claims

---

[108] Morocco, Written Submission, International Court of Justice: Pleadings, Oral Arguments, Documents: Western Sahara, vol. III, at 170. Also see Benjelloun, Morocco, Oral Pleadings, International Court of Justice: Pleadings, Oral Arguments, Documents: Western Sahara, vol. IV, at 213.

[109] It is interesting to note that in parts of its historical overview Mauritania uses the chronology of the Hegiran Calendar, a common practice throughout the Muslim world, but unusual before the ICJ: Mauritania, Written Submission, International Court of Justice: Pleadings, Oral Arguments, Documents: Western Sahara, vol. III, at 67.

[110] For a general rebuttal of Spanish Sahara's separate identity, see Morocco, Written Submission, International Court of Justice: Pleadings, Oral Arguments, Documents: Western Sahara, vol. III, at 161.

[111] Morocco, Written Submission, International Court of Justice: Pleadings, Oral Arguments, Documents: Western Sahara, vol. III, at 183.

with an equally ill-conceived construction of the Ṣaḥrāwī nation as much more distinct and fully formed than the historical record suggests.

Mauritanian and Moroccan historical accounts of Arab rule and the onslaught of colonialism are supported by Judge Ammoun, who devoted attention to this obscured past. For example, Judge Ammoun supported Moroccan arguments about the sovereign nature of the Sulṭan's rule extending across western parts of the Sahara and argued that colonialism's aim was to cut off the territory from these ties of allegiance, religion and rule. Berman characterises Judge Ammoun's opinion as yet another attempt at narrative authenticity: 'certain phases of history are valorized as authentic parts of the national heritage, others as mutations by a foreign, specifically European, invader.'[112] Judge Ammoun regarded colonialism as disruptive to the historical evolution of the territory's 'genuine' development.[113] Instead of embracing foreign influences, such as self-determination, it was possible with such an historical understanding to regard the Opinion's natural resolution as resulting in Western Sahara's re/integration with two of its territorial neighbours.

Although all States and judges were aware of the many conventions of competency required of them at the Peace Palace, this did not entail the consistent use of one legal grammar. Competency through language had to evolve in the particular forum; all speakers realised the relevance of distinguishing law from its many others, but they each articulated this boundary-drawing in slightly different ways. All narratives struggled with maintaining a clear line between law and politics: at times emotion and interpretation were vital, but it was difficult to gauge the line, given institutional biases. At the very least, it is clear that the Court required a semblance of separation between law and politics: facts could not simply speak for themselves, but had to be translated through the medium of relatively dispassionate discourse that displayed a respect for the primacy of the Court and the discipline of international law; pure historical and social scientific arguments were largely feared and overlooked by the Court.

4) *Constituting Selfhood before the Court: Legal Personality, Identity Politics and the Multicultural Limits of International Law*

A diversity of argumentative strategies was also mirrored by the substantive positions of the parties. Spain's motivations centred on its desire for apology and absolution: it wanted to show that its policies in the Sahara had always reflected

---

[112] N. Berman, 'Sovereignty in Abeyance: Self-Determination and International Law' (1988–1989) 7 *Wisconsin International Law Journal* 51, at 101.

[113] Ibid., at 102.

its overriding sympathy and support for the territory's indigenous, regionally autonomous inhabitants, the Ṣaḥrāwīs. Spain characterised neighbouring States' authority as weak and devoid of legal value. Spain's wholly European vision of international legal doctrine discounted and denied the validity of non-European modes of governance over the territory. Spain embodied a pure, positivist version of international law, which at times became a caricature of the worst aspects of a narrowly defined European consciousness.

Both Morocco and Mauritania directly challenged the continuing application of exclusively European norms when they asked, 'Est-ce à dire que seules les théories européennes de l'État, tant pour le passé que pour le présent et pour le futur, soient les seules valables?'[114] Morocco countered the European state model with the Sharīfian system of rule, which exhibited a much closer relationship between secular and religious affairs. Mauritania also acknowledged the importance of its membership within *dār al-islām* as discussed in Chapter Two, but because it could not characterise the Shinqīṭī entity as a state in the pre-colonial period, it instead tried to endow this nomadic community with international legal personality directly.[115] Although the Moroccan and Mauritanian positions diverged on legal and factual points, they both championed the cause of particularism: their experiences required specific, European international legal tenets to be relaxed and expanded so as to become more universal. In invoking the *particular*, these States were implicitly questioning the *universal* basis of contemporary international law.

Mauritania and Morocco used the forum of the ICJ simultaneously to rewrite the historical record and to construct a self-image not beholden to colonialism. As in the case of narrative strategies explored above, however, narrative substance was also structured by the inescapable imprint of international law's past *and* present configurations. Some of the Moroccan and Mauritanian perspectives on this past as well as their references to non-European law tried to push the boundaries of traditional international law. The bench recognised this call to universalism, but ultimately could do little more than effect an uneasy and legally dissatisfying compromise between these competing approaches to territorial control. In this last section we will explore the Moroccan and Mauritanian reliance on and critique of public international law and concurrently consider the success of such arguments in the eyes of Spain, Algeria and the Court.

[114] Isoart, Morocco, Oral Pleadings, International Court of Justice: Pleadings, Oral Arguments, Documents: Western Sahara, vol. IV, at 261.

[115] Shaw, *supra* n. 8, at 136–137.

a) *Allegiances of the Faithful: The Moroccan Sulṭan and Islamic Rule in the Sahara*

Morocco presented the most sustained discussion of Arab-Islamic rule in the pre-colonial and colonial era to support its case of control over Western Sahara both before and during much of Spain's colonial presence. In advancing such a narrative, Morocco offered an alternative historical account to that of the dominant, colonial version, which saw Africa as open to occupation, or at best, cession. Morocco's pleadings offer one of the most well developed accounts of Islamic *siyar* before the ICJ,[116] reminding the Court of Islam's sophisticated legal tradition. Morocco, however, did not simply invoke Islamic legal principles in contradistinction to dominant international legal narratives. Instead, Morocco, like Mauritania in its discussion of *terra nullius*, also relied on various international law doctrines relating to the acquisition of territory to offer further support for its claims of immemorial possession. Morocco was covering all bases by trying to expand the cultural boundaries of international law while also applying 'pure' rules to the past.[117] For example, Morocco invoked the norm of territorial integrity and a number of treaties between itself and European powers.[118] Conversely, it also relied on international law to deny Spanish rights because of ineffective control, the invalidity of secret treaties as well as the inapplicability of the hinterland rule.[119] Morocco's construction of its statehood through a combination of European and non-European legal norms and the Court's assessment of the latter is considered after a brief summary of Moroccan depictions of Islamic approaches to authority.

Morocco discounted the first question about *terra nullius*, because its entire case rested on a demonstration of legal ties *of a sovereign nature* between the international legal subject of the Sharīfian Empire and the tribes of Western Sahara. At the most basic level, Morocco was conscious of reminding the Court

[116] W. S. D. Cravens, 'The Future of Islamic Arguments in International Boundary Disputes between Islamic States' (1998) 55 *Washington & Lee Law Review* 529, at 530. *Siyar* is discussed in Chapter Two, at 67–68.

[117] Knop also argues that while 'Morocco relied on the universal rules for the acquisition of sovereignty, it also sought to persuade the International Court of Justice that the interpretation of the rules should be particularized so as to take account of the special structure of the Sherifian state.' Knop, *supra* n. 3, at 137.

[118] Treaties discussed in Morocco, Written Statement, International Court of Justice: Pleadings, Oral Arguments, Documents: Western Sahara, vol. III, at 194–195. For a useful overview of Moroccan-European relations of equality in the eighteenth century, see C. R. Pennell, 'Accommodation between European and Islamic Law in the Western Mediterranean in the Early Nineteenth Century' (1994) 21 *British Journal of Middle East Studies* 159.

[119] Morocco, Written Statement, International Court of Justice: Pleadings, Oral Arguments, Documents: Western Sahara, vol. III, at 142–169.

of its multicultural mandate; international law can and should abandon its predilection for the European nation-state:

> Pour apprécier la nature et la valeur des liens juridiques existant entre le Maroc et le Sahara occidental, il est donc essential d'abandonner le schéma constitutionnel de l'Etat européen du XIXe siècle, car il est le produit d'une situation économique et sociale localisée qui ne trouve pas application sur le territoire du Maghreb extrême.[120]

The argument was that because of its desert environment, political relations in Western Sahara were different from the temperate climes north of the Mediterranean;[121] tribal organisation was the norm.[122] Aridity, low inhabitation rates and nomadic movements across large swathes of land throughout much of the Sulṭan's domains further produced a bifurcated system of authority, where relatively centralised control over the *bled makhzen* (land of the storehouse, or governance)[123] contrasted with more tenuous connections with the *bled siba* (the land of dissidence).[124] Although familiar attributes of sovereignty may have been scant in *bled siba*, which according to Morocco corresponded with southern Morocco and northern Western Sahara, Morocco argued that this was a secondary detail because of the way in which Islam and its overseer, the Sulṭan or Khalīfa, united the faithful in a fusion of divine and human rule as was discussed in Chapter Two.[125] All the Saharan tribes mentioned the Sulṭan

[120] Isoart, Morocco, Oral Pleadings, International Court of Justice: Pleadings, Oral Arguments, Documents: Western Sahara, vol. IV, at 256–257.

[121] 'Les données géographiques, physiques et climatiques déterminent l'état des relations politiques.' Ibid.

[122] Again, Morocco was mindful of the contrast between North West Africa and Europe in producing tribalism: 'Les liens existant entre les tribus et le souverain marocain ne sont pas, bien sûr, comparables aux modèles européens, ils sont en revanche parfaitement adaptes aux réalités tribales.' Morocco, Written Statement, International Court of Justice: Pleadings, Oral Arguments, Documents: Western Sahara, vol. III, at 182.

[123] It is useful to conceive of storehouse here as the state's repository of taxes, because the ability to collect taxes was the main distinguishing feature between the *bled makhzen* from the *bled siba.* J. Castellino, 'Territory and Identity in International Law: The Struggle for Self-Determination in the Western Sahara' (1999) 28 *Millennium: Journal of International Studies* 523, at 533.

[124] Morocco, Written Statement, International Court of Justice: Pleadings, Oral Arguments, Documents: Western Sahara, vol. III, at 179–180.

[125] Morocco summaries the nature of the Sulan's authority in the following terms: 'dès le début de l'État musulman, s'établit un équilibre entre les autorités tribales qui sont l'expression d'une opinion publique embryonnaire mais qui sont tout de même l'expression d'une opinion publique de base et l'authorité charismatique du prophète. Naissant alors les deux grandes traditions politiques musulmanes: l'authorité théocratique fondée sur l'obéissance à la parole de Dieu [via the Qur'ān]; l'authorité politique fondée sur l'approbation de la communauté, approbation consignée dans un acte d'allégeance personelle, d'abord au prophète, puis à son successeur le calife.' Isoart, Morocco, Oral Pleadings, International Court of Justice: Pleadings,

in their prayers and he was largely responsible for the appointment of leadership positions, such as *qāḍīs* or leaders/judges for the tribes. During the period of heightened European interference in the nineteenth century, Morocco conceded that it 'était certainement affaibli par les menées étrangères et par des lacunes internes de structures',[126] but it remained a united society; resistance to colonialism further supported its thesis.[127]

The Court was willing to embrace Morocco's emphasis on personal and religious ties of allegiance, but only up to a point; the familiar concepts of European relations with territory as well as 'sovereignty' were hard to displace for long. The nature of the UNGA's question to Court about legal ties was vague enough to elicit a wide range of possible interpretations and a number of judges spent time conflating or distinguishing legal ties *vis-à-vis* ties of 'sovereignty'. The Court seemed to embrace the particularity of Morocco by acknowledging its own mode of rule. Judge Forster regarded these differences as allowing a degree of leeway in a finding of legal ties that could be understood as sovereign.[128]

The Court, however, adopted a narrower definition that still tried to remain concessionary and culturally aware: Morocco had established *some* legal ties, but not of a *sufficiently* sovereign nature. What would have been sufficient in this case? Further, what did the Court mean by 'sovereignty'? Roussellier compares the ICJ's position here with some of its earlier jurisprudence, where Moroccan personality had been recognised.[129] If the basis of Moroccan sovereignty in the earlier case had been its connections with tribes that often inhabited at least the northern parts of Western Sahara, it would seem that the ICJ in its 1975 Advisory Opinion was drawing an artificial and inconsistent line across Moroccan territory.[130] Roussellier then asks why could not the Court 'declare

Oral Arguments, Documents: Western Sahara, vol. IV, at 259. Also, see Chapter Two, at 65–70.

126 Morocco, Written Statement, International Court of Justice: Pleadings, Oral Arguments, Documents: Western Sahara, vol. III, at 177.

127 Ibid., at 187–194.

128 ICJ Reps (1975) (sep. op. Forster), at 95.

129 Namely, *Case Concerning Rights of Nationals of the United States of America in Morocco (France/United States)* (1952) ICJ Reps, p. 176. The same argument would apply in relation to the *Nationalities Decrees* Case, where the PCIJ regarded Morocco as under protection, rather than as a colony *per se*: *Nationality Decrees Issued in Tunis and Morocco (Advisory Opinion)* (1923) PCIJ, Series B, No. 4. For an excellent reading of the pleadings and their ambiguity about the nature of protection and selfhood, see N Berman, 'The *Nationality Decrees Case*, or, Of Intimacy and Consent' (2000) 13 *Leiden Journal of International Law* 265. Also see, J. Crawford, *The Creation of States in International Law* (Cambridge: Cambridge University Press, 2nd edition, 2006), at 510.

130 '[t]he Court is caught in an apparent contradiction. On the one hand, it acknowledged Morocco's sovereignty as then French Protectorate – including and in particular over the Bled

some parts of the Territory of Western Sahara...parts of Bled Siba, instead of a mere projection or extension of the limited display of the Moroccan sultan's authority'?[131] The Court wanted to stress its support for Western Sahara's self-determination. However, it also did not want to be seen as disregarding the cultural traditions of Morocco and Mauritania. Indeterminate references to sovereignty aided the Court in its task of effecting a compromise of sorts that in reality gave very little ground: Western standards of the state prevailed so as to support the silenced and still stateless Ṣaḥrāwīs. Or in the words of Nesiah, 'the discussion of self-determination is expressive of the Court's desire to lay out its own normative commitments by pulling Western Sahara into the normative and jurisprudential framework of international law, a statist or administrative framework of territory.'[132]

In a similar territorial focus, Judge Ammoun explored the Islamic arguments of Morocco in some detail to hold that there had existed legal ties of a sovereign nature over Western Sahara. Judge Ammoun was able to agree with the majority Opinion up to a point in its recognition of legal ties, but '[w]ithout sufficiently convincing reasons...it minimizes the nature of those ties by maintaining that they consisted in an allegiance of the Saharan population to the Sulṭan of Morocco.'[133] In contrast, Judge Ammoun saw these ties as much more significant because the sulṭan 'personified the State' in its legislative, executive and religious aspects.[134] Judge Ammoun largely agreed with Morocco's use of treaty evidence and the testimony of geographers from the time to support its case for 'legal ties of a political character between the territory of Western Sahara and the Kingdom of Morocco.'[135] Throughout his separate opinion, although Judge Ammoun stressed the *particular* nature of authority in *dār al-islām*, he also noted its *territorial* qualities, thus linking the particular with the 'universal' given of territory. Accordingly, the Court should not have discounted the importance of territorial control within the Sulṭan's domain, because '[t]hose people did not live suspended between the sky and the ground.'[136]

Nesiah depicts Ammoun as trapped in the 'double bind' of a colonialised international law. His opinion 'offers an exemplary instance where statist repre-

---

Siba – but, on the other hand, it rejected Morocco's claim of territorial sovereignty on Western Sahara though it has ascertained that some Tekna tribes from southern Morocco, a [sic] Bled Siba as well, have migrated into the Western Sahara Territory.' Roussellier, *supra* n. 62, at 63.

131 Ibid.

132 Nesiah, *supra* n. 93, at 15.

133 ICJ Reps (1975) (sep. op. Ammoun), at 83.

134 Ibid.

135 Ibid., at 102.

136 Ibid., at 101.

sentations of territory continue to be visited and revisited, repeated and transformed, as an ongoing problematic of postcolonial nationhood.'[137] Although Judge Ammoun tried to expand the narrow confines of a European-based law, he ultimately ended up applying 'the criteria of statist territory' for Morocco's relationship with Western Sahara.[138] Thus Ammoun's separate opinion as well the Advisory Opinion itself 'illustrates the ICJ's adherence to the traditional Western legal concept of territorial sovereignty and its unwillingness to give real consideration to arguments based on principles of Islamic international law.'[139]

b) *Nomadic Co-sovereignty in the Bilād Shinqīṭī*[140]

Like Morocco, Mauritania invoked the particular conditions of the desert as well as Islamic notions of authority in its attempt to provide a broader definition of international legal personality for the two Advisory Opinion questions regarding *terra nullius* and legal ties.[141] Mauritania, however, was not able to rely on a pre-colonial political entity such as its Sharīfian counterpart, because there 'existait à l'époque dans la région du Sahara occidental, ensemble qui, comme chacun le sait, n'avait pas la qualité d'État et dans lequel allait se créer plus tard la République islamique de Mauritanie.'[142] The absence of a state did not necessarily undermine the Mauritanian case based on overlapping nomadic co-sovereignty across modern-day Mauritania and Western Sahara. Nevertheless, Mauritania was aware of the conceptual difficulties that the Court would encounter in abandoning statist and legal preconceptions for its preference for social research:

> les situations que constatent les historiens, les géographes, les ethnologues, les sociologies et politologues et qui traduisent dans les termes de bled siba et Bilad Chinguiti sont certainement difficiles à appréhendrer pour le juriste qui est habitué à des notions tranchées comme celles d'État, de frontière, etc.[143]

---

[137] Nesiah, *supra* n. 93, at 20.

[138] Ibid., at 19.

[139] Cravens, *supra* n. 116, at 531.

[140] 'La thèse mauritanienne distingue la partie nord du Sahara occidental de sa partie sud. Le Nord relève du bled siba marocain, c'est domain de mouvance des Tekna marocains, le Sud fait parte intégrante du pays de Chinguiti.' Salmon, Oral Pleadings, International Court of Justice: Pleadings, Oral Arguments, Documents: Western Sahara, vol. IV, at 425.

[141] For an overview of Mauritanian state/society structures, see Salem, *supra* n. 21.

[142] Mauritania, Written Statement, International Court of Justice: Pleadings, Oral Arguments, Documents: Western Sahara, vol. III, at 58.

[143] Yedali Ould Cheikh, Mauritania, Oral Pleadings, International Court of Justice: Pleadings, Oral Arguments, Documents: Western Sahara, vol. IV, at 423.

The challenges of Mauritania's unconventional material and arguments were exacerbated by the proceedings' inevitable inter-temporal law focus: not only was Mauritania (as well as Morocco) trying to expand international law in the postcolonial era, but it was inviting the Court to revisit a past little known for its respect for tribal personality. As in the case of Morocco's exploration of territorial titles, Mauritania presented a number of innovative arguments from this area of law, but the Court's silence on such matters left their cogency untested.[144]

The heart of Mauritania's case in proving its legal ties over a non-*terra nullius* entity combined a detailed examination of its former social structure with a call for international law to move beyond its statist assumptions. Mauritania acknowledged that many jurists and other writers in the colonial period had operated within a linear framework of human history, where tribal, Muslim societies were seen as behind those of the West.[145] However, Mauritania was at pains to demonstrate that '[l]'absence d'institution étatique ne signifait pas anarchie, puisqu'on a vu les liens multiples et, en particular, les liens de droit saharien qui répondaient parfaitement aux necessités de la vie nomade dans une société préétatique.'[146] Mauritania devoted considerable energy to an examination of non-legal material supporting its claim to an independent, unified and sophisticated model of rule based on the overlapping nomadic movements of interdependent tribes.[147] Studies of wells, cemeteries and the position of women all reinforced the argument that the prevailing model of social organisation was

[144] One of the most interesting ideas raised by Mauritania was its characterisation of European domination over tribal peoples. Classical international law determines the mode of territorial acquisition through a combination of legal personality, treaty and the physical act of conquest. Thus for example, where a territory is populated by an internationally recognised people, only cession via treaty or conquest is possible. Many protectorates in Africa were the product of 'trinket treaties' that resulted in cession, but the mixture of force as well as the ambiguous status of various signatories blurred the lines between cession, occupation and conquest as was discussed in Part II's Introduction, at 105–109. Mauritania adds to this a subtler form of domination, language: 'Aucune pressure militaire quelconque n'accompagne les négociations. Les explorateurs qui s'aventurent dans les régions sous la domination des tribus font figure de héros téméraires. C'est par la diplomatie et l'argumentation qu'ils convainquent leurs interlocuteurs à signer de telles conventions.' Mauritania, Written Statement, International Court of Justice: Pleadings, Oral Arguments, Documents: Western Sahara, vol. III, at 55. Shaw also argues that the shape of the Opinion's argument placed far too much reliance on the legal effects of trinket treaties, Shaw, *supra* n. 8, at 133.

[145] '[E]n ignorant la réalité socio-culturelle, des penseurs européens ont purement et simplement nié l'État musulman et ont prétendu que la notion de souveraineté n'y avait jamais dépassé le stade de la tribu.' Salmon, Mauritania, Oral Pleadings, International Court of Justice: Pleadings, Oral Arguments, Documents: Western Sahara, vol. V, at 296.

[146] Ibid.

[147] Generally, see Mauritania, Written Statement, International Court of Justice: Pleadings, Oral Arguments, Documents: Western Sahara, vol. III, at 58–87.

the only sustainable option in the Saharan context.[148] Furthermore, even with its sophistication established, Mauritania claimed that international law's mandate did not rest on the internal aspects of a territory's political system. On the eve of Western Sahara's and Mauritania's colonisation, jurists could appreciate the primacy of people above the state in recognising legal personality: 'vers 1880 la notion de people est une notion juridique indéniable.'[149]

Membership in *dār al-islām* was not only a useful tool for Morocco; Mauritania as well as Algeria invoked the concept to appeal to the universalism of international law. For Mauritania, an absence of defined borders was of secondary importance because the Bilād Shinqīṭi 'est reconnu dans tous les pays arabes comme une expression précise.'[150] Within the confines of *dār al-islām*, the Bilād Shinqīṭi retained an independent status,[151] especially *vis-à-vis* its stronger neighbour, the Sharīfian Empire. Algeria's counsel, Bedjaoui, also considered the impact of membership in *dār al-islām* as an alternative approach to European conceptions of *terra nullius*. According to Bedjaoui, inclusion in *dār al-islām ipso facto* entailed the presence of defined authority and the corresponding impossibility of *terra nullius*:

> On peut formuler donc la réponse ainsi: «Non le Sahara n'était pas un territoire sans maître parce qu'il appartenait à Dar el Islam.» En utilisant une telle approche, non seulement votre haute juridiction accepterait de reconnaître qu'elle est la haute Cour de toutes les nations et de tous les systèmes juridiques qui doivent coexister en bonne entente sur cette terre, mais elle redrait justice à toutes les sociétés bafouées par la colonisation.[152]

For Bedjaoui, the Court could move beyond its colonial past even within the strictures of inter-temporal law by considering legal systems other than the European version of the late nineteenth century.

The Opinion never explicitly acknowledged Bedjaoui's suggestion, but the Court's treatment of Morocco's and especially Mauritania's claims suggests that

---

148 Mauritania, Written Statement, International Court of Justice: Pleadings, Oral Arguments, Documents: Western Sahara, vol. III, at 63–83.

149 Salmon, Mauritania, Oral Pleadings, International Court of Justice: Pleadings, Oral Arguments, Documents: Western Sahara, vol. V, at 297.

150 Mauritania, Written Statement, International Court of Justice: Pleadings, Oral Arguments, Documents: Western Sahara, vol. III, at 67.

151 '[L]a culture chinguitienne fait partie de formes similaires du monde arabo-musulman. Mais ce qui est significatif, c'est qu'elle est le fait d'un peuple pasteurs et le seul peuple de pasteurs de la zone aride à être dans ce cas. C'est ce qui lui confrère vigeur interne et rayonnement extérieur.' Ould Maouloud, Mauritania, Oral Pleadings, International Court of Justice: Pleadings, Oral Arguments, Documents: Western Sahara, vol. IV, at 367.

152 Bedjaoui, Algeria, Oral Pleadings, International Court of Justice: Pleadings, Oral Arguments, Documents: Western Sahara, vol. IV, at 489.

this call for a cosmopolitan international law was ultimately rejected. Indeed, the Court found it even more difficult to appreciate the legal nature of Mauritanian rule than its Moroccan counterpart. Like Spain, the Court was hard-pressed in conceptualising the factual and legal reality of the Shinqīṭi entity and its congruity with modern day Mauritania. The Opinion included a discussion of the legal requirements for legal personality as expounded in the *Reparations* Case and applied by Mauritania in the pleadings. As per Mauritania's central thesis, the ICJ in its 1949 Opinion had observed that the 'subjects of international law in any legal system are not necessarily identical in their nature or in the extent of their rights and their nature depends upon the needs of the community.'[153] After an examination of the evidence, however, the 1975 bench could not find any basis 'for considering the emirates and the tribes which existed in the region to have constituted, in another phrase used by the Court in the *Reparations* Case, "an entity capable of availing itself of obligations incumbent upon its Members".'[154]

Perhaps in a bid to appear less dismissive of Mauritania's tribal thesis and its faith in the universal ramifications of its particular experience, the Court's negation of sovereign ties gave way at least to recognition of some lesser legal rights.[155] In a tribute to Spain's own dichotomisation of law and fact, Judge De Castro was even more strident in his rejection of Mauritania's legal existence: 'To endeavour to deduce from the existence of ethnic, cultural and geographical analogies, the existence of legal ties is like leaping into an abyss.'[156]

The Court's dispositive statement for the second question can now be quoted in full to appreciate the dilemma the Court faced in balancing the Ṣaḥrāwīs' right to self-determination with Mauritanian and Moroccan calls to universalism and multiculturalism of (neo)colonial desires:

> The materials and information presented to the Court show the existence, at the time of Spanish colonization, of legal ties of allegiance between the Sultan of Morocco and some of the tribes living in the territory of Western Sahara. They equally show the existence of rights, including some rights relating to land, which constituted legal ties between the Mauritanian entity, as understood by the Court, and the territory of Western Sahara. On the other hand, the Court's conclusion is that the materials and information presented to it do not establish any tie of territorial sovereignty between the territory of Western Sahara and the Kingdom of Morocco or the Mauritanian entity. Thus the Court has not found legal ties of such a nature

[153] *Reparation for Injuries Suffered in the Service of the United Nations* (1949) ICJ Reps, p. 178, quoted in ICJ Reps (1975), at 64.

[154] Ibid.

[155] 'To confine the question to ties of sovereignty would, moreover, be to ignore the special characteristics of the Saharan region and peoples... and also to disregard the possible relevance of other legal ties to the various procedures concerned in the decolonization process.' ICJ Reps (1975), at 64. For a similar perspective, see ICJ Reps (1975) (sep. op. Dillard), at 125–126.

[156] ICJ Reps (1975) (sep. op. De Castro), at 165.

as might affect the application of resolution 1514 (XV) in the decolonization of Western Sahara and, in particular, of the principle of self-determination through the free and genuine expression of the will of the peoples of the Territory.[157]

This passage with its twists and turns belies the Court's confusion over its role in balancing competing claims of particularism.

5) *Conclusion*

The *Western Sahara* Case fell under the Court's advisory jurisdiction, but through a combination of its subject matter, its participants and its institutional parameters, the arguments delivered at the bar and the bench were in constant contention. The most fundamental point of dispute was not about how to demarcate territorial boundaries or legal personality, but rather the location of law in contrast to politics. Both the strategies used and the narratives evoked all suggested slightly different and shifting interpretations of this relationship at the heart of international law. It has been shown above that this desire for demarcating the law/politics dichotomy structured each judge's, as well as each state's, discursive delivery: emotion, language and the use of the social sciences and history were all interpreted differently in quests for authenticity and legitimacy. This observation supports my assumption that the law/politics dichotomy is one of the main structuring devices – or grammars – of international law. A certain flexibility of narrative delivery was also reflected in doctrinal diversity where Mauritania, Morocco and Algeria all attempted to expand the experiential and cultural foundations of international law by inviting the Court to recognise Arab-Islamic systems of governance.

Although mindful of its consultative role in the UNGA's decolonisation thrust, the Court was also aware of the need to appear receptive to non-European legal traditions. The bench was caught between inclinations to respect self-determination on the one hand, with a desire to embrace Islamic legal traditions on the other. Which vision of the self should triumph in the Peace Palace? The Court's difficulties were exacerbated not only by the unacknowledged context of colonial and neo-colonial aggression towards Western Sahara but even more so by the indeterminate nature of international law itself. In particular, the bench's elastic interpretation and application of 'sovereignty' destabilised the boundaries of international law. Spain had called on the Court to guarantee the sanctity of a state-based notion of legal personality lest such ill-defined examples of the

[157] ICJ Reps (1975), at 68.

Shinqīṭī entity lead historical and present realities into chaos.[158] Ultimately, the Court responded to such a request in its findings that the 'legal ties' of Mauritania and Morocco were less than 'sovereign' because they lacked a sufficiently territorial basis. The Court thus prioritised the norm of self-determination for Western Sahara's people over and above the claims of regional powers. The Court, however, never acknowledged the existence of this norm conflict between self-determination and 'legal ties'; it was easier to revert to a policy choice rather than offer a detailed analysis of how international law would offer the tools for such conflict resolution.

By failing to settle the conflict between self-determination of non-European legal ties the Court reinforced broader themes at work throughout the hearings, including the relationship between particularism and the universalism as well as European and non-European approaches to rule. These themes, and the underlying tension between law and politics, point to the continuing relevance of exclusion and cultural particularism in international law. Attempts to ignore, rewrite or move beyond unpalatable aspects of international law's past, present and future were all canvassed, but European colonialism remained one of the only narrative constants for each participant. International law was drawn on as a resource for liberation both by Mauritania and Morocco *vis-à-vis* their colonial repression, as well as by Spain and the Court for Western Sahara's liberation. By invoking international law for this purpose, however, it was inevitable that histories of European control and international legal predilection for the state form should also emerge. As was the case in Chapters Three and Four, North African states confronted the postcolonial paradox: could international law be used to advance their interests in a way that did not entail an endorsement of a narrative sympathetic to European colonialism? It was both ironic and yet predictable that the Court sought to grant selfhood and statehood to a people whose territory it never defined and whose legal personality remained elusive and unspoken.[159] The Peace Palace may well be far from the Sahara, but the

[158] For example, see Arias-Salgado, Spain, Oral Pleadings, International Court of Justice: Pleadings, Oral Arguments, Documents: Western Sahara, vol. V, at 58.

[159] Knop captures some of these themes in her work on the case, when she argues that the 'court throughout used a broad concept of legality to domesticate the exotic relationships of the Sahara, bringing them inside international law by recognizing them as legal. Simultaneously, its narrow concept of sovereignty denied these relationships equal status with the European master's by refusing to consider them as sovereign. This double movement of acceptance and rejection, legality and sovereignty, was characteristic of the court's interpretation of legal ties and legal entity, just as it had been of its interpretation of *terra nullius*. The court's treatment of *terra nullius* recognized the legal existence of the tribes that inhabited Western Sahara, but was silent on their sovereignty.' Knop, *supra* n. 3, at 157.

Court still managed to dream of sandcastles for the silenced and still-stateless Ṣaḥrāwīs.

6) *Postscript*

Morocco and Mauritania presented an impressive range of arguments before the ICJ in their bid to distract world attention from political developments in the Sahara. Both States contributed to producing an Opinion supportive of Western Saharan independence *and yet also cognisant* of their respective 'legal ties'. In contrast with the Court's concessionary tones, Moroccan action during and after the proceedings indicated its unabashed designs of re/claiming Western Sahara: it did not need the endorsement of the Court for its eventual occupation of the entire territory, after Mauritania's withdrawal from the south in 1979. Nevertheless, it is instructive to note that Morocco's King Ḥassan recognised the utility of international legal rhetoric and appreciated the way in which he could use the Opinion's ambiguity to his advantage. Once the Opinion was handed down, the King did not reject the Court's finding *per se*. Instead, he distorted its primary support for self-determination:

> the opinion of the Court can only mean one thing: the so-called Western Sahara was part of Moroccan territory over which the sovereignty was exercised by the Kings of Morocco and that the population of this territory considered themselves and were considered to be Moroccans...To-day Moroccan demands have been recognized by the legal advisory organ of the United Nations.[160]

After this speech, the fate of Western Sahara was sealed: Moroccan occupation has brought mass flight by the bulk of Western Sahara's population, Moroccan settlers and concerted phosphate extraction. Further, in a reflection of Chapter Six's theme, Morocco's occupation has also brought the construction of a wall (or berm) dividing the territory between Moroccan control of the coast and its mineral wealth on one side, and Western Sahara's impoverished people in the desert as well as western Algeria, on the other. After a number of years of UN neglect, numerous policies, including various international and regional diplomatic initiatives and a UN peacekeeping effort, have thus far failed to achieve Ṣaḥrāwīs self-determination.[161]

---

[160] Press Release of the Permanent Mission to the United Nations on 16 October 1975, quoted in UN Doc. S/PV.1849, 11 (1975), in Franck, *supra* n. 24, at 711.

[161] For studies of post-Opinion policies regarding Western Sahara, see C. Dunbar, 'Saharan Stasis: Status and Future Prospects of the Western Sahara Conflict' (2000) 4 *Middle East Journal* 522; Franck, *supra* n. 24; P. S. Martin, 'Nationalism, Identity and Citizenship in The Western Sahara' (2005) 10 *Journal of North African Studies* 565; J. Mundy, 'Neutrality or Complicity?

One of international law's best-known articulations of the self-determination norm has achieved very little beyond the confines of the courtroom. It remains to be seen in the next chapter how the Court has managed more recently to guarantee self-determination in the face of equally complex and competing arguments on law and politics in its *Wall* Opinion.

The United States and the 1975 Moroccan Takeover of the Spanish Sahara' (2006) 11 *Journal of North African Studies* 275; L. E. Smith, 'The Struggle for Western Sahara: What Future for Africa's Last Colony?' (2005) 10 *Journal of North African Studies* 545; International Crisis Group, Report N. 65, 'Western Sahara: The Cost of the Conflict', 11 June 2007; International Crisis Group, Report N. 66, 'Western Sahara: Out of the Impasse', 11 June 2007. The latest UN Security Council initiatives are outlined in Resolution 1754, 30 April 2007: S/RES/1754 (2007).

Chapter Six

Discourses of Division? Law, Politics and the ICJ Advisory Opinion on the Legal Consequences of the Construction of a Wall in the Occupied Palestinian Territory

1) *Introduction*

The situations of Western Sahara and Palestine have much in common. Both remain territories under foreign rule in the face of widespread support for their peoples' self-determination. It is also significant that out of a small list of ICJ Advisory Opinions about self-determination, these two hail from the Arab world. As suggested in the previous chapter, Advisory Opinions are especially useful for exploring the range of legal grammars used in ICJ disputes because of the increased number of participating states. This was particularly so in the 2004 *Wall* Case. Several states presented either written submissions or oral presentations both supportive and dismissive of the Court's role in adjudicating Israel's construction of a wall in the Palestinian Occupied Territories (OPT) and its legal effects. Like Western Sahara, participants expressed their support or opposition towards the exercise of ICJ jurisdiction through the grammar of the law/politics dichotomy. States opposing the ICJ's jurisdiction characterised the United Nations General Assembly request (UNGA) for an opinion as politically driven. The Court could not fulfil its role in such a context, and, further, it would hamper other initiatives. Supporters of the Court, on the other hand, were seemingly required to leave their politics at the courtroom door. Once the Court granted jurisdiction, however, many states showed how politics was an integral part of proceedings. The Court itself was also conscious of the political significance of the matter, and thus this Case is a valuable site for exploring different characterisations of international law and its relationship with politics.

Unlike the other cases discussed in this book, the *Wall* Opinion is not a classic territorial dispute. The UNGA requested the Court to comment on the legal implications of the wall's construction for Israel and third states. Boundaries remained ill-defined throughout the dispute, allowing participating states to discuss the legal regime created by the wall in broader terms. Like other cases discussed here, however, the centrality of territory underlay much of the discussion. The UNGA Advisory Opinion request was circumscribed, but both states and members of the Court touched on broader, 'political' considerations of the Arab-Israeli conflict. In particular, the importance of selfhood and territory informed many positions. Thus, the *Wall* Opinion can be seen as a classic (post) colonial contest over international legal personality: in a world of nation-states, securing territory is vital. This was also seen in the *Western Sahara* Case where the central characters of the Case, the Ṣaḥrāwī people, existed in a legal limbo. Because of their unfilfiled claim over territory as well as their unsecured international legal status, the Ṣaḥrāwī were not able to speak in the Peace Palace. In the present Case, however, the Court welcomed Palestine's legal team along with delegations from some inter-governmental organisations (IGOs).

The Chapter is not concerned with most of the substantive aspects of the Case, because doctrinal issues relating to occupation and state responsibility fall outside the scope of this research, with its focus on territory. The Opinion did, however, raise some reflections on the relationship between self-determination and territory, and these areas are explored briefly. Of greater significance for the book is the way the Case allows us to understand how the law/politics dichotomy, one of international law's fundamental conceptual structures, functions in adjudication. What relationship was there between the construction of arguments and their portrayal of law and politics? Further, debates about word usage provide us with an opportunity of assessing some of the parameters of the international law lexicon. Which words, expressions, and especially, concepts and feelings are capable of expression within an international legal forum? After surveying the dispute's background and proceedings, the chapter will map some of these legal grammars along with its lexicon and then appraise the success of such strategies.

2) *Background to the Opinion*

a) *Brief Overview of the Arab-Israeli Conflict*

After four wars,[1] two peace treaties,[2] innumerable diplomatic initiatives and the Israeli occupation of the Palestinian West Bank and Gaza Strip as well as parts of Syria, Egypt and Lebanon,[3] the Arab-Israeli conflict remains far from

---

[1] Namely, the 1948 War, the Suez Canal Crisis 1956, the Six Day War of 1967 and the Yom Kippur War of 1973.

[2] Between Israel and Egypt in 1979 and between Jordan and Israel in 1994.

[3] The West Bank and Gaza in Palestine, Syria's Golan Heights and Egypt's Sinai Peninsula were occupied after the Six Day War of 1967 and all but the Sinai remain under Israeli occupation. Southern Lebanon was occupied by Israel between 1982 and 2000.

resolved. Its complexity and the passions it arouses have prevented international law from playing a central role, and yet the conflict spans a number of seminal international legal issues, many of which were explored in the *Wall* Advisory Opinion.[4]

Despite the fact that Palestine has been under Israeli occupation for over forty years, its fortunes have always been linked not only with its occupier but also with international institutions and international law. Further, the narrative of Palestine contains many central themes in postcolonial accounts of international law during the modern period. Although the end of World War I had ushered in a powerful discourse supportive of self-determination, this was only applicable to European peoples. We saw in Chapter Two how 'Ottoman military defeat by the British and French during the First World War produced a radical change throughout the whole Middle East.'[5] Secret treaties signed during the war assured French and British interests.[6] The realisation of these agreements did not produce typical colonial administrations, however, but the League of Nations Mandate, which 'was used to legitimise British and French government of their Middle East possessions.'[7] During the war, Britain also assured the interests of its national Zionist lobby. Through the efforts of the Zionist Federation in Britain, the Cabinet endorsed a statement drafted by the Federation's leaders.[8] This document, which came to be known as the 1917 Balfour Declaration, noted that Britain 'viewed with favour the establishment in Palestine of a national home for the Jewish people, it being clearly understood that nothing should be done which might prejudice the civil and religious rights of existing non-Jewish communities in Palestine.'[9] Crawford argues that it remains unclear whether Britain's responsibilities under the League Covenant should have precluded its support of Jewish

---

[4] Crawford argues that the bulk of international law literature on the conflict has been partisan. For an overview of some of this material and a thorough consideration of the legal aspects of statehood for Palestine and Israel, see J. Crawford, 'Israel (1948–1949) and Palestine (1998–1999): Two Studies in the Creation of States', G. S. Goodwin-Gill, & S. Talmon, (eds.), *The Reality of International Law: Essays in Honour of Ian Brownlie* (Oxford: Clarendon Press, 1999), 95–124; and J. Crawford, *The Creation of States in International Law* (Cambridge: Cambridge University Press, 2nd edition, 2006), 421–448.

[5] R. Owen, State, *Power and Politics in the Making of the Modern Middle East* (London: Routledge, 2nd edition, 2000), at 9. See Chapter Two, at 84–85.

[6] Namely, the Sykes-Picot Agreement of 1916: Exchange of Letters between France and Great Britain respecting the Recognition and Protection of an Arab State in Syria, 9/6 May 1916, 221 CTS 323; Exchange of Notes between France and Great Britain modifying the Agreement of 9/6 May 1916, 25/30 May 1916, 222 CTS 13.

[7] Owen, *supra* n. 5, at 8.

[8] J. Quigley, *The Case for Palestine: An International Law Perspective* (Durham; London: Duke University Press, revised, 2005), at 8.

[9] Quoted in Quigley, ibid.

interests and whether it really was possible to juggle such competing interests.[10] What at least is clear is that Britain was unable to resolve this tension and that the seeds of conflict can be traced to the fundamental incompatibility between Mandate responsibilities contained in Article 22 of the League Covenant and the Balfour Declaration.[11]

Up until Britain's withdrawal from Palestine in 1948, relations between Jewish and Arab populations had produced not only serious local tensions but also international attention from the newly formed UN. As the Arab League remarked in its oral statement in the *Wall* Advisory Opinion, the 'issue of Palestine is the longest-lived problem on the agenda of the United Nations.'[12] Despite the formation of dedicated committees about Palestine's future as a well as the General Assembly-endorsed Partition Plan,[13] disagreement was so pronounced that war broke out between Zionist and Arab forces soon after Britain's flight from Mandatory responsibility. The international consequences of this war included the creation of the state of Israel;[14] agreement on the 1949 Armistice Line (often referred to as the Green Line) dividing Israel from the Jordanian-administered West Bank; a large mass of Arab refugees[15] who would come to rest their hopes increasingly on the promise of self-determination rather than the luke-warm reception offered by Arab states; as well as the seeds of deep-seated animosity between Israel and its Arab neighbours.

---

[10] Crawford, 'Israel (1948–1949) and Palestine (1998–1999)', *supra* n. 4, at 104–106.

[11] Article 22 of the Covenant is discussed in Chapter Two at 85–86. For an overview of Britain's difficulties faced in honouring the Balfour Declaration under the Mandate, see I. Pappe, *A History of Modern Palestine: One Land, Two Peoples* (Cambridge: Cambridge University Press, 2004), at ch. 3.

[12] Mr. Bothe, Oral Statement of the League of Arab States, 25 February 2004, CR 2004/5, at 22. Available at: http://www.icj-cij.org/docket/files/131/1521.pdf.

[13] The Partition Plan was included within Resolution 181(11), 29 November 1947. For a general overview of the events precipitating the 1948 war, see J. Quigley, 'Sovereignty in Jerusalem' 45 *Catholic University Law Review* (1996) 765, at 769–771.

[14] Israel also became a member of the United Nations on 11 May 1949 as a result of General Assembly Resolution 273 (III). The territory comprising the new state of Israel was much larger than that envisaged under the UN 1947 Partition Plan and so some Arab states in their *Wall* Case submissions still regarded Israel's UN membership as based on its compliance with the territorial plans of the partition. However, UN membership is not conditional and Crawford points out ('Israel (1948–1949) and Palestine (1998–1999) *supra* n. 4, at 108–110) that the best explanation for Israel's formation was as an act of force leading to secession (requiring stable and effective government). Israel would have been able to demonstrate this capacity by January 1949.

[15] Halliday suggests that the figure was around 1.4 million. F. Halliday, *The Middle East in International Relations: Power, Politics and Ideology* (Cambridge: Cambridge University Press, 2005), at 94.

Regional tensions came to their climax in the 1967 War. After only six days, the war ended with the Israeli occupation of territories east of the Green Line (including East Jerusalem) as well as the Golan Heights in Syria and Egypt's Sinai Peninsula. Almost immediately after the occupation of Palestinian lands Israel's actions were condemned by the UN Security Council (UNSC) in Resolution 242. UN resolutions following the conflict accepted the cease-fire lines (including the 'Green Line' delimiting the West Bank) but rejected the 'conferring of any title to the territory occupied by Israel.'[16] Since 1967 Palestine has remained a central concern of the UN, and yet independence is as elusive now as it was with the creation of the Mandate. Both the UNGA and the UNSC have issued countless resolutions on specific aspects of the conflict. The central themes to emerge from these include the Palestinian right to self-determination, the non-recognition of Israeli sovereignty over the territory and its status instead as a belligerent occupier under the ambit of international humanitarian law (IHL), the importance of regional peace agreements, the illegality of Israeli settlements, and the need for both Palestinians and Israelis to cease the cycle of violence perpetrated by both public and private actors against civilians.[17]

Only a year before the UNGA requested the Court's assistance, a 'Roadmap' was first mooted as a way of ameliorating regional tensions. The Roadmap laid out steps to be followed by Palestine and Israel and it was to be overseen by the UN, the United States (US), the European Union (EU) and Russia.[18] These countries came to be known as the Quartet and they continued their efforts throughout the Advisory Opinion proceedings.

Palestine's occupation is a classic example of neocolonialism in a postcolonial age. In the *Wall* Case, postcolonial states employed the language of international law in pursuit of the Palestinian cause of self-determination, which suggests that international law was being used as a weapon of the weak in their attempt to solidify a world free of colonialism.[19] Whether international law as a body of norms is capable of supporting such aims is the subject of discussion below.

[16] Q. Wright, 'The Middle East Problem' (1970) 64 *American Journal of International Law* 270, at 272.

[17] For a comprehensive list of UN resolutions relating to Palestine, see http://www.arableagueonline.org/las/english/level2_en.jsp?level_id=701.

[18] For some background about the Roadmap, see International Crisis Group, Report N. 14, 'A Middle East Roadmap to Where?', 2 May 2003, available at http://www.crisisgroup.org/home/index.cfm?id=1659&l=1. The Roadmap was endorsed by the UNSC in Resolution 1515, 19 November 2003: S/RES/1515 (2003).

[19] Power disparities were illustrated in Professor Salmon's speech on behalf of Palestine: 'Advocating negotiations between the wolf and the lamb implies ensuring minimum protection for the lamb.', Oral Statement of Palestine, at 59, para. 7, 23 February 2004, CR 2004/1, (translation). Available at http://www.icj-cij.org/docket/files/131/1505.pdf.

b) *Bringing the Conflict before the Court: The Request for an Advisory Opinion*

Although Palestine has been a constant on the agendas of the UNGA and UNSC, it was not until Israel's construction of a wall that the UNGA sought the assistance of the ICJ. We saw in the introduction to Part III that only the UNSC, UNGA or specialised UN bodies acting within the scope of their mandate can request an Advisory Opinion from the Court.[20] Under the Charter, the power of the UNGA to make a request is further limited by Article 24, which establishes that the UNSC has 'primary responsibility for the maintenance of international peace and security.' Although this provision can be read to prohibit all UNGA involvement in affairs under the Council's consideration, Article 24 only stipulates 'primary responsibility'.[21] Further, in 1950, the UNGA passed its 'Uniting for Peace' resolution, which provides that

> if the Security Council, because of lack of unanimity of the permanent members, fails to exercise its primary responsibility for the maintenance of international peace and security in any case where there appears to be a threat to the peace, breach of the peace, or act of aggression, the General Assembly shall consider the matter immediately with a view to making appropriate recommendations to members for collective measures... If not in session at the time, the General Assembly may meet in emergency special session within twenty-four hours of the request therefor.[22]

The Tenth UNGA Emergency Special Session had been convened in 1997 to discuss Israeli settlements in the Occupied Palestinian Territories (OPT) after a veto by the US in the Security Council.[23] The Tenth Session was reconvened on 20 October 2003 in the wake of another US veto of a Council Resolution, which was partially concerned with the construction of a wall in the OPT.[24]

The minutes from the Emergency Special Sessions preceding the Advisory Opinion pleadings indicate that political and legal positions about the Court's role in the Case and the legal issues raised were already clearly established. Many UN member states that spoke during the 2003 Emergency Special Sessions also went on to present submissions to the Court and there is very little internal discrepancy in their positions.[25] Although stances on legality or illegality and the applicable law used remained relatively constant, there was a significant shift in

---

[20] See Part III's Introduction, at 185–186.

[21] This is discussed by the Court in the *Wall* Opinion: ICJ Reps (2004), at para. 24.

[22] 3 November 1950, 377(V).

[23] For resolutions passed on this issue in the session, see A/RES/ES-10/2, 5 May 1997; A/Res/ES-10/3, 30 July 1997; A/RES/ES-10/4, 19 November 1997.

[24] Draft Resolution S/2003/980, 14 October 2003.

[25] For ease of expression, 'states' will be used to denote state, and quasi-state entities (such as Palestine) where I am discussing general UN activities by its member states and permanent observers.

the language and imagery used in the two settings. Speaking before fellow UN members in a highly charged political setting, speakers were more confident in employing 'inflammatory' language.[26] Speakers in the UN setting also appeared more confident about using or abusing international law for their own purposes.[27] The use of legalese was rare. It would seem that the atmosphere of the Court produced a marked difference in the behaviour of parties. These observations suggest that states regard the practice and discourse of international law used in ICJ adjudication as qualitatively distinct from political debate.

After heated discussions, a number of resolutions were passed about the wall's construction and the scope for requesting an Advisory Opinion. In Resolution ES-10/13 calling for Israel to 'stop and reverse the construction of the wall in the Occupied Palestinian Territory, including in and around East Jerusalem' as well as report by the Secretary-General on Israel's compliance,[28] 144 states supported the Resolution with four against and twelve abstaining.[29] Shortly after the Secretary-General's report was received and after the Security Council veto, Kuwait on behalf of the Arab group and Malaysia on behalf of the Non-Aligned Movement (NAM) sought the reconvention of the Emergency Special Session to respond to the report's findings. The various references made to the Arab and NAM positions throughout the meetings suggest a mutual position not only about the wall's illegality but also the need for an Advisory Opinion.[30] In this vein and after much hyperbole, a resolution requesting the Court's Advisory Opinion was put to the vote and passed. Like other earlier resolutions, Resolution ES 10/14 condemned the wall's construction.[31] Its call for the Court's intercession, however, aroused caution in many – particularly European – states and the resolution passed with a smaller majority (111, with 55 abstentions and

[26] In the words of the President of the 26th Emergency Special Session, 'I really want to caution against the language being used in matters that are ticklish debates which sometimes have the tendency of being inflammatory and not necessarily helping the cause. I really want to make it clear, that for whatever reason – and I do not really care who is upset – I really object to any analogy that is made, particularly from the inside, which may have a tendency to describe as in the Assembly as inmates in an asylum. I think that we can find better language to use in terms of describing the debates that are taking place here'. E/ES-10/PV.26, 19 July 2004, at 3.

[27] For example, 'it is abundantly clear that the construction of the expansionist annexation wall by the occupying Power is a war crime and, I reiterate, a war crime of such seriousness and intensity that it constitutes a crime against humanity.' Mr. Al-Kidwa, UN Observer of Palestine, A/ES-10/PV.21, 20 October 2003, at 3.

[28] A/RES/ES-10/13, 27 October 2003.

[29] A/ES-10/PV.22, 21 October 2003, at 2–3.

[30] Generally see A/ES/10/PV.23, 8 December 2003.

[31] A/RES/ES-10/14, 12 December 2003.

7 against).[32] Despite this, numbers were sufficient in transferring the debate from New York to The Hague.[33]

3) *The Decision of the Court*[34]

In its resolution, the UNGA had asked the Court to give its advice on the following question:

> What are the legal consequences arising from the construction of the wall being built by Israel, the occupying Power, in the Occupied Palestinian Territory, including in and around East Jerusalem, as described in the report of the Secretary-General, considering the rules and principles of international law, including the Fourth Geneva Convention of 1949, and relevant Security Council and General Assembly resolutions?[35]

The Court provided its response in the form of an Opinion as well as a number of separate opinions and one dissenting declaration.[36] The bench went about answering this question by first considering whether it had jurisdiction and if it was proper to exercise its jurisdiction.

a) *Jurisdiction*

The Court's jurisdiction was challenged on a number of grounds. First, the Court had to consider whether the Emergency Special Session request was valid. The Court accepted the nexus between the Uniting for Peace Resolution and the UNGA's request to hold that there were no reasons to regard the request as

---

[32] A/ES/10/PV.23, 8 December 2003, at 20–21.

[33] It must be pointed out that this was not the only ICJ case dealing with Palestine. Others include: *Reparation for Injuries Suffered in the Service of the United Nations (Advisory Opinion)* (1949) ICJ Reps, p. 174; and *Applicability of the Obligation to Arbitrate under Section 21 of the United Nations Headquarters Agreement of June 26 1947 (Advisory Opinion)* (1988) ICJ Reps, p. 12.

[34] For summaries of the case, see P. H. F. Bekker, 'The World Court Rules that Israel's West Bank Barrier Violates International Law', *ASIL Insights*, July 2004, S. C. Breau, 'Legal Consequences of the Construction of a Wall in the Occupied Palestinian Territory: Advisory Opinion, 9 July 2004' (2005) 54 *International and Comparative Law Quarterly* 1003; N. Lubell, 'The ICJ Advisory Opinion and the Separation Barrier: A Troublesome Route' (2005) 35 *Israel Yearbook of Human Rights* 283; and N. Strapatsas, 'Case Note on the ICJ Advisory Opinion on the Legal Consequences of the Construction of the Wall in Occupied Palestinian Territory' (2005) 35 *Israel Yearbook of Human Rights* 251.

[35] A/RES/ES-10/14, at 3.

[36] Judges Koroma, Higgins, Kooijmans. Al-Khasawneh, Elaraby and Owada issued separate opinions; and Judge Buergenthal issued a dissenting declaration.

invalid.[37] Second, a number of submissions argued that the UNGA request was insufficiently 'legal' as per Article 96 of the Charter;[38] that the request lacked clarity; and that it was too political. The Court drew on its jurisprudence to show that none of the objections raised constituted grounds for declining its jurisdiction.[39] It held that the request centred on a sufficiently legal matter.[40] In the words of Judge Koroma, the question was 'eminently legal'.[41] The Court was not concerned that the wording of the UNGA's request was somewhat vague, as it pointed out that such a situation simply required 'clarification in interpretation, and such necessary clarifications have frequently been given by the Court.'[42] Lastly, 'the Court cannot accept the view... that is has no jurisdiction because of the "political" character of the question'.[43] The Opinion relied on ICJ decisions, especially *Legality of the Threat of Use of Nuclear Weapons*,[44] to rebut this argument.[45] The Court acknowledged the existence of politics in its work, but maintained that politics and many other issues were inherent aspects of international law and did not negate the quality of the *legal* question under consideration. Accordingly, the Court found it had jurisdiction to give the requested Advisory Opinion.[46] The Court may have acknowledged the political context, but its judgment on the merits demonstrated how it strove to overlook tensions beyond the Courtroom. As is typical, the language of the Opinion was used to avoid many of the complexities highlighted from a reading of the pleadings.

b) *Propriety*

Although the Court affirmed its jurisdiction, it also considered whether there were elements of the UNGA's request 'that would render the exercise of the Court's jurisdiction improper and inconsistent with the Court's judicial function'.[47] A substantial body of jurisprudence has grown up around this question, which

---

[37] ICJ Reps (2004) at para. 35.

[38] Article 96 states: 'The General Assembly or the Security Council may request the International Court of Justice to give an advisory opinion on any legal question.' Italics added.

[39] ICJ Reps (2004), at paras. 38–41.

[40] ICJ Reps (2004), at para. 37.

[41] ICJ Reps (2004) (sep. op. Koroma), at para. 3.

[42] ICJ Reps (2004), at para. 38.

[43] ICJ Reps (2004), at para. 41.

[44] *Legality of the Threat or Use of Nuclear Weapons (Advisory Opinion)* (1996) ICJ Reps, p. 26.

[45] ICJ Reps (2004), at para. 41.

[46] ICJ Reps (2004), at para. 42.

[47] ICJ Reps (2004), at para. 43.

generally focuses on whether there would be any 'compelling reasons'[48] leading to its jurisdiction being declined. The Opinion restated a well-known fact that the ICJ had never declined jurisdiction on these grounds and acknowledged its special responsibility as the 'principal judicial organ of the United Nations'.[49] One of the most important reasons against its jurisdiction was the proposition advanced in a number of submissions that 'the request concerns a contentious matter between Israel and Palestine'[50] lacking Israeli consent. Here, the Court reaffirmed that advisory opinions as opposed to contentious cases do not *ipso facto* require a state's consent, and that previous opinions had been rendered in the absence of consent.[51] So as to distinguish the PCIJ case of *Eastern Carelia*,[52] the Court relied on *Western Sahara's* dictum that jurisdiction could be upheld despite a lack of consent as well as the presence of a bilateral dispute as long as this was not 'incompatible with the Court's judicial character'.[53] The Court acknowledged that Israel and Palestine had 'expressed radically different views'.[54] It also recognised an aspect of the Case partly comprised a bilateral dispute, however, as in the *Western Sahara* Case, it chose to focus on the relationship between its advisory jurisdiction and the mandate of the General Assembly. It held that the construction of the wall 'to be directly of concern to the United Nations.'[55] The Opinion would primarily function as judicial assistance to the Charter-determined duties of the General Assembly, rather than act as an alternative forum for a bilateral dispute. By using these arguments the Court could carve out a legal niche for itself within the broader context of the 'political' conflict.

The Court considered and refuted four more challenges to its competence: that the Opinion would impede negotiations between the parties; that the Court lacked adequate factual materials on the Case, especially because of the absence of Israeli consent; that the Opinion would serve no useful purpose; and

---

[48] *Certain Expenses of the United Nations (article 17, paragraph of the Charter) (Advisory Opinion)* (1962) ICJ Reps, p. 155.

[49] Citing United Nations Charter art 92, ICJ Reps (2004), at 156, para. 44.

[50] ICJ Reps (2004), at 157, para. 46.

[51] Judge Burgenthal also noted this point, but placed much greater weight on it, arguing that fairness would have been improved if Israel were permitted to appoint a judge *ad hoc*. ICJ Reps (2004) (sep. op. Burgenthal), at 265–267.

[52] *Status of Eastern Carelia (Advisory Opinion)*, 1923, P.C.IJ., Series B, No. 5. Judge Burgenthal in his dissent also pointed out that in the case that as Russia was not a member of the League it had therefore not consented to have its disputes heard by the PCIJ at all. However, in this case, Israeli membership of the UN created a qualitatively different scenario. ICJ Reps (2004) (sep. op. Burgenthal), at 263, para. 9.

[53] *Western Sahara (Advisory Opinion)* ICJ Reps. (1975), at 25, paras. 32–33, in ICJ Reps (2004), at 158, para. 47.

[54] ICJ Reps (2004), at 158, para. 48.

[55] ICJ Reps (2004), at 159, para. 49.

that Palestine did not come to the proceedings in good faith.[56] First, with very little investigation of the ensuing negotiations, the Court erred on the side of jurisdiction when it argued that opinions differed as to the possible relationship between an Opinion and negotiations. Ultimately, it did not regard potential interference 'as a compelling reason to decline' jurisdiction.[57] On the requirement of sufficient information, the Court again distinguished *Eastern Carelia* to hold that the current Case did not require factual material only available from a non-consenting party.[58] Instead, 'the Court has at its disposal the report of the Secretary-General, as well as a voluminous dossier submitted by him to the Court', the submissions from the pleadings and, lastly, material available in the 'public domain'.[59] Third, in relation to the contention that the Opinion would be of no value, the Court held that it 'cannot substitute its assessment of the usefulness of the opinion requested for that of the organ that seeks such opinion'.[60] Both the UNGA and UNSC would be free to 'draw [their own] conclusions'.[61] Finally, the Court dismissed Israel's contention that Palestine's responsibility for acts of violence meant that it came to the Case in bad faith and without 'clean hands'.[62] This was not a 'pertinent' consideration because the Case involved a request by the UNGA rather than a bilateral dispute *per se*.[63]

Judges Higgins and Kooijmans criticised aspects of the Court's reasoning in relation to its competence. Their reservations centred on the bilateral and political aspects of the Case as well as the Opinion's ill-founded reliance on the *Namibia* decision.[64] Both separate opinions indicate that the Court's compromise was an awkward one. Nevertheless, there was sufficient agreement for fourteen of its members to accept the UNGA's request and consider the matter on its merits.

c) *Merits*

The Opinion's discussion of the legal principles lacked detail. The Court's decision has especially been questioned in relation to its 'somewhat light treatment

---

[56] ICJ Reps (2004), at paras. 46–65.
[57] ICJ Reps (2004), at 160, para. 53.
[58] ICJ Reps (2004), at paras. 55–58.
[59] ICJ Reps (2004), at 161–162, para. 57. Cf Judge Burgenthal's disagreement on this point, ICJ Reps (2004) (sep. op. Burgenthal), at 268, para. 22.
[60] ICJ Reps (2004), at 163, para. 62.
[61] Ibid.
[62] ICJ Reps (2004), at 163, para. 63.
[63] ICJ Reps (2004), at 164, para. 64.
[64] *Legal Consequences for States of the Continued Presence of South Africa in Namibia (South West Africa) notwithstanding Security Council Resolution 276 (1970) (Advisory Opinion)* (1971) ICJ Reps, p. 12. ICJ Reps (2004) (sep. op. Higgins), at 207, at paras. 1–11; ICJ Reps (sep. op. Kooijmans), at 219, at paras. 23–25.

of international humanitarian law', human rights law, as well as the requirements of self-defence.[65] These factors fall outside of the chapter's focus, but it is useful to note that the Court adopted its usual approach in obfuscating norm conflict and relying on formalism.[66] It must also be remembered that a number of states that had made submissions did not address issues of substance because they had requested the Court to decline its jurisdiction. Thus the available material from both the Court as well as various parties was somewhat superficial.

Before the Court could consider the legal consequences of the wall's construction, it needed to determine what bodies of law applied and whether any breaches had occurred within the OPT. At the outset, it distinguished between those parts of the wall west of the Green Line (in Israel proper) and those in the OPT. It held that only the latter were of relevance because any state was free to construct walls within its own territory.[67] Before it considered the applicable laws, it discussed the territorial status of the OPT since the time of the Mandate. Although the Opinion did not consider the territorial status of Palestine between 1948 and 1967,[68] it highlighted League of Nations principles pertaining to the territory: non-annexation and 'the well-being and development of peoples'.[69]

---

[65] ICJ Reps (2004) (sep. op. Higgins), at 213, para. 25. For some responses to the Court's treatment of IHL, human rights and self-defence issues, see A. Imseis, 'Critical Reflections on the International Humanitarian Law Aspects of the ICJ Wall Advisory Opinion' (2005) 99 *American Journal of International Law* 102; F. Mégrét, 'A Sacred Trust of Civilization' (2005) 1 *Journal of International Law & International Relations* 305; S. D. Murphy, 'Self-Defense and the Israeli Wall Advisory Opinion: An Ipse Dixit from the ICJ?' (2005) 99 *American Journal of International Law* 62; A. M. Smith, 'Good Fences Make Good Neighbors?: The "Wall Decision" and the Troubling Rise of the ICJ as a Human Rights Court' (2005) 18 *Harvard Human Rights Journal* 251; C. J. Tams, 'Light Treatment of a Complex Problem: The Law of Self-Defence in the Wall Case' (2005) 16 *European Journal of International Law* 963; R. Wedgwood, 'The ICJ Advisory Opinion on the Israeli Security Fence and the Limits of Self-Defence' (2005) 99 *American Journal of International Law* 52.

[66] Judge Higgins characterised the majority's strict definition of self-defence as only applying between states as 'formalism of an unevenhanded sort.' ICJ Reps (2004) (sep. op. Higgins), at 215, para. 34.

[67] ICJ Reps (2004), at 164, para. 67.

[68] Judge Al-Khasawneh applauded this approach of the Opinion's and explained the underlying motives of the Court: 'The Court followed a wise course in steering away from embarking on an enquiry into the precise prior status of those territories not only because such an enquiry is unnecessary for the purpose of establishing their present status as occupied territories affirming the *de jure* applicability of the Fourth Geneva Convention to them, but also because the prior status of the territories would make no difference whatsoever to their status as occupied territories except that they were *terra nullius* when they were occupied by Israel, which no one would seriously argue given that discredited concept is of no contemporary application, besides being incompatible with the territories' status as a former mandatory territory.' ICJ Reps (2004) (sep. op. Al-Khasawneh), at 237, para. 8.

[69] Citing ICJ Reps (1950), p. 131, in ICJ Reps (2004), at 165, para. 70.

What was clear for the Court at least was the status of Palestine after the June War in 1967: it was under Israeli belligerent occupation. This recognition of Palestine's occupied status is confirmed by numerous UNSC resolutions issued since 1967.[70]

Echoing the Mandate ideals, the Court first identified both the right of self-determination and the prohibition against the use of force as constituting the general legal principles applicable. It cited the *East Timor* Case[71] in support of the notion that 'the right of self-determination of peoples today is a right *erga omnes*'.[72] This right therefore applied to Israeli policies, which included building the wall, transferring its population to settlements in the OPT, and the resulting flight of Palestinians from the territory. These acts impeded the Palestinian right to self-determination and are discussed further below in this chapter's comparison of the pleadings and the Opinion. Although supportive of the notion of self-determination generally in the OPT, Judges Higgins and Kooijmans argued that there was no direct relationship between the wall and this right; it could only be appreciated with regard to the broader context, and this was beyond the scope of the UNGA's request.[73] Judge Higgins pointed out that the wall did not change the territorial status of Palestine: both before and after its construction Palestine would remain an occupied territory.[74] This view placed too little weight on what the Opinion described as the expansionist aims embodied by the wall; the Court regarded the walls' construction as constituting *de facto* annexation.[75] In such a case, the right of self-determination was being breached. Most of the Court was unwilling to accept Israeli statements about the 'temporary'[76] nature of the structure and thus interpreted the right of self-determination in a more contextual and flexible manner than Judges Kooijmans and Higgins. These difficulties of definition faced by the bench indicate how international legal discourse is ill-equipped to express hypothetical, future scenarios with possible legal implications attached.

After examining the various laws applicable and instances of Israeli breaches, the Court discussed the legal consequences for both Israel and third states.

---

70 Particularly, UNSC Resolution 242 (1967), 22 November.

71 *East Timor (Australia/ Portugal) (Merits)* ICJ Reps (1995), p. 102.

72 ICJ Reps (2004), at 172, para. 88.

73 ICJ Reps (2004) (sep. op. Higgins) p. 214, para. 30. ICJ Reps (2004) (sep. op. Kooijmans), at 228, para. 32.

74 ICJ Reps (2004) (sep. op. Higgins), at 213–214, paras. 30–31.

75 Cf. Kretzmer's critique on the Court's unsatisfying treatment of future acts: D. Kretzmer, 'The Advisory Opinion: the Light Treatment of International Humanitarian Law' (2005) 99 *American Journal of International Law* 88, at 92.

76 According to Israel, the Wall's construction is 'a non-violent and temporary measure of last resort.' Written Statement of Israel, 30 January 2004, at para. 1.16. Available at http://www.icj-cij.org/docket/files/131/1579.pdf.

As the Court had determined that the wall's construction was in breach of the right to self-determination, IHL and human rights law, it held that Israel must respect such obligations. Israel was required to stop and reverse the wall's construction. Relying on the *Factory at Chorzów* Case,[77] the Court further held that Israel was required to make reparations or, where this was not possible, to compensate the victims for the damage suffered during the wall's construction.[78] As for third states, the Opinion stated that self-determination as well as aspects of IHL were 'of an *erga omnes* character'[79] permitting no derogation.[80] Thus, in its *dispositif* the Court held:

> *(3)* A. By fourteen votes to one,[81]
> The construction of the wall being built by Israel, the occupying Power, in the Occupied Palestinian Territory, including in and around East Jerusalem, and its associated regime, are contrary to international law;
> B. By fourteen votes to one,
> Israel is under an obligation to terminate its breaches of international law; it is under an obligation to cease forthwith the works of construction of the wall being built in the Occupied Palestinian Territory...to dismantle forthwith the structure therein situated, and to repeal or render ineffective forthwith all legislative and regulatory acts relating thereto...
> C. By fourteen votes to one, Israel is under an obligation to make reparation for all damage caused by the construction of the wall in the Occupied Palestinian Territory...
> D. By thirteen votes to two,[82] All States are under an obligation not to recognize the illegal situation resulting from the construction of the wall and not to render aid or assistance in maintaining the situation created by such a construction...
> E. By fourteen votes to one,[83] The United Nations...should consider what further action is required to bring to an end the illegal situation...[84]

Judge Buergenthal did not support the Court's jurisdiction and so he voted consistently against all dispositive paragraphs. Although Judge Higgins voted for paragraph *3* (D), she expressed reservations about its operation, because it called for states 'to ensure compliance by Israel with international humanitarian law.'[85] Judge Kooijmans also argued that there was no positive duty for States in the Fourth Geneva Convention regarding breaches and that it was not practicable for the Court to rule on this anyway.[86] Finally, it was unclear from the Court's

---

[77] *Factory at Chorzów (Merits)* (1928) P.C.I.J., Series A, No. 17.
[78] ICJ Reps (2004), at 198, para. 153.
[79] ICJ Reps (2004), at 199, para. 157.
[80] ICJ Reps (2004), at 200, para. 159.
[81] Judge Buergenthal in dissent to paragraphs 3 A, B & C.
[82] Judges Buergenthal and Kooijmans in dissent.
[83] Judge Buergenthal in dissent.
[84] ICJ Reps (2004), at para. 163.
[85] ICJ Reps (2004) (sep. op. Higgins), at 207, at paras. 37–39.
[86] ICJ Reps (2004) (sep. op. Kooijmans), at 219, paras. 46–50.

discussion whether it was eliding the term *erga omnes* with *jus cogens*, especially in relation to the right of self-determination.[87]

Despite the Opinion's rather sketchy and shallow treatment of many aspects of the Case, it still provides a useful statement on many international legal principles and needs to be appreciated for what it is: a difficult compromise reached by fourteen out of the Court's fifteen members. For Falk 'the degree of consensus is rather remarkable, given the controversial subject matter, and the far-reaching and drastic responses given to the General Assembly's question.'[88] Damrosch and Oxman are less forthcoming with praise for the Opinion, because substantial agreement between the judges 'came at the price of a lowest-common-denominator approach to the reasoning of the opinion'.[89] O'Keefe echoes these sentiments, arguing that the Opinion 'is often unsatisfying in methodological and stylistic terms... [and it] is too prone to bald, *ex cathedra* pronouncements of law and fact, which give little indication of the Court's reasoning'.[90] At times the Opinion's 'certain delphic quality'[91] may have been necessary because of the tense legal and political issues the Case straddled, but O'Keefe argues that the Court need not have been so 'exceedingly spare' in its approach.[92] An opportunity to clarify some particularly pertinent issues, such as the emerging norm relating to self-defence, as well as the finer points of IHL, was wasted. In her separate opinion, Higgins opines that she did not feel compelled to add to the Opinion because of any major discrepancies with what was written; rather, her 'regrets are... about what [the Court] has chosen *not* to write.'[93]

As shown by Higgins, the silences of the Court tell us a great deal about international law and its relevance to the dispute. In the following sections, I compare positions taken in the pleadings with both the statements and silences of the Court.

---

[87] See generally, A Orakhelashvili, 'International Public Order and the International Court's Advisory Opinion on Legal Consequences of the Construction of a Wall in the Occupied Palestinian Territory' (2005) 43 *Archiv des Völkerrechts* 240.

[88] R. A. Falk, 'Towards Authoritativeness: The ICJ Ruling on Israel's Security Wall' (2005) 99 *American Journal of International Law* 42, at 43.

[89] L. F. Damrosch, & B. H. Oxman, 'Agora: ICJ Advisory Opinion on Construction of a Wall in the Occupied Palestinian Territory: Editors' Introduction' (2005) 99 *American Journal of International Law* 1, at 1.

[90] R. O'Keefe, 'Legal Consequences of the Construction of a Wall in the Occupied Palestinian Territory: A Commentary' (2004) 37 *Revue belge de droit international* 92, at 126; Scobbie concurs with this position: I. Scobbie,'Smoke, Mirrors and Killer Whales: the International Court's Opinion and the Israeli Barrier Wall' (2004) 5 *German Law Journal* 1107, at 1107.

[91] O'Keefe, Ibid., at 126.

[92] Ibid., at 127.

[93] Emphasis added, ICJ Reps (2004) (sep. op. Higgins), at 207, para. 20.

4) *Contesting the Court's Jurisdiction*

In contrast with contentious ICJ cases, Advisory Opinions offer much greater scope for the participation of a range of states as well as IGOs and in the case of Palestine, nascent state entities.[94] States are under no compulsion to submit written or oral arguments and non-state entities must first secure the permission of the Court.[95] The prestige, prominence and authority of the Court may induce states to act, but there are also other considerations such as resources and priorities to take into account. In the *Wall* pleadings many states participated, but many also chose to play no part. Links can be made between the relative regard for the proceedings among the states participating and their method of engagement. There was a much greater number of written as opposed to oral submissions, and often those states requesting the Court to decline its jurisdiction – namely, various EU states, the US, Israel and some others – only submitted written arguments. There was an overwhelming consensus among these states on the issue of jurisdiction: negotiations through the prism of the Roadmap were to take priority over legal proceedings likely to jeopardise this process. Such a stance suggests that these mostly First World states regarded the role of the ICJ as of limited value in such a highly 'political' matter. It would also seem that states were strongly influenced by regional and strategic affiliations.[96] The views espoused in these written submissions indicated a tendency to set clear boundaries

[94] Despite significant scholarly attention generated by the *Wall* Opinion, very little work has considered the pleadings. In cases where authors have looked at the pleadings at all, they have tended to focus excessively on Israel's written submission. For those authors who regarded the case as a bilateral dispute, they seized on the Israeli position and juxtaposed it with the Opinion. Some authors who have considered other submissions include: I. Scobbie, 'Words my Mother Never Taught me – "In Defense of the International Court"' (2005) 99 *American Journal of International Law* 76; and G. R. Watson, 'The "Wall" Decision in Legal and Political Context' (2005) 99 *American Journal of International Law* 6.

[95] Article 66, Statute of the International Court of Justice. In the Wall Opinion, the Court decided to invite submissions from Palestine, the Organisation of Islamic Conference (OIC) and the Arab League. In the case of Palestine, it grounded its reasons on A/RES/ES-10/14 (discussed above), the Secretary-General's report a well as Palestine's 'special status of observer [in the UN] and that...[Palestine] is co-sponsor of the draft resolution requesting the advisory opinion'. As for the Arab League and the OIC, 'these two international organizations were likely to be able to furnish information on the question.' President Shi, Opening Address, Public Sitting, CR 2004/1, 23 February 2004, at 15.

[96] According to Hirsch, regional interests may well be of greater importance for Israeli compliance than any commitment to the international community as represented in the ICJ as well as the UNGA's request: 'This social influence of international reference groups indicates that the position of states belonging to the Western group regarding the recent Advisory Opinion is of significance to Israeli decision makers, even if it is not translated into coherent sanctions.' M. Hirsch, 'The Impact of the Advisory Opinion on Israel's Future Policy: International Relations Perspective' (2005) 1 *Journal of International Law and International Relations* 319, at 340.

between legal and political spheres in international life with law being deemed as only appropriate in limited situations. It should also be noted that all states parties to the Roadmap's Quartet, namely Russia, the US and the EU submitted that the Court should decline to exercise its jurisdiction.

While strong agreement existed among mostly First World states in relation to the ICJ's minor role, there was a similar pattern for Third World,[97] and particularly Arab, states regarding the importance and place of international law and the ICJ in resolving the protracted conflict. Many Third World states regarded the Case to be of great importance.[98] There were a disproportionate number of Third World states submitting oral (as well as written) statements and a connection can be made between the relative importance that these states placed on the proceedings and their participation. Saudi Arabia declared in the hearings that '[t]his is the first time... Saudi Arabia has made an oral presentation to the International Court of Justice.'[99] Other Third World states expressed their awareness of the 'momentousness of the occasion'[100] by declaring their reverence for the Court in more florid language than their First World counterparts.[101] This was especially so for small states, such as Belize and Cuba, which were cognisant of their minor international influence, but still wanted to make a contribution to the proceedings.

As in the case of the Quartet states and Israel, there were identifiable allegiances and alliances within the pleadings as well as a degree of cross-referencing across submissions.[102] The NAM[103] along with the Arab Group at the UN (which happens to comprise NAM members) were the co-sponsors of the original UNGA

---

[97] Exceptions included: Palau, Micronesia and the Marshall Islands continued in their strong allegiance with the US on matters relating to Israel and asked for the Court to decline jurisdiction. This was also the case for Cameroon, despite its membership in the Organisation of Islamic Conference. Finally, although was a relatively united European stance, some states broke away from this or were more sympathetic to the legal process.

[98] For example, Written Submission of Yemen, http://www.icj-cij.org/docket/files/131/1581.pdf; and Professor Sorel, Oral Statement of Belize, 24 February 2004, CR 2004/3, at 14.

[99] Ambassador Shobokshi, Oral Statement of the Kingdom of Saudi Arabia, 23 February 2004, CR 2004/2 at 43, para. 1.

[100] Professor Sorel, Oral Pleadings of Belize, 24 February, CR 2004/3, at 14, para. 1.

[101] See especially Oral Statement of Malaysia, 24 February 2004, CR 2004/4; Oral Statement of Madagascar, 24 February 2004, CR 2004/4; and Oral Statement of South Africa, 23 February 2004, CR 2004/2. These states all spoke in the Emergency Special Sessions as well.

[102] Sudan provides an example of inter-Arab cross-referencing to other Arab states: 'At the outset, we would like to associate ourselves with the Written Statements submitted to this Court by both the League of Arab States and the Organization of Islamic Conference (OIC), and we fully endorse their legal arguments, opinions and conclusions on the matter. We also subscribe to the views and legal arguments presented by Palestine and by other delegations appearing before this Court.' Ambassador Idris, Oral Statement of Sudan, 25 February 2004, CR 2004/5, at 14, para. 2.

[103] For a full list of NAM members, see http://www.nam.gov.za/background/members.htm.

resolution requesting the Opinion, and many submissions acknowledged these links. The Organisation of Islamic Conference (OIC) also submitted both written and oral pleadings and many of its members are both members of the NAM[104] and the Arab League.[105] It is not surprising then that the OIC was invited to participate in the hearings. Palestine is a member, but also, more importantly, Article 2 of the OIC Charter lists one of the Organisation's principal objectives as being: 'to coordinate efforts for the safeguarding of the Holy Places and support of the struggle of the people of Palestine, to help them regain their rights and liberate their land'.[106] The OIC has a committee overseeing the implementation of this Article 'on the Arab-Israeli conflict in view of the fundamental connection between the Al-Quds[107] [Jerusalem] question and the conflict.'[108] At the time of the pleadings, Morocco's King Muhammed VI was the chair of Al-Quds committee and Morocco listed this as a factor in its participation.[109]

Similarly, the Arab League emphasised its own motivations in the pleadings as being directly 'at the top of the League of Arab States' agenda since its creation in 1945.[110] The League's Pact asserted the right of Palestine to independence. Accordingly, Palestine was granted the full membership in the Arab League.'[111] The matter of Palestine led to Egypt's decade-long suspension as well as the temporary transferral of the League's headquarters in Cairo after Egypt's peace treaty with Israel in 1979. Ultimately, the NAM, the Arab League and the OIC need not have given international law, and its embodiment in the form of the ICJ, such attention. Many member states of these organisations have been actively involved in diplomatic efforts regarding both the conflict and the wall

[104] For example, in its written submission, Bangladesh highlighted its membership of both the NAM and OIC and linked this with its position in the pleadings. Oral Statement of Bangladesh, 23 February 2004, CR 2004/2, at 59.

[105] In addition, both the Arab League and the OIC are Observer Organisations within the NAM.

[106] A copy of the Charter can be found on the OIC's website: http://www.oic-oci.org/.

[107] Al-Quds (القدس) is the Arabic name for Jerusalem, which is the third most holy site for Muslims. This is reflected in the derivation of the name: the word is based on the verb *qadasa* قدس (to be holy) and the literal meaning of quds is holiness, sacredness, sanctity: Cowan, J. M. (ed.), *The Hans Wehr Dictionary of Modern Written Arabic* (Ithaca, NY: Spoken Languages Services, 4th ed, 1994). The use of Al-Quds instead of Jerusalem is a highly symbolic act on the part of Arabs who have come to see 'Jerusalem' as signifying a unified Jewish capital, see Y. Suleiman, *A War of Words: Language and Conflict in the Middle East* (Cambridge: Cambridge University Press, 2004), at 175.

[108] This statement can also be found on the OIC's website, http://www.oic-oci.org/.

[109] Written Submission of the Kingdom of Morocco, at 1, http://www.icj-cij.org/docket/files/131/1585.pdf.

[110] The members of the Arab League are listed in the Introduction at 7, footnote 16.

[111] Written Submission of the League of Arab States, 28 January 2004, para. 2.1. http://www.icj-cij.org/docket/files/131/1545.pdf.

in particular. However, their choice to support the legal process suggests a commitment to legal institutions as well as a faith in international legal principles. The link between the language of faith and international law for Third World states is explored further below.

A few observations about the relative quality of the legal teams and statements presented are worthwhile before considering the nature of the pleadings themselves. Written submissions varied dramatically in terms of their quality of style and length and as well as considered treatment of legal arguments. In instances where states placed great weight on the jurisdiction and substantive findings of the Court, submissions were often detailed and well-polished, as in the case of Saudi Arabia, the the Arab League, the OIC, Malaysia, South Africa and particularly, Jordan and Palestine.[112] In contrast, many states opposed to the jurisdiction of the Court submitted shorter and often perfunctory documents. Israel however had a strong interest in blocking the pleadings and so its written submission was quite detailed, in relation not only to jurisdiction but also, inadvertently, substance. From a quick perusal of both the drafting style and the legal teams employed, it is clear that there were disparities in the time and resources outlaid in the proceedings.[113] Palestine's legal team in particular comprised a host of eminent international law experts, who were given the liberty to work on the Case as they saw fit; they were not under any instructions from Ramallah.[114] This fact alone is significant;[115] it suggests that Palestine's faith in

---

[112] Written Submission of Saudi Arabia, http://www.icj-cij.org/docket/files/131/1543.pdf; Written Submission of the League of Arab States, *supra* n. 111; Written Submission of the Organisation of Islamic States, http://www.icj-cij.org/docket/files/131/1589.pdf; Written Submission of Malaysia, http://www.icj-cij.org/docket/files/131/1625.pdf; Written Submission of South Africa, http://www.icj-cij.org/docket/files/131/1597.pdf; Written Submission of Jordan, http://www.icj-cij.org/docket/files/131/1559.pdf; and Written Submission of Palestine, http://www.icj-cij.org/docket/files/131/1555.pdf.

[113] Syria's submission for example contained numerous errors and was utterly incoherent at times. A sample of its style illustrates this: 'The second: is what the second article referred to when expecting three cases in which the state could not have the state of emergency as a pretext. The first of these cases refers that it is not allowed to have the state of emergency as a pretext to violate a clear rule of the international law. These rules are not to be disobeyed for any reason. **Consequently, we say here that catching the others' territories by force, settling, imposing the public punishment policy and adopting racial separation policy are on top of clear international rules that could not be violated or disobeyed with the pretext of existence.**' Written Submission of the Syrian Arab Republic, 30 January 2004, 24, http://www.icj-cij.org/docket/files/131/1567.pdf, (emphasis in original).

[114] For an account about Palestine's legal team, see P. H. F. Bekker, 'The World Court's Ruling Regarding Israel's West Bank Barrier and the Primacy of International Law: An Insider's Perspective' (2005) 38 *Cornell International Law Journal* 553, at 557.

[115] In particular, it should be noted that a member of the Palestinian team, James Crawford, has written on the territorial status of Palestine before, essentially holding that it does not

the processes of international law – as embodied in the discipline's finest – meant that no political direction was needed. Instead, international legal principles could speak for themselves.

5) *Strategies of Argument*

This section is concerned with two strategic devices employed by the parties in presenting their respective positions: the use of language and the use of history. Both of these strategies reveal underlying Third World normative evaluations about the role of international law in a postcolonial era as explored in this book's other case studies.

a) *Speaking before the Court*

States participating in the pleadings did not necessarily share the same vocabulary or understanding of international law. Whether such discrepancies can be explained as simply different dialects or different languages will be assessed in the Conclusion. It is also evident from a comparison of the language used in the lead up to the Opinion in the Emergency Special Sessions, that parties were aware of the unique discourse that the Advisory Opinion elicited – language of the pleadings was far less emotive and florid.

Choice of language was of importance for both the parties and the Court in relation to the name of the Case and its focus, the wall. Although, the Court must have been aware of the controversy over terminology, it chose not to delve into this.[116] In explaining its use of the word 'wall' (as opposed to 'fence' or 'barrier'), the Court simply stated that other words 'are no more accurate if understood in the physical sense.'[117] However, the Court did qualify its use of the word later in the Opinion by describing the surrounding circumstances as creating a 'régime':[118] the wall was more than a simple edifice, it took on complex qualities with legal consequences. This idea can be attributed to a number of submissions from Arab states, such as Palestine and Jordan.[119]

---

yet manifest the qualities of statehood, *supra* n. 4; J. Crawford 'The Creation of the State of Palestine: Too Much Too Soon?' (1990) 1 *European Journal of International Law* 307; and Crawford, *The Creation of States in International Law, supra* n. 4, at 421–448.

116 Scobbie also acknowledged this controversy in his discussion of the Opinion. Scobbie, 'Words My Mother Never Taught Me', *supra* n. 94, at 76, footnote 1.

117 ICJ Reps (2004), at 164, para. 67.

118 For example, ICJ Reps (2004), at 191, para. 134.

119 'The wall, far from being a simple self-standing security measure, is thus to be understood as a *regime* serving Israeli policy towards the annexation of the West Bank or substantial parts thereof' (emphasis added), Written Submission of Jordan, *supra* n. 112, at 97, para. 5.151;

Within the pleadings themselves, there is an unambiguous correlation between Third World support for the Court's jurisdiction and their use of the term, 'wall'. Every Arab state and most Third World states (except those not in favour of the request: the Pacific states and Cameroon), supported this pattern. Jordan's Prince Al-Hussein voiced the Third World position when he argued before the Court that the Case 'concerns a wall. And not just "a" wall, but a very specific wall…[that] is not just a simple fence.'[120] For those Western states asking the Court to decline jurisdiction, many chose to use the term, 'barrier' instead, and this conjures up the image of a structure less total than a wall. The use of the term 'fence' was associated with Israel's position and is 'highly symbolic', suggesting, as it does, an insubstantial and semi-permanent structure.[121] Israel consistently used (and continues to use) the term and only a few states followed suit in their submissions, all of which favoured negotiations over the Opinion.[122] Israel went into detail about this:

> The use of the term 'wall' in the resolution requesting an opinion is neither happenstance nor oversight. It reflects a calculated media campaign to raise pejorative connotations in the mind of the Court of great concrete constructions[123] of separation as the Berlin Wall, intended to stop people escaping from tyranny.[124]

This notion of the Berlin Wall was explored by the Arab League in its oral statement, and was the only delegation to do so.[125] The broader idea of separation,

'The Wall is not a physical structure. It is a whole regime.' Mr. Al-Kidwa, Oral Statement of Palestine, 23 February 2004, CR 2004/1, at 18, para. 4; Written Submission of Palestine, *supra* n. 112, at 4, para. 11.

120 Written Submission of Jordan, *supra* n. 112, at 53.

121 In the words of Professor Sorel, Belize's counsel, 'Like the General Assembly, I shall use the word "Wall", not forgetting that other, highly symbolic expressions are used by Israel to describe this construction referred to as "security fence" then "security barrier".' Oral Statement of Belize, CR 2004/3, at 15, footnote 3.

122 Written Submission of Belgium, http://www.icj-cij.org/docket/files/131/1635.pdf; Written Submission of the European Union,_http://www.icj-cij.org/docket/files/131/1615.pdf.

123 This statement is directly contradicted by the Arab League, which argued that Israel was denying the effects of the wall 'by calling the "fence" a temporary security measure. But this claim veils the true situation. It is public notice that major parts of the Wall are built in a very solid way, concrete structures, ditches, and so on.' Professor Bothe, Oral Statement of the League of Arab States, CR 2004/5, at p. 29. This position is corroborated by footage on B'Tselem's (a prominent Israeli human rights organisation) website: http://www.btselem.org/English/Photo_Archive/List.asp?x_Concatenate=15&z_Concatenate=LIKE,%27%25,%25%27.

124 Written Submission of Israel, *supra* n. 76, at 10, para. 2.7.

125 Oral Statement of the League of Arab States, Mr. Bothe, CR 2004/5, 25 Febraury, at 21–22.

however, was expressed by some other Arab states, which referred to the 'apartheid wall'[126] and the 'segregation wall'.[127]

Language choice over 'wall' was bolder in the political setting of the earlier Emergency Special Settings discussed above. During the Emergency Special Sessions, speakers were more forthright in their language. Prominent parties in the Case also spoke at the Sessions and followed the Palestinian delegate's condemnatory language regarding the wall, using phrases such as 'expansionist annexation wall' (Palestine),[128] 'expansionist conquest wall' (Palestine),[129] 'Israeli expansionist wall' (Malaysia speaking for NAM)[130] and 'that expansionist wall' (OIC).[131] Israel also employed much more inflammatory language to describe the wall: 'this is the Arafat fence. This is the fence that Arafat built.'[132] None of these expressions were employed before the Court; the participants were aware of international law's particular lexicon and translated their perspectives accordingly.

In both the pleadings and the Opinion itself, ideas of 'existence' were touched on through certain linguistic techniques. As in the case of the use of 'wall', the Court refused to be drawn into these debates on Palestine's existence: '[a]s regards the principle of the right of peoples to self-determination, the Court observes that the existence of a "Palestinian people" is no longer in issue.'[133] However, Palestine was described by Italy as existing 'still in an inchoate state',[134] and Israel was able to demonstrate this idea by always using quotation marks when discussing Palestine; it would seem that for some states Palestine was in a state of limbo.[135] In a postcolonial context where selfhood is best secured through statehood, Palestine's unresolved status fitted uncomfortably with international law's preference for precision and clarity. Perhaps the international legal lexicon was stretched to its limit with such an example, and states exploited this lacuna for their own agendas. Language usage was of such importance for Malaysia that it specifically addressed the issue during the pleadings: 'Malaysia takes strong exception to the pejorative way in which Israel refers to Palestine throughout its Written Statement, such as the use of inverted commas to refer to Palestine'.[136]

---

126 Written Submission of the League of Arab States, *supra* n. 111, at 7 para. 1.4.

127 Written Submission of Kuwait, 30 January 2004, http://www.icj-cij.org/docket/files/131/1561.pdf.

128 A/ES-10/PV.21, at 3.

129 Ibid., at 9.

130 Ibid.

131 Ibid.

132 A/ES-10/PV.23, 6.

133 ICJ Reps (2004), at 182–183, para. 118.

134 Written Submission of Italy, http://www.icj-cij.org/docket/files/131/1593.pdf, p. 4.

135 See generally, Wrriten Submission of Israel, *supra* n. 76.

136 Mr. Albar, Oral Statement of Malaysia, 24 February 2004, CR 2004/4, p. 24.

Syria also adopted the technique *vis-à-vis* Israel by employing quotation marks when referring to anything Israeli including Prime Minister, Ariel Sharon.[137]

Israel's existence as a recognised state has been a contested issue for both Arab and Muslim states more generally. Many continue to refuse not only to make peace with Israel or enter into diplomatic relations, but even to acknowledge its existence.[138] This dissonance between legal fact and political predisposition was illustrated in parts of the written submission of the OIC, where the presence of Israel remained ambiguous; it was unclear whether the OIC was recognising it or not.[139] This example indicates that choices over language were of primary concern for certain states participating in the Case. Some words and phrases stretched international law's lexicon, which tends to comprise 'neutral', 'non-emotional' language so as to preserve the underlying grammar of the law/politics dichotomy.

Many parties employed inflammatory language in the UNGA Emergency Special Sessions and this was carried over to a lesser extent in the advisory pleadings themselves. Chapter One explored some of Koskenniemi's ideas, including his argument that international law cannot be used as a discourse to express the full range of human emotions; 'certain values cannot be translated to the idiom of legal reason.'[140] Did emotional discourses remain within the bounds of legal language and was this discourse understood in the courtroom? This is a question that cannot be answered with any precision, but it would seem from the Court's rejection of the more extreme phrases employed that their use fell on deaf ears; their meaning was lost on the border between 'legal' and 'non-legal' language. Words and expressions such as 'apartheid', 'bantustantisation', 'racial discrimination', 'ghettoisation', Israel as coloniser and its behaviour towards Palestinians

[137] However, it should be noted that Syria's submission was so poorly drafted that occasionally quotation marks were forgotten, but the intention was clear nevertheless.

[138] This is also reflected in one of most widespread English/Arabic dictionaries, *Al-Mawrid*. Under 'I', in the English section, it is only possible to find an entry for the adjective, 'Israeli'. A noun for the place does not exist in this dictionary.

[139] Written Submission of the Organisation of Islamic Conference, 30 January 2004, *supra* n. 112, at 6–7.

[140] M. Koskenniemi, 'Faith, Identity, and the Killing of the Innocent: International Lawyers and Nuclear Weapons' (1997) 10 *Leiden Journal of International Law* 137, at 156. Also see Chapter One, at 38. A particularly emotive outburst came from Cuba: 'It is totally impossible to estimate the degree of mourning imposed on Palestinian families, of pain to the mothers of the Palestinian children who have died as a result of violence exerted by the occupying Power, and the systematic humiliation to which the Palestinian people are subjected.' Written Statement of Cuba, 30 January 2004, http://www.icj-cij.org/docket/files/131/1629.pdf, at 1. Israel's submission was equally impassioned through its outrage over suicide bombings, Written Submission of Israel, *supra* n. 76.

as rendering them in a category of 'sub-humans'[141] were used frequently in the pleadings. However, their use was exclusively by Third World states, particularly Arab states. It is possible to argue that Third World states had a more expansive notion of the role that international law could play in highly contested matters and used a lexicon supportive of such ideas. The action of these states echoes Kritsiotis' supposition about international law's expanding linguistic and participation base: these states were trying to refashion the lexicon and grammar of international law and thus the spheres of its application.[142] Here, Third World states had argued for the Court's jurisdiction along the familiar lines of the matter conforming to a 'legal' issue. Once inside the Peace Palace, Third World states maintained an awareness of legal niceties in toning down some of their rhetoric. However, the debates over word use and occasional flights into inflammatory language challenged clear divisions between law and politics. Given the Court's response, it would also appear that much of this language remained on the margins of international law, or even outside it.

b) *The Use of History*

Because historical narratives are related to a case's substance, it is not surprising that those mainly First World states rejecting the jurisdiction of the Court overlooked matters from the past. Choices about the relationship between international law as well as its ability to confront its own past informed states' support for or opposition to jurisdiction. Although former imperial powers, such as France and Britain, submitted substantial written dossiers, neither revisited their own responsibility in the creation of the Mandate system. Either they were uncomfortable with their record or wanted it left unexamined because they regarded the past as irrelevant to the wall's construction, starting as it did only a few years before the Advisory Opinion proceedings.

As a strategy of legal argument, the First World position can be contrasted with approaches taken by many Arab parties. Although Arab and non-Arab submissions within the Third World grouping were quite evenly balanced, only Arab parties (including the partly-Arab OIC) discussed the historical record in

141 Written Statement of the Organisation of Islamic Conference, *supra* n. 112, at para. 42. This idea of 'sub-human' conjures up imagery of the Holocaust and this device is quite deliberate on the OIC's part. In the preceding section the submission makes a direct connection between the European Holocaust and the role of European guilt in the creation of Israel. The OIC is not so subtly reminding readers that Jews were rendered as sub-human in living memory and it is suggesting that the Jewish state is now behaving in a similar fashion towards Palestinians because of Israeli disregard for fundamental human rights principles. Also see Written Submission, at para. 20.

142 D. Kritsiotis 'The Power of International Law as Language' (1997–1998) 34 *California Western Law Review* 397. Also see Chapter One, at 35.

any detail. This indicates greater Arab sensitivity to the past even though many other Third World states had also experienced colonial rule. For a number of Arab states, participation in the *Wall* Case was an opportunity not only to revisit the past, but also to offer their own narrative about events that are seen to have direct influence today. This desire to rewrite the past also occurs in the other cases, where a Third World desire to decolonise history has been noted. Jordan's introductory comment highlighted the central role of historical narrative in legal proceedings:

> In addressing the issues which arise in these proceedings, Jordan is constrained to note that the substance of the matter which is the subject of these advisory proceedings raises some very major issues of law and fact, particularly the historical facts going back more than 50 years. Those facts shape the legal issues which call for consideration in these advisory proceedings. Moreover, the legal issues themselves are exceedingly complex and in many respects controversial, and require the most careful analysis.[143]

Other Arab parties echoing these sentiments included Palestine, Egypt, Sudan, the Arab League and the OIC. There was also a degree of reliance between Arab states on each other's submissions, such as in the case of Egypt: 'Since various memoranda submitted to the Court by Arab countries and the League of Arab Nations, have elaborately depicted the historical background of this issue, therefore, the Arab Republic of Egypt would like to refer thereto in order to avoid repetition.'[144] This statement suggests shared positions on both the importance of history as well as its content.

All Arab submissions considering the historical record as well as the Court's summary of the past began their analysis at the time of the Mandate, thus indicating consensus about the historical trajectory relevant for the Advisory Opinion. Although both the Court's Opinion and Arab submissions highlighted the Mandate ideals of sacred trust and (eventual) independence, the Court's 'neutral' account of the period obscured colonialist agendas, such as the role of European powers in the Mandatory system and its allocation of responsibility as well as the impact of the Balfour Declaration on Arab inhabitants of Palestine.

A thorough investigation of the historical record was not required of the Court; it was asked to consider the legal consequences arising from recent events. Many Arab submissions devoted considerable attention to history, however, because the past was seen as inextricably linked to the case at hand. Similarly, Judge Elaraby from Egypt distinguished himself from others on the bench through his emphasis on the historical record:

---

143 Written Statement of Jordan, *supra* n. 112, at 6, para. 1.6.

144 Written Statement of the Arab Republic of Egypt, http://www.icj-cij.org/docket/files/131/1547.pdf, at 16.

> An historical survey...may appear as academic, without relevance to the present events. The present is however determined by the accumulation of past event and no reasonable and fair concern for the future can possibly disregard a firm grasp of past events. In particular, when on more than one occasion the rule of law was consistently side-stepped.[145]

In his section on the legal status of the OPT, Judge Elaraby sought to show how the Case for Palestine's non-annexation by Israel could be bolstered by an examination of the historical record;[146] the past and the present were interdependent. Like the deconstruction of the law/politics dichotomy, certain submissions challenged a closely related international legal grammar, the law/history dichotomy.

In their strategic use of history Arab parties and the OIC not only demonstrated their greater reliance on history as a method of international legal argument but also explored some substantive and ongoing themes at work within international law. Neither international law itself nor colonial practice were regarded neutrally; each submission's narrative was flavoured by a normative evaluation of international society's characteristics in the past and the present.

We saw in Chapter One that TWAIL in particular is interested in tracing the ongoing relationship between colonialism and the law. Chimni has categorised TWAIL II as having a more critical and structural approach to international law than TWAIL I.[147] TWAIL II authors are sceptical about international law's capacity to be truly inclusive of non-European, postcolonial peoples. International law is portrayed as structured by its colonial past, and despite Third World participation in the international system as sovereign, independent states, international law continues its colonialist, civilising tendencies in new forms. TWAIL I approaches, however, are generally much more optimistic and are imbued with faith in the potentiality of international law as liberator.

Where the historical record is considered in Arab and OIC submissions, there is a strong resemblance to TWAIL I approaches: international law's relationship with past colonial practices is distinguished from its inclusive and anti-colonialist qualities in the post-1945 world. Many Arab and NAM states described Israel's actions in the Emergency Special Sessions and pleadings as 'colonial', thus trying to demonstrate that colonialism persists in the postcolonial era. However, these accounts also tended to suggest that Israel's actions were exceptional and contrary to international law; as the Court itself pointed out, the prohibition against the acquisition of territory by force is now a fundamental legal doctrine.[148]

---

145 ICJ Reps (2004) (sep. op. Elaraby), at 246, para. 2.1.

146 Ibid., at para. 2.5.

147 B. S. Chimni, 'Towards a Radical Third World Approach to International Law' (2002) 5 *International Centre for Comparative Law and Politics Review* 14.

148 ICJ Reps (2004), at para. 117.

For many Third World states, there was a conviction that international law has qualitatively changed; norms against territorial annexation show that European colonialism is an event of the past, even if it did result in lasting effects on the ground for Palestinian self-determination. Rather than mistrust international law's capacity for liberation, as many TWAIL II writers do, it seems that Arab historical accounts acknowledged the role of history not so much to remind us about European colonialism *per se* but to make us aware of how similar Israeli practices are with events of the past. Thus the recounting of historical events to highlight themes in legal doctrine was a strategic device for a number of Arab states as well as the OIC. We were made aware of the Arab endorsement of international law's vital role – as well as its legitimacy – in international society today; international law contained the capacity to bring colonialism to an end.

6) *The Promise of Doctrine?*

Having surveyed some strategic devices of argument, this final section turns to matters of substance. Third World and First World perspectives are contrasted and compared with the Court's doctrinal position on the issues of conquest, self-determination and human rights norms. The final part of this section comes full circle by looking again at the issue of the Court's jurisdiction to reflect on the role of the ICJ in resolving even the most 'political' of disputes.

The first two interrelated legal principles applicable in the *Wall* Opinion related to the prohibition against the acquisition of territory through the use of force and the right to self-determination. Here, the Court cited Article 2(4) of the UN Charter banning the use of force.[149] It then linked this general prohibition to the action of territorial annexation – conquest – by referring to the Declaration on Principles of International Law concerning Friendly Relations and Co-operation among States (Resolution 2625(XXV) as well as ICJ jurisprudence to confirm that this rule was customary.[150] The Opinion then discussed the right to self-determination also by relying on UNGA Resolution 2625 (XXV), its jurisprudence 'on a number of occasions' and common Article 1 in the two human rights covenants.[151] Later, the Court went on to hold that the right to self-determination was *erga omnes*, but it remained unclear whether

[149] ICJ Reps (2004), at para. 87.

[150] 'Declaration on Principles of International Law Concerning Friendly Relations and Co-operation among States in Accordance with the Charter of the United Nations', 24 October 1970, ICJ Reps (2004), at 171, at para. 87. Also see Part III Introduction, at 185–190.

[151] International Covenant on Civil and Political Rights (1966) 999 UNTS 171; and International Covenant on Economic, Social and Cultural Rights (1966) 993 UNTS 3, ICJ Reps (2004), at 171–172, at para. 88.

the Court was actually referring to the notion of *jus cogens* as well.[152] This area of law remains unclear and many pleadings reflected this confusion.[153]

Uncertainty about norm conflict was also evident in submissions from Third World states. Parties generally gave only cursory consideration to the principles of conquest and self-determination, but they were also referred to as constituting the core of international legal norms for a number of states. For example, Palestine regarded the norm against the acquisition of territory to be so well-accepted that it did not need to cite any authorities in its submission; international law was irrefutable here.[154] Many states specifically relied on UNGA Resolution 2625 (XXV) and some sought to rely on the Kellog-Briand Pact of 1928.[155] Most First World states did not consider the merits of the Case, but even where they did, there was more of a tendency to explore IHL and human rights issues.[156] Norms about conquest and self-determination were of far greater concern to Third World states, including Arab states. For states only recently endowed with full international legal personality could appreciate the primacy of statehood more than their First World counterparts.

How did Third World states approach the question of human rights and their application in the OPT? In its Opinion the Court had discussed the scope for human rights derogation in some detail to hold that Israel was still bound by a number of human rights norms.[157] No state argued that human rights law was inapplicable in the OPT, because in the words of South Africa, such norms apply to the individual and not the state.[158] Commentary on human rights in general was minimal, but the unquestioning way in which parties recognised provisions as applicable in all contexts is significant. For example, Lebanon stated that human rights treaties 'now embody unquestionable universal values'.[159] The OIC echoed

[152] For a discussion about Judge Al-Khasawneh's implicit linking of the two concepts, see I. Scobbie, 'Unchart(er)ed Waters?: Consequences of the Advisory Opinion on the Legal Consequences of the Construction of a Wall in the Occupied Palestinian Territory for the Responsibility of the UN for Palestine' 16 (2005) *European Journal of International Law* 941, at 949.

[153] See for example, Written Statement of Jordan, *supra* n. 112, at paras. 5.37, 5.100.

[154] Written Statement of Palestine, *supra* n. 112, at 156, para. 347.

[155] The Kellogg-Briand Pact, 27 August 1928, 94 LNTS 57. Written Submissions of Cuba, *supra* n. 140; Written Statement of Senegal, http://www.icj-cij.org/docket/files/131/1643.pdf; and Written Statement of Morocco, *supra* n. 109. This agreement was not mentioned by the Court.

[156] For example, see Written Statement of the United Kingdom, 30 January 2004, http://www.icj-cij.org/docket/files/131/1605.pdf, at 23–24; Written Statement of Ireland, 30 January 2004, http://www.icj-cij.org/docket/files/131/1613.pdf, at paras. 2.1–2.14.

[157] ICJ Reps (2004), 192–194, at paras. 136–137.

[158] Written Submission of South Africa, *supra* n. 112, at 22, para. 55.

[159] Written Statement of Lebanon, 30 January 2004, http://www.icj-cij.org/docket/files/131/1563.pdf, 8, para. 37.

these sentiments 'by strongly reaffirming the inalienable and universal nature of human rights regardless of the circumstances in which a particular group finds itself.'[160] Although Gross has argued that the elision of human rights and IHL protections can weaken the position of persons in occupied territories,[161] Third World states overlooked these subtleties in support of 'the more law, the better' approach.

Although debate persists within some quarters about the Western biases inherent in human rights norms,[162] Arab states did not subscribe to such views in their submissions. On the contrary, their positions demonstrate support for such norms and sometimes detailed analysis of how human rights norms apply on the ground. For example, Palestine considered in its written statement the ramifications of the wall's construction on the various human rights of the Palestinian population. It traced the actions of individuals and communities in their daily lives and indicated that human rights guarantees are embedded in all levels of social and political life. In his written statement for Palestine, Professor Vaughan Lowe argued that human rights in the Case fell into two categories: those affected directly by the construction of the wall (such as property seizures), and rights violated as a consequence (such as restrictions on movement). This position indicates how human rights were presented as far more than rigid rules; context and law were interdependent.[163] Thus, Third World states used norms on human rights, self-determination and the prohibition against conquest as a shield in their defence of Palestinian (and postcolonial) interests. The promise of doctrine in the courtroom was embraced, rather than rejected as in the case of most First World states.

Matters of jurisdiction and propriety also reflected normative positions about the role of the ICJ and international law within international society. Overall, most consideration was given by both the Court and the various parties to the matter of jurisdiction. Submissions often relied on very similar material to reach opposite positions. This indicates that international law (especially the jurisprudence of the Court in relation to the exercise of its jurisdiction) was interpreted and applied by actors in different ways to serve different ends. All submissions were informed by a particular reading of the relationship between

---

[160] Written Statement of the Organisation of Islamic Conference, *supra* n. 112, 12, at para. 42.

[161] A. M. Gross, 'Human Proportions: Are Human Rights the Emperor's New Clothes of the International Law of Occupation?' (2007) 18 *European Journal of International Law* 1.

[162] See for example, A. E. Mayer, 'Universal Versus Islamic Human Rights: A Clash of Cultures or a Clash within a Construct?' (1994) 15 *Michigan Journal of International Law* 307; and A. An-Na'im, 'Islam and Human Rights: Beyond the Universality Debate', Proceedings of the 94th Annual Meeting of the American Society of International Law (2000), at 95.

[163] Professor Vaughan Lowe, Oral Statement of Palestine, CR 2004/1, 23 February 2004, at paras. 15–26.

law and politics and, more specifically, how the 'peaceful settlement of this dispute'[164] fitted into such a relationship. In the pleadings, those parties favouring the Court's jurisdiction also tended to be more supportive of international law's primary role in resolving international disputes.[165] Both positions also acknowledged current diplomatic efforts in relation to the Road Map. However, there were strong differences over the relationship between the advisory function of the Court and negotiations – that is, law and politics. Submissions from both perspectives highlighted their support for negotiations and also detailed their direct role in such efforts.[166]

Like many First World states, Arab states have participated in negotiations to solve the Arab-Israeli conflict, but they did not see negotiations as precluding international law's role. Instead, Arab submissions embraced negotiations within the wider context of international law, where the Advisory Opinion was one important legal device in advancing the aim of Israeli compliance with international legal principles. Thus international law and international politics were not regarded as opposites but as mutually interdependent forces within international society.

First World states, on the other hand, typically sought to construct a clear line (or wall) between political, diplomatic processes and international law. The starkest example of this position was provided by the US, which hardly mentioned international law at all. Instead, detailed discussion about diplomatic efforts demonstrated how international law was irrelevant and unhelpful in relation to the wall's construction and the Arab-Israeli conflict in general.[167] European positions were more nuanced in their approach to the Advisory Opinion. EU states voted *en masse* for Resolution ES 10/13 calling on Israel to stop its construction of the wall. However, even though these legal ramifications were clear, the process of seeking Israeli compliance was seen as a political one.[168] A request

---

164 Professor Sorel, Oral Statement of Belize, CR 2004/3, at 14.

165 As embodied in the Arab League's statement: 'The current request means the General Assembly has recognised the importance of the role of law in the solution of the problem.' Professor Bothe, Oral Statement of the League of Arab States, CR 2004/5, at 22.

166 For example, both Egypt and Saudi Arabia draw attention to their efforts in previous negotiations to demonstrate that their support for the Advisory Opinion is not about taking sides; they are supportive of both legal and political processes and think that they can rely on each other to an extent. Written Submission of Egypt, *supra* n. 144, at 3; and Oral Statement of Saudi Arabia, CR 2004/2, p. 46, at para. 16.

167 Written Statement of the United States of America, http://www.icj-cij.org/docket/files/131/1583.pdf.

168 Written Submission of Germany, http://www.icj-cij.org/docket/files/131/1599.pdf, p. 3; Written Statement of the Netherlands, http://www.icj-cij.org/docket/files/131/1627.pdf; Written Statement of Spain, http://www.icj-cij.org/docket/files/131/1633.pdf; and Written Statement of Italy, *supra* n. 134.

for an Advisory Opinion was inappropriate, requiring as it would that the Court step into political territory.

Some First World states were more supportive of the Court's wider role. For example, although it was part of the EU bloc, France's submission wavered in its support for an Advisory Opinion. It discussed substantive issues of IHL and human rights and deferred responsibility by arguing that questions of jurisdiction should be left to the Court.[169] Other EU states, such as Ireland, Cyprus and Malta were less forthright in their positions, but all supported the Advisory Opinion request and the Court.[170] Although Switzerland had abstained in the UNGA request for an Advisory Opinion, it shifted its position once the resolution was passed; it deferred to the will of the international community as embodied in the UNGA.[171] Similar motivations informed Sweden's submission in support of the Opinion, despite its EU membership.[172] From their brief statements on the matter, it would seem that First World states supportive of the Court's jurisdiction respected the Court as an institution of international law. Also, the status of the UNGA was regarded as significant and was seen as being able to straddle the political and legal spheres of international life. In the words of Syria, such First World states also saw the UNGA Emergency Special Session as 'an expression of the international community'.[173]

Two academic perspectives about the relative weight to ascribe to ICJ Advisory Opinions illustrate First and Third World perspectives about the nature of international society and international law's place within it. On the one hand, Pomerance criticises the Court's decision to exercise its jurisdiction in the *Wall* opinion. She argues that the Court increasingly has come to act under a 'duty-to-cooperate' because of its institutional role as the principal judicial organ of the UN.[174] Pomerance's analysis tries to limit the effect of the Court and the UN more generally in international life: there should be no analogy made between the ICJ and international law or the UN and international society. The ICJ has become a UN Court (rather than a World Court) administering UN law (rather than international law).[175] Falk, on the other hand, tends to concur with the

---

[169] Written Submission of France, http://www.icj-cij.org/docket/files/131/1591.pdf, at 17, para. 74.

[170] Written Statement of Ireland, *supra* n. 156; Written Statement of Malta, http://www.icj-cij.org/docket/files/131/1623.pdf; Written Statement of Cyprus, http://www.icj-cij.org/docket/files/131/1617.pdf.

[171] Written Submission of Switzerland, http://www.icj-cij.org/docket/files/131/1577.pdf, at paras. 1–6.

[172] Written Statement of Sweden, http://www.icj-cij.org/docket/files/131/1631.pdf.

[173] Written Submission of Syria, *supra* n. 113, at 2.

[174] M. Pomerance, 'The ICJ's Advisory Opinion and the Crumbling Wall between the Political and the Judicial' (2005) 99 *American Journal of International Law* 26, at 30.

[175] Ibid., at 41.

majority of Third World submissions in support of jurisdiction: the UN request for an Advisory Opinion was significant and should be respected. Rather than see the UN in narrow terms like Pomerance, Falk reminds us that it is 'the embodiment of an inchoate organized international community.'[176] Although a number of First World submissions relied on the case of *Eastern Carelia* to argue that jurisdiction should be declined, Falk reminds us that there was not the same relationship between the PCIJ and the League of Nations as is the case with the UN and the ICJ.[177] From the UN Charter, '"[j]udicial" needs to be interpreted to encompass not only...contentious disputes...but also the role of the Court in declaring and developing international law within the scope of the operations of the UN system.'[178] Professor Crawford's oral statement for Palestine supported these sentiments, when he argued that the Court does 'not give just another political opinion'.[179] Instead, it offers a legal perspective sufficiently autonomous and distinct from international political life to act as an 'authoritative'[180] source of regulation and legitimacy.[181]

Submissions seeking the Court's jurisdiction are indicative of broader faith and reliance on not only the ICJ but also international law itself. Various Third World submissions also made a connection between the UN's long history of involvement with the Palestinian cause and self-determination more generally to advance their claims about the central role of its principal judicial organ, the ICJ. Arab states in particular regarded the Case as of singular importance in affirming their faith in international law. Saudi Arabia was optimistic about the effects of an opinion in quelling violence on both sides, stating that an opinion 'may give hope that the rule of law will be respected.'[182] For Palestine, the stakes were much higher. Mr. Al-Kidwa, Palestine's representative at the UN, and its first speaker in the pleadings, stated that if the wall's construction and self-determination's denial continued, it would 'destroy [the Palestinians'] faith

---

176 Falk, *supra* n. 88, at 46, footnote 21.

177 Ibid., at 46. Palestine also distinguished the ICJ from the PCIJ by arguing that the ICJ is more explicitly connected to the UN as its principal judicial organ. Written Statement of Palestine, *supra* n. 112, at paras. 60–61.

178 Falk, ibid., at 48. Madagascar also advocated greater use of the ICJ advisory function: 'Madagascar deplores the under-exploitation of the invaluable resource represented by the advisory procedure.' Mr. Alfred Rambeloson, Oral Pleading of Madagascar, CR 2004/4, at 20.

179 Professor Crawford, Oral Statement of Palestine, CR 2004/1, at 33, para. 33.

180 Mr. Albar, Oral Statement of Malaysia, CR 2004/4, at 23.

181 Belize regarded the ICJ and international law in similar terms: 'The law is clearly a reflection of politics and its role as a social regulator is rooted in a reality that is at once political, economic and social, since it would otherwise be nothing. The Court is therefore acting quite logically when it detaches the legal aspects from their broader context, as it must do in the present case.' Professor Sorel, Oral Pleading of Belize, CR 2004/3, at 17, para. 13.

182 Ambasador Shobokshi, Oral Statement of Saudi Arabia, CR 2004/2, at 54.

in the rule of international law and the international community's ability to uphold it in the face of such grievous violations.'[183] Palestine's position and its support by Arab states required the ICJ, the UN and international law to play central roles in the particular case pertaining to the wall, as well as the Arab-Israeli conflict. As was the case relating to their concern about the protection of Holy Sites in the OPT,[184] Arab states regarded the Advisory Opinion as being about more than legal doctrine or political negotiations; the Case was a test of their faith in international law itself.

7) *Conclusion*

This chapter has shown that states and IGOs can operate in legal pleadings with very different perspectives about the strategic qualities of international law as well as its substantive content. The ways in which language was used provided some indication about the relative importance states placed on emotion and legal terminology. I have shown in this chapter that Third World, and especially Arab, states were more comfortable in stretching the lexicon of international law across the boundaries of standard 'neutral', non-emotional discourse. This was reinforced by the way in which such states spoke openly about their trust in international law; international law was about more than legal doctrine, it also required a level of faith from the participants in the proceedings. The scope of international law was extended further in the accounts of various Arab submissions and the Separate Opinion of Judge Elaraby. Arab sensitivities about the relevance of history to present legal matters provided a more contextual narrative about the Case. Images of colonialism in the past and the present also tended to reinforce TWAIL I perspectives, which are supportive of the emancipatory potential of modern international law for non-European peoples.

The ways in which parties participated in the Case and the positions taken on the jurisdiction of the Court demonstrated the relative respect such states placed not only in the ICJ but also, in international law. Third World states

[183] Mr. Al-Kidwa, Oral Statement of Palestine, CR 2004/1, at 24.

[184] Arab states in particular as well as some other submissions highlighted the importance of preserving Christian, Jewish and Muslim Holy Sites for all worshippers in Jerusalem. For example, see Sir Arthur Watts, Oral Statement of Jordan, CR 2004/4, at 56, para. 8; Written Submission of Palestine, *supra* n. 112, at 74, para. 174; Written Submission of Morocco, *supra* n. 109, at 8; Oral Statement of Saudi Arabia, CR 2004/2, at 58–59, para. 55; Written Submission of Sweden, *supra* n. 172, at para. 11; Oral Statement of Bangladesh, CR 2004/2, at 64; Oral Statement of the League of Arab States, CR 2004/5, at 31. The Court (in relative terms) devoted a lot of attention to this issue in its judgment as well: ICJ Reps (2004), at 188–189, para. 129.

tended to demonstrate greater reverence for the Court and its formal function. At the same time, however, they supported the work of the UNGA and viewed the resolution requesting an Advisory Opinion as indicative of international public opinion. Thus the spheres of international politics and international law were distinguished in such submissions but were also seen as interdependent and inclusive of Third World states. For First World states unsupportive of the jurisdiction of the Court, international law tended to garner more formal engagement, as evidenced by less inflammatory language and requests for the Court to decline its jurisdiction. International law was regarded as being of only limited use in international life. The broader goals discussed by Third World states, such as self-determination and an end to colonialism, were overlooked in most First World submissions, and negotiations were contrasted with international law to indicate a clear demarcation between legal and political spheres.

Reactions to the *Wall* Opinion were diverse and varied. Once the Opinion was handed down, Palestine and Israel maintained their earlier positions about the value of the ICJ and international law in resolving the conflict. According to Palestine's representative at the UN

> As for the Palestinian people, the advisory opinion has been having a positive – not a negative – impact on Palestinian society. People are seeing that international law can bring them justice. As a result, the law and compliance with it will take in even more importance and prominence within this society. This will be instrumental in developing and ingraining a culture of respect for the law... this advisory opinion provides a tremendous lesson on the primacy of the law and its rules, and everyone, especially in the region, must see this.[185]

Israel's representative, on the other hand, argued that

> a disservice was done by the [General] Assembly not just to the International Court of Justice but to the balanced and non-selective application of the rule of law... The reputation and credibility of international judicial institutions are the worse for it[186]

The Court negotiated a path through these positions to render its judgment, which included as much as it omitted. As in the case of Third World submissions, the ICJ showed that international law could play a role in even the most divisive of issues. To bolster its jurisdiction as well as its contribution to the conflict, however, the Court retreated behind doctrinal defences. In its Opinion the Court employed familiar devices of the law/politics dichotomy: the dispute

[185] Mr. Al-Kidwa, UN Observer of Palestine, UN GA Emergency Special Session, 24th mtg (16th July, 2004), UN Doc A/ES-10, PV.24, at 9.

[186] Mr. Gillerman, UN representative of Israel, UN GA Emergency Special Session, 27th mtg (20th July, 2004), UN Doc A/ES-10/PV.27, at 7.

was sufficiently legal, norm conflict was downplayed, language was 'neutral' and historical legacies were reduced to their most minimal and least political form.

Postcolonial states were comfortable operating in this discursive environment, but their strategic and substantive legal grammars did not simply mimic the tone of the Court. Instead, Third World, and especially Arab, states used the Advisory Opinion to expand the Court's legal lexicon. These states maintained a faith in international law through the ICJ advisory jurisdiction while also placing the proceedings in a broader context by resorting to historical narratives and emotive discourse. The Court did not respond to most of these devices, but it is significant that they were used. More noteworthy was the fact that both the Court and Third World states showed that international law could play a role in the conflict. Agreement over the centrality of self-determination and conquest indicated that both postcolonial states and the Court were in sympathy about the territorial confines of contemporary international law. International legal personality was the *sina qua non* for Third World states, who in coming to the Peace Palace confirmed their support and acceptance for the Court and much of the law it applied. In contrast to the dissatisfaction anticipated from the Court's majority judgment in the *Qatar/Bahrain* dispute, it is anticipated that many Third World states are only now beginning to sense a 'bitter taste' from events occurring *outside* of the courtroom.[187] The wall's construction continues unabated and with it, faith in a postcolonial law is shaken.

[187] Here, I am referring to the minority judgment's concern about Bahrain's and Qatar's response to the Court's 2001 ruling. See Chapter Four, at 180.

Conclusion

ICJ territorial adjudication is about more than geographical demarcation; it is also an exercise in discursive boundary-drawing. The book has highlighted how states and members of the Court engage in an ongoing dialogue about the boundaries of law and its linguistic limitations. On entering the Court's discursive domain, states bring a number of expectations and hopes about international law. To be heard, though, these aspirations have to be translated into a particular language, with its own grammar and lexicon. The cases have shown that international law contains some linguistic diversity, perhaps allowing us to speak of international legal *dialects*. As illustrated by the Arabic language with its multitude of distinctive articulations, understanding a range of dialects requires sophisticated linguistic capacities. Native speakers of Arabic can understand a range of local lexicons and syntactical forms, but meanings are not always clear. In relation both to Arabic and international law, we can ask, when are the boundaries between dialect and language crossed? When is it necessary to employ a translator? More importantly, can concepts and sensibilities be articulated across linguistic divides?

Koskenniemi's idea about the silences of international law is relevant here. International law cannot speak of everything and for everyone;[1] it is a limited and limiting discourse. For the International Court of Justice hearing territorial claims in a postcolonial era, this is of fundamental importance. 'New' states entering the Court are required to speak a pre-established language structured through a radical division between law and politics and between the past and the present. Some of the arguments employed on behalf of Arab states have destabilised dominant approaches to international law, both through strategic and substantive devices. Here, I revisit some of these devices to answer my two central research questions.

The first research question I asked was, 'what are the structures of legal argument that emerge in ICJ territorial disputes involving Arab states?' Broadly, these patterns were explored through the lenses of strategic and substantive devices. These two devices are not mutually distinct, however. They are both informed

[1] M. Koskenniemi, 'Faith, Identity, and the Killing of the Innocent: International Lawyers and Nuclear Weapons' (1997) 10 *Leiden Journal of International Law* 137; and M. Koskenniemi 'The Silence of Law/The Voice of Justice', L. Boisson de Chazournes & P. Sands (eds.), *International Law, the International Court of Justice and Nuclear Weapons* (Cambridge: Cambridge University Press, 1999), 488–510.

by the law/politics dichotomy, which is the main grammar used in international legal discourse. We saw in Chapter One that critical approaches to international law have shown how mainstream accounts of international law, either in the academy or adjudicative bodies, have tried to quarantine law from the indeterminacy of politics. If doctrine can be distinguished from political choice, then its neutrality and legitimacy is easier to preserve. Indeterminacy, however, lies at the heart of the international legal project, which does not gain its structure and stability through normative rules; rather, international law as language is shaped through a combination of institutional biases, legal grammars, and a lexicon built from European experiences of authority over territory.

Throughout the four cases, variations on the law/politics dichotomy shaped the way parties engaged with the Court. In discussions about the Court's jurisdictional role, for example, it was important to portray the ICJ as separate from the wider context of the case at hand. Questions about the 'legal' nature of a case are especially important in advisory opinions, and the *Western Sahara* Case and the *Wall* Case illustrated a variety of ways of defining 'legal' disputes. Both cases highlighted how Third World states are more comfortable with introducing contextual matters before the Court. These broader considerations, however, did not affect the Court's 'legal' role, because many of these states also displayed a profound faith in the promise of doctrine. Particularly in the *Wall* Case, postcolonial states seized upon international legal principles in an effort to strengthen their quest for Palestinian selfhood and statehood within the international legal community. In the *Wall* pleadings many Third World states were content to adopt TWAIL I-like postures, supportive of international law's decolonising reach. Yet we saw that such gestures sometimes sat uncomfortably with ongoing structural realities of legal speech that rarely permits detailed considerations of the colonial past and thus, the colonial present. In trying to cling to the promise of international law, these states only reinforced the limited confines in which international legal discourse and adjudication can operate.

The advisory opinions also allowed a comparison of the argumentative registers used by the parties. Typically, Third World states presented their claims in more emotive and inflammatory language than their First World counterparts. Perhaps the tenor of such arguments was not heard by the Court, because we saw that for much of the time the bench did not engage with such rhetorical flushes. The Court could not respond to all of the needs of these states and it had to retreat to the familiar territory of constrained, neutral language. In the case of the *Wall* Opinion, we could sense that the Court was eager to provide a response to the claims of mostly Third World states. Within the limits set by the request by the UNGA, the Court affirmed that law can play a role even in the most contentious of cases. To preserve the integrity of the Court and the law it applies, however, the Court also showed us that deference to the law/politics dichotomy is vital.

States toned down their language before the bench in invoking their cause of law as a weapon to secure Palestinian self-determination.

Questioning the boundaries of law was a constant motif in Chapters Three, Four and Five, where an examination of territorial claims necessitated a journey into the murky practices of colonial domination. Both Libya in Chapter Three as well as Qatar in Chapter Four revealed a record of European intimidation and bias in the construction of treaties and resulting boundaries. These states provided an opportunity for the Court to re-evaluate the 'legal' effects of such 'political' events. Treaties created in the context of coercion or arbitral awards tainted by the pursuit of petroleum profits undermined the distinction between law and politics. These narratives also questioned the legitimacy of a postcolonial legal order that has rarely delved into its own past. On both occasions, the Court indicated that such probing of the past was outside its remit. Here the Court was caught in a double bind. Should it acknowledge the way politics had infused colonial practice to lend greater legitimacy to certain Third World claims and thus undermine law's determinacy? Or should the law/politics dichotomy be maintained by depicting colonial acts as simple confirmations of doctrine, thereby weakening the legitimacy of the law for Third World states trying to rewrite its past? We saw time and again that the Court opted for the latter option, whose effects were not confined to the past. By confirming colonial practices, the Court also revealed a law less than universal and one that struggles to translate non-European experiences during and after colonialism.

The Court's denial of historical complexity was a constant throughout the cases, emphasising that the grammars of argument in territorial adjudication require constructions of a past supportive of dominant images of contemporary international law. Yet the Peace Palace witnessed conflicting accounts about the legacies of colonialism as well as the tools of historical analysis. For example, while states like Spain in Chapter Five and Chad in Chapter Three suggested that historical narration was an uncomplicated affair, other states argued that the selection of particular documents and maps and their interpretation produced conflicting historical perspectives. States with minimal archival material to bolster their case faced a double bind: should they rely on materials drawn up in the interests of their former colonisers? Or should they try to convince the Court of their claims in a manner radically different from ICJ institutional conventions? Third World states often had no choice but to use material of their former colonisers, but it was surprising how this material was not scrutinised more rigorously by both the bench and the bar. Historical narratives had to be simplified for the task of rendering legal statements, and often this entailed uncritical reliance on European, as well as Ottoman, archival material.

The Court was not capable of adjudicating these historical nuances, but when it did enter the annals of history it displayed an inability to grapple with the contingencies of choice. Further, where the Court was forced to deliberate on contrasting historical accounts, it generally favoured colonial discourses. We saw this most explicitly in relation to the classification of 'colonial protectorates' in the *Cameroon/Nigeria* Case discussed in the introduction to Part II.[2] There, the Court adopted a European, colonial interpretation of legal title to dismiss the validity of African personality; the politics of colonialism was favoured over a Pandora's Box of territorial instability and legal uncertainty. This policy choice, also known as *uti possidetis juris*, has come to dominate African territorial cases, but its reception has been less than total in the Arab world. Regardless of regional practices, however, the Court's jurisprudence has consistently shown that *uti possidetis* is the dominant norm to apply in postcolonial territorial matters, and the Court's motivations are explicable. Both African elites and the majority of international lawyers regard colonial lines across the continent as the price to be paid for more legitimate reappraisals of indigenous effective control and its clash with former colonisers.

Historical narratives also supported positions about the substantive content of international law. Perhaps the most important aim of historical narration for Third World states was based on a desire to decolonise international law. By challenging European accounts of international law, these states were not trying to subvert international law; rather, they were trying to strengthen it. Third World submissions like those of Algeria's in *Western Sahara*, Qatar's in *Qatar/Bahrain* and Libya's in *Libya/Chad* all tried to incorporate Arab-Islamic traditions into the fabric of international law. By detailing cultural particularities, these states could boost international law's universal reach. If non-European modes of rule were recognised by the Court, territorial adjudication could expand the lexicon of international law. We saw, however, that the Court was reluctant to accept these overtures because they would have threatened its foundational grammar of the law/politics dichotomy in revealing international law's contingent past. Operating in a discourse framed largely by European statehood, the Court had to limit the legal effects of such arguments, and in so doing, it affirmed the centrality of European experiences in international law's past *and* present configurations. The rich Arab record provided the Court with a chance to extend international law's cultural boundaries, but we have seen that it was only prepared to take a few tentative steps into the Sahara or swim a few strokes off the shores of the Gulf.

Many would not be surprised by these findings, as they can be read to support narratives explored in Chapter One about increasing Third World participation in ICJ proceedings and a corresponding acceptance of international rules. Third World states have willingly brought their claims to the Court cognisant of its

[2] *Land and Maritime Boundary between Cameroon and Nigeria (Cameroon/Nigeria; Equatorial Guinea Intervening)* (2002) ICJ Reps, p. 303, discussed at 107–108.

limited cultural and historical capacities. The story, however, is more complex. Each case demonstrated that Third World states both acknowledged ICJ conventions and also tried to stretch the boundaries of international law through a number of devices. Substantively, non-European approaches to authority challenged dominant European models, but, time and again, the Court rejected the implications of historical revision. Where states like Chad sought stable boundaries, it was 'paradoxically required by the circumstances to espouse some particularly unacceptable propositions of colonialist discourse.'[3] These are the words of Judge Rezek in his declaration from the *Bakassi Peninsula* Case, but the idea is apt here for the way in which it encapsulates the postcolonial paradox. Third World states through their legal counsel seek to secure their statehood, but they must do so in a discourse that is not of their own making.

If we return to debates about reasons for the Court's increased docket and Third World participation, the findings of Chapter Six contrast with those in the other cases. In Chapter One, I was sceptical about equating increased Third World participation with wholescale acceptance and approval of both the ICJ and international law. I suggested that Third World participation must be understood discursively before trying to explain this phenomenon. Chapters Three, Four and Five have all suggested that Third World participation has come at a price: in many instances colonial legacies have been reinforced so that particular renderings of the past will have significant effects into the future. Perhaps some postcolonial states, like Chad, will be pleased with such an outcome, but from the way the Court ignored so much of colonialism's dark sides, it is doubtful that a service was rendered in enhancing international law's wider legitimacy. Perhaps litigation is a useful resource and Third World states have now a wealth of evidence to show them what the likely results of territorial adjudication would be: certainty and doctrine as triumphant over historical redress. Unprecedented Third World participation in the *Wall* Opinion could be construed as acceptance on the part of much of the postcolonial world, indicating that international law's strengths *and* weaknesses are now recognised and embraced. In their optimism and faith in the ICJ process, these Third World states followed closely in the footsteps of TWAIL I scholars eager to reap the rewards of membership within international society. Yet the other cases have shown us that ICJ litigation and international legal language can only speak of certain experiences and deliver limited outcomes.

These observations allow us to answer my second research question, which asked, 'what do these structures of legal argument reveal about the scope for universalising the discourse of international law?' There is no simple answer to this question because of the tension between inclusion and exclusion within inter-

[3] *(Cameroon/Nigeria; Equatorial Guinea Intervening)* (2002) ICJ Reps (sep. op. Rezek), at 489.

national legal discourse. We have seen that the Peace Palace doors are now open for all states to enter, but at what financial cost, under which rules and in whose language? Third World states seeking to affirm their statehood via adjudication through a language forged in the crucible of colonialism can try to expand the cultural reach of international law, and thus its universalism, but such practices also reveal the limits of inclusion. Adjudicative argument is significant, but it is not enough to generate linguistic renewal *per se* and we have seen that rarely was the Court willing or able to understand many of the dialects used in the Peace Palace. Non-European histories and experiences were discussed, but were usually rejected by the Court through its silence. The cases have suggested that only the narrowest margin of linguistic change is permitted in most instances, but that at least a number of minority opinions and Third World states were willing to push the boundaries of international legal language. Thus the scope for universalising international law remains a limited one.

I have shown in this book that mapping legal grammars in ICJ adjudication is a valuable device in probing linguistic patterns of the discipline. A discursive reading of Arab territorial disputes highlights how critical approaches provide useful tools for interrogating both legal speech and its silences. Although this research has revealed that legal discourse has a constricted lexicon and grammar, it has also shown that speech is never static. Thus, international law contains within it many dialects with their nascent grammars and lexicons awaiting our appraisal and engagement. We just need to listen.

Glossary

À titre de souverain (Fr.): those acts reflecting the exercise of sovereign power.
Accord cadre (Fr.): framework agreement.
Ahdname (Turk.): decree of the sulṭan.
Ahl al-ḥall wa'l-'aqd (Ar.) [the people of loosening and binding]: the group of electors of the khalīfa.
Ahl al-kitāb (Ar.) [people of the book, or *dhimmīs*]: non-Muslims believing in God: Christians, Jews, Sabians and Zoroastrians.
Al-'arabiyya al-qawmiyya (Ar.): pan-Arabism.
Al-khulafā' al-rāshidūn: (Ar.) [the rightly guided Caliphs]: Abū Bakr, 'Umr, 'Uthmān, 'Alī, who ruled in turn after the Prophet's death in 632. This period is known as *'asr al-sā'ada* (the Era of Felicity).
Al-sharq al-awsaṭ (Ar.) [The Middle East], a term also used regularly in Arabic parlance.
Al-umma al-arabiyya (Ar.): the Arab nation.
Amān: (Ar.): protection of life, property and freedom often applying as a writ of safe conduct for envoys and foreigners in Muslim lands.
'aqd al-bay'a (Ar.): contract of allegiance to the caliph or sulṭan.
Bai'a (Ar.): oath of allegiance, e.g. for far-flung tribes accepting the spiritual oversight of the Sulṭan of Morocco.
Bled al-makhzen (Ar.): lands of the government (or literally, storehouse). This term was used in the *Western Saharan* Advisory Opinion to distinguish between those lands over which the Sulṭan of Morocco had direct control (*bled al-makhzen* and those he did not, *bled al-siba*).
Bled al-siba (Ar.): lands of dissidence. This term was used to describe peripheral areas of the Moroccan Sulṭan's rule before colonialism, when ties of allegiance through religion existed rather than any real territorial control.
Caid (Ar.): an administrative official of a tribe appointed by the sulṭan, e.g. in Western Sahara.
Compromis (Fr.): an agreement by which states in dispute may agree to take that dispute to the ICJ.
Dār al-ḥarb (Ar.): land of war, or that part of the world not under Muslim rule.
Dār al-islām (Ar.): land of peace, or that part of the world under Muslim rule.
Dār al-ṣulḥ (Ar.): land of reconciliation or treaty between Muslim and non-Muslim powers.
Dawla (Ar.): state.
De lege ferenda (Lat.): law as it should be.
De lege lata (Lat.): law as it currently stands.
Dhimma (Ar.): where non-Muslims accept Muslim rule in exchange for protection and the payment of a poll tax (*jizya*). Such an agreement cannot be concluded with apostates.
Dirah (Ar.): territory within which a tribe moves.
Dispositif (Fr.): operative paragraph(s) of a judgment.
Effectivités (Fr.): state activities of a sovereign kind.
Erga omnes (Lat.) [against all]: rules applicable and binding on all states regardless of consent. For example, the prohibition on genocide is binding on all states whether or not they are party to conventions detailing its prohibition.
Ex iniuria non oritur jus (Lat.): an illegal act cannot produce legal rights.

Fiqh: (Ar.) ['understanding']: the science of Muslim law.

Forum prorogatum (Lat.)*:* where state parties impliedly consent to the jurisdiction of the ICJ for a specific dispute.

Ḥadīth (Ar.): collections of the sayings of the Prophet, one of the sources of Islamic law.

Ḥajj (Ar.): the annual pilgrimage to Mecca. One of the five obligations for a Muslim, along with prayer, fasting during Ramaḍān, the *shahāda* (the profession of faith in Allah and his prophet, Muhammed), and *zakāt*, or charity.

Ḥarbī (Ar.): a person from *dār al-ḥarb*.

Hudna (Ar.): meaning truce or armistice, often in relation to 10-year truces concluded between Muslim and non-Muslim powers.

*Ijmā*ʿ (Ar.): one of the four sources of *sharīʿa*, based on the consensus of legal/religious scholars.

Ijtihād (Ar.): independent human reasoning. This phase in the development of legal doctrine formally ended in the tenth century.

Imām (Ar.): teacher, or the title of a scholar adept in Islamic studies.

In personam (Lat.): relating to jurisdiction over an individual person.

Intifāḍa (Ar.): shaking off, uprising. Usually associated with two episodes of Palestinian resistance against Israel's occupation of the West Bank and the Gaza Strip, which began in 1987 and 2000.

Jihād: (Ar.): literally meaning struggle, used to refer to the waging of Muslim war throughout *dār al-ḥarb.*

Jizya: (Ar.) poll tax imposed on *dhimmīs*, instead of *zakat* and/or military service, expected of able-bodied Muslim males.

Jus ad bellum (Lat.): rights to wage war, or 'just war'.

Jus cogens (Lat.) [compelling law]: peremptory norms of general international law.

Jus in bello (Lat.): the rules applicable once hostilities have commenced.

Jus inter gentes (Lat.): law between nations, i.e. international law.

Jus naturale (Lat.): natural law.

Kaimakam: (Turk.) governor of a *kaza*.

Kaza: (Turk.) Ottoman administrative district, a unit smaller than a *sanjak*.

khādim al-ḥaramayn al-sharīfayn (Ar.) [servant of the two holy shrines]: A title given to the Caliph as overseer of Mecca and Medina.

Khalīfat rasūl allāh (Ar.): successor of the messenger of God. The full title bestowed on a *khalīfa* by Sunnis.

Kharaj (Ar.): land tax imposed in Muslim lands on *dhimmīs*.

Madhhab (Ar.): jurisprudential school of Islamic fiqh: Malikī, Shāfiʿī, Ḥanbalī, Ḥanafī.

Mujtahid (Ar.): a practitioner of *ijtihād*, or independent reasoning.

mustaʾmin (Ar.): protected person, referring to non-Muslims such as traders and ambassadors who were afforded basic rights and protections within *dār al-islām*.

Opinio iuris (Lat.): behaviour demonstrating a sense of legal obligation; this is one of the sources of customary international law.

Pacta sunt servanda (Lat.): [agreements must be honoured].

Qawm (Ar.): people.

Qawmiyya (Ar.): pan-Arabism, or Arab nationalism.

Qiyas (Ar.): reasoning by analogy from existing principles. This is one of the four sources of the *sharīʿa*.

Qurʾān (Ar.) ['the recitation']: the central text of Islam, believed to be the word of God, revealed to his Prophet and written down after Muhammed's death in 632.

Res communis (Lat.): a thing belonging to all and therefore not capable of being placed under state sovereignty, such as the high seas and outer space.

Res judicata (Lat.) [a thing that has been judged]: The rule refers to the practice whereby arbitral bodies do not consider a case that has already been determined by another arbitral body.
Res nullius (Lat.): things or land not under the territorial sovereignty of a state, but able to be so (in contrast with *res communis*).
Res sic stantibus (Lat.) [things standing so, or remaining the same]: agreements entered into on the basis that circumstances will remain unchanged.
Sanjak (or, *sancak*) (Turk.): an Ottoman subprovince.
Sharīʿa (Ar.) [path to water]: Islamic law.
Sheikh (Ar.): elder man of a tribe; an Islamic authority.
Shīʿa: (Ar.): referring to those Muslims who saw Muhammed's rule being continued through ʿAlī and his descendents. Shīʿas are the second largest group within the Muslim world after Sunnis.
Siyar (Ar.) [the conduct of rulers]: The system of international law developed by Muslim states/ empires for their relations with non-Muslim powers.
Sulṭan (Ar.) [deriving from the word for power]: title of a political ruler in contrast to a religious leader or teacher, *Imām*.
Sunna: (Ar.) [manner of acting; rule of conduct; mode of life]: lessons learned from the life of the Prophet, mainly through the *ḥadīth*. It is one of the four sources of law.
Sunni: (Ar.): deriving from the word *sunna*, meaning words or actions or the example of the Prophet. Sunnis followed Abu Bakr and are the vast majority of Muslims today.
Tanzimat (Turk.): Generally used to refer to the period between 1839–1876 when the Ottoman Empire implemented a number of reforms.
Taqlīd (Ar.) [imitation]: marks the end of the official period of *ijtihād* in the tenth century whereby Muslims were expected to respect the authority of legal scholars of past generations – the personal interpretation of sources was henceforth forbidden.
Terra nullius (Lat.): land belonging to no-one and available to be claimed by a sovereign power.
Travaux préparatoires (Fr.): Preparatory work; the preliminary drafts, minutes, conferences etc. contributing to the final draft of a treaty.
Umma (Ar.): this can be translated as community or nation, but it always refers to the community of Muslims and its boundaries are not defined by territory or state rule, but belief.
Uti possedetis juris (Lat.; Roman Law) [as you possess]: A decree of the Praetor that the ownership of property in question should remain in possession of the person. In international law, it is the idea that old administrative boundaries will become international boundaries when a political subdivision achieves independence. Based on the Latin phrase: *uti possidetis, ita possideatis* (as you possess, so may you possess).
Vali (Turk.): administrative ruler of a *vilayet*.
Vilayet (Turk.): largest administrative unit within the Ottoman Empire.
Watan (Ar.): nation.
Wataniyya (Ar.): nationalism.
Zāwiyya (Ar.) [corner]: used in the Maghreb as the name of a religious school. The term was used in the *Libya/Chad* case in relation to the Senūsī religious order's outposts in the Sahara.

Bibliography

Primary Sources

Bahrain, *Case Concerning Maritime Delimitation and Territorial Questions between Qatar and Bahrain (Qatar/Bahrain)*, Counter-Memorial Submitted by the State of Bahrain, Questions of Jurisdiction and Admissibility, 3 vols., 1992.

Bahrain, *Case Concerning Maritime Delimitation and Territorial Questions between Qatar and Bahrain (Qatar/Bahrain)*, Rejoinder Submitted by the State of Bahrain, Questions of Jurisdiction and Admissibility, 1992.

Bahrain, *Case Concerning Maritime Delimitation and Territorial Questions between Qatar and Bahrain (Qatar/Bahrain)*, Memorial Submitted by the State of Bahrain (Merits), 7 vols., 1996.

Bahrain, *Case Concerning Maritime Delimitation and Territorial Questions between Qatar and Bahrain (Qatar/Bahrain)*, Counter-Memorial Submitted by the State of Bahrain (Merits), 3 vols., 1997.

Bahrain, *Case Concerning Maritime Delimitation and Territorial Questions between Qatar and Bahrain (Qatar/Bahrain)*, Reply Submitted by the State of Bahrain (Merits), 2 vols., 1999.

Chad, *Case Concerning the Territorial Dispute (Libyan Arab Jamahiriya/Chad)*, Memorial Submitted by the Republic of Chad, 6 vols., 1991.

Chad, *Case Concerning the Territorial Dispute (Libyan Arab Jamahiriya/Chad)*, Counter-Memorial Submitted by the Republic of Chad, 4 vols., 1992.

Chad, *Case Concerning the Territorial Dispute (Libyan Arab Jamahiriya/Chad)*, Reply Submitted by the Republic of Chad, 3 vols., 1992.

International Court of Justice, *Western Sahara*, Written Statements and Documents, 3 vols., 1981.

International Court of Justice, *Western Sahara*, Oral Statements, 2 vols., 1981.

Libya, *Case Concerning the Territorial Dispute (Libyan Arab Jamahiriya/Chad)*, Memorial Submitted by the Great Socialist People's Libyan Arab Jamahiriya, 6 vols., 1991.

Libya, *Case Concerning the Territorial Dispute (Libyan Arab Jamahiriya/Chad)*, Counter-Memorial Submitted by the Great Socialist People's Libyan Arab Jamahiriya, 3 vols., 1992.

Libya, *Case Concerning the Territorial Dispute (Libyan Arab Jamahiriya/Chad)*, Reply Submitted by the Great Socialist People's Libyan Arab Jamahiriya, 3 vols., 1992.

Libya/Chad, CR 1993/14, 14 June 1993.

Libya/Chad, CR 1993/15, 15 June 1993.

Libya/Chad, CR 1993/16, 16 June 1993.

Libya/Chad, CR 1993/18, 18 June 1993.

Libya/Chad, CR 1993/19, 21 June 1993.

Libya/Chad, CR 1993/20, 22 June 1993.

Libya/Chad, CR 1993/21, 25 June 1993.

Libya/Chad, CR 1993/22, 28 June 1993.

Libya/Chad, CR 1999/23, 29 June 1993.

Libya/Chad, CR 1993/24, 30 June 1993.

Libya/Chad, CR 1993/25, 1 July 1993.

Libya/Chad, CR 1993/26, 2 July 1993.

Libya/Chad, CR 1993/27, 6 July 1993.
Libya/Chad, CR 1993/28, 7 July 1993.
Libya/Chad, CR 1993/29, 8 July 1993.
Libya/Chad, CR 1993/30, 12 July 1993.
Libya/Chad, CR 1993/31, 13 July 1993.
Libya/Chad, CR 1993/32, 14 July 1993.

Qatar, *Case Concerning Maritime Delimitation and Territorial Questions between Qatar and Bahrain (Qatar/Bahrain)*, Memorial Submitted by the State of Qatar. Questions of Jurisdiction and Admissibility, 3 vols., 1992.

Qatar, *Case Concerning Maritime Delimitation and Territorial Questions between Qatar and Bahrain (Qatar/ Bahrain)*, Reply Submitted by the State of Qatar. Questions of Jurisdiction and Admissibility, 2 vols., 1992a.

Qatar, *Case Concerning Maritime Delimitation and Territorial Questions between Qatar and Bahrain (Qatar/Bahrain)*, Memorial Submitted by the State of Qatar (Merits), 17 vols., 1996.

Qatar, *Case Concerning Maritime Delimitation and Territorial Questions between Qatar and Bahrain (Qatar/Bahrain)*, Counter-Memorial Submitted by the State of Qatar (Merits), 6 vols., 1997.

Qatar, *Case Concerning Maritime Delimitation and Territorial Questions between Qatar and Bahrain (Qatar/ Bahrain)*, Interim Report (Merits), 3 vols., 1998.

Qatar, *Case Concerning Maritime Delimitation and Territorial Questions between Qatar and Bahrain (Qatar/Bahrain)*, Reply Submitted by the State of Qatar (Merits), 7 vols., 1999.

Qatar/Bahrain (Merits), CR 2000/5, 29 May 2000.
Qatar/Bahrain (Merits), CR 2000/6, 30 May 2000.
Qatar/Bahrain (Merits), CR 2000/7, 31 May 2000.
Qatar/Bahrain (Merits), CR 2000/8, 5 June 2000.
Qatar/Bahrain (Merits), CR 2000/9, 5 June 2000.
Qatar/Bahrain (Merits), CR 2000/10, 6 June 2000.
Qatar/Bahrain (Merits), CR 2000/11, 8 June 2000.
Qatar/Bahrain (Merits), CR 2000/12, 9 June 2000.
Qatar/Bahrain (Merits), CR 2000/13, 13 June 2000.
Qatar/Bahrain (Merits), CR 2000/14, 13 June 2000.
Qatar/Bahrain (Merits), CR 2000/15, 14 June 2000.
Qatar/Bahrain (Merits), CR 2000/16, 15 June 2000.
Qatar/Bahrain (Merits), CR 2000/17, 20 June 2000.
Qatar/Bahrain (Merits), CR 2000/18, 21 June 2000.
Qatar/Bahrain (Merits), CR 2000/19, 22 June 2000.
Qatar/Bahrain (Merits), CR 2000/21, 27 June 2000.
Qatar/Bahrain (Merits), CR 2000/22, 28 June 2000.
Qatar/Bahrain (Merits), CR 2000/25, 29 June 2000.

Written Submission in the *Wall* Opinion, Republic of Guinea, 15 January 2004.
Written Submission in the *Wall* Opinion, Kingdom of Saudi Arabia, 27 January 2004.
Written Submission in the *Wall* Opinion, the League of Arab States, 28 January 2004.
Written Submission in the *Wall* Opinion, Arab Republic of Egypt, 28 January 2004.
Written Submission in the *Wall* Opinion, Republic of Cameroon, 28 January 2004.
Written Submission in the *Wall* Opinion, the Russian Federation, 29 January 2004.
Written Submission in the *Wall* Opinion, Australia, 29 January 2004.
Written Submission in the *Wall* Opinion, Palestine, 29 January 2004.
Written Submission in the *Wall* Opinion, Secretary-General of the United Nations, 29 January 2004.

Written Submission in the *Wall* Opinion, Hashemite Kingdom of Jordan, 30 January 2004.
Written Submission in the *Wall* Opinion, Kuwait, 30 January 2004.
Written Submission in the *Wall* Opinion, Lebanon, 30 January 2004.
Written Submission in the *Wall* Opinion, Canada, 30 January 2004.
Written Submission in the *Wall* Opinion, the Syrian Arab Republic, 30 January 2004.
Written Submission in the *Wall* Opinion, Swiss Confederation, 30 January 2004.
Written Submission in the *Wall* Opinion, Israel, 30 January 2004.
Written Submission in the *Wall* Opinion, Republic of Yemen, 30 January 2004.
Written Submission in the *Wall* Opinion, United States of America, 30 January 2004.
Written Submission in the *Wall* Opinion, the Kingdo of Morocco, 30 January 2004.
Written Submission in the *Wall* Opinion, Republic of Indonesia, 30 January 2004.
Written Submission in the *Wall* Opinion, the Organisation of Islamic Conference, 30 January 2004.
Written Submission in the *Wall* Opinion, the French Republic, 30 January 2004.
Written Submission in the *Wall* Opinion, The Sudan, 30 January 2004.
Written Submission in the *Wall* Opinion, Italy, 30 January 2004.
Written Submission in the *Wall* Opinion, Republic of South Africa, 30 January 2004.
Written Submission in the *Wall* Opinion, Federal Republic of Germany, 30 January 2004.
Written Submission in the *Wall* Opinion, Japan, 30 January 2004.
Written Submission in the *Wall* Opinion, Kingdom of Norway, 30 January 2004.
Written Submission in the *Wall* Opinion, Kingdom of Great Britain and Northern Ireland, 30 January 2004.
Written Submission in the *Wall* Opinion, Islamic Republic of Pakistan, 30 January 2004.
Written Submission in the *Wall* Opinion, Czech Republic, 30 January 2004.
Written Submission in the *Wall* Opinion, Greece, 30 January 2004.
Written Submission in the *Wall* Opinion, Ireland, 30 January 2004.
Written Submission in the *Wall* Opinion, the European Union, 30 January 2004.
Written Submission in the *Wall* Opinion, Republic of Cyprus, 30 January 2004.
Written Submission in the *Wall* Opinion, Republic of Brazil, 30 January 2004.
Written Submission in the *Wall* Opinion, Republic of Namibia, 30 January 2004.
Written Submission in the *Wall* Opinion, Malta, 30 January 2004.
Written Submission in the *Wall* Opinion, Malaysia, 30 January 2004.
Written Submission in the *Wall* Opinion, the Kingdom of the Netherlands, 30 January 2004.
Written Submission in the *Wall* Opinion, Republic of Cuba, 30 January 2004.
Written Submission in the *Wall* Opinion, Kingdom of Sweden, 30 January 2004.
Written Submission in the *Wall* Opinion, Spain, 30 January 2004.
Written Submission in the *Wall* Opinion, Kingdom of Belgium, 30 January 2004.
Written Submission in the *Wall* Opinion, Republic of Palau, 30 January 2004.
Written Submission in the *Wall* Opinion, Federated States of Micronesia, 30 January 2004.
Written Submission in the *Wall* Opinion, Republic of the Marshall Islands, 30 January 2004.
Written Submission in the *Wall* Opinion, Republic of Senegal, 30 January 2004.
Written Submission in the *Wall* Opinion, Democratic People's Republic of Korea, 30 January 2004.
The *Wall* Opinion, CR 2004/1, 23 February 2004.
The *Wall* Opinion, CR 2004/2, 23 February 2004.
The *Wall* Opinion, CR 2004/3, 24 February 2004.
The *Wall* Opinion, CR 2004/4, 24 February 2004.
The *Wall* Opinion, CR 2004/5, 25 February 2005.

Secondary Sources

Abbott, K. 'Modern International Relations Theory: A Prospectus for International Lawyers' (1989) 14 *Yale Journal of International Law* 335.

Abel, R. L. 'The Underdevelopment of Legal Professions: A Review Article on Third World Lawyers' (1982) *American Bar Foundation Research Journal* 871.

ABILA Committee on Intergovernmental Settlement of Disputes, 'Reforming the United Nations: What About the International Court of Justice?' (2006) 5 *Chinese Journal of International Law* 39.

Abi-Saab, G. 'The Newly Independent States and the Rules of International Law: An Outline' (1962) 8 *Howard Law Journal* 95.

——. 'The Third World and the Future of the International Legal Order' (1973) 29 *Revue égyptienne de droit international* 27.

——. 'International Law and The International Community: The Long Road to Universality', R. St. J. Macdonald (ed.), *Essays in Honour of Wang Tieya* (Dordrecht: Martinus Nijhoff, 1994) 31–41.

——. 'The International Court as a World Court', V. Lowe & M. Fitzmaurice (eds.), *Fifty Years of the International Court of Justice: Essays in Honour of Sir Robert Jennings* (Cambridge: Cambridge University Press, 1996) 3–16.

Abou-el-Haj, R. A. 'The Social Uses of the Past: Recent Arab Historiography of Ottoman Rule' (1982) 14 *International Journal of Middle East Studies* 185.

AbūSulaymān, A. A. *Towards an Islamic Theory of International Relations* (Herndon, VA: The International Institute of Islamic Thought, 2nd edition, 1994).

Aceves, W. J. 'Institutionalist Theory and International Legal Scholarship (1997) 12 *American University Journal of International Law and Policy* 227.

Adede, A. O. 'Judicial Settlement in Perspective', A. S. Muller, D. Raič & J. M. Thuránszky (eds.), *The International Court of Justice: Its Future Role after Fifty Years* (Boston; The Hague: Martinus Nijhoff, 1997) 47–81.

Ago, R. 'Pluralism and the Origins of the International Community' (1977) *Italian Yearbook of International Law* 3.

Ahmida, A. A. *The Making of Modern Libya: State Formation, Colonization, and Reisistance, 1830–1932* (New York: State University of New York, 1994).

Ajibola, B. A. 'Dispute Resolution by the International Court of Justice' (1998) 11 *Leiden Journal of International Law* 123.

Ajomo, M. A. 'International Law, the United Nations and Decolonization', E. G. Bello & B. A. Ajibola (eds.), *Essays in Honour of Judge Taslim Olawale Elias: vol. I Contemporary International Law and Human Rights* (Dordrecht: Martinus Nijhoff, 1992) 77–92.

Akbarzadeh, S. & Connor, K. 'The Organization of the Islamic Conference: Sharing an Illusion' (2005) 12 *Middle East Policy* 79.

Akinsanya, A. 'The Afro-Arab Alliance: Dream or Reality' (1976) 75 *African Affairs* 511.

Al-Arayed, J. S. *A Line in the Sea: The Qatar v. Bahrain Border Dispute in the World Court* (Berkeley: North Atlantic Books, 2003).

Al-Enazy, A. H. '"The International Boundary Treaty" (Treaty of Jeddah) Concluded between the Kingdom of Saudi Arabia and the Yemeni Republic on June 12, 2000' (2002) 96 *American Journal of International Law* 161.

Alexandrov, S. A. 'The Compulsory Jurisdiction of the International Court of Justice: How Compulsory Is It?' (2006) 5 *Chinese Journal of International Law* 29.

Alexandrowicz, C. H. *An Introduction to the History of the Law of Nations in the East Indies (16th, 17th, 18th Centuries)* (Oxford: Clarendon Press, 1967).

——. 'New and Original States: The Issue of Reversion to Sovereignty' (1969) 45 *International Affairs* 465.
Al Faruqi, I. R. 'The Ideal Social Order in the Arab World' (1969) 11 *Journal of Church & State* 239.
Al-Ghunaimi, M. T. *The Muslim Conception of International Law and the Western Approach* (The Hague: Martinus Nijhoff, 1968).
Allain, J. *International Law in the Middle East: Closer to Power than Justice* (Aldershot: Ashgate, 2004).
Allcock, J. B. et al. *Border and Territorial Disputes* (Harlow, Essex: Longman, 3rd ed., 1992).
Allott, P. 'The International Court of Justice and the Idea of Justice', V. Lowe & M. Fitzmaurice (eds.), *Fifty Years of the International Court of Justice: Essays in Honour of Sir Robert Jennings* (Cambridge: Cambridge University Press, 1996) 17–39.
——. 'International Law and the Idea of History' (1999) 1 *Journal of the History of International Law* 1.
Al-Qāsimī, S. M. *The Myth of Arab Piracy in the Gulf* (London: Routledge, 1988).
Amin, S. H. *International and Legal Problems of the Gulf* (London: Middle East and North African Studies Press, 1981).
Amr, M. S. M. *The Role of the International Court of Justice as the Principal Judicial Organ of the United Nations* (The Hague; New York: Kluwer, 2003).
Anand, R. P. 'Attitude of the Asian-African States Toward Certain Problems of International Law', F. E. Snyder & S. Sathirathai (eds.), *Third World Attitudes Toward International Law: An Introduction* (Dordrecht; Boston: Martinus Nijhoff, 1987) 5–22.
——. *Studies in International Law and History: An Asian Perspective* (Leiden: Martinus Nijhoff, 2004).
Anderson, L. 'Nineteenth-Century Reform in Ottoman Libya' (1984) 16 *International Journal of Middle East Studies* 325.
Andrews, J. A. 'The Concept of Statehood and the Acquisition of Territory in the Nineteenth Century' (1978) 94 *Law Quarterly Review* 408.
Anghie, A. '"The Heart of My Home": Colonialism, Environmental Damage, and the Nauru Case' (1993) 34 *Harvard International Law Journal Law* 445.
——. 'Francisco de Vitoria and the Colonial Origins of International Law' (1996) 5 *Social and Legal Studies* 321.
——. 'Finding the Peripheries: Sovereignty and Colonialism in Nineteenth Century International Law' (1999) 40 *Harvard International Law Journal* 1.
——. 'Civilization and Commerce: The Concept of Governance in Historical Perspective' (2000) 45 *Villanova Law Review* 887.
——. 'Time Present and Time Past: Globalization, International Financial Institutions, and the Third World' (2000) 32 *New York University Journal of International Law and Politics* 243.
——. 'C. G. Weeramantry at the International Court of Justice' (2001) 14 *Leiden Journal of International Law* 829.
——. 'Colonialism and the Birth of International Institutions: Sovereignty, Economy, and the Mandate System of the League of Nations' (2002) 34 *New York University Journal of International Law and Politics* 513.
——. 'Cultural Difference and International Law: The League of Nations and its Two Visions of the Nation-State' (2002) 5 *International Centre for Comparative Law and Politics Review* 4.
——. 'International Financial Institutions', C. Reus-Smit (ed.), *The Politics of International Law* (Cambridge: Cambridge University Press, 2004) 217–237.
——. *Imperialism, Sovereignty and the Making of International Law* (Cambridge: Cambridge University Press, 2005).

——. 'The Evolution of International Law: Colonial and Postcolonial Realities' (2006) 27 *Third World Quarterly* 739.
Anghie, A. & Chimni, B. S. 'Third World Approaches to International Law and Individual Responsibility in Internal Conflicts' (2003) 2 *Chinese Journal of International Law* 77.
An-Na'im, A. A. 'Why should Muslims Abandon *Jihad*? Human rights and the Future of International Law' (2006) 27 *Third World Quarterly* 785.
Anscombe, F. F. *The Ottoman Gulf: The Creation of Kuwait, Saudi Arabia, and Qatar* (New York: Columbia University Press, 1997).
Antunes, N. S. M. 'The *Eritrea-Yemen* Arbitration: First Stage – The Law of Title to Territory Re-Averred' (1999) 48 *International and Comparative Law Quarterly* 362.
——. 'The 1999 *Eritrea-Yemen* Maritime Delimitation Award and the Development of International Law' (2001) 50 *International and Comparative Law Quarterly* 299.
Arend, A. 'Do legal rules matter? International Law and International Politics' (1998) 38 *Virginia Journal of International Law* 107.
Argüello-Gomez, C. J. 'Some Procedural and Substantive Aspects of the *Libya/Chad* Case' (1996) 9 *Leiden Journal of International Law* 167.
Armstrong, D. *Revolution and World Order: The Revolutionary State in International Society* (Oxford: Clarendon Press, 1993).
——. 'Law, Justice and the Idea of World Society' (1999) 75 *International Affairs* 547.
Ayoob, M. 'The Third World in the System of States: Acute Schizophrenia or Growing Pains?' (1989) 33 *International Studies Quarterly* 67.
Ayubi, N. N. *Over-stating the Arab State: Politics and Society in the Middle East* (London: I. B. Tauris, 1995).
Badr, G. M. 'A Survey of Islamic International Law', C. Evans & M. W. Janis (eds.), *Religion and International Law* (Cambridge, MA: Martinus Nijhoff, 1999) 95–101.
Bain, W. *Between Anarchy and Society: Trusteeship and the Obligations of Power* (Oxford: Oxford University Press, 2003).
Barakat, H. *The Arab World: Society, Culture, and State* (Berkeley: University of California Press, 1993).
Barker, J. *International Law and International Relations* (London & New York: Continuum, 2000).
Barnett, M. 'Institutions, Roles, and Disorder: The Case of the Arab State System' (1993) 37 *International Studies Quarterly* 271.
——. 'Sovereignty, Nationalism, and Regional Order in the Arab States System' (1995) 49 *International Organization* 479.
Barnett, M. N. *Dialogues in Arab Politics: Negotiations in Regional Order* (New York: Columbia University Press, 1998).
Barrie, G. N. 'Uti Possidetis versus Self-Determination and Modern International Law: In Africa the Chickens are Coming Home to Roost' (1988) *Tijoskrif vir die Suid-Afrikaanse Reg* 451.
Bassiouni, M. C. 'Protection of Diplomats under Islamic Law' (1980) 74 *American Journal of International Law* 609.
Baxi, U. 'What may the "Third World" expect from International Law?' (2006) 27 *Third World Quarterly* 713.
Beck, R. J. 'International Law and International Relations: The Prospectus for Interdisciplinary Collaboration' (1995) 1 *Journal of International Legal Studies* 119.
Beckett, J. A. 'Countering Uncertainty and Ending Up/Down Arguments: *Prolegomena* to a Response to NAIL' (2005) 16 *European Journal of International Law* 213.
Bederman, D. J. 'The 1871 London Declaration, Rebus Sic Stantibus and a Primitivist View of the Law of Nations' (1988) 82 *American Journal of International Law* 1.

Bederman, D. 'Review Essay: Constructivism, Positivism, and Empiricism in International Law: Legal Rules and International Society' (2001) 89 *Georgetown Law Journal* 469.

Bedjaoui, M. *Towards a New International Economic Order* (Paris: UNESCO, 1979).

——. 'The 1980–1988 Gulf War and Universal Law: The Severe Judgment of World Legal Scholarship upon the Belligerents', I. F. Dekker & H. H. G. Post (eds.), *The Gulf War of 1980–1988: The Iran-Iraq War in International Legal Perspective* (Dordrecht: Martinus Nijhoff, 1992) 279–299.

——. 'Celebration of the Fiftieth Anniversary of the International Court of Justice' (1996) 8 *African Journal of International Comparative Law* 617.

Bekker, P. H. F. 'The World Court Rules that Israel's West Bank Barrier Violates International Law', *ASIL Insights*, July 2004.

——. 'The World Court's Ruling Regarding Israel's West Bank Barrier and the Primacy of International Law: An Insider's Perspective' (2005) 38 *Cornell International Law Journal* 553.

——. 'International Legal Aid in Practice: The ICJ Trust Fund' (1993) 87 *American Journal of International Law* 659.

——. 'The 2005 Record of the International Court of Justice' (2006) 5 *Chinese Journal of International Law* 371.

Benvenisti, E. *The International Law of Occupation* (Princeton: Princeton University Press, 1993).

Berman, N. 'Sovereignty in Abeyance: Self-Determination and International Law' (1988–1989) 7 *Wisconsin International Law Journal* 51.

——. 'Legalizing Jerusalem or, of Law, Fantasy, and Faith' (1996) 45 *Catholic University Law Review* 823.

——. 'In the Wake of Empire', (1999) 14 *American University International Law Review* 1515 (First Annual Grotius Lecture, American Society of International Law).

——. 'The *Nationality Decrees Case*, or, Of Intimacy and Consent' (2000) 13 *Leiden Journal of International Law* 265.

——. '"The Appeals of the Orient": Colonized Desire and the War of the Riff', K. Knop (ed.), *Gender and Human Rights* (Oxford: Oxford University Press, 2004) 195–230.

——. 'Les ambivalences impériales', in H. Ruiz & E Jouannet (dir.), *Droit. international et impérialisme en Europe et aux États-Unis* 131 (Paris: UMR. de Droit Comparé, 2007) (author's translation).

Beydoun, K. A. 'Dar al-Islam Meets "Islam as Civilization": An Alignment of Politico-Theoretical Fundamentalisms and the Geopolitical Realism of this Worldview' (2004–2005) 4 *UCLA Journal of Islamic & Near Eastern Law* 143.

Bien-Aime, T. 'A Pathway to the Hague and Beyond: The United Nations Trust Fund Proposal' (1989–1990) 22 *New York University Journal of International Law & Politics* 671.

Bishai, W. B. 'Negotiations and Peace Agreements between Muslims and Non-Muslims in Islamic History', S. A. Hanna (ed.), *Medieval and Middle Eastern Studies: In Honor of Aziz Suryal Atiya* (Leiden: Brill, 1972) 50–61.

Blay, S. K. N. 'Self-Determination *versus* Territorial Integrity in Decolonization' (1985) 25 *Indian Journal of International Law* 386.

Blaydes, L. E. Jr., 'International Court of Justice does not find "legal ties" of such a nature to affect self-determination in the decolonization process of Western Sahara' (1976) 11 *Texas International Law Journal* 354.

Bodansky, D. '*Non Liquet* and the Incompleteness of International Law', L. Boisson de Chazournes & P. Sands (eds.), *International Law, the International Court of Justice and Nuclear Weapons* (Cambridge: Cambridge University Press, 1999) 153–170.

Boisard, M. A. 'On the Probable Influence of Islam on Western Public and International Law' (1980) 11 *International Journal of Middle East Studies* 429.

Boisson de Chazournes, L. & Sands, P. 'Introduction', L. Boisson de Chazournes & P. Sands (eds.), *International Law, the International Court of Justice and Nuclear Weapons* (Cambridge: Cambridge University Press, 1999) 1–24.

Boutros-Ghali, B. 'The Arab League (1945–1970)' (1969) 25 *Revue égyptienne de droit international* 67.

Bowett, D. W. 'The Dubai/Sharjah Boundary Arbitration of 1981' (1994) 65 *British Yearbook of International Law* 103.

Boyle, J. 'Ideals and Things: International Legal Scholarship and the Prison-house of Language' (1985) 26 *Harvard Journal of International Law* 327.

Breau, S. C. 'Legal Consequences of the Construction of a Wall in the Occupied Palestinian Territory: Advisory Opinion, 9 July 2004' (2005) 54 *International and Comparative Law Quarterly* 1003.

Brower, C. N. & Sharpe, J. K. 'International Arbitration and the Islamic World: The Third Phase' (2003) 97 *American Journal of International Law* 643.

Brownlie, I. *African Boundaries: A Legal and Diplomatic Encyclopaedia* (London: C. Hurst, 1979).

——. 'Boundary Problems and the Formation of New States', D. Freestone, S. Subedi & S. Davidson (eds.), *Contemporary Issues in International Law: A Collection of the Josephine Onoh Memorial Lectures* (The Hague: Kluwer, 2002).

Burrows, M. '"Mission civilisatrice": French Cultural Policy in the Middle East, 1860–1914' (1986) 29 *Historical Journal* 109.

Byers, M. 'Custom, Power and the Power of Rules: Customary International Law from an Interdisciplinary Perspective (1995) 17 *Michigan Journal of International Law* 109.

Byman, A. 'The March on the Spanish Sahara: A Test of International Law' (1976–1977) 6 *Denver Journal of International Law & Policy* 95.

Cammett, M. 'Defensive Integration and Late Developers: The Gulf Cooperation Council and the Arab Maghreb Union' (1999) 5 *Global Governance* 379.

Campbell, A. M. 'International Law – Maritime Delimitation and Territorial Dispute – Qatar v. Bahrain, 1994 I.C.J. 112 (July 1)' (1996) 19 *Suffolk Transnational Law Review* 573.

Caplan, P. 'Introduction: Anthropology and the Study of Disputes', P. Caplan (ed.), *Understanding Disputes: The Politics of Argument* (Oxford: Providence, 1995) 1–10.

Carty, A. 'Review Article: Visions of the Past of International Society: Law, History or Politics?' (2006) 69 *Modern Law Review* 644.

Cass, D. Z. 'Re-Thinking Self-Determination: A Critical Analysis of Current International Law Theories' (1992) 18 *Syracuse Journal of International Law* 21.

——. 'Navigating the Newstream: Recent Critical Scholarship in International Law' (1996) 65 *Nordic Journal of International Law* 341.

Cassese, A. *Self-Determination of Peoples: A Legal Reappraisal* (Cambridge: Cambridge University Press, 1995).

——. 'The International Court of Justice and the Right of Peoples to Self-Determination', V. Lowe & M. Fitzmaurice (eds.), *Fifty Years of the International Court of Justice: Essays in Honour of Sir Robert Jennings* (Cambridge: Cambridge University Press, 1996) 351–363.

Castellino, J. 'Territory and Identity in International Law: The Struggle for Self-Determination in the Western Sahara' (1999) 28 *Millennium: Journal of International Studies* 523.

——. *International Law and Self-Determination: The Interplay of the Politics of Territorial Possession with Formulations of Post-Colonial 'National' Identity* (The Hague: Martinus Nijhoff, 2000).

Castellino, J. & Allen, S. *Title to Territory in International Law: A Temporal Analysis* (Aldershot: Ashgate, 2003).

Castenada, J. 'The Underdeveloped Nations and the Development of International Law' (1961) 15 *International Organization* 38.

Chakrabarty, D. 'Postcoloniality and the Artifice of History: Who Speaks for "Indian" Pasts?' (1992) 37 *Representations* 1.

Charlesworth, H. 'Feminist Methods in International Law' (1999) 93 *American Journal of International Law* 379.

——. 'International Law: A Discipline in Crisis' (2002) 65 *Modern Law Review* 377.

——. 'Judge *ad hoc* of the International Court of Justice', T. McCormack & C. Saunders (eds.), *Sir Ninian Stephen: A Tribute* (Carleton, Vic: Melbourne University Press, 2007) 176–189.

Charlesworth, H. & Chinkin, C. *The Boundaries of International Law: A Feminist Analysis* (Manchester: Manchester University Press, 2000).

Charney, J. I. 'Universal International Law' (1993) 87 *American Journal of International Law* 529.

Chesterman, S. 'Law, Subject and Subjectivity in International Relations: International Law and the Postcolony' (1996) 20 *Melbourne University Law Review* 979.

Chimni, B. S. 'Towards a Radical Third World Approach to Contemporary International Law' (2002) 5 *International Centre for Comparative Law and Politics Review* 14.

——. 'Third World Approaches to International Law: A Manifesto', A. Anghie et al. (eds.), *The Third World and International Order: Law, Politics and Globalization* (Leiden: Martinus Nijhoff, 2003) 47–73.

——. 'Towards a TWAIL Theory of Interpretation: Some Notes', Conference Paper, Third World Approaches to International Law Conference, Albany Law School 20–21 April 2007.

Chinkin, C. 'The Peaceful Settlement of Disputes: New Grounds for Optimism?', McDonald, R. St. John (ed.), *Essays in Honour of Wang Tieya* (Dordrecht; Boston: Martinus Nijhoff, 1994) 165–179.

——. 'A Mirage in the Sand? Distinguishing Binding and Non-Binding Relations between States' (1997) 10 *Leiden Journal of International Law* 223.

Choueiri, Y. M. 'Review: The Middle East: Colonialism, Islam and the Nation-State' (2002) 37 *Journal of Contemporary History* 649.

Cockayne, J. D. R. 'Islam and International Humanitarian Law: From Clash to a Conversation between Civilizations' (2002) 84 *International Review of the Red Cross* 597.

Colby, E. 'How to Fight Savage Tribes' (1927) 21 *American Journal of International Law* 279.

Coleman, A. 'The International Court of Justice and Highly Political Matters' (2004) 4 *Melbourne Journal of International Law* 29.

Collier, J. G. 'The International Court of Justice and the Peaceful Settlement of Disputes', V. Lowe & M. Fitzmaurice (eds.), *Fifty Years of the International Court of Justice: Essays in Honour of Sir Robert Jennings* (Cambridge: Cambridge University Press, 1996) 364–372.

Collier & Lowe, V. *The Settlement of Disputes in International Law: Institutions and Procedures* (Oxford: Oxford University Press, 1999).

Colson, E. 'The Contentiousness of Disputes', P. Caplan (ed.), *Understanding Disputes: The Politics of Argument* (Oxford: Providence, 1995) 65–82.

Coplin, W. D. & Rochester, J. M. 'The Permanent Court of International Justice, the International Court of Justice, the League of Nations, and the United Nations: A Comparative Empirical Survey' (1972) 66 *American Political Science Review* 529.

Craven, M. 'What Happened to Unequal Treaties? The Continuities of Informal Empire' (2005) 74 *Nordic Journal of International Law* 335.

Cravens, W. S. D. 'The Future of Islamic Arguments in International Boundary Disputes between Islamic States' (1998) 55 *Washington & Lee Law Review* 529.

Crawford, J. 'The Creation of the State of Palestine: Too Much Too Soon?' (1990) 1 *European Journal of International Law* 307.
——. 'The General Assembly, the International Court and Self-Determination', V. Lowe & M. Fitzmaurice (eds.), *Fifty Years of the International Court of Justice: Essays in Honour of Sir Robert Jennings* (Cambridge: Cambridge University Press, 1996) 585–605.
——. 'Israel (1948–1949) and Palestine (1998–1999): Two Studies in the Creation of States', G. S. Goodwin-Gill & S. Talmon (eds.), *The Reality of International Law: Essays in Honour of Ian Brownlie* (Oxford: Clarendon Press, 1999) 95–124.
——. 'The Right of Self-Determination in International Law: Its Development and Future', P. Alston (ed.), *Peoples' Rights* (Oxford: Oxford University Press, 2001) 7–67.
——. *The Creation of States in International Law* (Cambridge: Cambridge University Press, 2nd edition, 2006).
Crone, P. *God's Rule: Government and Islam* (New York: Columbia University Press, 2004).
Cutler, C. 'The "Grotian Tradition" in International Relations' (1991) 17 *Review of International Studies* 41.
Cutler, C. A. 'Critical Historical Materialism and International Law: Imagining International Law as Praxis', S. Hobden & J. M. Hobson (eds.), *Historical Sociology of International Relations* (Cambridge: Cambridge University Press, 2002) 181–199.
Damis, J. *Conflict in Northwest Africa: The Western Sahara Dispute* (Stanford, Hoover Institute Press, 1983).
Damrosch, L. F. (ed.), *The International Court of Justice at a Crossroads* (Dobbs Ferry, NY: Transnational, 1987).
Damrosch, L. F. & Oxman, B. H. 'Agora: ICJ Advisory Opinion on Construction of a Wall in the Occupied Palestinian Territory: Editors' Introduction' (2005) 99 *American Journal of International Law* 1.
Davidson, L. & Goldschmidt, A. Jr., 'The Roots of Arab Bitterness', K. Yambert (ed.), *The Contemporary Middle East* (Boulder, CO: Westview Press, 2006) 27–40.
Daweesha, A. *Arab Nationalism in the Twentieth Century: From Triumph to Despair* (Princeton: Princeton University Press, 2003).
Deeb, M.-J. *Libya's Foreign Policy in North Africa* (Boulder: Westview Press, 1991).
Dennis, M. J. 'Application of Human Rights Treaties Extraterritorially in Times of Armed Conflict and Military Occupation' (2005) 99 *American Journal of International Law* 119.
De Puy, A. 'Bringing Down the Barrier: A Comparative Analysis of the ICJ Advisory Opinion and the High Court of Justice of Israel's Ruling on Israel's Construction of a Barrier on Occupied Territory' (2005) 13 *Tulane Journal of International and Comparative Law* 275.
Deringil, S. 'Legitimacy Structures in the Ottoman State: The Reign of Abdülhamid II (1876–1909)' (1991) 23 *International Journal of Middle East Studies* 345.
De Waart, P. J. I. M. 'International Court of Justice Firmly Walled in the Law of Power in the Israeli-Palestinian Peace Process' (2005) 18 *Leiden Journal of International Law* 467.
Distefano, G. 'The Conceptualization (Construction) of Territorial Title in the Light of International Court of Justice Case Law' (2006) 19 *Leiden Journal of International Law* 1041.
Doornbos, M. 'The African State in Academic Debate: Retrospect and Prospect' (1990) 28 *Journal of Modern African Studies* 179.
Douzinas, C. 'Theses on Law, History and Time' (2006) 7 *Melbourne Journal of International Law* 13.
Dupuy, P.-M. 'Between Individual and the State: International Law at a Crossroads', L. Boisson de Chazournes & P. Sands (eds.), *International Law, the International Court of Justice and Nuclear Weapons* (Cambridge: Cambridge University Press, 1999) 449–461.

——. 'The Danger of Fragmentation or Unification of the International Legal System and the International Court of Justice' (1998–1999) 31 *New York University Journal of International Law & Politics* 791.

Dunbar, C. 'Saharan Stasis: Status and Future Prospects of the Western Sahara Conflict' (2000) 4 *Middle East Journal* 522.

Dunoff, J. L. et al., *International Law Norms, Actors, Process: A Problem-Oriented Approach* (New York: Aspen, 2002).

ElBaradei, M. 'The Egyptian-Israeli Peace Treaty and Access to the Gulf of Aqaba: A New Legal Regime' (1982) 76 *American Journal of International Law* 532.

El-Erian, A. 'The International Court of Justice and the Concept of Universality' (1981) 19 *Columbia Journal of Transnational Law* 197.

Eickelman, D. F. & Piscatori, J. *Muslim Politics* (Princeton: Princeton University Press, 1996).

Elias, T. O. *The International Court of Justice and Some Contemporary Problems: Essays on International Law* (The Hague: Martinus Nijhoff, 1983).

——. *New Horizons in International Law* (Dordrecht; Boston: Martinus Nijhoff, 2nd, 1992).

El Moudden, A. 'The Idea of the Caliphate between Moroccans and Ottomans: Political and Symbolic Stakes in the 16th and 17th Century-Maghrib' (1995) 82 *Studia Islamica* 103.

Evans, M. D. 'Case Concerning Maritime Delimitation and Territorial Questions between Qatar and Bahrain (*Qatar v. Bahrain*), Jurisdiction and Admissibility' (1995) 44 *International and Comparative Law Quarterly* 691.

——. 'The Maritime Delimitation between Eritrea and Yemen' (2001) 14 *Leiden Journal of International Law* 141.

——. 'Case Concerning Maritime Delimitation and Territorial Questions between Qatar and Bahrain (*Qatar v Bahrain*)' (2002) 51 *International and Comparative Law Quarterly* 709.

Eyffinger, A. *The International Court of Justice 1946–1996* (The Hague: Kluwer, 1996).

Falk, R. *Reviving the World Court* (Charlottesville: University Press of Virginia, 1986).

——. 'Self-Determination under International Law: The Coherence of Doctrine versus the Incoherence of Experience', W. Danspeckgruber (ed.), *The Self-Determination of Peoples: Community, Nation and State in an Interdependent World* (Boulder, CO: Lynne Reinner, 2002) 31–66.

——. 'Towards Authoritativeness: The ICJ Ruling on Israel's Security Wall' (2005) 99 *American Journal of International Law* 42.

——. 'International Law and the Future' (2006) 27 *Third World Quarterly* 727.

Falk, R. & Weston, B. H. 'The Israeli-Occupied Territories, International Law, and the Boundaries of Scholarly Discourse: A Reply to Michael Curtis' (1991) 32 *Harvard International Law Journal* 457.

Faroqhi, S. *The Ottoman Empire and the World Around It* (London: I. B. Tauris, 2004).

Fatouros, A. A. 'International Law and the Third World' (1964) 50 *Virginia Law Review* 783.

Fidler, D. P. 'A Kinder, Gentler System of Capitulations? International Law, Structural Adjustment, and the Standards of Liberal, Globalized Civilization' (2000) 35 *Texas International Law Journal* 387.

——. 'The Return of the Standard of Civilization' (2001) 2 *Chicago Journal of International Law* 137.

——. 'Revolt Against or From Within the West? TWAIL, the Developing World and the Future Direction of International Law' (2003) 2 *Chinese Journal of International Law* 29.

Finnemore, M. 'Are Legal Norms Distinctive?' (2000) 32 *New York University Journal of International Law and Politics* 699.

Foda, E. *The Projected Arab Court of Justice: A Study in Regional Jurisdiction with Specific Reference to the Muslim Law of Nations* (The Hague: Martinus Nijhoff, 1957).

Ford, C. A. 'Siyar-ization and its Discontents: International Law and Islam's Constitutional Crisis' (1995) 30 *Texas International Law Journal* 499.

Forsythe, D. P. 'The International Court of Justice at Fifty', A. S. Muller, D. Raič & J. M. Thuránszky (eds.), *The International Court of Justice: Its Future Role after Fifty Years* (The Hague; Boston: Martinus Nijhoff, 1997) 385–405.

Franck, T. M. 'The Stealing of the Sahara' (1976) 70 *American Journal of International Law* 694.

——. 'The Theory and Practice of Decolonization: the Western Sahara Case', R. Lawless & L. Monahan (eds.), *War and Refugees: The Western Saharan Conflict* (London; New York: Pinter, 1986) 9.

——. 'Postmodern Tribalism and the Right to Secession', C. Brölmann et al. (eds.), *Peoples and Minorities in International Law* (The Hague: Kluwer, 1993) 3–27.

——. 'Fairness and the General Assembly Advisory Opinion', L. Boisson de Chazournes & P. Sands (eds.), *International Law, the International Court of Justice and Nuclear Weapons* (Cambridge: Cambridge University Press, 1999) 511–519.

Frankenberg, G. 'Critical Comparisons: Re-Thinking Comparative Law' (1985) 26 *Harvard International Law Journal* 411.

Gareau, J.-F. 'Shouting at the Wall: Self-Determination and the Legal Consequences of the Construction of a Wall in the Occupied Palestinian Territory' (2005) 18 *Leiden Journal of International Law* 489.

Gathii, J. T. 'Alternative and Critical: The Contribution of Research and Scholarship on Developing Countries to International Legal Theory' (2000) 41 *Harvard International Law Journal* 263.

——. 'Neoliberalism, Colonialism and International Governance: Decentring the International Law of Governmental Legitimacy' (2000) 98 *Michigan Law Review* 1996.

——. 'Rejoinder: TWAILing International Law' (2000) 98 *Michigan Law Review* 2066.

——. 'Geographical Hegelianism in Territorial Disputes Involving Non-European Land Relations: An Analysis of the Case Concerning *Kasikili/Sedudu Island* (Botswana/Namibia)' (2002) 15 *Leiden Journal of International Law* 581.

——. 'Imperialism, Colonialism, and International Law' (2007) 54 *Buffalo Law Review* 1013.

Gaubatz, K. T. & MacArthur, M. 'How International is "International" Law?' (2000–2001) 22 *Michigan Journal of International Law* 239.

Gause, F. G. III, 'Sovereignty, Statecraft and Stability in the Middle East' (1992) 45 *Journal of International Affairs* 441.

Glenn, H. P. *Legal Traditions of the World: Sustainable Diversity in Law* (Oxford: Oxford University Press, 2000).

Goffman, D. *The Ottoman Empire and Early Modern Europe* (Cambridge: Cambridge University Press, 2002).

Gong, G. *The Standard of "Civilization" in International Society* (Oxford: Clarendon Press, 1984).

Gongora, T. 'War Making and State Power in the Contemporary Middle East' (1997) 29 *International Journal of Middle East Studies* 323.

Greig, D. W. 'Sovereignty, Territory and the International Lawyer's Dilemma' (1988) 26 *Osgoode Hall Law Journal* 127.

Grewe, W. H. *The Epochs of International Law*, M. Byers (trans.) (New York; Berlin: de Gruyter, 2000).

Gross, A. M. 'Human Proportions: Are Human Rights the Emperor's New Clothes of the International Law of Occupation?' (2007) 18 *European Journal of International Law* 1.

Gross, L. 'Underutilization of the International Court of Justice' (1986) 27 *American Journal of International Law* 571.

Grovogui, S. N. *Sovereigns, Quasi-Sovereigns, and Africans: Race and Self-Determination in International Law* (Minneapolis: University of Minnesota Press, 1996).

Guillaume, G. 'The Future of International Judicial Institutions' (1995) 44 *International & Comparative Law Quarterly* 848.

Haddad, M. 'The Rise of Arab Nationalism Reconsidered' (1994) 26 *International Journal of Middle East Studies* 201.

——. 'Arab Religious Nationalism in the Colonial Era: Rereading Rashīd Riḍa's Ideas on the Caliphate' (1997) 117 *Journal of the American Oriental Society* 253.

Hall, B. S. 'The Question of "Race" in the Pre-colonial Southern Sahara' (2005) 10 *Journal of North African Studies* 339.

Hallaq, W. B. *A History of Islamic Legal Theories: An Introduction to Sunnī uṣūl al-fiqh* (Cambridge: Cambridge University Press, 1997).

——. *The Origins and Evolution of Islamic Law* (Cambridge: Cambridge University Press, 2005).

——. 'The Quest for Origins or Doctrine? Islamic Legal Studies as Colonialist Discourse' (2003) 2 *UCLA Journal of Islamic and Near Eastern Law* 1.

Halliday, F. *The Middle East in International Relations: Power, Politics and Ideology* (Cambridge, Cambridge University Press, 2005).

Hanauer, L. S. 'The Irrelevance of Self-Determination Law to Ethno-National Conflict: A New Look at the Western Sahara Case' (1995) 9 *Emory International Law Review* 1333.

Harland, C. 'International Court of Justice Elections: A Report on the First Fifty Years' (1996) 34 *Canadian Yearbook of International Law* 303.

Hassouna, H. A. *The League of Arab States and Regional Disputes: A Study of Middle East Conflicts* (Leiden: Oceana, 1975).

Heard-Bey, F. 'Conflict Resolution and Regional Co-operation: The Role of the Gulf Co-operation Council 1970–2002' (2006) 42 *Middle Eastern Studies* 199.

Herbst, J. 'The Creation and Maintenance of National Boundaries in Africa' (1989) 43 *International Organization* 673.

Herman, L. L. 'An Analysis of the World Court Judgment in the Western Sahara Case' (1976–1977) 41 *Saskatchkewan Law Review* 133.

Higgins, R. 'The June War: The United Nations and Legal Background' (1974) 2 *The Arab-Israeli Conflict* 535.

——. 'Judge Dillard and the Right to Self-Determination' (1982–1983) 23 *Virginia Journal of International Law* 387.

——. *Problems and Process: International Law and How We Use It* (Oxford: Clarendon Press, 1994).

——. 'Some Observations on the Inter-temporal Rule in International Law', J. Makarczyk (ed.), *Theory of International Law at the Threshold of the 21st Century: Essays in Honour of Krysztof Skubiszewski* (The Hague: Kluwer, 1996) 173–181.

——. 'A Babel of Judicial Voices? Ruminations from the Bench' (2006) 55 *International & Comparative Law Quarterly* 791.

Highet, K. 'The Peace Palace Heats Up: The World Court in Business Again?' (1991) 85 *American Journal of International Law* 646.

Hirsch, M. 'The Impact of the Advisory Opinion on Israel's Future Policy: International Relations Perspective' (2005) 1 *Journal of International Law and International Relations* 319.

Hodges, T. *Western Sahara: The Roots of a Desert War* (Westport: L. Hill, 1983).

Hourani, A. *Arabic Thought in the Liberal Age 1798–1939* (Cambridge: Cambridge University Press, 1962, reissued 1983).

——. *A History of the Arab Peoples* (London: Faber & Faber, 1991).

——. 'How Should We Write the History of the Middle East?' (1991) 23 *International Journal of Middle East Studies* 125.

Huliaras, A. 'Qadhafi's Comeback: Libya and Sub-Saharan Africa in the 1990s' (2001) 100 *African Affairs* 5.

Hurd, I. *After Anarchy: Legitimacy and Power in the United Nations Security Council* (Princeton: Princeton University Press, 2007).

İlhan, M. M. 'The Ottoman Archives and Their Importance for Historical Studies: With Special Reference to Arab Provinces' (1991) C. LV *Belleten* 415.

Imseis, A. 'On the Fourth Geneva Convention and the Occupied Palestinian Territory' (2003) 44 *Harvard Journal of International Law* 65.

——. 'Critical Reflections on the International Humanitarian Law Aspects of the ICJ *Wall* Advisory Opinion' (2005) 99 *American Journal of International Law* 102.

International Crisis Group, Report N.14, 'A Middle East Roadmap to Where?', 2 May 2003.

International Crisis Group, Report N.65, 'Western Sahara: The Cost of the Conflict', 11 June 2007.

International Crisis Group, Report N.66, 'Western Sahara: Out of the Impasse', 11 June 2007..

Jackson, S. A. *Islamic Law and the State: The Constitutional Jurisprudence of Shihāb al-Dīn al-Qarāfi* (Leiden: Brill, 1996).

Janis, M. W. 'The International Court of Justice: Advisory Opinion on the Western Sahara' (1976) 17 *Harvard Journal of International Law* 609.

Jennings, R. Y. *The Acquisition of Territory in International Law* (Manchester: Manchester University Press, 1963).

——. 'Universal International Law in a Multicultural World', M. Bos & I. Brownlie (eds.), *Liber Amicorum for The Rt. Hon. Lord Wilberforce* (Oxford: Clarendon Press, 1987) 39–51.

——. 'The International Court of Justice after Fifty Years' (1995) 89 *American Journal of International Law* 493.

——. 'The Proper Work and Purposes of the International Court of Justice', D. Raič & J. M. Thuránszky (eds.), *The International Court of Justice: Its Future Role after Fifty Years* (The Hague; Boston: Martinus Nijhoff, 1997) 33–45.

——. 'The Role of the International Court of Justice' (1998) 68 *British Yearbook of International Law* 1.

——. 'International Courts and International Politics', D. Freestone et al. (eds.), *Contemporary Issues in International Law: A Collection of Josephine Onoh Memorial Lectures* (The Hague: Kluwer, 2002) 13–28.

Jessup, P. C. 'Diversity and Uniformity in the Law of Nations' (1964) 58 *American Journal of International Law* 341.

Johnson, C. 'Eritrea-Yemen Arbitration' (2000) 13 *Leiden Journal of International Law* 427.

Joffé, G. 'The International Court of Justice and the Western Sahara Dispute' R. Lawless & L. Monahan (eds.), *War and Refugees: The Western Sahara Conflict* (London; New York: Pinter, 1987).

——. 'Concepts of Sovereignty in the Gulf Region', R. Schofield (ed.), *Territorial Foundations of the Gulf States* (London: UCL Press, 1994) 78–93.

——. 'Qadhafi's Islam in Local Historical Perspective', D. Vandewalle (ed.), *Qadhafi's Libya, 1969–1994* (New York: St Martin's Press, 1995) 139–154.

——. 'Libya's Saharan Destiny' (2005) 10 *Journal of North African Studies* 605.

Kahan, R. 'Building a Protective Wall around Terrorists – How the International Court of Justice's Ruling in the Legal Consequences of the Construction of a Wall in the Occupied Palestinian Territory Made the World Safer for Terrorists and More Dangerous for Member States of the United Nations' (2005) 28 *Fordham International Law Journal* 827.

Kaikobad, K. H. 'Some Observations on the Doctrine of Continuity and Finality of Borders' (1984) 54 *British Yearbook of International Law* 119.

——. 'The Quality of Justice: '*Excès de Pouvoir'* in the Adjudication and Arbitration of Territorial and Boundary Disputes', G. S. Goodwin-Gill & S. Talmon (eds.), *The Reality of International Law: Essays in Honour of Ian Brownlie* (Oxford: Clarendon Press, 1999) 293–321.

Karpat, K. H. 'The Transformation of the Ottoman State, 1789–1908' (1972) 3 *International Journal of Middle East Studies* 243.

Karsh, E. & Karsh, I. *Empires in the Sand: The Struggle for Mastery in the Middle East 1789–1923* (Cambridge, MA: Harvard University Press, 1999).

Kassim, A. F. 'The Advisory Opinion of the International Court of Justice on the Legal Consequences of the Construction of a Wall in the Occupied Palestinian Territory: Significance and Implications' (2003–2004) 10 *Yearbook of Islamic and Middle Eastern Law* 457.

Katona, D. 'Challenging the Global Structure through Self-Determination: An African Perspective' (1998–1999) 14 *American University Law Review* 1439.

Kayali, H. *Arabs and Young Turks: Ottomanism, Arabism, and Islamism in the Ottoman Empire, 1908–1918* (Berkeley: University of California Press, 1997).

Keal, P. *European Conquest and the Rights of Indigenous Peoples: The Moral Backwardness of International Society* (Cambridge: Cambridge University Press, 2003).

Keddie, N. R. 'Is There a Middle East?' (1973) 4 *International Journal of Middle East Studies* 255.

Keene, E. *Beyond the Anarchical Society: Grotius, Colonialism and Order in World Politics* (Cambridge: Cambridge University Press, 2002).

Kelly, J. B. 'The Buraimi Oasis Dispute' (1956) 32 *International Affairs (Royal Institute of International Affairs)* 318.

——. *Arabia, the Gulf and the West* (London: Weidenfeld & Nicolson, 1980).

Kelsay, J. 'Al-Shaybani and the Islamic Law of War' (2003) 2 *Journal of Military Ethics* 63.

Kennedy, D. 'Primitive Legal Scholarship' (1986) 27 *Harvard International Law Journal* 1.

——. 'The Sources of International Law' (1987) 2 *American University Journal of International Law and Policy* 1.

——. 'A New Stream of International Law Scholarship' (1988) 7 *Wisconsin International Law Journal* 1.

——. 'International Law and the Nineteenth Century: History of an Illusion' (1996) 65 *Nordic Journal of International Law* 385.

——. 'The *Nuclear Weapons* case', L. Boisson de Chazournes & P. Sands (eds.), *International Law, the International Court of Justice and Nuclear Weapons* (Cambridge: Cambridge University Press, 1999) 462–472.

——. 'When Renewal Repeats: Thinking against the Box' (1999–2000) 32 *New York University Journal of International Law and Politics* 335.

——. *The Dark Sides of Virtue: Reassessing International Humanitarianism* (Princeton, Princeton University Press, 2004).

——. 'Sovereignty: Responding to Anghie and Aravamudan' (2006) 41 *Texas International Law Journal* 1.

——. 'The Last Treatise: Project and Person (Reflections on Martti Koskenniemi's *From Apology to Utopia*) (2006) 7 *German Law Journal* 982.

——. Keynote Address, Third World Approaches to International Law Conference, Albany Law School, 20–21 April 2007.

Keohane, R. 'International Relations and International Law: Two Optics' (1997) 38 *Harvard International Law Journal* 487.

Khadduri, M. 'International Law', M. Khadduri & H. J. Liebesny (eds.), *Law in the Middle East: Origin and Development of Islamic Law, vol. 1* (Washington: Middle East Institute, 1955) 349–372.
——. *War and Peace in the Law of Islam* (Baltimore: John Hopkins Press, 1955).
——. 'Islam and the Modern Law of Nations' (1956) 50 *American Journal of International Law* 358.
——. *The Islamic Law of Nations: Shaybānī's Siyar* (Baltimore: John Hopkins Press, 1966).
——. *The Islamic Conception of Justice* (Baltimore, John Hopkins University Press, 1984).
Khan, H. M. 'Nothing is Written: Fundamentalism, Revivalism, Reformism and the Fate of Islamic Law' (2002) 24 *Michigan Journal of International Law* 273.
King-Irani, 'Exiled to a Liminal Legal Zone: Are we all Palestinians Now?' (2006) 27 *Third World Quarterly* 923.
Kirgis, F. L. Jr., 'The Degrees of Self-Determination in the United Nations Era' (1994) 88 *American Journal of International Law* 304.
Klabbers, J. 'Qatar v. Bahrain: the concept of "treaty" in international law' (1995) 33 *Archiv des Völkerrechts* 361.
——. 'The Relative Autonomy of International Law or The Forgotten Politics of Interdisciplinarity' (2005) 1 *Journal of International Law & International Relations* 35.
Klabbers, J. & Lefeber, R. 'Africa: Lost between Self-Determination and *uti possidetis*', C. Brölmann et al. (eds.), *Peoples and Minorities in International Law* (Dordrecht; Boston: Kluwer, 1993) 37–76.
Knop, K. 'Re/Statements: Feminism and State Sovereignty in International Law' (1993) 3 *Transnational Law and Contemporary Problems* 293.
——. *Diversity and Self-Determination in International Law* (Cambridge: Cambridge University Press, 2002).
Korhonen, O. 'Liberalism and International Law: A Centre Projecting a Periphery' (1996) 65 *Nordic Journal of International Law* 481.
——. 'New International Law: Silences, Defence or Deliverance?' (1996) 7 *European Journal of International Law* 1.
——. *International Law Situated: An Analysis of the Lawyer's Stance towards Culture, History and Community* (The Hague: Kluwer, 2000).
Korman, S. *The Right of Conquest: The Acquisition of Territory by Force in International Law and Practice* (Oxford: Clarendon Press, 1996).
Koskenniemi, M. 'The Future of Statehood' (1991) 32 *Harvard International Law Journal* 397.
——. 'L'affaire du différend territorial (Jamahiriya Arabe Libyenne c. Tchad) Arrêt de la Cour Internationale de Justice du 3 février 1994' (1994) 40 *Annuaire français de droit international* 442.
——. 'National Self-Determination Today: Problems of Legal Theory and Practice' (1994) 43 *International and Comparative Law Quarterly* 241.
——. 'Preface' (1996) 65 *Nordic Journal of International Law* 337.
——. 'Faith, Identity, and the Killing of the Innocent: International Lawyers and Nuclear Weapons' (1997) 10 *Leiden Journal of International Law* 137.
——. 'The Silence of Law/The Voice of Justice', L. Boisson de Chazournes & P. Sands (eds.), *International Law, the International Court of Justice and Nuclear Weapons* (Cambridge: Cambridge University Press, 1999) 488–510.
——. 'Letter to the Editors of the Symposium' (1999) 93 *American Journal of International Law* 351.
——. *The Gentle Civilizer of Nations: The Rise and Fall of International Law 1870–1960* (Cambridge: Cambridge University Press, 2002).

——. 'The Epochs of International Law (Book Review)' (2002) 51 *International & Comparative Law Quarterly* 746–751.

——. 'International Law and Imperialism', D. Freestone, S. Subedi & S. Davidson (eds.), *Contemporary Issues in International Law: A Collection of the Josephine Onoh Memorial Lectures* (The Hague: Kluwer, 2002) 197–218.

——. 'Legal Universalism: Between Morality and Power in a World of States', S. Cheng (ed.), *Law, Justice, and Power: Between Reason and Will* (Stanford, Stanford University Press, 2004) 46–69.

——. 'International Law and Hegemony: A Reconfiguration' (2004) 17 *Cambridge Review of International Affairs* 197.

——. *From Apology to Utopia: The Structure of International Legal Argument* (Cambridge: Cambridge University Press, 2nd edition, 2005).

——. 'The Fate of Public International Law: Between Technique and Politics' (2007) 70 *Modern Law Review* 1.

Koury, S. 'The I.C.J. Advisory Opinion on the Wall: A Prelude to State Action?' (2003–2004) 10 *Yearbook of Islamic and Middle Eastern Law* 463.

Kratochwil, F. 'Thrasymmachos Revisited: On the Relevance of Norms and the Study of Law for International Relations' (1984) 37 *Journal of International Affairs* 343.

Kretzmer, D. 'The Advisory Opinion: the Light Treatment of International Humanitarian Law' (2005) 99 *American Journal of International Law* 88.

Kritsiotis, D. 'The Power of International Law as Language' (1997–1998) 34 *California Western Law Review* 397.

——. 'When States Use Armed Force', C. Reus-Smit (ed.), *The Politics of International Law* (Cambridge: Cambridge University Press, 2004) 45–79.

Kwiatkowska, B. 'The Eritrea-Yemen Arbitration: Landmark Progress in the Acquisition of Territorial Sovereignty and Equitable Maritime Boundary Delimitation' (2001) 32 *Ocean Development & International Law* 1.

——. 'The *Qatar v. Bahrain* Maritime Delimitation and Territorial Questions Case' (2002) 33 *Ocean Development and International Law* 227.

Lachs, M. 'Evidence in the Procedure of the International Court of Justice: Role of the Court', E .G Bello & B. A. Ajibola (eds.), *Essays in Honour of Judge Taslim Olawale Elias: vol. I Contemporary International Law and Human Rights* (Dordrecht; Boston: Martinus Nijhoff, 1992) 265–276.

Landauer, C. 'Wilhelm Grewe, *The Epochs of International Law* (Book Review)' (2003) 16 *Leiden Journal of International Law* 191–201.

Lapidoth, R. 'The Strait of Tiran, the Gulf of Aqaba and the 1979 Treaty of Peace between Egypt and Israel' (1983) 77 *American Journal of International Law* 84.

Lapidus, I. *A History of Islamic Societies* (Cambridge: Cambridge University Press, 2nd edition, 2002).

Lauterpacht, E. 'The Juridical and the Meta-Juridical in International Law', J. Makarczyk (ed.), *Theory of International Law at the Threshold of the 21st Century: Essays in Honour of Krysztof Skubiszewski* (The Hague: Kluwer, 1996) 215–234.

——. '"Partial" Judgments and the Inherent Jurisdiction of the International Court of Justice' V. Lowe & M. Fitzmaurice (eds.), *Fifty Years of the International Court of Justice: Essays in Honour of Sir Robert Jennings* (Cambridge: Cambridge University Press, 1996) 465–486.

Lauterpacht, H. 'The Mandate under International Law in the Covenant of the League of Nations', *International Law: Being the Collected Papers of Hersch Lauterpacht*, vol. 3 (Cambridge: Cambridge University Press, 1977) 29–84.

Lee, S. 'Continuing Relevance of Traditional Modes of Territorial Acquisition in International Law and a Modest Appraisal' (2000) 16 *Connecticut Journal of International Law* 1.

Le Gall, M. 'The Ottoman Government and the Sanusiyya: A Reappraisal' (1989) 21 *International Journal of Middle East Studies* 91.

Levy, G. J. 'Advisory Opinion on the Western Sahara' (1975–1976) 2 *Brooklyn Journal of International Law* 289.

Liebesny, H. J. 'The Development of Western Judicial Privileges', M. Khadduri & H. J. Liebesny (eds.), *Law in the Middle East: Origin and Development of Islamic Law, vol. 1* (Richmond, VA: William Byrd Press, 1955) 309–333.

Lombardini, M. 'The International Islamic Court of Justice: Towards an International Islamic Legal System?' (2001) 14 *Leiden Journal of International Law* 665.

Lustick, I. S. 'The Absence of Middle Eastern Great Powers: Political "Backwardness" in Historical Perspective' (1997) 51 *International Organization* 653.

Lydon, G. 'Writing Trans-Saharan History: Methods, Sources and Interpretations across the African Divide' (2005) 10 *Journal of North African Studies* 293.

Lynch, M. *State Interests and Public Spheres: The International Politics of Jordan's Identity* (New York: Columbia University Press, 1999).

Mahmassani, S. 'The Principles of International Law in the Light of Islamic Doctrine' (1966) 117 *Recueil des Cours* 201.

Maluwa, T. *International Law in Post-Colonial Africa* (The Hague: Kluwer, 1999).

——. 'International Law-Making in Post-Colonial Africa: The Role of the Organization of African Unity' (2002) 49 *Netherlands International Law Review* 81.

Marasinghe, L. 'Third World Jurisprudence of the Twenty-First Century', A. Anghie & G. Sturgess (eds.), *Legal Visions of the 21st Century: Essays in Honour of Judge Christopher Weeramantry* (The Hague: Kluwer, 1998) 49–71.

Martin, P. S. 'Nationalism, Identity and Citizenship in The Western Sahara' (2005) 10 *Journal of North African Studies* 565.

May, R. & Massey, S. 'The OAU Intervention in Chad: Mission Impossible or Mission Evaded?' (1998) 5 *International Peacekeeping* 46.

Mayer, A. E. 'War and Peace in the Islamic Tradition and International Law', J. Kelsay & J. T. Johnson (eds.), *Just War and Jihad: Historical and Theoretical Perspectives on War and Peace in Western and Islamic Traditions* (New York: Greenwood Press, 1991) 195–226.

McCorquodale, R. & Pangalangan, R. 'Pushing Back the Limitations of Territorial Boundaries' (2001) 12 *European Journal of International Law* 867.

McHugo, J. 'The Judgment of the International Court of Justice in the Jurisdiction and Admissibility Phase of *Qatar v. Bahrain*: An Example of the Continuing Need for "Fact-Scepticism"' (1997) 28 *Netherlands Yearbook of International Law* 171.

McKeon, R. W. Jr., 'The Aouzou Strip: Adjudication of Competing Territorial Claims in Africa by the International Court of Justice' (1991) 23 *Case Western Reserve Journal of International Law* 147.

McKinnon Wood, H. 'The Treaty of Paris and Turkey's Status in International Law' (1943) 37 *American Journal of International Law* 262.

McWhinney, E. *The International Court of Justice and the Western Tradition of International Law: The Paul Martin Lectures in International Relations and Law* (Dordrecht; Boston: Martinus Nijhoff, 1987).

——. 'Western and Non-Western Legal Cultures and the International Court of Justice' (1987) 65 *Washington University Law Quarterly* 873.

——. '"Internationalizing" The International Court: The Quest for Ethno-cultural and Legal-systemic Representativeness', E. G. Bello & B. A. Ajibola (eds.), *Essays in Honour of Judge Taslim Olawale Elias: vol. I Contemporary International Law and Human Rights* (Dordrecht; Boston: Martinus Nijhoff, 1992) 277–289.

——. 'The International Court of Justice and International Law-making: The Judicial Activism/Self-Restraint Antinomy' (2006) 5 *Chinese Journal of International Law* 3.

Mégrét, F. 'A Sacred Trust of Civilization' (2005) 1 *Journal of International Law & International Relations* 305.

Menage, V. L. 'The English Capitulation of 1580: A Review Article' (1980) 12 *International Journal of Middle East Studies* 373.

Merrills, J. G. 'International Boundary Disputes in Theory and Practice: Precedents Established', J. Dahlitz (ed.), *Peaceful Resolution of Major International Disputes* (New York: United Nations, 1999) 95–112.

——. 'The International Court of Justice and the Adjudication of Territorial and Boundary Disputes' (2000) 13 *Leiden Journal of International Law* 873.

Mgbeoji, I. 'The Civilised Self and the Barbaric Other: Imperial Delusions of Order and the Challenges of Human Security' (2006) 27 *Third World Quarterly* 855.

Mickelson, K. 'Rhetoric and Rage: Third World Voices in International Legal Discourse' (1998) 16 *Wisconsin International Law Journal* 353.

Miéville, C. *Between Equal Rights: A Marxist Theory of International Law* (London: Pluto, 2006).

Milano, E. *Unlawful Territorial Situations in International Law: Reconciling Effectiveness, Legality and Legitimacy* (Leiden: Brill, 2006).

Moinuddin, H. *The Charter of the Islamic Conference and Legal Framework of Economic Co-operation among its Member States* (Oxford: Clarendon, 1987).

Morgan, E. 'The Law of Betrayal in the Wild West Bank' (2005) 1 *Journal of International Law and International Relations* 345.

Mosler, H. 'Political and Justiciable Legal Disputes: Revival of an Old Controversy?', B. Cheng & E. D. Brown (eds.), *Contemporary Problems in International Law: Essays in honour of Georg Schwarzenberger on his Eightieth Birthday* (London: Stevens & Sons, 1988) 216–229.

Mubiala, M. 'La Contribution des États Africains a la Renaissance de la Cour Internationale de Justice' (1995) *African Yearbook of International Law* 173.

Mundy, J. 'Neutrality or Complicity? The United States and the 1975 Moroccan Takeover of the Spanish Sahara' (2006) 11 *Journal of North African Studies* 275.

Munya, P. M. 'The International Court of Justice and Peaceful Settlement of African Disputes: Problems, Challenges and Prospects' (1998) 7 *Journal of International Law & Practice* 159.

Murphy, S. D. 'Self-Defense and the Israeli *Wall* Advisory Opinion: An *Ipse Dixit* from the ICJ?' (2005) 99 *American Journal of International Law* 62.

Mutua, M. 'Why Redraw the Map of Africa: A Moral and Legal Inquiry' (1994–1995) 16 *Michigan Journal of International Law* 1113.

——. 'Critical Race Theory and International Law: The View of an Insider-Outsider' (2000) 45 *Villanova Law Review* 841.

——. Keynote Address, Third World Approaches to International Law Conference, Albany Law School, 20–21 April 2007.

Nahas, M. 'State-Systems and Revolutionary Challenge: Nasser, Khomeini, and the Middle East' (1985) 17 *International Journal of Middle East Studies* 507.

Naldi, J. 'The Organization of African Unity and the Saharan Arab Democratic Republic' (1982) 26 *Journal of African Law* 152.

Naldi, G. J. 'The Statehood of the Saharan Arab Democratic Republic' (1985) 25 *Indian Journal of International Law* 448.

Nesiah, V. 'Placing International Law: White Spaces on a Map' (2003) 16 *Leiden Journal of International Law* 1.

Newman, D. 'Real Spaces, Symbolic Spaces: Interrelated Notions of Territory in the Arab-Israeli Conflict', P. F. Diehl (ed.), *A Road Map to War: Territorial Dimensions of International Conflict* (Nashville: Vanderbilt University Press, 1999) 3–34.

Nyang, S. 'Religion and the Maintenance of Boundaries: An Islamic View', D. Miller & S. H. Hashmi (eds.), *Boundaries of Justice: Diverse Ethical Perspectives* (Princeton: Princeton University Press, 2001) 202–212.

Öberg, M. D. 'The Legal Effects of Resolutions of the UN Security Council and General Assembly in the Jurisprudence of the ICJ' (2005) 16 *European Journal of International Law* 879.

Obregón, L. 'Between Civilisation and Barbarism: Creole interventions in international law' (2006) 27 *Third World Quarterly* 815.

Oda, S. 'Comment', D. Bowett et al. (eds.), *The International Court of Justice: Process, Practice and Procedure* (London: British Institute of International & Comparative Law, 1997) 94–101.

Oduntan, G. 'The Demarcation of Straddling Villages in Accordance with the International Court of Justice Jurisprudence: The Cameroon-Nigeria Experience' (2006) 5 *Chinese Journal of International Law* 79.

Okafor, C. 'After Martyrdom: International Law, Sub-State Groups, and the Construction of Legitimate Statehood in Africa' (2000) 41 *Harvard International Law Journal* 503.

O'Keefe, R. 'Legal Consequences of the Construction of a Wall in the Occupied Palestinian Territory: A Commentary' (2004) 37 *Revue belge de droit international* 92.

Okere, B. O. 'The Western Sahara Case' (1979) 28 *International & Comparative Law Quarterly* 296.

Oliver, R. *The African Experience: From Olduvai Gorge to the 21st Century* (Boulder, CO: Westview, 2000, 2nd edition).

Onuma, Y. 'When was the Law of International Society Born? – An Inquiry into the History of International Law from an Intercivilizational Perspective' (2000) 2 *Journal of the History of International Law* 1.

——. 'Is the International Court of Justice an Emperor without Clothes?' (2002) 8 *International Legal Theory* 1.

——. 'International Law in and with International Politics: The Functions of International Law in International Society' (2003) 14 *European Journal of International Law* 105.

Orakhelashvili, A. 'International Public Order and the International Court's Advisory Opinion on Legal Consequences of the Construction of a Wall in the Occupied Palestinian Territory' (2005) 43 *Archiv des Völkerrechts* 240.

——. 'The International Court and "Its Freedom to Select the Grounds upon which it Will Base its Judgment"' (2007) 56 *International & Comparative Law Quarterly* 171.

Otto, D. 'Subalternality and International Law: The Problems of Global Community and the Incommensurability of Difference' (1996) 5 *Social & Legal Studies* 337.

Owen, R. *State, Power and Politics in the Making of the Modern Middle East* (London: Routledge, 2nd edition, 2000).

Pahuja, S. 'The Postcoloniality of International Law' (2005) 46 *Harvard International Law Journal* 459.

——. 'Review: Antony Anghie, *Imperialism, Sovereignty and the Making of International Law*' (2006) 69 *Modern Law Review* 486.

Panaite, V. 'The Re'ayas of Tributary-Protected Principalities (the 16th–18th Century)' (2003) 1 *Romano-Turcica* 83.

Pappe, I. *A History of Modern Palestine: One Land, Two Peoples* (Cambridge: Cambridge University Press, 2004).

Parvin, M. & Sommer, M. 'Dar Al-Islam: The Evolution of Muslim Territoriality and its Implications for Conflict Resolution' (1980) 11 *International Journal of Middle East Studies* 1.

Paulson, C. 'Compliance with Final Judgements of the International Court of Justice since 1987' (2004) 98 *American Journal of International Law* 434.

Paulus, A. L. 'International Law after Postmodernism: Towards Renewal or Decline of International Law?' (2001) 14 *Leiden Journal of International Law* 727.

Peck, C. & Lee, R. S. (eds.), *Increasing the Effectiveness of the International Court of Justice: Proceedings of the ICJ/UNITAR Colloquium to Celebrate the 50th Anniversary of the Court* (Boston: Martinus Nijhoff).

Peck, M. C. *Historical Dictionary of the Gulf Arab States* (Lanham, MD: Scarecrow Press, 1997).

Pennell, C. R. 'Accommodation between European and Islamic Law in the Western Mediterranean in the Early Nineteenth Century' (1994) 21 *British Journal of Middle East Studies* 159.

Piscatori, J. 'Order, Justice, and Global Islam', R. Foot et al. (eds.), *Order and Justice in International Relations* (Oxford: Oxford University Press, 2003) 262–292.

——. *Islam in a World of Nation-States* (Cambridge: Cambridge University Press, 1986).

Plant, G. 'Maritime Delimitation and Territorial Questions between Qatar and Bahrain' (2002) 96 *American Journal of International Law* 198.

Pomerance, M. 'The Advisory Role of the International Court of Justice and its "Judicial" Character: Past and Future Prisms', A. S. Muller et al. (eds.), *The International Court of Justice* (The Hague: Kluwer, 1997) 271–323.

——. 'The ICJ and South West Africa (Namibia): A Retrospective Legal/Political Assessment' (1999) 12 *Leiden Journal of International Law* 425.

——. 'The ICJ's Advisory Opinion and the Crumbling Wall between the Political and the Judicial' (2005) 99 *American Journal of International Law* 26.

Porras, I. M. 'On Terrorism: Reflections on Violence and the Outlaw' (1994) *Utah Law Review* 119.

Post, H. 'Adjudication as a Mode of Acquisition of Territory? Some observations on the Iraq-Kuwait Boundary Demarcation in Light of the Jurisprudence of the International Court of Justice' V. Lowe & M. Fitzmaurice (eds.), *Fifty Years of the International Court of Justice: Essays in Honour of Sir Robert Jennings* (Cambridge: Cambridge University Press, 1996) 237–263.

Prott, L. V. 'Role, Consensus and Opinion Analysis at the International Court of Justice' (1983) 14 *Netherlands Yearbook of International Law* 69.

Purvis, N. 'Critical Legal Studies in Public International Law' (1991) 32 *Harvard International Law Journal* 81.

Quataert, D. *The Ottoman Empire 1700–1922* (Cambridge: Cambridge University Press, 2nd edition, 2005).

Quigley, J. 'Sovereignty in Jerusalem' (1996) 45 *Catholic University Law Review* 765.

——. *The Case for Palestine: An International Law Perspective* (Durham; London: Duke University Press, revised, 2005).

Rajagopal, B. 'From Resistance to Renewal: The Third World, Social Movements, and the Expansion of International Institutions' (2000) 41 *Harvard International Law Journal* 529.

——. *International Law from Below: Development, Social Movements and Third World Resistance* (Cambridge: Cambridge University Press, 2003).

——. 'Counter-hegemonic International Law: Rethinking Human Rights and Development as Third World Strategy' (2006) 27 *Third World Quarterly* 767.

Ramcharan, B. G. 'Recourse to the Law in the Settlement of International Disputes: Western Sahara' (1998) *African Yearbook of International Law* 205.

Ratner, S. R. 'Drawing a Better Line: *Uti Possidetis* and the Borders of New States' (1996) 90 *American Journal of International Law* 590.

——. 'Land Feuds and their Solutions: Finding International Law beyond the Tribunal Chamber' (2006) 100 *American Journal of International Law* 808.

Ratner, S. R. & Slaughter, A.-M. 'Appraising the Methods of International Law: A Prospectus for Readers' (1999) 93 *American Journal of International Law* 291.

Rehman, J. *Islamic State Practices, International Law and the Threat from Terrorism* (Portland: Hart, 2005).

Reichel, C. 'Maritime Delimitation and Territorial Questions between Qatar and Bahrain' (1998) 26 *Denver Journal of International Law and Policy* 725.

Reisman, W. M. 'African Imperialism' (1976) 70 *American Journal of International Law* 801.

——. 'Protecting Indigenous Rights in International Adjudication' (1995) 89 *American Journal of International Law* 350.

——. 'The Government of the State of Eritrea and the Government of the State of Yemen' (1999) 93 *American Journal of International Law* 668.

——. 'Islamic Fundamentalism and Its Impact on International Law and Politics', M. W. Janis & C. Evans (eds.), *Religion and International Law* (Cambridge, MA: Martinus Nijhoff, 1999) 357–384.

——. 'The Political Consequences of the General Assembly Advisory Opinion', L. Boisson de Chazournes & P. Sands (eds.), *International Law, the International Court of Justice and Nuclear Weapons* (Cambridge: Cambridge University Press, 1999) 473–487.

——. 'Unratified Treaties and Other Unperfected Acts in International Law: Constitutional Functions' (2002) 35 *Vanderbilt Journal of Transnational Law* 729.

Reus-Smit, C. 'The Politics of International Law', C. Reus-Smit (ed.), *The Politics of International Law* (Cambridge: Cambridge University Press, 2004) 14–44.

Ricciardi, M. M. 'Title to the Aouzou Strip: A Legal and Historical Analysis' (1992) 17 *Yale Journal of International Law* 301.

Riedel, E. H. 'Confrontation in the Western Sahara in the Light of the Advisory Opinion of the International Court of Justice of 16 October 1975: A Critical Appraisal' (1976) 19 *German Yearbook of International Law* 405.

Riles, A. 'Aspiration and Control: International Legal Rhetoric and the Essentialization of Culture' (1993) 106 *Harvard Law Review* 723.

——. 'The View from the International Plane: Perspective and Scale in the Architecture of Colonial International Law' (1995) 6 *Law and Critique* 38.

Romano, C. P. R. 'International Justice and Developing Countries: A Quantitative Analysis' (2002) 1 *Law & Practice of International Courts and Tribunals* 367.

——. 'International Justice and Developing Countries (Continued): A Qualitative Analysis' (2002) 1 *Law & Practice of International Courts and Tribunals* 539.

Rosenne, S. 'The Qatar/Bahrain Case: What is a Treaty? A Framework Agreement and the Seising of the Court' (1995) 8 *Leiden Journal of International Law* 161.

——. 'Decolonisation in the International Court of Justice' (1996) 8 *African Journal of International and Comparative Law* 564.

——. *Rosenne's The World Court: What it is and How it Works*, T. D. Gill (ed.), (Leiden: Martinus Nijhoff, 2003, 6th ed).

Roussellier, J. E. 'Elusive Sovereignty – People, Land and the Frontiers of the Desert: The Case of the Western Sahara and the International Court of Justice' (2007) 12 *Journal of North African Studies* 55.

Ruskola, T. 'Legal Orientalism' (2002) 101 *Michigan Law Review* 179.

Sabet, A. G. 'The Islamic Paradigm of Nations: Towards a Neoclassical Approach' (2003) 31 *Religion, State and Society* 179.

Said, E. *Orientalism: Western Conceptions of the Orient* (London: Penguin, 1978).

——. 'Secular Interpretation, the Geographical Element, and the Methodology of Imperialism', G. Prakash (ed.), *After Colonialism: Imperial Histories and Postcolonial Displacements* (Princeton: Princeton University Press, 1995) 21–39.

Salem, Z. O. A. 'Mauritania: A Saharan Frontier-state' (2005) 10 *Journal of North African Studies* 491.

Salmon, J. & Sinclair, I. 'Special Features of the *Qatar* v. *Bahrain* Case before the ICJ' (2003) 2 *Studi di dirrito internazionale in onoro de Arangio-Ruiz* 1167.

Sarin, M. L. 'The Asian-African States and the Development of International Law', F. E. Snyder & S. Sathirathai (eds.), *Third World Attitudes Toward International Law: An Introduction* (Dordrecht: Martinus Nijhoff, 1987) 33–51.

Sathirathai, S. 'An Understanding of the Relationship between International Legal Discourse and Third World Countries' (1984) 25 *Harvard Journal of International Law* 395.

Sayigh, Y. 'The Gulf Crisis: Why the Arab Regional Order Failed' (1991) 67 *International Affairs* 476.

Schofield, R. 'Borders and Territoriality in the Gulf and the Arabian Peninsula during the Twentieth Century', R. Schofield (ed.), *Territorial Foundations of the Gulf States* (London: UCL Press, 1994) 1–77.

Schwarzenberger, G. 'Title to Territory: Response to a Challenge' (1957) 51 *American Journal of International Law* 308.

——. 'The Standard of Civilisation in International Law' (1955) 17 *Current Legal Problems* 212.

Schwebel, S. M. 'Authorizing the Secretary-General of the United Nations to Request Advisory Opinions of the International Court of Justice' (1984) 78 *American Journal of International Law* 869.

——. 'What Weight to Conquest?' (1970) 64 *American Journal of International Law* 344.

——. *Justice in International Law* (Cambridge; New York: Grotius Publications, 1994).

——. 'The Impact of the International Court of Justice', M. Shahabuddeen (ed.), *Boutros Boutros-Ghali: Amicorum discipulorumque liber: Paix, développement, démocratie*, vol. 1 (Brussels: Bruylant, 1998) 663–674.

Scobbie, I. 'Towards the Elimination of International Law: Some Radical Scepticism about Sceptical Radicalism' (1990) 61 *British Yearbook of International Law* 339.

——. 'Smoke, Mirrors and Killer Whales: the International Court's Opinion and the Israeli Barrier Wall' (2004) 5 *German Law Journal* 1107.

——. 'Words my Mother Never Taught me – "In Defense of the International Court"' (2004) 99 *American Journal of International Law* 76.

——. 'Unchart(er)ed Waters?: Consequences of the Advisory Opinion on the *Legal Consequences of the Construction of a Wall in the Occupied Palestinian Territory* for the Responsibility of the UN for Palestine' (2005) 16 *European Journal of International Law* 941.

Scott, S. V. 'International Law as Ideology: Theorizing the Relationship between International Law and International Politics (1994) 5 *European Journal of International Law* 313.

——. 'Beyond 'Compliance': Reconceiving the International Law-Foreign Policy Dynamic' (1998) 19 *Australian Yearbook of International Law* 35.

——. *International Law in World Politics: An Introduction* (Boulder, CO: Lynne Rienner, 2004).

Secosan, I. 'Western Sahara: Reminiscence of Colonization in Africa' (2005) 2 *International Studies Review* 15.

Setear, J. K. 'An Iterative Perspective on Treaties: A Synthesis of International Relations Theory and International Law (1996) 37 *Harvard International Law Journal* 139.

Shahabuddeen, M. 'The International Court of Justice: The Integrity of an Idea', R. S. Pathak & R. P. Dhokalia (eds.), *International Law in Transition: Essays in Memory of Judge Nagendra Singh* (Dordrecht; Boston: Martinus Nijhoff, 1992) 341–361.

——. 'Developing Countries and the Idea of International Law', R. St. J. McDonald (ed.), *Essays in Honour of Wang Tieya* (Dordrecht; Boston: Martinus Nijhoff, 1994) 721–736.

——. 'The World Court at the Turn of the Century', A. S. Muller, D. Raič & J. M. Thuránszky (eds.), *The International Court of Justice: Its Future Role after Fifty Years* (The Hague; Boston: Martinus Nijhoff, 1997) 3–29.

——. 'The Evolution of the Global Legal Framework', M. Shahabuddeen (ed.), *Boutros Boutros-Ghali: Amicorum discipulorumque liber: Paix, développement, démocratie*, vol. 1 (Brussels, Bruylant, 1998)701–724.

Shahvar, S. 'Iron Poles, Wooden Poles: The Electric Telegraph and the Ottoman-Iranian Boundary Conflict, 1863–1865' (2007) 34 *British Journal of Middle East Studies* 23.

Shalakany, A. A. 'Arbitration and the Third World: A Plea for Reassessing Bias under the Specter of Neoliberalism' (2000) 41 *Harvard International Law Journal* 419.

Shaw, M. N. 'The Western Sahara Case' (1978) *British Yearbook of International Law* 119.

——. *Title to Territory in Africa: International Legal Issues* (Oxford: Clarendon Press, 1986).

——. 'The Heritage of States: The Principle of *uti possidetis juris* Today' (1997) 67 *British Yearbook of International Law* 75.

——. 'Peoples, Territories and Boundaries' (1997) 8 *European Journal of International Law* 478.

——. '"Peaceful Resolution of 'Political Disputes": The Desirable Parameters of ICJ Jurisdiction', J. Dahlitz (ed.), *Peaceful Resolution of Major International Disputes* (New York: United Nations, 1999) 49–75.

Simmons, B. A. 'Capacity, Commitment, and Compliance: International Institutions and Territorial Disputes' (2002) 46 *Journal of Conflict Resolution* 829.

Simpson, G. J. '*Mabo*, International Law, *terra nullius* and the Stories of Settlement: An Unresolved Jurisprudence' (1993–1994) 19 *Melbourne University Law Review* 195.

——. 'The Diffusion of Sovereignty: Self-Determination in the Postcolonial Age' (1996) 32 *Stanford Journal of International Law* 255.

Simpson, G. 'The Situation on the International Legal Theory Front: The Power of Rules and the Rule of Power' (2000) 11 *European Journal of International Law* 439.

——. *Great Powers and Outlaw States: Unequal Sovereigns in the International Legal Order* (Cambridge: Cambridge University Press, 2004).

Sinclair, I. 'The Court as an Institution: Its Role and Position in International Society', D. D. Bowett et al., *The International Court of Justice: Process, Practice and Procedure* (London: British Institute of International & Comparative Law, 1997) 21–26.

Sinha, S. P. 'Perspective of the Newly Independent States on the Binding Quality of International Law', F. E. Snyder & S. Sathirathai (eds.), *Third World Attitudes Toward International Law: An Introduction* (Dordrecht; Boston: Martinus Nijhoff, 1987) 23–31.

Skouteris, T. 'Fin de NAIL: New Approaches to International Law and its Impact on Contemporary International Legal Scholarship' (1997) 10 *Leiden Journal of International Law* 415.

Skouteris, T. & Korhonen, O. 'Under Rhodes' Eyes: The "Old" and the "New" International Law at Looking Distance' (1998) 11 *Leiden Journal of International Law* 429.

Slaughter Burley, A.-M. 'International Law and International Relations Theory: A Dual Agenda' (1993) 87 *American Journal of International Law* 205.

Slaughter, A.-M., Tulumello, A. S. & Wood, S. 'International Law and International Relations theory: A new generation of interdisciplinary scholarship' (1998) 92 *American Journal of International Law* 367.

Slaughter, A.-M. & Ratner, S. R. 'The Method is the Message' (1999) 93 *American Journal of International Law* 410.
Smith, A. M. 'Good Fences Make Good Neighbors?: The "Wall Decision" and the Troubling Rise of the ICJ as a Human Rights Court' (2005) 18 *Harvard Human Rights Journal* 251.
Smith, L. E. 'The Struggle for Western Sahara: What Future for Africa's Last Colony?' (2005) 10 *Journal of North African Studies* 545.
Smith, M. A. 'Sovereignty over Unoccupied Territories – The Western Saharan Decision' (1977) 9 *Case Western Journal of International Law* 135.
Spiermann, O. '*Lotus* and the Double Structure of International Legal Argument', L. Boisson de Chazournes & P. Sands (eds.), *International Law, the International Court of Justice and Nuclear Weapons* (Cambridge: Cambridge University Press, 1999) 131–152.
Steiger, H. 'From the International Law of Christianity to the International Law of the World Citizen – Reflections on the Formation of the Epochs of the History of International Law' (2000) 3 *Journal of the History of International Law* 180.
Stevens, J. 'Recreating the State' (2006) 27 *Third World Quarterly* 755.
Strawson, J. 'Islamic Law and English Texts' (1995) 6 *Law and Critique* 21.
Sugihara, T. 'The Judicial Function of the International Court of Justice with Respect to Disputes Involving Highly Political Issues', A. S. Muller, D. Raič & J. M. Thuránszky (eds.), *The International Court of Justice: Its Future Role after Fifty Years* (The Hague; Boston: Martinus Nijhoff, 1997) 117–138.
Suleiman, Y. *A War of Words: Language and Conflict in the Middle East* (Cambridge: Cambridge University Press, 2004).
Sumner, B. T. 'Territorial Disputes at the International Court of Justice' (2004) 53 *Duke Law Journal* 1779.
Tams, C. J. 'Light Treatment of a Complex Problem: The Law of Self-Defence in the *Wall* Case' (2005) 16 *European Journal of International Law* 963.
Tanaka, Y. 'Reflections on Maritime Delimitation in the *Qatar/Bahrain* Case' (2003) 52 *International and Comparative Law Quarterly* 53.
Tashjian, J. S. 'Contentious Matters and the Advisory Power: The ICJ and Israel's Wall' (2005) 6 *Chicago Journal of International Law* 427.
Thayer, L. E. 'The Capitulations of the Ottoman Empire and the Question of their Abrogation as it Affects the United States' (1923) 17 *American Journal of International Law* 207.
Thirlway, H. 'The Drafting of ICJ Decisions: Some Personal Recollections and Observations' (2006) 5 *Chinese Journal of International Law* 15.
——. '*International Legal Argument in the Permanent Court of Justice: The Rise of the International Judiciary* (Book Review)' (2007) 101 *American Journal of International Law* 246.
Thomas, C. 'Critical Race Theory and Postcolonial Development Theory: Observations on Methodology' (2000) 45 *Villanova Law Review* 1195.
Thomas, S. 'The Global Resurgence of Religion, International Law and International Society', E. Carolyn & M. W. Janis (eds.), *Religion and International Law* (Cambridge, MA: Martinus Nijhoff, 1999) 321–338.
Tiefenbrun, S. W. 'The Role of the World Court in Settling International Disputes: A Recent Assessment' (1997) 20 *Loyola of Los Angeles International & Comparative Law Journal* 1.
Tieya, W. 'The Third World and International Law' R. St. J. Macdonald & D. M. Johnston (eds.), *The Structure and Process of International Law: Essays in Legal Philosophy Doctrine and Theory* (The Hague; Boston: Martinus Nijhoff, 1983) 955–976.
Tilly, C. 'War Making and State Making as Organized Crime', P. Evans (et al.) (eds.), *Bringing the State Back In* (Cambridge; New York: Cambridge University Press) 169–191.

Tinker, C. 'Dispute Resolution and International Law: The United Nations Dialogue among Civilizations' (2001) 17 *New York Law School Journal of Human Rights* 985.

Toyoda, T. 'L'aspect univeraliste du droit international européen du 19ème siècle et le statut juridique de la Turquie avant 1856' (2006) 8 *Journal of the History of International Law* 19.

Tomuschat, C. 'World Order Models A Disputation with B. S. Chimni and Yasuaki Onuma' (2006) 8 *International Community Law Review* 71.

Udombana, N. J. 'The Ghost of Berlin Still Haunts Africa! The ICJ Judgment on the Land and Maritime Boundary Dispute between Cameroon and Nigeria' (2003) *African Yearbook of International Law* 13.

Wallace-Bruce, N. L. 'Africa and International Law – The Emergence of Statehood' (1985) 23 *Journal of Modern African Studies* 575.

Warner, C. W. 'The Rise of the State System in Africa' (2001) 27 *Review of International Studies* 65.

Watson, G. R. 'The "Wall" Decision in Legal and Political Context' (2005) 99 *American Journal of International Law* 6.

Wedgwood, R. 'The ICJ Advisory Opinion on the Israeli Security Fence and the Limits of Self-Defence' (2005) 99 *American Journal of International Law* 52.

Weeramantry, C. G. 'Expanding the Potential of the World Court', N. Jasentuliyana (ed.), *Perspectives on International Law* (Boston: Kluwer, 1995) 309–346.

——. 'The Function of the International Court of Justice in the Development of International Law' (1997) 10 *Leiden Journal of International Law* 309.

——. *Islamic Jurisprudence: An International Perspective* (Kuala Lumpur: The Other Press, 2001).

——. *Universalising International Law* (Leiden: Martinus Nijhoff, 2004).

Westbrook, D. 'Islamic International Law and Public International Law: Separate Expressions of World Order' (1993) 33 *Virginia Journal of International Law* 819.

Wight, M. *Systems of States: Edited with an introduction by Hedley Bull* (Leicester: Leicester University Press, 1977).

Wild, P. B. 'The Organization of African Unity and the Algerian-Moroccan Border Conflict: A Study of New Machinery for Peacekeeping and the Peaceful Settlement of Disputes Among African States' (1966) 20 *International Organization* 18.

Wilkinson, J. C. *Arabia's Frontiers: The Story of Britain's Boundary Drawing in the Desert* (London: I. B. Tauris, 1991).

Wright, Q. 'The Middle East Problem' (1970) 64 *American Journal of International Law* 270.

Wright, J. *Libya, Chad and the Central Sahara* (London: Hurst, 1989).

Zacher, M. W. 'The Territorial Integrity Norm: International Boundaries and the Use of Force' (2001) 55 *International Organization* 215.

Zaman, R. A. 'Islamic Perspectives on Territorial Boundaries and Autonomy', D. Miller & S. H. Hashmi (eds.), *Boundaries and Justice: Diverse Ethical Perspectives* (Princeton & Oxford: Princeton University Press, 2001) 182–202.

Zawati, H. M. *Is Jihād a Just War? War, Peace, and Human Rights under Islamic and Public International Law* (Lewiston, NY: Edwin Mellen Press, 2001).

Zoubir, Y. H. 'The Western Sahara Conflict: A Case Study in Failure of Pre-Negotiation and Prolongation of Conflict' (1996) 26 *California Western International Law Journal* 173.

Zoubir, Y. H. & Benabdallah-Gambier, K. 'Morocco, Western Sahara and the Future of the Maghreb' (2004) 9 *Journal of North African Studies* 49.

Zubaida, S. *Law and Power in the Islamic World* (London: I. B. Tauris, 2003).

Zunes, S. 'Implications of the U.S. Reaction to the World Court Ruling against Israel's "Separation Barrier"' (2004) 11 *Middle East Policy* 72.

Index